W9-BVO-750

Lineberger Memorial

Library

[QUINTILIAN]

The Lesser Declamations

I

LCL 500

CONTENTS

CONTENTS

s/o B/kwl. 4/06 21.60

LOEB CLASSICAL LIBRARY® is a registered trademark
of the President and Fellows of Harvard College

Library of Congress Catalog Card Number 2005046792
CIP data available from the Library of Congress

ISBN 0-674-99618-6

Composed in ZephGreek and ZaphText by
Technologies 'N Typography, Merrimac, Massachusetts.
Printed and bound by Edwards Brothers, Ann Arbor, Michigan

[QUINTILIAN]

THE LESSER DECLAMATIONS

VOLUME I

EDITED AND TRANSLATED BY

D. R. SHACKLETON BAILEY

HARVARD UNIVERSITY PRESS

CAMBRIDGE, MASSACHUSETTS

LONDON, ENGLAND

2006

CONTENTS

ACKNOWLEDGMENT

I wish to express my appreciation of Philippa Goold's editorial and proofreading assistance in the publication of this edition. It was marked by expert knowledge of the material and rare meticulosity and critical acumen.

DRSB

INTRODUCTION

Higher education in Rome was an education in rhetoric, the art and practice of verbal persuasion, and the prime didactic tool was the academic declamation. The teacher composed and delivered speeches, put into the mouth of a prosecutor or defendant at an imaginary trial (*controversiae*) or of an actor in a more or less historical situation (*suasoriae*). They would be accompanied by explanations and precepts (*sermones*—talks). The learners in their turn would follow the example set, composing and delivering in class.

The "Lesser Declamations" ascribed to Quintilian (145 preserved out of an original 388) are one of a number of such collections surviving in Greek and Latin. They take various forms. In this collection of *controversiae*, perhaps from the second century A.D., the declamations are usually prefaced by a pedagogic *sermo* from "the master" (Winterbottom's term); though not seldom it provides little relevance to the declamation that follows and is so opaquely phrased that one pities the pupils it is supposed to edify. The "Greater Declamations," also ascribed to Quintilian but of later, probably much later, date, have no introductory matter but their titles and themes. In addition we have in the work of the elder Seneca of Cordoba (born c. 55 B.C.) extracts, allegedly from memory, assigned

1

to celebrated professors active in his younger days.

In the introduction to his edition (1984) Winterbottom provides a clear and concise survey of the problems surrounding our collection. Was it, as Ritter and Leo thought, "a series of lecture notes taken at the school of Quintilian"? More likely in Winterbottom's opinion (p. xiii) "the *Nachlass* of a *rhetor*, inefficiently edited and published after his death . . . not notes taken down at another's lecture, but notes made by a lecturer for his own purposes. The lack of system will reflect the editor's inefficiency or lack of understanding in the ordering of a confused archive . . . The *sermones* will be the notes, to be expanded in front of the class, on the treatment of each topic. The *declamationes* will be fair copies for dictation or performance." Not inconceivably some of them might be the work of pupils, preserved by the rhetor along with his own. Whether or not they are in some measure derived from the famous Quintilian, it is clear that their author was intimately acquainted with his *Orator's Education*.

The value of the collection lies in its character as exemplifying the nature of the training in the rhetorical schools. The declaimers strive to impress, by striking epigrams (*sententiae*) and ingenious, often perverse, argument. This kind of training is reflected in post-republican Latin literature, poetry and prose—even in the elder Pliny's vast encyclopedia. Any page of Seneca the philosopher and dramatist (son of the "rhetor") or Lucan or Statius, to say nothing of Virgil or Ovid, is likely to show how deeply impregnated the author was by his early exposure to the system. Even Martial, often regarded as an exception, was in his fashion one of its products; the conceits of a piece like Martial

11.18 spring from the same psychological mold that produced the *sententiae*.

Of the manuscripts, oldest and best, a swarm of corruptions notwithstanding, is tenth-century A, beginning at Declamation 244; the previous 243 have left no trace except the numbering. A's first folio, containing 244 and the beginning of 245, survives only in a copy (Pi) taken by Pithoeus (Pierre Pithou) for his edition of 1580.

Two fifteenth-century manuscripts, B and C, begin at Declamation 252.13. As evidence for the text itself, as opposed to its transmission, they are negligible. Their common parent or ancestor (β) is identified with a manuscript E of German provenance (Bischoff, see Winterbottom, p. xxii) surviving in two fragments containing parts of 354–57 and 372–81. E was roughly contemporary with and independent of A, but from the same archetype. To BC Winterbottom added a third, D, as probably an independent witness to B; it starts from the same point. But contamination cannot be excluded (Winterbottom, p. xxii n. 17) and its evidence is to be taken with caution.

Winterbottom's list of eight major editors begins with the editio princeps (Parma 1494; "often content to print gibberish") and ends with C. Ritter (Leipzig 1884), who, in conjunction with E. Rohde of "Psyche" fame, contributed a quantity of corrections, many of which established themselves in the text. A century later came Winterbottom, followed in 1989 by my Teubner (Stuttgart). This too was nothing if not innovative and most of its innovations are retained in this edition, but some are dropped and others added. Special mention is also due to the work of two out-

standing critics, L. Håkanson and W. S. Watt (see Abbreviations).

Pursuant to the character of the Loeb series I make concessions to readability and resort to the cross of despair *in extremis*.

Winterbottom's edition includes a pioneer commentary that leaves many problems unsolved or unattempted; and in the notes to my translation I have aired some disagreements. But my debt to it as a standby and stimulus will be apparent to anyone who troubles to make a comparison. Two points call for special mention. First, following Håkanson's similar practice in his text of Calpurnius Flaccus, he places many passages between double brackets as irrelevant or redundant in their present context but, in his opinion, part of the "master's" *Nachlass* from which the collection was assembled. I have followed suit, and unless otherwise stated the double brackets in my text are to be attributed to him. In Winterbottom's view these "are a sign not of the corrupt nature of our manuscript transmission but of the circumstances in which the collection was formed. They, like other features of the *Declamations*, strongly suggest that the Master, though their author, did not prepare them for publication." They "will arise from the second thoughts that the Master will have added in his margins over a long teaching career" (p. xii).

Second, as befits an editor of Quintilian (Oxford Text) and Seneca "Rhetor" (Loeb Classical Library), Winterbottom's commentary pays much attention to rhetorical technique, an element not included in the brief notes to my translation.

The *Lesser Declamations* as a whole have not previously appeared in translation.

ABBREVIATIONS AND SIGLA

Aer.	P. Aerodius (ed. Paris 1563)
Bu.	P. Burman (ed. Leiden 1720)
ed. Leid.	(ed. Leiden 1665)
ed. princ.	(Parma 1494)
Fr.	P. Francius in Bu.*
Gron.	J. F. Gronovius in ed. Leid.
Hå.[1]	L. Håkanson, *Cl. et Mediev.* Dissert. 9 (1973) 310–17
Hå.[2]	in Wi.
Hå.[3]	*Gnomon* (1985) 648–50
HSCP	*Harvard Studies in Classical Philology*
Lat.	L. Latinius in Bu.
Obr.	U. Obrecht (ed. Strassburg 1698)
OLD	*Oxford Latin Dictionary*
Pith.	P. Pithoeus (ed. Paris 1580)
Ranc.	Ranconetus (see J. C. Orelli, *M. Tulli Ciceronis Orator Brutus Topica . . .* (Zurich 1830), xcvii–ci)
Ri.	C. Ritter (ed. Leipzig (Teubner) 1884)
Ro.	E. Rohde in Ri.
Sch.	J. Schulting in Bu.

* "Francius Clarius" (Wi. xxvii and 465) did not exist: see my Teubner edition, note on p. v.

ABBREVIATIONS

SB[1]	D. R. Shackleton Bailey, *HSCP* 87 (1983) 230–39
SB[2]	Ibid. 92 (1989) 367–404
SB[3]	ed. Stuttgart (Teubner) 1989
SB[4]	this edition
Watt[1]	W. S. Watt, *Illinois Classical Studies* 9 (1984) 53–78. See also in Wi.
Watt[2]	*Würzburger Jahrbücher fur das Altertum* 21 (1996–97) 289–308
Wi.	M. Winterbottom (ed. Berlin 1984)

For further bibliographical detail see Winterbottom's bibliography (pp. xxviii–xxix of his edition) and Håkanson's report in *Aufstieg und Niedergang der römischen Welt*, II (1986) 2272–2306.

SIGLA

A	Montepessulanus H 126
Pi	Pithoeus' copy of A's first folio
B	Monacensis lat. 309
C	Vaticanus Chigianus H 261
B	Vaticanus Palatinus lat. 1558
β	consensus BCD or BC
E	see Introduction
⟦ ⟧	see Introduction

DECLAMATIONES MINORES

‹Adultera a marito exule occisa›

Imprudentis caedis damnatus quinquennio exulet. Adulterum cum adultera liceat occidere. ‹Imprudentis caedis damnatus cum ante expletum poenae quinquennium noctu domum ad visendam uxorem reversus esset,[1] in adulterio eam deprehendit; occidit. Reversus post quintum annum caedis reus est.›

‹DECLAMATIO›

1   . . . manifestum est, et in hac tamen civitate extra controversiam praecipue . . . positum . . . . eos[2] qui a se homines occisos esse fateantur teneri lege. Qui distingues? ‹Ex›igis sanare adulteras? Occidisti.[3] Quis igitur dubitat hoc in ‹hac›[4] civitate a legibus permissum? 'Adulterum' inquit 'cum adultera liceat occidere': quid aliud feci? 'Sed non licuit occidere tibi': et in hoc omnem calumniam suam contrahit, ‹ut›[5] neget mihi licuisse occidere: primum quod ius civis non habuerim eo tempore quo exul eram;

---

[1] Wi.: revertisset Ri.
[2] ‹non omnes continuo› eos tempt. Ri.
[3] SB4: distingues igit . sa . . ere. Occidisti adulteros Pi.
[4] Ro.
[5] Ri.

⟨Adulteress killed by exiled husband⟩[1]

Let one found guilty of involuntary homicide be exiled for five years. Let it be lawful to kill an adulterer along with an adulteress.[2] ⟨A person found guilty of involuntary homicide returned at night to visit his wife before completing his five years of punishment. Finding her in adultery, he killed her. Returning after the five years, he is charged with homicide.⟩

DECLAMATION

* * * is clear, and anyway in this of all communities it is beyond dispute that ⟨not all⟩ persons admitting to a homicide ⟨automatically⟩ come under the law. How shall you distinguish * * * Do you require that I cure adultresses? You killed them. So who doubts that this is legal in this community? "Let it be lawful to kill an adulterer along with the adulteress," so it runs. Isn't that just what I did? "But you had no right to kill," and his whole quibble boils down to this, his denial of my right to kill: first, because I did not have citizen rights during my time in exile and laws

---

1 Missing title and theme were reconstructed by Ritter and precursors.

2 Preserved in Pithoeus' copy of the first page of A, much of which was illegible (see Introduction).

2　nec ad me iura pertinuisse quod exulo. Si in perpetuum
exilium missus essem, forsitan posset de hoc quaeri, an ad
leges pertinuerim, cum illud ex lege fieret quod exularem.
Quinquennale vero exilium ⟨num⟩[6] dubium est quin
. . . . processerit absente me, neque erat causa
propter quam vis inferretur ei qui imprudens occidisset.

3　Non damnabatur animus,[7] aut sceleris ea poena erat. 'Sed
ut pertinuerit' inquit 'ad te lex, ⟨occidere⟩[8] tamen tibi non
licuit, cum ad occidendum venire non licuerit. Lex enim
quinquennio te iubet exulare.' Puta me contra ius redisse
⟨et⟩ sic ⟨mecum⟩ in praesentia ⟨age⟩[9] tamquam contra
ius redissem. Non tamen mihi obicere debes quod occide-
rim, sed quod ⟨reversus sim⟩[10] . . . tingente fecisse contra

4　leges . . . . contra illam tamen legem[11] feci . . . . ad iudicium
pertinet . . . . . sic etiam redire mihi licuisse . . . . . hoc rerum
. . . . . . occidere licere. Ergo lex qu . . . . significat omnia
. . . . quae adversus adulteros scripta est ut contra alias
leges . . . . . ab exilio, nec homines occidere licuit. Sed
quemadmodum homine . . . . erant ita rever . .

5　　　　　　　　　　SERMO

Locus potens,[12] [quomodo][13] quantum liceat adversus
adulteros. Sed in hac controversia facere oportet quod in
omnibus[14] fere, ut quotiens communem dixerimus locum
ad proprium revertamur. Communis est locus adversus
adulteros omnes, proprius adversum hos adulteros.

6 *SB*[4] (*cf.* 248.5, 14): non *iam* coni. *SB*[3]
7 *Pith.*: -mo Pi　　8 *Ro.*: *lac. ind.* Pi
9 *Ro.*: si (*lac.*) in praesentia (*lac.*) Pi
10 *Wi., duce Ri.*　　11 *Ri.*: legi Pi
12 *Ro.*: pat- Pi　　13 *Ri.*
14 *Ri.*: commun- Pi

did not apply to me because I am in exile.[3] Now if I had been sent into exile for life, perhaps there might be a question whether I was relevant to laws, since my being in exile resulted from the law. But is ⟨there any⟩ doubt that the five-year exile * * * proceeded in my absence, and there was no reason for violence to be used against a person who had killed involuntarily? My intention was not found guilty, nor was that the punishment of a crime. "But," says he, "even if the law applied to you, you had no license ⟨to kill⟩ because you had no license to come for that purpose. For the law orders you to be in exile for five years." Suppose I did return contrary to the law and ⟨proceed with me⟩ for the present as though I had returned contrary to the law: all the same, you should not charge me with killing but with having returned illegally * * *[4]

DISCUSSION

An effective topic, how much is allowed against adulterers. But in this controversy as in pretty well all others: whenever we have discussed a common topic, we go back to the particular. The common topic is against all adulterers, the particular against these adulterers.

[3] The prosecutor argues that the law permitting the killing of adulterers taken in the act does not cover the killer because as an exile the laws do not apply to him. The defendant seems to reply that this is not true of exiles for involuntary homicide, which is not a crime. But the detail of the argument is obscure in the absence of the original theme.

[4] I do not attempt to translate the following fragments.

6

DECLAMATIO

Itane mulier impune peccarit[15] quae calamitatem viri sui
pro occasione habuit . . . . bus erat, cui quinquennium
breve videbatur. Aequale enim illud fuit adult . . . . . narra-
batur cuius opinio . . . . dum frequens; sed paene conti-
nuum ac perpetuum fuit. Ne quis autem existimet nunc[16]
adulterium unius tantum vindicandum: ‹pertinet›[17] ad
exemplum totius civitatis.

245

‹Depositi infitiator›[1]

Qui depositum infitiatus fuerit, quadruplum solvat. Qui
filium luxuriosum relinquebat, pecuniam apud amicum
deposuit et mandavit ut redderet emendato. Petit adulescens pecuniam *[2] Ille quadruplum petit.

1

SERMO

. . . . videtur hic adulescens . . . . . . tamen asper exactor .
quoniam[3] persona nobis proponitur amici, et amici hoc
ipso de quo agitur probati. Nam ita facilius ostendemus
omnia eum fecisse adulescentis ipsius causa, si ne reus quidem usquam ad odium compellitur.

[15] *Wi.*: -assit Pi	[16] *Sch.*: cum Pi
[17] *Sch.*: *lac. ind.* Pi	[1] *Pith. in indice*
[2] *lac. ind. Pith.*	[3] *hinc incipit* A

[1] This I take to be the sense of what is missing, as indicated in
SB[1] in revision of Rohde's supplement, and propose the following
sequence: Father deposits money with a friend, enjoining him not
to return it to his loose-living son after his death until said son
mends his ways. Father dies and Son demands the money. Instead

DECLAMATION

Shall the woman then sin with impunity, having used her
husband's calamity as an opportunity? * * * thought five
years too short a period * * * but it was almost continuous
and perpetual. Let no one think that only an individual's
adultery is now to be avenged; ‹it concerns› an example to
the whole community.

245

‹Denier of deposit›

Whoso denies a deposit, let him pay fourfold. A man who
was leaving behind a loose-living son deposited money
with a friend with instructions to return it to the son if
he reformed. The young man claimed the money ‹but lost
the case. Later he reformed and the friend offered the
money›.[1] The other now sues for fourfold.

DISCUSSION

This young man seems * * * but a harsh exactor * * * since
we are presenting the persona of a friend, and a friend
proved such by the very thing here at issue. For it will be
easier for us to show that all he did was for the young man's
own sake if even under prosecution he is at no point driven
into hostility.

of quoting Father's instructions, the friend denies the deposit (for
his reason see s.6). Son brings suit and loses. Later he reforms and
the friend offers to return the money and returns it (s.7). Son sues
him for four times the sum as penalty for his denial. "Offered the
money" rather than "returned the money" as showing that the
initiative came from the friend—the son had not repeated his
demand.

13

2
DECLAMATIO

'Qui depositum infitiatus fuerit, quadruplum solvat.' Infitiari est depositum nolle solvere. Itaque ne actio quidem haec dari potest nisi adversus eum qui damnatus fuerit. Eo enim tempore quaeratur necesse est an habeat pecuniam et an infitietur; neque omnino quadruplum solvere debet nisi simplam ⟨debere⟩[4] convictus. Quare si hanc tantum negasset aliquando et postea obtulisset, non tamen poterat videri quadruplo obligatus, cum hoc ipsum quadruplum cum ea summa abierit[5] quae negabatur.[6] Quid si et absolu-
3 tus est iudicio, cum in quadruplum damnari poterat? Neque enim ideo debet quadruplum solvere quia potuit ne simplum quidem solvere. Si ipsam pecuniam quae a patre tuo apud amicum ⟨deposita est repetere⟩[7] velles, non liceret tamen tibi rem iudicatam retractare. Hoc ergo fieri potest, ut rem non potueris repetere, poenam repetas?

4
SERMO

Haec circa ius, illa circa aequitatem. Qui quadruplum ab infitiatore petit, illa dicere solet: 'Oportet poenam esse avaritiae et adfici supplicio cupiditates; neque enim aliter fides constare potuerit apud homines[8] nisi metu contineantur.[9] Depositum [hoc][10] eo magis vindicandum est

---

[4] s. d. *Wi.*, *auct. Ri.*: simul A
[5] *SB*[3]: habue- A   [6] *Ro.*: negatur A
[7] *Ri.*, *auct. Bu.* (*lac. fere xxv litt. in* A): *anne* quondam *vel* aliquando *addendum?*   [8] *Ro.*: omnes A
[9] *Bu.*: -atur A   [10] *Ro.*

---

[2] The friend.
[3] Without the matter going to court. The offer to repay cancel-

"Whoso denies a deposit, let him pay fourfold." To deny a deposit is to refuse to pay it. Therefore even permission to proceed on this charge cannot be granted except against a person found guilty. For at that time it has to be asked whether he has the money and whether he denies; and there can be no question of owing fourfold except in the case of a person who has been adjudged ⟨to owe⟩ the amount simple. So if he[2] had merely refused to pay this amount at some point and had subsequently offered to do so,[3] all the same he could not appear obliged to pay fourfold, since this very fourfold disappeared along with the sum which was refused. Add that he was judged not liable when he could have been ordered to pay fourfold. For he ought not to pay fourfold because it was open to him not to pay even the sum simple.[4] If you had chosen ⟨to reclaim⟩ the actual amount ⟨which was deposited⟩ by your father with his friend, even so you would not have been permitted to reopen a matter already judged. Can it be then that you were unable to claim the sum but claim the penalty?

So much on the law, this on equity: a person claiming fourfold from a denier usually speaks as follows: "There ought to be a penalty for avarice and greedy behavior should be chastised; for good faith cannot be maintained among men unless they are held in check by fear. A deposit should

led the debt. Penalty could only arise from a claim denied by the debtor and then validated by a court, but there had been no such validation; on the contrary, a court had rejected the son's claim.

    4 "A sarcastic remark" (Wi.).

quod fere secreta sunt citra probationem.' Non potest omnino in hoc arguere avaritiam.

5

Depositum quo tempore petisti? Luxuriosus adhuc. Si voluisset confiteri habere se pecuniam, nondum tamen debebat. Non est in depositis simplex condicio. Deponitur aliquid quod quandocumque repetitur reddendum est; deponitur aliquid in tempus. Hoc quomodo depositum erat? Ut acciperes cum luxuriari desisses. Quo tempore repetebas adhuc luxuriabaris. Non debebatur ergo, nec potest videri infitiatus quod eo tempore negavit quo illi extorqueri non posset vel confitenti. 'Quare tamen negare maluit quam hoc iure uti?' Quoniam te luxuriosum spes adhuc pecuniae faciebat. An non hoc est quod te fecerit frugi? Didicisti tibi pecuniam ‹frugalitate›[11] et labore servandam.

6

7

At mehercule vereor ne cito obtulerit. Sine dubio tu discussam luxuriam vis probare avaritia; at[12] haec ipsa accipiendae pecuniae fames alias videtur prodere cupiditates. Satis erat homini frugi quod accepisti. Itaque et alias quoque condiciones frugalitati tuae ponit amicus paternus: si vixeris quomodo videris fecisse, si tenendi potius patrimonii quam auferendi habueris curam, est adhuc quod tibi

---

[11] *Ri.* (*lac. fere xv litt. in* A) [12] *Pith.*: et A

---

[5] Why not with a receipt—though in this case, the depositor being dead, there might well be none.

[6] The return of the money showed that the friend's refusal to repay had not been motivated by greed.

[7] *Iure* refers to the authority given by the depositor to his friend.

be championed all the more because deposits are usually secret and not provable."[5] In this case he can't denounce avarice at all.[6]

DECLAMATION

At what time did you claim the deposit? When you were still a loose-liver. If he had wanted to admit possession of the money, he ought not to have done so at that point. With deposits there is more than one situation. One deposit has to be returned whenever it is reclaimed, another is for a time. How was this deposited? You were to get it when you had stopped your loose living. At the time you were reclaiming it you were still living loose. Therefore it was not owing and he cannot appear to have denied what he refused to hand over at a time when it could not have been wrung from him even if he had admitted possession. "But why did he prefer to deny rather than use this right?"[7] Because the hope of the money was still keeping you living loosely. Or is it not this that has made you reform? You have learned that you must keep money by ‹frugality› and hard work.

But upon my word I am afraid he made the offer too soon. No doubt you wish to show by greed that you have shaken off loose living! But this very hurry to get the money seems to betray other cupidities. For a man of sober habit what you did get[8] would have been enough. So your father's friend places yet other conditions on your frugality: if you live as you seem to have done, if you are more concerned to keep your patrimony than to take other

---

[8] From the friend—the original deposit. The son may also have inherited something from his father.

possit tribuere‹. Reddidit›[13] patrimonium paternum; sed
adhuc habet suum.

246

Soporatus fortis privignus

Qui fortiter fecerat, bello imminente, soporem ab noverca
subiectum bibit. Causam dixit tamquam desertor. Absolutus accusat novercam veneficii.

1   DECLAMATIO

Etiamsi, iudices, eventus proximae causae satis videri potest etiam in hanc quoque pronuntiasse, primum tamen
doloris mei professionem dissimulare non possum, quod
novercam ante accusare non potui. Debeo quidem sententiis iudicum omnia; homo tamen gravissimam iniuriam
passus adhuc tantum absolutus sum. Verum me quamvis
praecipitem[1] in hoc iudicium agat ultio, tamen ne[2] illud
quidem periculum fallit: hodie constituetis an merito absolutus sim. Inter summa discrimina rei publicae, ‹si›[3]
2   non fuit venenum,[4] ego deserui. Si quid[5] autem ad hanc
praeteritorum indignationem adicere etiam forma ipsa[6]
iudicii potest, illud certe est quod nulla possit tolerare
patientia, quod se mihi contendit noverca beneficium
dedisse. Vos aestimabitis quid de persona hac sentiatis:

---

[13] *SB*[1]   [1] *Opitz (cf. Watt*[1]): -pua A: -pue *Pith.*
[2] t. ne *Ri.*: talis A   [3] *SB*[2]
[4] *post* venenum *lac. unius lineae in* A
[5] *Ri.*: quis A   [6] *Ri.*: -am –am A

people's, there is still something he can do for you. ⟨He has returned⟩ your paternal patrimony; but he still has his own.

246

The hero[1] stepson drugged

A man who had become a hero, when war was imminent, drank a sleeping-draught offered him by his stepmother. He stood trial as a deserter. Acquitted, he accuses his stepmother of poisoning.

DECLAMATION

Gentlemen of the jury, even though the result of the recent trial may appear to have constituted a sufficient verdict against this woman too, yet to begin with I cannot refrain from protesting my chagrin in that I was unable to accuse my stepmother previously. I am profoundly grateful for the jury's votes; but I am a man who has suffered a grievous injury and as yet I have merely been acquitted. But although desire for revenge drives me headlong into this court, I am none the less aware of a danger: you will today determine whether I deserved to be acquitted. The commonwealth was in grave peril and, ⟨if⟩ it was not poison, I deserted. And if the very form of this trial can add anything to this indignation at what is past, here at least is something that no patience could tolerate, my stepmother's contention that she did me a kindness. You, gentlemen, will judge what you are to think of her persona: a mother would not

---

[1] Wi. regularly so renders *vir fortis*, the standard term in declamation for a soldier whose conspicuous bravery entitled him to claim a public reward. Likewise "became a hero" for *fortiter fecit*.

non fecisset hoc mater; certe, quod mihi satis est, pater
non fecit.

3   SERMO

Quotiens finiendum erit, primum intueri debebitis quid
utraque pars velit, deinde id quod vult quam brevissime
complecti. Quare negat venenum esse qui pro rea[7] dicit?
Quia non occiderit neque sit mortiferum. Quare dicit venenum esse qui accusat? Quoniam medicamentum sit et
efficiat aliquid contra naturam. Ergo non est satis id modo
videri venenum quod occidat, sed haec omnia venena sunt
⟨quae * ⟩.[8] 'Ad tuam quidem finitionem etiam mortiferum
istud erit: nam cum id ageres ut desererem, desertorem
poena sequatur, etiam id quod deesse huic medicamento
videbatur adieceras.[9]'

4   DECLAMATIO

Veneficii accuso. Veneficam dico quae soporem dedit.
Unde tibi ⟨in⟩[10] hos usus venena? Notiora sunt quaedam
pernicie et experimento deprehenduntur, adeo ut aliqua
publice dentur. Hoc quid est? Quid[11] tu vis vocari? In tempus venenum, quo mens aufertur, quo corpus gravatur,
quo membra solvuntur. Saepe in scelere virtutis est nosse
[veneni][12] modum. Eo magis ⟨venenum est⟩[12] quod vide-
mus copia ⟨quadam⟩[13] constare, quod temperamento
quodam, ut stetur citra mortem. Si quis accusare te vene-

---

[7] *Gron.*: reo A   [8] *Wi.*
[9] *Ro.*: -res *ut vid.* A
[10] *Pith.*
[11] *Gron.*: quod A
[12] *SB*[2]
[13] *SB*[3]

have done it. Assuredly (and this is enough for me) my father did not do it.

Whenever a definition has to be made, you will need first to look at what each side wants and then to wrap up what each side wants as briefly as possible. Why does the advocate for the defense deny that it was poison? Because it did not kill, it is not death-bringing.[2] Why does the prosecutor say it is poison? Because it is a drug and produces something against nature. Therefore it is not enough that merely what kills should be regarded as poison, but everything is poison ⟨which⟩[3] * * * "According to your definition also that substance will be death-bringing; for since you tried to make me a deserter and death is the punishment for such, you had added what this drug seemed to lack."

I accuse of poisoning. I say that the woman who gave the sleeping-draught is a poisoner. Where did you find poisons to serve these purposes? Certain substances are well known by their destructive effect and detected by experiment, so much so that some of them are publicly administered.[4] What is this? What do you want it called? A poison for the occasion, by which mind is taken away, body weighed down, limbs paralyzed. In crime knowing the right measure is often a virtue. When we see that it is ⟨a particular⟩ quantity and a particular mixture that makes the effect stop short of death, ⟨it is poison⟩ all the more.

---

2 Implying the defense's definition of poison as "a substance that kills."   3 For the possible content of the gap see Wi.

4 As hemlock to Socrates.

ficii voluisset illo tempore quo sane non vacabat, si protulisset corpus meum, quod non solum motu sui,[14] familiae conclamatione excitari non potuit sed belli tumultu et fragore signorum et trepidatione totius civitatis, victurum promitteres?

5   Veneficium scientia docui, veneficium periculo docui; volo dicere et de animo. Potionem istam cui dedisti? Quo tempore dedisti? Privigno dedisti. Si alio tempore dedisses, deceptam te putarem; nunc excogitasti potionem quae

6 me lege occideret.[15] Equidem, si me interroges, vixisse me illo tempore non arbitror. Quid enim ⟨eram⟩,[16] pro di immortales? aut in qua parte naturae locavit me noverca? Bellum mihi nuntiatum est, et hominem quem non peregrinatio detinuit, non absentia ulla a periculo civitatis rele-

7 gavit, ⟨somnus vinxit⟩.[17] Quid actum[18] sit manente me intra muros commilitones mei narraverunt; dicitur ingens fuisse proelium, commissa utrimque acies, dubia saepe victoria et huc atque illuc spes inclinata, cum interim miles in quo plurimum fiduciae, in quo maximum momentum videbatur, in nulla parte visus auditur. Quid plus contingere potuit hosti si perissem? Non alio modo audivi bella

8 quam avorum proavorumque temporibus. At si mihi detur emendatio praeteritorum, utinam noverca illud statim venenum dedisset quo vita auferretur! Illa potione consump-

---

[14] *SB*[3]: corporis A   [15] *Fr.*: -rit A
[16] *Watt*[1] (*cf. Wi.*)   [17] *Ro.*
[18] *Gron.*: acta A[1]: acti A[2]

---

[5] This is the argument at the end of the *sermo*. It should have been set out in the declamation, the rest of which, as we have it, does not deal with intent.

Suppose someone had chosen to accuse you of poisoning at that juncture (when to be sure there was too much else to do): if he had produced my body, which could not be aroused—I won't say by the moving of it and the lamentation of the household but by the hubbub of war and the noise of signals and the commotion of the whole community, would you have guaranteed that I would live?

I have shown that poisoning is proved by the expertise and by the risk. I also want to speak of intent. To whom did you give that poison? When did you give it? You gave it to your stepson. If you had given it at another time, I should think you were disappointed. As it is, you thought up a poison that would kill me legally.[5] For my part, if you ask me, I don't think I was alive at that time. For what ⟨was⟩ I, in heaven's name? Or in what part of nature did my stepmother locate me? News of the war reached me, and I, a man whom no foreign travel detained nor any absence kept from the community's peril—⟨sleep bound me fast⟩. My comrades in arms told me what happened while I remained within the walls. There was a tremendous battle, it is said, fighting joined on both sides, victory often in doubt, hope swinging to and fro: and all the while the warrior in whom most trust was placed, who was thought most likely to sway the issue, is reported as nowhere to be seen. What greater advantage could the enemy have had if I had been killed? I *heard* about the fighting just as though it had been in the days of our grandfathers or great-grandfathers. But if it were given me to redress the past, I only wish my stepmother had given me a lethal sort of poison right away.

tum tota civitas ad rogum tulisset, celebrasset laudes;
etiam temporis discrimen multum attulisset admirationis.
Illa dicerent homines: 'non tulissemus haec si vixisset.'

9 'Ego' inquit 'tamen[19] animo bono feci.' Erubescite, ma-
tres, quae amplexae armatos iam liberos impiae tamen iam
estis meae[20] exemplo. Inventa est tota civitate ⟨una
quae⟩[21] magis amaret, una quae parceret: noverca. Non
dico de his adhuc quae secuta sunt, non illam iudicii contumeliam; interim tamen, quid mihi potuit gravius accidere?
Quam ego, dii deaeque, perdidi occasionem! Obtulerat
deus tempus merita geminandi; venerat dies approbandi

10 quod fortiter feceram id non Fortunam fuisse. Felices
commilitones mei: hostium terga vidistis, calcastis cadave-
ra, victoriam publicam clamore laeto[22] rettulistis[23]; at ego
'quando pugnandum est?' interrogavi, longamque illam
novercae noctem tandem emensus non mente, non gradu
constiti, ac mihi vicisse cives meos accusator indicavit.

11 Videor ex magna parte iam[24] approbasse causam proximo iudicio. Quo enim modo absolutus sum nisi illa accusatori dicerem: 'vis tenuit et devincta[25] mens'?

19 *Pith.*: tantum A
20 *SB*[1]: mei A
21 *Pith.*
22 *SB*[4]: -ti A
23 *SB*[1]: retu- A
24 *Ro.*: etiam A
25 *Sch., Gron.*: -icta A

Had that draught killed me, the entire community would have borne me to the pyre, sung my praises. Even the time gap would have brought much admiration. People would have said: "We should never have borne all this[6] if he had lived." "Ah, but," she says, "I meant well." Take shame, you mothers who embraced your children in arms but are made unnatural now by the example of mine![7] In the whole community was found <one> more loving, one that spared: my stepmother! I say nothing as yet of what followed, nothing of the insult of that trial. But in the meanwhile, could anything harder to bear have befallen me? Gods and goddesses, what an opportunity I lost! God had given me the opportunity to double my deserts. The day had come to show that my former bravery was not Fortune's doing. Happy my comrades! You saw the enemy's back, trod on his corpses, brought back the public victory in a shout of joy; but as for me, "when are we to fight?" I asked, and after finally enduring that long night of my stepmother's making, I was unsteady in mind and feet and my accuser informed me that my countrymen had won the day.

I think that I already to a great extent established my case at the recent trial. For how was I acquitted except by telling my accuser: "I was held by force and a mind in chains"?

---

[6] The sufferings of war (though it had ended in victory (s.10)).

[7] A stepmother is occasionally called a mother (*TLL* VIII. 430.1), but this is sarcasm. The patriotic mothers, he says, were put to shame by this stepmother's behavior.

247

Raptoris divitis bona

Mariti bona uxor accipiat. Adulescens locuples rapuit;
priusquam optaret puella, misit ad eam propinquos rogatum ut nuptias haberet. Auditis illa precibus tacuit et flevit.
Percussit se adulescens. Priusquam expiraret, optavit illa
nuptias. Petunt bona propinqui et uxor.

1 SERMO

Demonstranda vobis est via: videte quid utraque pars velit,
quid utraque pars dicat, et illud quam fieri potest brevissime et significantissime comprehendite. Ut puta, dicit
haec puella: 'Uxor sum: nuptias enim optavi. Optando statim maritum habere illum coepi: necesse enim erat illi
marito esse si viveret; nec tempore fit matrimonium[1] sed
iure.' [Haec erto hec comprehendenda sunt finitionibus.][2]

2 Dicit pars diversa: 'Non fuisti uxor. Non substitisti[3] cum
illo. Optione tradita es quidem illi, sed statim discessit post
vocem.' Hoc finitione comprehendendum est: 'uxor est
quae femina viro nuptiis collocata in societatem vitae venit.' [Tum non est tradita.][4] Illa quid dicit? 'Uxor est cuius
cum viro matrimonium factum est.' †Pars diversa hoc
dicit.†

3 Finitio interim dicitur falsa, interim parum plena. Nos
neque falsam possumus dicere partis adversae finitionem
neque parum plenam, nec tam in subvertenda ea morari

[1] *Gron.*: patri- (*ex* pari-) A[2]
[2] *Wi.*
[3] *Fr.*: subsisti A
[4] *Wi.*

26

247

The property of a rich rapist

Let the wife get her husband's property. A rich young man committed rape. Before the girl made her option,[1] he sent his relatives to her to ask her to marry him. After hearing their pleas, she wept in silence. The young man stabbed himself. Before he died, she opted for marriage. The relatives and the wife claim the property.

DISCUSSION

I have to show you the way. See what each side wants, what each side says, and wrap it up as briefly and meaningfully as can be done. Suppose the girl says: "I am his wife, for I opted for marriage. By so opting I immediately started to have him as my husband. For he was bound to be my husband if he lived, and marriage does not happen by time but by status." The other side says: "You were not his wife. You did not settle down with him. True, you were handed over to him by your option, but he passed away immediately after the word was spoken." This must be wrapped up by a definition: "a wife is a woman placed with a man through a wedding who comes to share his life." What does *she* say? "A wife is a woman who has entered into matrimony with a man."

A definition is sometimes said to be false, sometimes incomplete. We cannot say that the opposition's definition is false or incomplete, and we ought not to spend time in sub-

---

[1] As in 262, the theme assumes knowledge of the (declamatory) law of rape: the victim has to choose between letting the rapist be executed and marrying him.

debemus quam in confirmanda nostra. Sit ergo, ut non infirmanda [finitionis genus],⁵ ita [ad]⁵ convincenda nimis
4 plena esse.⁶ Possumus enim dicere: 'ea quae viro per nuptias tradita in societatem vitae venit', sed non tantum haec uxor (sicut non negaremus uxorem si ita finiretur⁷: 'uxor est quae per nuptias a parentibus in matrimonium tradita in societate ‹vitae›⁸ multis annis fuit,' ‹cum tamen›⁹ illud 'a parentibus tradita' non necessarium in finitione uxoris
5 sit). Ista falsa quidem non sunt, sed plerisque detractis erit adhuc uxor. Fingamus enim factas esse nuptias, consecutam statim alterius mortem: erit profecto uxor, etiam te confitente, [tradita]¹⁰ etsi¹¹ in societate vitae non fuerit.' Quomodo ergo ista societas vitae adiecta non quidem mentitur sed adicit ‹non›¹² necessarium, ita illud quoque 'nuptiis collocata' efficit uxorem, sed non hoc solummodo
6 [erit].¹³ Fingamus enim nuptias quidem fecisse nullas, coisse autem liberorum creandorum gratia: non tamen uxor non erit, quamvis nuptiis non sit collocata. Videamus igitur, si ista supervacua et circumfusa sunt, ‹qualis›¹⁴ finitio huic nomini sufficiat. Neque enim hoc intueri debetis, quid desit, sed quid satis sit.

⁵ *Wi.*
⁶ *Wi.*: plenam. non A¹ (*de* A² *non liquet*)
⁷ *Sch.*: -remus A
⁸ *Leo*
⁹ *Ro.*
¹⁰ *SB*³
¹¹ *Fr.*: si A
¹² *Leo, auct. Sch.*
¹³ *Leo*
¹⁴ *Ro.*

verting it so much as in confirming our own. So let it not be
invalidated but convicted of over-amplitude. For we can
say: "A wife is a woman who, being handed over to a man
through a wedding, comes to share his life" but "wife" does
not apply exclusively to her (just as, if it were so defined: "a
wife is a woman who, being handed over into matrimony
by her parents through a wedding, has lived for many years
in partnership ⟨of life⟩," we should not deny that such a
woman is a wife ⟨although⟩ "handed over by her parents"
is not necessary in the definition of "wife"). These defini-
tions are not false, but after much has been detracted
she will still be a wife. For let us suppose that a marriage
has taken place and that death of one of the parties immediately followed: she will surely be a wife, even by your
admission, although she was not in partnership of life. So
just as that added "partnership of life" is not a lie but
an ⟨un⟩necessary addition, so also that phrase "placed
through a wedding" makes a wife, but this is not the only
qualification.[2] For let us suppose that she has not entered
into any marriage but had intercourse for the purpose of
creating children: she will not not be a wife, although she
has not been placed through a wedding. Let us see, therefore, if these items are superfluous extras, ⟨what sort of⟩
definition will suffice for this name.[3] For you ought not to
be looking for what is lacking[4] but for what is sufficient.

[2] Partnership in life is not *sine qua non* to wifely status. But if
this is not a case for double brackets, the "Master" slips. His new
argument (*fingamus . . . collocata*) makes the definition incomplete. It is also inconsistent with s.7 init.

[3] Wife.   [4] Inaccurately = "could be added." But *quid
esse possit* (SB[2]) would be logical.

7

DECLAMATIO

Dixi uxorem esse cuius cum viro matrimonium factum est.
Quid amplius? Nam sicut coitus atque congressus citra ius
non efficeret uxorem, ita uxor etiam citra haec manet. Id ex
cotidianis et in frontem incurrentibus approbari potest.
Nam, ut ab ipsis ‹verbis›[15] incipiam, [comprehendo][16]
uxorem duxisse [dici][16]: hoc ante noctem, hoc ante con-
gressum, hoc primo statim iure. Et fortasse in aliis possit
videri necessarium expectare: hic[17] de nuptiis ‹non› con-
viximus.[18] 'Est quidem ius matrimonii expletum, tamen
expecto et coitum et (id quod petis[19]) patrimonium[20] iun-
gendum.' Haec in eiusmodi condicione non sunt expectan-
da, quia antecesserint. Raptor si non occiditur, iam maritus
8   est. Id sic quoque accipitur: qui maritus erit, non est cae-
lebs; quae uxor, non vidua aut virgo. De utraque vos persona ergo volo interrogare. Putemus statim optione finita
quaeri de adulescente: diceresne illum esse caelibem? Ac
si diceres, illa[21] occurrerent[22]: 'Dic igitur caelibem. Uxorem potest aliam ducere?' Virginem hanc aut viduam non
diceres. Ac de altero[23] quaeri supervacuum est. Si virginem[24]: interrogo an esset ‹alius›[25] aliquis cuius nuptiarum
habitura esset ius puella. Crederem igitur neque illam
virginem esse constare et illum non esse caelibem. Si haec

15 *Hå.*[2]   16 *SB*[3]   17 *Ro.*: haec A
18 non c. *SB*[2]: convicimus A
19 *SB*[2]: peto A   20 *Gron.*: matri- A
21 *Sch.*: ille A
22 *SB*[3]: -urret A: -urreret *Sch.*
23 *coni. Wi.*: -ra A
24 *SB*[2]: viduam A
25 *SB*[2]

DECLAMATION

I have said that a wife is a woman of whom matrimony has been made with a man. What more? For just as coition and intercourse short of the law would not make a wife,[5] so a wife is still a wife even short of them. That can be established by everyday examples that meet us head on. For to begin with the ⟨words⟩ themselves, "to have married a wife," this comes before the night, comes before intercourse, comes as soon as there is status. And perhaps in other cases it could seem necessary to wait: in this one we did ⟨not⟩ cohabit after the marriage. [6] "True, the status of matrimony has been completed, but all the same I wait, both for coition and for combining of patrimony—which is what you are claiming." In a situation of this sort these items are not to be waited for since they have already occurred. If the rapist is not put to death, he is already husband. That is also accepted thus: he who shall be a husband is not a bachelor; she who shall be a wife is not a widow or a spinster. So I should like to put a question to you about both personae. Let us suppose that immediately after the option you are asked about the young man: would you have called him a bachelor? And if you said yes, you would face the following: "All right, call him a bachelor. Can he marry another woman?" You would not call *her* a spinster or a widow—as for the latter there is no need to ask: if a spinster, I ask whether there was anyone ⟨else⟩ whom the girl could lawfully have married. I should therefore have believed it agreed that neither was she a spinster nor he a

[5] See note 2 above.   [6] There had been no formal wedding, but it is contended that the victim's choice constituted one—retrospective to the rape (SB[2]).

uxor et ille maritus, nunc quaero cuius ille maritus, cuius
9   haec uxor. 'Nuptias tamen in domo ‹desidero›.'[26] Nuptiae
in aliis sint sane necessariae (quamquam ne id quidem
utique ius exigit, causam tamen [in domo][27] hanc habent,
ostendendae voluntatis, ‹parentum voluntate›[28] filiam tibi
aut †eam ipsam† coniungi quae sui habet potestatem):
10 hic[29] quod nuptiae efficiunt, optio fecit. Videamus an
etiam fortius atque vehementius: quippe illic voluntas, hic
etiam necessitas quaeritur. Ausim dicere utique in hoc genere litis nullas esse digniores quae retineant maritorum
hereditates quam eas quae uxores ex raptu esse coeperunt,
quoniam post raptum nulla uxor est nisi beneficio suo. Ac
forsitan inde etiam lex ista descendit.
11   Ad illa libet pervenire ad quae pars diversa vocat: an
haec digna sit quae uxoris nomen accipiat. Si hoc tantum
dicerem: meruit hereditatem pro iniuria, posset tamen videri hereditas ista genus quoddam satisfactionis. Amata
est ab adulescente: debet hoc quoque valere in portione
litis huiusce; nihil ille maluit quam ista bona, etiamsi viveret, esse communia. Ille fecit his bonis hanc legem.[30] 'Spe-
ravit de ea adulescens, ‹non amavit›[31]: ideo rogare ausus
est.' *

---

[26] *Wi.* (-ras *Ri.*)   [27] *Wi.*
[28] *SB*[3]   [29] *Ro.*: hoc A
[30] convenire *vel sim. excidisse susp. Wi.*   [31] *SB*[2]

---

[7] Not in fact (not *coitus* at least), but in effect. But perhaps add
non: "since that has not taken place, no need to wait."

[8] Taking *litis* as partitive gen. with *hoc*, *faute de mieux*.

[9] See crit. note.

[10] That she would choose marriage rather than death.

bachelor. If she was a wife and he a husband, I now ask: whose husband was he, whose wife was she? "All the same, ⟨I desiderate⟩ a wedding in the home." Granted, if you will, that a wedding is necessary in other cases (though the law does not absolutely require even that, but there is a reason—to show will, i.e. that the daughter is united with you ⟨by will of her parents,[7]⟩ or, in the case of a woman who is her own mistress, by her own will): in this case the option effected whatever a wedding effects. Let us see if we can put it even more strongly and emphatically: there it is a question of will, here of necessity as well. I should venture to assert absolutely that no women in this category of suit better deserve to retain marital inheritances than those who have begun to be wives as a result of rape, since after rape nobody is a wife except by her own benefaction. And it may be that this is the origin of that law.

Now I want to answer the opposition's challenge: is she worthy to receive the title of wife? If I were merely to say that she deserved the inheritance in return for the injury, that inheritance might still be regarded as a sort of compensation. The young man loved her; this element in this suit ought to carry its proportional weight.[8] He wanted nothing more, even if he lived, than that this property should be common. *He* made this law for his property.[9] "The young man had hopes of her,[10] this is why he dared to ask; ⟨he did not love her."[11] I am sorry for this excellent and too sensitive young man, that you should so interpret his feelings.⟩

[11] I give the words in quotation marks to the relatives and place after them those double-bracketed in s.15.

12   Nuptias petiit puella (non dico nunc de iure): cogitate
quantum beneficium dare voluerit, immo, quod ad ipsam
pertinet, dederit: remisit iniuriam raptae virginitatis ea cui
13 lex et morte[32] vindicare permisit. 'Sed sero hoc dedit.'
Etiamsi huius tarditate factum esset, non illius festina-
tione, noli tamen mirari pudicam si castitas non statim irae
suae imperare potuit. Satis praestat rapta quae non cito op-
14 tat. 'At enim iam vulnerato optavit, quoniam moriturum
sciebat; captavit hereditatem.' Num igitur animum puellae a primis temporibus raptor ignoravit? Magnum cle-
mentiae argumentum: cui potestas adeundi magistratus
statim, permissa[33] continuo vox qua se et iniuriam suam
ulcisceretur, finiret onera pudoris sui, audît rogantes diu.
Primum hoc praeiudicium eius est quae exorari possit:
15 rogari velle pro erogato[34] est. Hoc tantum non satis erat,
iudices, si dicerem 'non negavit'? Atqui dolor erumpit,
et numquam fere ira[35] silentio continetur. ⟦Miseret me
adulescentis optimi alioqui et nimis verecundi quod sic
animum eius interpretamini.⟧

    Satis[36] erat dicere: non negavit. Audeo dicere, iudices:
promisit. Neque ⟨enim⟩[37] unum promittendi genus est.

---

[32] *Sch., Gron.*: -em A
[33] *Bu.*: em- A
[34] *Ri.*: ro- A   [35] *Ro.*: i. f. A
[36] *SB¹, Wi.*: -ius A   [37] *Sch.*

---

[12] Forget the legal entitlement. She deserves the property for
what she did for him.

[13] Obscure, but perhaps: if that was the girl's attitude, would
he not have known from the start and killed himself before? To
which the relatives might answer: "How was he to know?"

The girl sought marriage (I am not speaking now of legal right[12]). Think how great a boon she wanted to give, or rather did give so far as in her lies: she forgave the injury of raped virginity when the law allowed her to avenge it by death. "But she gave this boon too late." Even if this had come of her tardiness, not his haste, don't be surprised at a modest girl if chastity could not all at once command its anger. A rape-victim who does not opt quickly grants enough. But you will say that she opted when he was already wounded, knowing he was going to die—she was after the inheritance. Was the rapist ignorant then from the outset of the girl's feelings?[13] It says a great deal for her clemency: she had the power to go before the magistrate straight away, she was free to speak immediately the word that would avenge herself and her injury, end the strain upon her modesty, but she listened long to the petitioners. First, this is a prior judgment by a woman who can be induced to forgive; the wish to be asked is as good as persuasion. Would it not be enough, gentlemen, if I simply said: "She did not refuse"? After all, indignation breaks out and anger is hardly ever contained in silence. [[I am sorry for this excellent and too sensitive[14] young man, that you should so interpret his feelings.]][15]

It would have been enough to say: "She did not refuse." Gentlemen, I venture to say: "She promised." <For> there is more than one way of making a promise. People's feel-

---

[14] Implying that he killed himself because he could not bear the shame (and not because he despaired of pardon).

[15] See note 11.

Voluntas hominum non tantum voce signata est. An vero si manum porrexisset[38] aut vultu adnuisset, dedisse fidem et confirmasse spem puella videretur: ⟨non videbitur⟩[39] quae facie adfectum, quae totis oculis misericordiam pro-

16 didit? Flevit: idem fecit quod illi qui rogabant. Ad mentionem periculi, ad mentionem carnificis, uberes lacrimas profudit. Certe non video adfectum qui occidat. 'Sed tacuit.' Alioqui hoc vos exigebatis ab ea quae modo virgo fuerat, quae hoc nomen paulo ante perdiderat, ut de nuptiis

17 loqueretur nisi ubi necesse erat? 'At post vulnus optavit.' Ecce maiorem misericordiam: suscepit raptoris sui misera curationem. Queritur quippe de Fortuna quod beneficium perdidit. Neque enim revellere[40] poterat tam alte exactam manum. Misera existimabat hoc eum fecisse causa misera-

18 tionis. Pervenit tamen aliqua ad illum laetitia datae salutis; etiamsi brevis, tamen grata est voluptas. Ad vocem eius auditam[41] certe oculos sustulit. Si nihil aliud, hoc certe solacii tulit, non mori se tamquam damnatum; non illum quamvis semianimem atque palpitantem invasit carnifex, non vulneratum cruentumque per ora populi traxit, non illi[42] caput vel exanime legi recisum est.

Pro ⟨raptor⟩[43] immitis, qui de summa clementia tam triste fecit exemplum!

[38] *Hå.*[2]: manu promisisset A
[39] *Gron.*
[40] *Ro.*: div- A
[41] *Bestius*: voce . . . audita A
[42] *Ro.* (*et* exanimi lege): illud A
[43] *SB*[1]

ings can be indicated by other means than words. If she had put out her hand or assented by her expression, the girl would have seemed to have given her word and confirmed his hope. <Will she not so seem> when she showed her emotion by her face, betrayed her pity in every look? She wept; she did the same as the petitioners. At the mention of danger, at the mention of the executioner, she shed copious tears. I certainly do not see the emotion of a killer. "But she said nothing." Anyway,[16] were you asking of one who had recently been a virgin and only just lost that title that she should speak of marriage when she did not have to? "But she opted *after* the stroke." There's pity all the greater: the poor girl undertook the treatment of her rapist. Surely she complains of Fortune in that she wasted her boon. For she could not pluck out the hand thrust in so deep. Poor girl, she thought he had done it to win pity! All the same, the joy of life granted did reach him in some measure; pleasure is welcome even when brief. He certainly raised his eyes when he heard her words. If nothing else, he had the consolation of not dying as a man condemned. The executioner did not assault him though half alive and palpitating, did not drag him wounded and bleeding before the public's eyes, his head was not cut off even after death to satisfy the law.

Ah cruel <rapist>, that made so sad an example out of supreme mercy!

---

[16] *Alioqui*, "of very indeterminate function here" (Wi.). But the drift may be "silence was not refusal and anyhow . . ."

248

Octo anni duplicis imprudentiae

Imprudentis caedis damnatus quinquennio exulet. Exulem intra fines liceat occidere. Qui caedem per imprudentiam commiserat, abiit in exilium. Ibi tertio anno exilii aliam caedem similiter commisit. Explevit tempus quinquennii ex eo tempore quo iterum occiderat. Redeuntem illum post octavum annum occidit quidam intra fines. Reus est caedis.

1   DECLAMATIO

Non continuo occisus homo ad crimen et ad damnationem pertinet, cum hoc interim legibus facere liceat. ⟦Quotiens autem licet, etiam oportet.⟧[1] Exulem occidere intra fines
2 licet. Id ius dupliciter efficitur. Aut enim redit cui omnino ⟨non⟩[2] licet, aut [non][3] redit ⟨cui non⟩[4] nisi ⟨post tempus⟩[5] licet. Nescio an ex iis duobus etiam iustius videatur occidi qui redit contra leges cum[6] aliquando iure rediturus sit. Illum enim sane cupiditas patriae et ultima desperatio
3 cogat aliquando furtum facere iuri. Praeterea cum aut ita revertantur exules tamquam in hoc fallant, aut ita tamquam iis facere liceat, aliquanto magis ii occidendi sunt qui palam contra ius revertuntur. Illis enim remissum furtum non utique nocet in exemplum, neque is qui se agnoscit

[1] *ita secl. SB*[3]
[2] *Sch., Gron., auct. Pith.*
[3] *Hå.*[2]
[4] *Hå.*[2], *auct. Sch., Ro.*
[5] *Ro.*
[6] *Ro.:* cum . . . qui A

248

Eight years for a double involuntary homicide

Let one found guilty of involuntary homicide be in exile for five years. Let it be lawful to kill an exile inside the borders. A man who had killed involuntarily went into exile. There in the third year of his exile he committed another homicide in a similar way. He completed the five-year period dating from the second homicide. As he was returning after the eighth year, somebody killed him inside the borders. He stands trial for murder.

DECLAMATION

The killing of a man does not automatically involve crime and conviction, since sometimes this is legally permissible. ⟦And when it is permissible, it is also incumbent.⟧ It is permissible to kill an exile inside the borders. That legal right arises in two ways: either the person returning is ⟨not⟩ permitted to return at all or the person returning ⟨is not⟩ permitted to return except ⟨after a time⟩. I incline to think that of the two the one who returns against the law when he would later return legally seems the more justly killed. The other might arguably be driven by homesickness and ultimate desperation to cheat the law. Furthermore, since exiles either return as eluding detection or as so licensed, those who return openly against the law deserve death considerably more. For in the former's case the remission of their cheat[1] does not necessarily make a harmful precedent and someone who acknowledges that he is returning

---

[1] Not punished because not discovered. But "remission" is loose.

contra ius reverti diu intra fines mansurus est. Is vero qui
contra legem sciens redit temptat iura vincere et in impudentia sua perseveraturus est.

4   Videamus nunc an huic qui[7] cum redisset[8] occisus est
reverti tempore illo liceat. 'Imprudentis caedis damnatus
quinquennio exulet.' Utrum hoc intellegimus, singulis
caedibus quinquennium esse constitutum? [an interest aliquid quotiens quisque peccaverit?][9] [[Nulla invenietur ratio qua duae caedes octo annis exulatum efficiant.]] Non,[10]
si imprudentis caedis damnatum quinquennio exulare
oportet, nihil intererit quot quisque occiderit. Ego igitur
hoc dico: quotiens commissa sit caedes, totiens quinquen-
5   nium esse ponendum. Et hoc satis firme tueri aliarum[11]
rerum exemplo possumus. Fingamus talem legem ut qui
furtum fecerit solvat quadruplum: *[12] ponamus quamlibet
poenam ei qui iniuriarum fuerit damnatus: num dubium
est quin quotiens iniuriam commiserit, totiens passurus sit
et poenam? Ergo si animadversio contra singula delicta
constituta est, hic bis deliquit: bis puniri debuit, decem
annis exilium implere debuit.

6   Sed ex eo, inquit, tempore quo sequentem caedem
commisit quinquennium explevit. Nihil mea refert utrum
sequenti caedi non reddiderit tempus quod debebat an
iam[13] priori. Nam si quinquennium ex triennio numeras,

[7] h. q. *Sch., Gron.*: sicut A
[8] *Gron.*: decessi- A
[9] *del. putavit Wi.*
[10] *SB*[3]: nam A
[11] *Gron.*: aliena- A
[12] *lac. ind.* A
[13] an iam *SB*[1]: etiam A

illegally will not stay long within the borders, whereas a man who wittingly[2] returns illegally is trying to defeat the law and is going to persist in his impudence.

Let us now see whether the man who was killed after his return had license to come back at that time. "Let one found guilty of involuntary homicide be in exile for five years." Do we understand this to mean that a five-year term is constituted for each separate homicide? ⟦No rationale will be discovered whereby two homicides result in a banishment for eight years.⟧ If one found guilty of involuntary homicide should be in exile for five years, that is not to say that it makes no difference how many people each person kills. So this is what I say: as often as homicide is committed, so often the five-year period is to be posited. And we can maintain this firmly enough by the example of other items. Let us imagine a law providing that one who steals pay fourfold ∗. And let us assume that there is a penalty, no matter what, for a person found guilty of injuries: is there any doubt that he will suffer that penalty as often as he commits an injury? So if the punishment is constituted against separate offences, this man has offended twice, he should have been punished twice, he should have completed his exile over ten years.

"But," says the defense, "he completed five years from the time he committed the second homicide." It is no concern of mine whether he failed to discharge the time he owed the second homicide or what he already owed the first. For if you count the five-year period from the three-

---

[2] In the first category the exile confessedly breaks the law. In the second (put obscurely) he claims that his return is legal, though he knows better.

illud prius non est satis plenum; si adsignas priori caedi
suum tempus, non coepit exulare sequenti caedi nisi post
quinquennium. Explica enim mihi medium illud bien-
7 nium. An hoc dicis: 'nihil interest'? ⟦Dic mihi quo modo
magis exulaverit quam si unum occidisset.⟧[14] Quod est istud contra leges compendium, ut idem illud biennium
prioris poenae ultimum sit, sequentis primum? Libet interrogare tamquam praesentem. Illo medio tempore utri
8 exulasti? Cuius hoc morti lex praestitit? ⟦Fingamus enim
duos statim occisos, ut duos ita etiam plures, et ad quem-
cumque numerum: nulla differentia est inter eum qui in
uno lapsus est et eum qui satisfactionem pluribus debet?
'Imprudentis caedis damnatus quinquennio exulet.' Ista
ratione statim poterat post quinquennium redire, siqui-
dem hoc dicere satis est: 'caedem imprudens commisit,
quinquennium exulavit.'⟧

9 Videamus nunc quam rationem secuta sit lex consti-
tuenda eiusmodi poena,[15] quam mehercule videtur mihi
prius[16] clementia quam iustitia constituisse. Pro vita[17]
hominis innocentis [pro vita][18] quinquennio denique con-
10 stituit absentiam. Ego quidem impudentiam illius vel in
hoc mirari satis non possum, quod festinavit tam cito in patriam reverti. Est enim ut sibi aliquis unum casum remittat
et semel lapsus errore se humanae necessitatis excuset; hic
vero qui commisit iterum idem quo exilium meruit, com-
putatis diebus atque horis, legem tantummodo inspexit,
non etiam crimina sua numeravit, nihil verecundiae suae

[14] *ita secl. SB*[3]   [15] *SB*[1]: -dae . . . –nae A
[16] *SB*[1]: priore A
[17] *SB*[1]: prae morte A
[18] *SB*[1] (*cf. Watt*[1])

year, that previous period is incomplete, whereas if you assign the first homicide its proper time, the exile begins his exile for the second homicide only after five years. Explain that middle two-year period to me. Or are you saying: "It doesn't matter?" ⟦Tell me how he has been in exile more than if he had killed once.⟧ What is this illegal abridgement, making that same two years the end of the earlier punishment and the beginning of the later? I should like to question him as though he were here present. On whose account were you in exile during that middle period? Whose was the death to which the law made this allocation? ⟦For let us imagine that two men were killed right away—or, as two, so more and up to any number: is there no difference between a man who made a mistake in the case of one and a man who owes satisfaction to more than one? "Let a man found guilty of involuntary homicide be in exile for five years." On your reasoning he could return at once after five years, if it is enough to say: "He committed homicide involuntarily, he has been in exile for five years."⟧

Let us see now what rationale the law followed in constituting such a punishment—and upon my word it seems to me to have so constituted more in mercy than in justice. In requital for the life of an innocent person it constituted an absence of just five years. For my part I cannot wonder enough at the impudence of him—just that he was in such a hurry to return to his country. A man may forgive himself one accident, excuse himself for a single false step on the ground that to err is human; but this man who repeated the same offence for which he deserved exile added up the days and the hours and merely looked at the law without also numbering his crimes or adding anything in satisfac-

adiecit, nihil pudori. Quis autem indignari potest eum interfectum qui occiderit duos? Nam si ulla hoc loco miseratio est, debet esse pro illis.

11   Haec dicerem tamquam de eo ad quem lex pertineret quae caedem imprudentem damnaret. Lex quomodo constituit? 'Imprudentis caedis damnatus quinquennio exulet.' Nihil mea interest an imprudens occiderit. Non enim ius ita[19] constitutum est ut qui imprudens occiderit quinquennio exulet, sed qui caedis damnatus imprudentis sit

12   quinquennio exulet. Hominem occidit in exilio fortasse imprudens: constitui tamen oportuit ab imprudente esse occisum. Nam quotiens aliquis interfectus est, aut id quaeritur, an omnino interfectus sit ab eo qui arguitur, aut id, an ab imprudente aut per imprudentem sit interfectus. Hic quidem certum erat ⟨ab illo⟩[20] interfectum esse hominem, sed ab imprudente interfectum[21] esse pronuntiari opor-

13   tuit. Non modo alterum quinquennium debuit legi, sed perpetuam [paene][22] poenam. Imprudentis caedis damnari genus absolutionis est. Hoc illi non contigit. Remittamus tamen in praesentia perpetuam poenam. De illo quis dubitabit, non posse eum damnari nisi post exactam iam quinquennii proprii poenam? Fingamus illi quinquennio peracto redire licuisse: accusari tum debebat, tum damnari,

---

[19] *Obr., auct. Sch., Gron.*: iustitia A
[20] *Ro.*
[21] *Ri.*: ita A
[22] *om. ed. Leid., del. Ro.*

---

[3] A strange doctrine. Could he not have been tried and sentenced to an additional five years, starting at the expiry of the first

tion of his remorse, his shame. And who can feel any indignation at the killing of a man who has slain two? If there is
any compassion here, it ought to be for them.

This is what I would have said if I were speaking of a
man who came under the law condemning involuntary homicide. What did the law lay down? "Let one found guilty
of involuntary homicide be in exile for five years." It is no
concern of mine whether he committed involuntary homicide. The law is not so framed as to require that he who has
committed involuntary homicide be in exile for five years
but that he who is found guilty of involuntary homicide be
in exile for five years. He killed a man while in exile, perhaps involuntarily; but it should have been determined
that the killing was involuntary. For whenever someone
has been killed, there are two questions: was he in fact
killed by the person accused or was he killed involuntarily,
directly or indirectly? In this case it was clear that a man
was killed <by the person in question>, but it should have
been declared that the killing was involuntary. Not only
did he owe the law another five years, but a punishment in
perpetuity. To be found guilty of involuntary homicide is a
sort of acquittal. This did not happen in his case. But let us
remit punishment in perpetuity for the present. Who will
have any doubt that he cannot be found guilty[3] until after
the punishment of the five years pertaining to him has
been completed? Let us suppose that after the five years
have expired he was free to return; he should then have

term? The declaimer says there had been no verdict of involuntary homicide on the second death, therefore no trial (none is
mentioned in the theme). Why then was the exile not free to return at the end of the five-year term?

45

tum in alterum quinquennium abire.[23]

14   Et, rogo, quid interest idem istud quo tempore exilii fecerit? Si peracto iam quinquennio aut in fine certe quinquennii hominem per imprudentiam occidisset, num dubium quin vobis considentibus[24] alterum quinquennium fuerit[25] debiturus? Ita bene illi cessit quod hominem citius occidit?

15   SERMO

Haec fere sunt quae in themate sunt posita. Qui[26] imprudens occidisse videatur, supervacuum habeo quaerere quicquam de animo illius, quamvis duos occiderit.

249

Abolitio adulteri fortis

Ne liceat cum adultera marito agere nisi prius cum adultero egerit. Coepit agere maritus cum eo quem adulterum esse dicebat. Bellum incidit. Inter moras iudicii fortiter pugnavit is qui accusabatur. Petît praemii nomine iudicii abolitionem; impetravit. Vult agere cum adultera. ⟨Praescribit.⟩[1] CD.

1   SERMO

An semper cum adultero prius agere necesse sit. An hic egerit. An, etiam si quid defuit actioni, quoniam tamen

[23] *Ro.*: abisset A	[24] *SB*[1] (*cf. SB*[2]): confite- A
[25] *Ri.*: erit A	[26] *SB*[1]: ut A
[1] *SB*[4]	

---

[1] See 246, note 1.
[2] The husband.

been accused, then found guilty, then go into exile for another five years.

And, I ask, what difference does it make at what point
of time during his exile he committed the same act? If he
had involuntarily killed a man after the five-year period
had been completed or at least as the five-year period was
ending, is there any doubt that he would have owed another five years, with you on the jury bench? Was he so
lucky in that he killed a man sooner?

DISCUSSION

These then, pretty much, are the points posited in the
theme. In the case of a man who is thought to have killed
involuntarily I hold it as superfluous to inquire as to intent,
although he killed twice.

249

Quashing of an adulterer hero

A husband shall not be free to sue an adulteress unless he
has previously sued the adulterer. A husband began a suit
against a man who he said was the adulterer. War inter-
vened. While the trial was hanging fire, the accused person
became a hero.[1] By way of reward he asked for the trial to
be quashed and gained his point. He[2] wishes to sue the
adulteress. ⟨She demurs.⟩[3] Speech in opposition.

DISCUSSION

Is it always necessary to sue the adulterer first? Has he
sued? Even if the suit is in some respect imperfect, yet,

[3] *Praescribit*: objects to a trial on the ground that the adulterer
has not been prosecuted.

publice iudicium[2] interceptum est, non debeat huius actionibus nocere. Quae mens fuerit praemium dantis rei publicae. Utrum uni abolitionem iudicii, an per coniunctionem[3] utriusque et adulterae dederit. Summum quod in omnibus controversiis est, utrum aequius sit.

2

Adulterii ream defero. Puto, hoc auribus vestris non novum crimen est; quod satis est, non ab hac coepi. Qualem causam pertulerim sic aestimare potestis: petitur altera abolitio. Ille optavit, haec praescribit, neuter negat. Postea videbo an isti oporteat tantum praestari quantum viro forti; interim semota personarum ratione ipsam excutere legem volo.

3   'Ne liceat' inquit 'cum adultera agere marito nisi prius cum adultero egerit.' Differo illa quae fecit, differo quae passus sum; hoc in praesentia dico, non utique semper exigi ut prius agatur cum adultero. Id vobis, iudices, facillime persuaderi poterit si non tam iniustos neque tam imprudentes existimatis legum latores fuisse ut necessitate constringerent[4] ea quae praestari non possent. Satis sine dubio lex ipsa dicendo 'ne prius cum adultera agatur quam cum adultero actum fuerit' ostendit se de iis loqui quorum

4 uterque accusari potest. Admonebo tamen uno aut altero argumento quantam lex ipsa, si ita accipitur, passura iniuriam sit. Fingamus enim adulterum vel sua voluntate vel [ita][5] interveniente fato statim decessisse: hoc iustum po-

---

2 *SB*[3]: -co –cio A
3 *Ri.*: -iecturam A
4 *coni. Wi.*: praes- A
5 *Wi.*

since the trial has been interrupted on public grounds, is it not right that his suit should not be adversely affected? What had the commonwealth in mind when it granted the reward? Did it grant the quashing of the trial to one person only or conjointly to the adulteress also? Finally, as in all controversies, which of the two is the more equitable?

DECLAMATION

I charge her with adultery. I imagine this charge does not come to your ears as something new. Enough that I am not starting with her. You can judge what sort of case I brought from the fact that a second quashing is sought. He opted, she demurs, neither denies. I shall consider later whether it is right that she be accorded as much as a hero. Meanwhile I want to analyze the law itself, setting personae aside.

"A husband," she says, "shall not be free to prosecute an adulteress unless he has previously prosecuted the adulterer." What she did, what I suffered, I leave till later. This only I say at present: that a prior action against the adulterer is not always absolutely required. That this is so, gentlemen of the jury, you can be most easily persuaded if you consider that the lawmakers were not so unjust or so unwise as to impose as necessary conditions requirements that could not be met. In saying "an adulteress shall not be sued before the adulterer has been sued" the law itself assuredly shows sufficiently that it is speaking of persons both of whom *can* be sued. But I shall bring one or two arguments to show how much damage the law itself will suffer if it be so interpreted. For let us suppose that the adulterer has died straight away either by his own will or by an intervention of fate: shall it possibly seem just that,

terit videri, ut, quoniam alterum debito supplicio Fata
5   subtraxerint, altera quoque impunitatem mereatur? Fingamus adulterum[6] conscientia criminis profugisse, nullo
modo facere sui potestatem: numquid exigetis ut ideo cum
adultera non agatur quoniam adulter crimen verum esse
6   confessus sit? Nullo modo id iustum videri potest. ⟦Nam is
qui dicit 'cum adultero prius agere debes', illud dicit: 'prius cum adultero age.' Fingamus autem[7] vel a te ipsa vel
ab alia nobis adulterii rea hanc [quoque][8] proponi prae-
scriptionem. Nonne illa patronorum defensio firmissima
erit: 'habes adulterum; lex te ab illo ordiri iubet: quid tran-
7   silis?' hoc in hac[9] non potest dici. Quis igitur credat eius
condicionis esse iura ulla ut aliquid non liceat et necesse
sit? Nam si mihi hoc ab ea dicitur: 'accusa prius adulterum,' ad te venio, res publica: accusare adulterum volo. ⟧[10]

8   Haec dicerem si non inchoassem, si nihil fecissem.
Nunc egi cum adultero, aut, qui[11] contentus essem voluntate [legis],[12] agere volui. ⟨Id⟩[13] per me stetit; habet lex
animum meum. Coepi, egi; nec lex utique ullo scripto hoc
comprehendit, ut mihi necesse sit agere usque ad finem.
Nam etsi iudices consedissent et absolvissent, ego tamen
egeram. Apparet igitur non exitu iudicii constare actionem
9   sed introitu. Igitur, si absolutus esset is quem tuum adulterum dicebam, agere mihi tecum licebat et ista praescriptio

     6 *Ri.*: alterum A
     7 *Ri.*: enim A
     8 *SB*[3]
     9 *SB*[1]: hanc A: hac causa *Watt*[1]
     10 *ita secl. SB*[3]
     11 a.q. *SB*[1]: et si A
     12 *Wi.*   13 *SB*[1], non *ante* stetit *Pith., edd.*

since the Fates have withdrawn one of the two from punishment he deserved, the other too gain impunity? Let us suppose that the adulterer in consciousness of guilt has taken flight, makes it impossible to get hold of him: will you demand that there be no proceedings against the adulteress because the adulterer has confessed that the charge is true? No way can this appear just. ⟦For he that says "you should first sue the adulterer," is saying "first sue the adulterer."[4] Let us suppose that this demurrer is put up for us either by you yourself[5] or by another woman charged with adultery. Will not the advocates' most solid defense be this: "You have the adulterer; the law requires you to begin with him. Why do you pass him over?" But in this woman's case that cannot be said. So who would believe that any laws can be of such a nature that a procedure is both not permitted and necessary? For if she says to me: "First charge the adulterer," I appeal to you, commonwealth: "I *want* to charge the adulterer."⟧

This is what I should have said if I had not begun, if I had done nothing. As it is, I *did* sue the adulterer, or rather, being content with purpose, I wanted to sue him. ⟨That⟩ depended on me; the law has my intention. I began, I sued; and nowhere in its text does the law state explicitly that I must sue to a finish. For even if the jury had sat and acquitted, none the less I had sued. It is evident therefore that suing does not consist in the end result of a trial but in its initiation. Accordingly, if the man whom I declared to be your adulterer had been acquitted, I should have been free to sue you and your demurrer would have been void: shall I

---

[4] Sheer inanity?
[5] A demurrer had been put up by the wife.

nulla esset: nunc non licebit agere quia se confessus est
absolvi non posse?

Egi. Puta enim eadem statim die qua reum detuli inter-
rogari te quid faciam †an ante†. Cum album descripsi, cum
iudices reieci, per illas omnes moras iudiciorum, longas nimium et pro nocentibus compositas, quid aliud feci quam
10 ut agerem? Non infitiaberis me agere coepisse. †Quid qui
agere coepit quia semel contigit num.†[14] Cum agere coepi,
⟨egi⟩[15]; neque enim videri possem[16] agere coepisse nisi
egissem. Ergo quantocumque tempore egi; nihil obest non
consummasse. Neque enim eum qui non vicit negaveris
pugnasse, neque eum qui fructus non percepit negaveris
possedisse, aut eum qui naufragium fecit[17] negaveris navi-
11 gasse. 'Sed abolitionem petît.' Vel hoc argumento satis
iusto probare possum egisse me. Tum igitur cum abolitio
petebatur quid ego eram? Actor, ut opinor, et accusator.
Quid ille erat? Reus, opinor. Atqui hoc nomen numquam
12 in eum adversum quem non agitur cadit. Tu hodie quid pu-
gnas? Ne adversus te agere incipiam. Nam eventus, ut tu
vis videri, dubius est, contra multa accidere possunt adhuc
propter quae iudicium ipsum non agatur. Praescribis tamen ne agam, id est, ne nomen tuum deferam, ne te legibus obligem. Qui[18] igitur tecum acturus sim statim, sic[19]
cum illo iam egi.

13 Sed[20] putemus non contineri actionem non finito iudicio: si tamen ⟨non⟩[21] mea culpa accidit quo minus iudi-

---

[14] quisquis a. c. ⟨agit⟩ (egit *Watt*[1]) quia s. c. rem *Ro.*, *auct.*
Obr.   [15] *Obr.*   [16] *Obr.*: possum A
[17] *Ri.*: fecerit A   [18] *SB*[3]: cum A
[19] *SB*[3]: si A   [20] egi. Sed *Ro.*: egissem A
[21] *Gron.*

now be forbidden to sue because he has confessed that he could not be acquitted?[6]

I sued. Suppose that on the very day on which I laid my charge you were asked what I was doing. When I copied the list,[7] when I challenged the jurors, through all those judicial delays, too long as they were and made up in the interest of the guilty, what else did I do but sue? You will not deny that I started to sue. Whoever begins to sue ⟨has sued,⟩ because once for all * * *. When I started to sue, ⟨I sued⟩; for I could not have been seen to begin without suing. So for however short a time, I sued; that I did not finish is nothing to the contrary. You would not say that a non-winner did not fight, or that an owner who received no returns did not own, or that the survivor of a shipwreck had not put to sea. "But he asked for a quashing." I can use this very argument as a sufficiently cogent proof that I had sued. So when the quashing was being asked for, what was I? A plaintiff, I imagine, and an accuser. What was he? A defendant, I imagine. But that name never applies to a person not being sued. What are you contending for to-day? To prevent me starting to sue you. For the outcome, as you would like it to appear, is in doubt and to the contrary many things can still happen to prevent the trial itself taking place. And yet you enter a demurrer to ban me from suing, that is to say from laying charge against you and legally constraining you. So, just as I am about to sue you straight away, so I have already sued him.

But let us suppose that no action[8] is involved when a trial is not concluded. If, however it was ⟨not⟩ my fault

---

6 By opting for the annulment of the suit against him.

7 Of jurors.   8 I.e. no prosecution.

cium finiretur, satis iniuriae passus sum in priore iudicio, et potest apud aequos iudices pro actione perfecta haberi quoniam mihi agenti consummare non licuit.

14   Dixi igitur ea quae ad causam pertinebant, neque semper priorem adulterum accusari posse, et a me actum esse, ⟨et⟩[22] etiamsi non esset perfecta actio, tamen quoniam re publica interveniente et lege viri fortis perfecta non esset, proinde eam haberi oportere ac si ego fecissem quidquid

15 volui. ⟦Propius accedere ad complexionem[23] huiusce rei volo. Crimen adulterii duos continet. Ex iis necesse est qui cum adultero prius agit agat et cum adultera. Num igitur hoc mihi dicere potes,[24] prius me agere tecum? Non potes.[25] Secundo te loco ream detuli, secundo loco produxi ad magistratus. At quidquid secundum est habeat aliquid prius necesse est. Haec natura ita sunt copulata ut, si cum adultero egi prius, tecum agam; si non egi, ago tecum prius tamquam cum adultero [iam egero].[26]⟧

16   Reliquum est intueri, iudices, voluntatem quoque rei publicae quae fuit tempore illo quo praemium dabat. Petît abolitionem vir fortis, ut opinor, sibi, nec potuit accipere

---

[22] *coni. Wi.*   [23] *SB*[1]: confessi- A
[24] *Ro., Ri.:* -est A
[25] tecum? Non p. *coni. Wi.:* t. n. oportet A
[26] *Ro.*

---

[9] It has been quashed in the preliminary stages before the court assembled.

[10] After the summing up in s.14 this passage looks like an afterthought by somebody. Two alternatives are presented: (a) the prosecution of one of the pair involving that of the other; (b) the prosecution of the adulteress following that of the lover. Applying

that the trial was not concluded,[9] I suffered enough injury in the former trial, and with fair judges it can be considered a completed action, since I as litigator was not permitted to consummate it.

So I have dealt with points that pertained to my case: that an adulterer cannot always be accused previously, that I did sue, that even though the action was not completed, yet, since the commonwealth interposed and it was not completed by reason of the hero's law, the action should be viewed as though I had done whatever I wished. ⟦I wish to come closer for a summary of this matter. The crime of adultery involves two persons. Of these two it must needs be that he who prosecutes the adulterer first also prosecutes the adulteress. So can you say to me that I am prosecuting you first? You cannot. I laid charge against you in the second place, I brought you before the magistrates in the second place. But whatever is second must have something prior. These things are so linked by nature that if I sued the adulterer first, I am suing you; If not, I am suing you first as though I were suing the adulterer.⟧[10]

It remains, gentlemen, also to examine what the commonwealth had in view when it gave the reward. The hero, I imagine, asked for the quashing on his own account and could not get any quashing except the one he asked for.

(b) there is no problem; the prosecutor will be in compliance with the law. But if his prosecution is disallowed as incomplete, he can apply (a), calling a prosecution of the adulteress a prosecution of the lover. That, however, nullifies the legal basis of the controversy, which by the word *prius* requires a separate prosecution of the lover. But it could be argued that the *intention* of the law would be met by prosecuting them jointly.

nisi quam petît. Alioqui si hoc tempore et suam abolitionem petisset et tuam, primum omnium duo praemia petisset; at,[27] quantumlibet meritis eius deberemus, nemo tamen passus esset duplici praemio unam honorari militiam.

17 Tuam abolitionem quare illi concesserimus? Nam abolitionis ipsi[28] concedendae ratio quaedam fuit; etiamsi peccavit, etiamsi gravem uni fecit iniuriam, redemit tamen
hoc virtute, redemit sanguine, redemit vulneribus: in te
quid spectabit[29] abolitio? Quod vitiis tuis et cupiditate illum quoque bonum alioqui, ut apparuit, civem adulterum
fecisti?

18 Scio, iudices, hactenus pertinere actionem ad hodiernum iudicium, nec quae sum obiecturus cum mihi accusare permiseritis hodie dicenda sunt. Quomodo deprehenderim, quo teste,[30] relinquo: illud tantum, qualem hanc
putetis esse feminam quae defendi noluit? Quamquam
hoc iam prior ille confessus est, qui, cum fortiter fecisset,
cum recenti meritorum gratia niteretur, plus tamen putavit apud vos valere [virtutem et][31] religionem et fidem ves

19 tram, sicut vere putavit. Hodierno igitur iudicio apparebit
an illi abolitionem petere necesse fuerit. Non estis exhortandi mihi ad tuendam castitatem, civitati ante omnia necessariam. Matrimoniis, etiamsi ego tacuerim, scitis contineri civitatem, [his populos,][32] his liberos et successionem
patrimoniorum et gradum hereditatum, his securitatem

27 *Obr.*: ut A
28 illi . . . ipsi *Ri.*: ipsi . . . illi A
29 *Ro.*: -avit A
30 *Sch.*: quos testes A
31 *SB*[3]
32 *SB*[4]

Otherwise, if at this time he had asked for quashing both in his own case and in yours, first of all he would have been asking for two rewards. But however much we owed him for what he did, no one would have tolerated that one military service be honored with a double reward. Why should we have granted him *your* quashing? For there was some sense in granting quashing to *him*. Even though he had done wrong, done grave injury to an individual, still he made amends for that by his courage, by his blood, by his wounds. But in your case what reason will there be for a quashing? Shall it be because by your vices and lust you made him too, otherwise, as plainly appeared, a good citizen, into an adulterer?

I know, gentlemen, that my plea concerns only today's proceedings and that I must not state today the evidence that I shall produce when you give me permission: how I caught them, what witnesses I had, I leave aside. I only ask what you think of this woman who did not wish to be defended—though to be sure the other, who came first, has already confessed this[11]: although a hero, although he could rely on your gratitude for his recent services, he thought that your oath and good faith carry more weight with you, and right he was. So the present proceedings will show whether he needed to ask for a quashing. It is not for me to exhort you to protect chastity, necessary as it is above all else to the community. You know without any words of mine that the community is bound up with marriages: children,[12] the passing on of patrimonies, the order of inheri-

---

[11] In getting his own trial quashed he as good as admitted her guilt as well as his.   [12] See crit. note. *His populos* does not belong with the other items; and only this community is in mind.

20 domesticam. Quomodo enim peregrinabimur? Quomodo ad colendos discedemus agros? Quae nobis securitas dabitur suscipientibus legationes publicas, euntibus in militiam, cum frequenter bella sint?

Potest vobis contingere ut et praemium viro forti dederitis et tamen adulterium vindicemus.

250

Sortitio ignominiosorum

Qui iniuriarum damnatus fuerit, ignominiosus sit. Ignominioso ne qua sit actio. Duo adulescentes invicem ‹iniuriarum›[1] agere coeperunt. Sortiti sunt utrius iudicium prius ageretur. Is qui sorte vicerat egit et damnavit iniuriarum. Damnato agere volenti praescribit.

1   SERMO

Patronum necessario dabimus. Nam etiam ut agere illi liceat, est tamen ignominiosus.

2   DECLAMATIO

'Ignominioso ne qua sit actio.' Si hodie primum deferret, necesse habebat pati condicionem fortunae suae. Nunc praescribendi tempus abiit. Tum enim praescribere debuisti, si poteras,[2] cum delatus es, et in hoc ipsum praescribere, ne deferret. Neque enim ulla praescriptio inchoata

---

¹ *Ro.*
² *Pith.*: potestis A

---

¹ In fact, he implies, it did not. There had been no prejudgment and he had agreed to the lottery.

tances, domestic security. For how shall we travel abroad?
How shall we leave to work our land? What security shall
we be given when we undertake public missions, go on
military service, since wars are of common occurrence?

You can have both: you have given the hero his reward
and yet we can punish adultery.

250

Persons under stigma cast lots

Let him who has been found guilty of injuries be under
stigma. Let no person under stigma have the right to bring
action. Two young men commenced reciprocal actions
⟨for injuries⟩. They drew lots to determine whose trial
should take place first. The winner prosecuted and convicted the other of injuries. When the other wants to bring
action, he enters a demurrer.

DISCUSSION

Of necessity we shall give him an advocate. For even
though he be free to bring action, he is none the less under
stigma.

DECLAMATION

"Let no person under stigma have the right to bring action." If he were laying charge today for the first time, he
would have no choice but to put up with the situation as his
fortune makes it. As it is, the time for a demurrer has gone
by. For you should have entered a demurrer, if it lay in your
power,[1] when the charge against you was brought, and the
demurrer should have been to just that—the bringing of
charge. For no demurrer prohibits the completion of pro-

iudicia peragi vetat, sed[3] inchoari aliquando prohibet. Actio isti cui praescribis data est, nec data solum verum etiam
3   inchoata: invicem rei fuistis. Quid enim? Tu initium putas actionis cum iudices consederint, cum ad dicendum surrexerit orator? Minime. ⟦Haec enim tu fecisti felicitate sortitionis.[4]⟧ Et lex quae ignominioso non dedit actionem hoc spectavit, ne omnino in causam educendi potestatem haberet, ne reum faciendi, ne in periculum perducendi. Quae si omnia iam facta sunt, tempus praescriptionis transiit.

4   Accedit et illud, quod quaerendum est: 'ignominioso ne qua sit actio iniuriarum:' ⟨utrum omnium an⟩[5] earum quae factae sint postea quam ignominiosus esse coepit? Fecit iniuriam aliquis [ei],[6] fecit frustra ignominioso. Videtur minus peccasse quam si aliquem civem, cui integer status esset, laesisset. Hunc contemptum utique noluit damnatis[7] lex esse nisi post damnationem. Hoc autem de quo quaeritur confitearis oportet actum esse ante damna-
5   tionem. ⟦Tam ignominioso noluit esse actionem quam ignominiae vindictam.⟧ Ut si ius emendi auferretur damnato, manerent tamen ea quae emisset antequam damnaretur.

Ergo non tempore praescribis, nec perire ea causa potest cuius origo ante damnationem est.
6   Haec dicerem cuicumque et in quacumque actione:

[3] *SB1, Wi.*: si A
[4] *Gron.*: actio- A
[5] *SB2* (an *iam Ro.*)
[6] *Wi.*
[7] *Gron.*: -ionis A

ceedings already commenced, only their commencement at any future time. Action had been granted to the object of your demurrer, and not only granted but actually begun: you were both charged reciprocally. For come, do you think action begins when the jury take their seats and the pleader rises to speak? Not a bit of it. ⟦For you did this because of the luck of the draw.⟧ And the law which denied a person under stigma the right to bring action aimed at depriving such absolutely of the power to bring to court, put on trial, set at risk. If all that has already taken place, the time for a demurrer has gone by.

Furthermore, we have to ask ⟨whether⟩ "let no person under stigma have the right to bring action for injuries" refers to ⟨all injuries or⟩ only to those that took place after he fell under stigma. Someone committed injury, committed it without consequence against a person under stigma; he is regarded as less guilty than if he had injured a citizen in good standing. The law definitely did not want this contempt to apply to convicted persons except after their conviction; but you have to admit that the offence in question was committed before the conviction. ⟦It[2] did not wish a person under stigma to have the right to bring action any more than it wished him the right to revenge his stigma.⟧ Just as a convicted person deprived of the right to make purchases would still remain in the possession of items purchased before his conviction.

Accordingly your demurrer is wrongly timed and a case that originated before conviction cannot disappear.

I should say all this to anybody in any action: in this case

---

2 The words double-bracketed are "clearly out of place" (Wi.), with the following comparison linked to what precedes them.

tecum agere invicem coepit, et agere coepit iniuriarum. Quantopere autem voluerit huiusmodi peragi iudicia legum lator ostendit cum iniuriarum damnatum ignominiosum esse voluit. Quare si apparuerit te malam causam habere, incipis rem iniquissimam postulare, ut tales poenas

7 quales praescribis ⟨is⟩[8] patiatur. Nam si tam gravem rem et tam intolerabilem lex iniuriam[9] putavit ut ei qui commisisset tale delictum omne ius poenae auferret, quaerendum de eo quoque est quod ⟨tu fecisti⟩.[10] Etenim[11] sorte factum est ut prior ageres, non quia atrocius erat quod querebaris. Quid porro? Hac ipsa sorte non hoc quaesitum est, uter prior ageret? Iam hoc ergo de quo contendimus constitutum est. Illa enim sorte duo iudicia ordinata sunt. Et tu,[12] cum accusares, eras reus, et proximo loco reus.

8 (Haec ad ius, illa ad aequitatem.)

Quid adeo iustum quam te damnari si iniuriam tum fecisti? Non enim ignominioso fecisti, et fortasse per te stetit ut iniuriam hic quoque faceret. Alioqui tu, si quam fiduciam haberes innocentiae tuae, nonne his ipsis quibus excludis illum confideres? Quid times? Accusabit te nemi-

9 nem postea accusaturus. Cecidit te; fecit iniuriam, confitebimur. Probabimus tamen istud iure accidisse. Quanta diffidentia in te causae est, qui post ista trepidas, et in nobis quanta fiducia, qui post hanc infelicitatem, post hanc fortunam confidimus dignos nos apud iudices futuros qui

8 *SB*[3]
9 *Gron.*: -arum A
10 *SB*[2]
11 *coni. Ro.* (*cf. SB*[2]): etiam A
12 *Ri.*: tum A[2]: dum A[1]

he commenced a reciprocal action against you and commenced it for injuries. How much our lawgiver wanted trials of this nature to be conducted to completion he showed when he wished a person convicted of injuries to be under stigma. So if it is evident that you have a bad case, you go about to demand something most inequitable, that <he> suffer penalties such as those to which you demur. For if the law considered injury so grave and intolerable a thing that it took away from him who had committed such an offence all right of punishment, enquiry should also be made into what <you did>. And indeed it was determined by lot that your case should come first, not because your grievance was the grosser. What further? This very lottery, was it not to determine which should bring action first? So the point on which we are at issue has already been settled. What else? For by that lot two trials were ordained. You too, though you were prosecuting, were a defendant, and a defendant next in place.

(So much for law, now for equity.)

What is so just as that you should be found guilty if you committed injury then? You did not do it to a person under stigma, and perhaps it was your doing that he too committed injury. Otherwise, if you had any confidence in your innocence, would you not be trusting yourself to these very processes from which you are excluding him? What are you afraid of? Your accuser will be a man who will never accuse anybody else. He struck you, committed an injury; we shall confess it—but we shall prove that you deserved it. How little faith you have in your case, to be in trepidation after that, and how much faith do we have, to be confident after this mishap, this adverse fortune, that before a jury we shall be worthy to receive retribution! Anyway, it is the

vindicemur? Iniquissimum alioqui est tantum fortunae
sortis illius licuisse ut hoc videatur quaesitum, uter ignominiosus esset.

251

Rapta sterilis repudiata

Intra quinquennium non parientem repudiare liceat.
Iniusti repudii sit actio. Quidam uxorem, quam ex raptu
habere coeperat secundum optionem, intra quinquennium non parientem dimisit. Agit illa iniusti repudii.

1
DECLAMATIO

Iniusti repudii accuso. Neminem adeo fore alienum a bonis moribus credo qui dubitet parum istud iuste factum
esse quo[1] quae summum dederat beneficium [vitae][2] ne id
2 quidem obtinuit apud maritum quod praestitit. Itaque calumniae[3] resistit, et impugnat iustum esse repudium quod
maritus iure aliquo fecerit. Ego porro non hanc interpretationem istius verbi vindico,[4] ut iura spectanda sint, sed
illud agi puto,[5] ut iustitia spectetur. Nam illud iniustum
repudium est quod iustitiae contrarium est.
3   Verumtamen si ad illa revocemur iura, nihil tamen ad
hanc pertinebit.[6] Istam enim legem et hoc beneficium ha-

---

[1] SB[4]: quod A   [2] SB[1]   [3] SB[4]: -ia A
[4] SB[4]: video A   [5] a. p. SB[1]: aliquando A
[6] *anne* pertinebunt?

---

[1] But the greatest of benefactions, life, still remained to her,
and the epigram is a misfire. Cf. s.5.

[2] The husband's "quibble" is that a thing done *iure*, legally,

height of injustice that the luck of that lottery reached so far as to let it appear that it was to determine which of the two would be under stigma.

251

A barren rape-victim divorced

Let there be a license to divorce a wife who has not given birth within five years. Let an action lie for unjust divorce. A man divorced his wife whom he had taken after raping her in accordance with option, not having given birth within five years. She prosecutes for unjust divorce.

DECLAMATION

I accuse of unjust divorce. I do not believe anyone will be so far estranged from good morals as to doubt that it was unjustly done that a woman who had made him the greatest of benefactions did not keep with her husband even what she gave.[1] So she resists the quibble,[2] and denies that the divorce which her husband has carried out with some juridical support is just. For my part I do not adopt[3] the interpretation of that word[4] which makes it refer to legalities,[5] but I think our business is to look at justice. For an unjust divorce is one that is contrary to justice.

All the same, if we were asked to consider those legalities, nothing will apply to this lady. Let those perhaps enjoy

---

could not be *iniustus*. *Calumnia* ("probably ablative" Wi.) attributes it absurdly to the wife; cf. Val. Max. 9.15.4 *neque calumniae petitoris . . . religio cessit*.

[3] See *OLD*, *vindico* 2d.
[4] *Iniusti*.
[5] *Iura*.

beant fortasse ii qui nuptias ex aequo fecerunt, qui traden-
tibus parentibus; ad eos vero ad quos necessitas pertinet
nuptiarum, nihil ista lex. Non magis enim repudiare licet
4 quam non nubere liceret. Duas enim poenas adversus raptores constituisse lex videtur, alteram mortis, alteram nuptiarum: leviorem hanc et beneficio propiorem, tamen et
ipsam[7] non sine necessitate. Quod si lege non defenderis,
profecto iniustum divortium est.

5 Sed fingamus te lege defendi: reliqua haec sit quaestio,
an facere debueris. Beneficium te accepisse summum manifestum est: vitam tibi dedit laesa, dedit vitam iuste irata,
dedit vitam perituro per supplicia, per dedecus. Pro his
nihil non praestari oporteret uxori. Quid aliud exegit quam
6 ut uxor esset? 'At enim non pariebat intra quinquennium.'
Si tibi eam parentes collocassent, aut ipsa nubendi tempus
elegisset, dicerem: 'non semper fecunditas properat, aliquando dilata veluti pleniores fructus reddit.' Haec vero et
rapta est antequam destinaretur, antequam idonea nuptiis
videretur, et habuit maritum in amores praecipitem, in
cupiditates pronum; [et cum invisa fuerit marito][8] potest
videri, quod non peperit, pudicitia, non sterilitate fecisse.
7 Tu porro quidquid licet, statim putas esse faciendum;
quidquid asperrimum leges, quidquid crudelissimum habent iura, occupas. Voluisses animum talem fuisse puellae
illo tempore quo ad genua iacebas? Haec vero non tantum
marito sed etiam rei publicae reddere plenam potest
rationem. Nam etiamsi non habet filium, at servavit tamen

---

[7] *Ri.*: et t. illa A   [8] *SB*[3]

---

[6] Lit. "handing over."

this law, this benefit, who have married on equal terms,
parents consenting;[6] but that law has nothing to do with
persons in whose case marriage was a necessity. They are
no more free to divorce than they would have been free not
to marry. For the law is seen to have laid down two penalties against rapists: one of death, the other of marriage.
The latter is the lighter, closer to a benefaction, but it too
involves compulsion. But if you are not defended by law,
then surely your divorce is unjust.

But let us suppose your defense is the law; there would
remain the question whether you ought to have done it.
That you received the greatest of benefactions is clear. Injured, she gave you your life; justly angry, she gave you
your life; as you were about to die in pain and ignominy,
she gave you your life. There is nothing that your wife
should not have been given in return: what else did she
exact of you except to be your wife? "Well, but she was not
giving birth within five years." If her parents had placed
her with you or she herself had chosen her time to wed, I
should say: "Fertility is not always in a hurry, sometimes it
yields ampler returns, so to speak, when delayed." But my
client was raped before a husband was chosen, before she
appeared ready for marriage, and she had a husband pre-
cipitate in his passions, headlong in his desires; it may be
thought that it was modesty, not barrenness, that made her
fail to give birth. You, moreover, think that whatever you
are free to do is to be done at once. Whatever is harshest in
the laws, whatever most cruel in the statutes, you seize
upon it. Would you have wished the girl to be so minded
when you were lying at her knees? She on the other hand
has a complete answer not only to her husband but to the
commonwealth. For even though she doesn't have a son,

67

iuvenem, tamen hominem, tamen civem.

252

Parasitus raptor candidatae

Inscripti maleficii sit actio. Raptor decem milia solvat. Pauperis et divitis filiae sacerdotium petebant. Rumor erat futurum ut pauperis filia sacerdos crearetur. Rapuit eam parasitus divitis. Decem ⟨milia⟩[1] accepta a divite solvit e lege. Accusat pauper divitem inscripti maleficii.

1   SERMO

Pleraeque controversiae sub hac lege positae duas quaestiones habent, ex ipsis eius[2] verbis tractas: an inscriptum sit quod obicitur et an maleficium sit: ⟨sed⟩,[3] quod frequenter dixi, non semper utramque: quoniam fere ubi de inscripto constat, quaeri solet de maleficio; si de maleficio
2   convenit, in controversiam venit an inscriptum sit. In hac controversia tertia quoque adiciatur quaestio necesse est [quae generalibus constat duabus][4]: an huius maleficium sit. Sed pro hac media eximitur. Non enim quaeri potest an sit maleficium: neque enim in rerum naturam cadit ut quisquam mortalium id maleficium neget cuius poenam solutam esse contendat. Quaeremus ergo an inscriptum sit et an huius maleficium sit.

  [1] *Pith.*
  [2] *SB*[2]: earum A
  [3] *Ro.*
  [4] *SB*[1], *Wi.*

yet she saved a young man, a human being, a citizen.

252

The parasite who raped a candidate

Let an action lie for unwritten wrongdoing. Let the rapist pay ten thousand. The daughters of a poor man and a rich man were candidates for a priesthood. Rumor had it that the poor man's daughter would be elected priestess. The rich man's parasite raped her. He paid the ten ‹thousand›, given him by the rich man, according to the law. The poor man accuses the rich man of unwritten wrongdoing.

DISCUSSION

Most controversies under this law have two questions, drawn from its actual words: is the alleged offense unwritten and is it wrongdoing? ‹But› as I have often said, not always both: for as a rule,[1] when "unwritten" is established, there is apt to be question about wrongdoing; whereas if there is agreement about wrongdoing, the controversy is about whether it is unwritten. A third question also must be added in this controversy: whether it is *his* wrongdoing. But in return for this, the middle question is eliminated. For there can be no question as to whether it is wrongdoing; for it is not in the Nature of Things for any mortal to deny that something for which he claims a penalty was paid was a wrongdoing. So we shall ask whether it is unwritten and whether the wrongdoing is his.

---

[1] Not always though. As in the present case, both might be agreed but the identity of the wrongdoer disputed.

69

3

DECLAMATIO

Inscripti maleficii agitur.

Cum maximam partem defensionis adversarius in hoc
ducat, ut inscriptum esse maleficium neget, poterat brevi
condicione decidi, ut diceret qua alia lege cum illo[5] consistere potuerim. Nunc callido et vetere ac diu iam excogitato
consilio legem non ad reum refert sed ad crimen; et, tamquam ego nihil aliud quam de amissa virginitate filiae que-
4 rar, recitat legem quae contra raptores scripta est. Ego
autem, etiamsi cum ipso agerem qui rapuerat, poteram
tamen, non contentus decem milibus quae accepi, in argumentum inscripti maleficii lege agere [etiam cum para-
sito].[6] Lex enim quae decem milia solvere raptorem pro
ablata virginitate voluit contra eos scripta est qui nihil
5 aliud egerunt. Differunt autem haec et personis et temporibus et locis. Nam ut pulsatus civis iniuriarum aget, si
magistratus erit maiestatis crimine obligabit,[7] si legatus
erit bello vindicabitur et iure gentium, et eadem pecunia
sublata ex privato furtum erit, ex sacrario temploque sacrilegium, sic raptor eius quae nihil aliud quam virginitatem
ultum ibit decem milia solvet, alia erit condicio eius qui
rapuerit in comitiis, qui rapuerit eam quae sacerdotium
petebat, immo, ne ingratus sim adversus beneficia populi,
6 iam, quantum in illo erat, acceperat. Longa ratio est, quoniam in argumentum causae huius ‹non› tantummodo[8] de
iniuria parasiti loquor. Tu autem mihi non debes recitare

---

[5] *Sch., Gron.*: alio A
[6] *SB*[1]
[7] crimine (*Pith.*) obligabit *Hå.*[2]: -men -tur A
[8] c. h. n. t. *SB*[4]: t. c. h. A

DECLAMATION

This is an action for unwritten wrongdoing.

Since my opponent puts most of his defense into his denial that unwritten wrongdoing is involved, the matter could have been settled by a brief stipulation: let him say under what other law I could have taken him to court. As it is, he comes up with a cunning strategy, old, long since thought out: he refers the law,[2] not to the defendant, but to the offense, and, as though my only complaint was about my daughter's lost virginity, he recites the law written against rapists. Now even if I were prosecuting the man who did the rape, I could go to law to prove unwritten wrongdoing, not content with the ten thousand I was paid. For the law that required the rapist to pay ten thousand for filched virginity was written against those who did nothing else. But these cases differ as to personae and times and places. A citizen who has been beaten will prosecute for injuries, but if he is a magistrate he will tie the man up in a charge of lese-majesty, if he is an envoy he will be avenged by war or international law. And the same money stolen from a private individual will be theft, but stolen from a shrine or temple it will be sacrilege. By the same token, the rapist of a female who will be avenging nothing but her virginity will pay ten thousand, but the case of a man who raped at the hustings or who raped a candidate for a priesthood (or rather, not to be unthankful for the people's favor, one who, so far as lay in them, had already been given it) will be different. It is a long argument, because I am <not> speaking only of the injury done by the parasite to prove this case. But you ought not to recite to me the law which

----

[2] I.e. produces a law referring . . .

legem quae contra parasitum scripta est, cum quo non ago, sed contra te, qui inscripti maleficii reus es lege. Neque enim hoc quod dicitur raptorem [decem milia][9] e lege solvere oportere ei solves qui dicat 'rapuisti', ⟨sed ei⟩[10] qui dicat 'raptorem summisisti', sed ei qui dicat 'comitia tur-
7 basti', sed ei qui dicat 'sacerdotium abstulisti.' Haec crimina si quam aliam[11] legem habent, transfer sane actionem meam; si nullam aliam habent, cur praescribis adversus maiorum diligentiam et exquisita ingenia quae ⟨iura⟩[12] scripserunt?

8 Est igitur inscriptum. An maleficium sit, si modo ista quae obieci vera sunt, neminem dubitaturum arbitror.

Illud tamen et iudicio non alienum et adfectibus meis necessarium est, dicere quantum maleficium sit. Diligentissime maiores hanc videntur excogitasse legem, quod, cum scirent nullam tantam esse prudentiam, nullam immo tam certam divinationem ut omnia quaecumque ingeniis malorum excogitari umquam potuissent providentia caventium videret, hac lege omnem malitiam veluti quadam indagine cinxerunt, ut quidquid aliarum legum effugisset
9 auxilium quasi extrinsecus circumdaretur. Ego autem, iudices, non de his qui hanc legem conscripserunt sed de ipsa rerum natura queror, in ipsis inscripti maleficii reis nullum discrimen esse servatum. Summisit aliquis raptorem: inscriptum maleficium est. Quid poenae adicitur quod adversus petitricem, quod adversus eam quae sacerdotium, ut dixi, iam prope acceperat, tantum etiam in ipsis

9 *Ri.*   10 *Ro.*   11 *Ro.*: eam A
12 *SB*[4] (ius *Sch.*)

---

3 So the penalty will be heavier.

was written against the parasite, whom I am not prose-cuting, but one written against yourself, who are on trial under the law of unwritten wrongdoing. Neither will you pay to one who says "you raped" what it is said the rapist ought to pay under the law ⟨but to one⟩ who says "you sub-orned a rapist,"[3] to one who says "you disrupted an elec-tion," to one who says "you took away my priesthood." If these charges have[4] any other law, by all means transfer my action, but if they have no other, why do you make a de-murrer contrary to the conscientiousness of our ancestors and the choice intellects of those who wrote ⟨our laws⟩?

So it is unwritten. Whether it is wrongdoing, provided my allegations are true, I do not think anyone will doubt.

But I think it not irrelevant to the trial and necessary to my feelings to say how great the wrongdoing is. Our ances-tors seem to have devised this law with the utmost care. They knew that no wisdom was large enough, or rather no divinatory power sure enough, to perceive with precau-tionary forethought everything that might ever be devised by the minds of villains. So with this law they put a sort of net, so to speak, around all wickedness, so that anything that escaped the remedy provided by other laws should be encircled, as it were, from outside. But for my part, gentle-men, I complain, not against those who wrote this law but against the very Nature of Things, that no distinction has been observed among those very persons charged with un-written wrongdoing. Someone suborned a rapist: it is un-written wrongdoing. What is added to the penalty because it was done against a woman seeking election, who, as I have said, had already almost got a priesthood? Even in the

---

[4] I.e. can be made under.

suppliciis habiturus lucri ⟨quod⟩[13] in compendio numeret quod plus malefecit?

10 Reliqua igitur una quaestio est, an hoc quod filiam meam rapuit, quod illo tempore, quod post illud populi iudicium, credatis non a divite effectum. Nihil argumenti ex moribus istius ducam, etiamsi qualis sit, quam dissolutus, quam luxuriosus ac perditus, satis vel uno argumento

11 probari potuit: parasitum habuit. Inter haec, ut opinor, posita est religionis vestrae cunctatio, iudices, ut dispiciatis utrum parasitus sua voluntate an quoniam id diviti praestabat rapuerit. 'Parasitus rapuit.' Quid ais? Tantum illi vacuit? Adeone saturitate apud te exundavit ut vilia scorta non quaereret? Qui omnibus contentus est, an solus oculos ad ingenuas et ad virgines et aliquem etiam petentes hono-

12 rem attolleret? Numquam hercule tam felicem istam servitutem esse crediderim ut impetus ad illicitas libidines haberet. Hoc dico: hanc tantum vult rapere parasitus. Age nunc,[14] ⟨si⟩[15] vultis, adiciam illud: unde manus illa qua expugnati sumus, unde tantus ac tam profusus[16] domus [tuae][17] tumultus, unde denique solvet quod lege debetur?

13 Si incredibile[18] est quod opponitur, iam certe relictum est ut ea pro te[19] fecerit.

Et hanc tamen partem excutiamus.[20] Summisit raptorem. Habuit enim causam: eundem honorem virgines competebant, nostra filia summoveri aliter non poterat.

---

13 SB[4]   14 Sch.: non A   15 SB[3]

16 cod. quidam: prorsus A

17 SB[3]

18 Sch.: cr- A

19 SB[1] (per te vel propter te Sch.): parte A

20 hinc incipit β

74

throes of execution he will gain, counting as so much profit the fact that his wrongdoing went further.

Therefore the only question remaining is whether you believe it was not the rich man's doing that he raped my daughter, and did so at that time and after that popular verdict. I shall not argue from the man's character; although what sort of a man he is, how dissolute, how loose-living and abandoned, could sufficiently be proved by a single piece of evidence: he had a parasite. Your hesitation, gentlemen, as persons under oath, is I suppose located in determining whether the parasite committed the rape of his own volition or did it as a service to the rich man. "The parasite committed rape." What are you saying? Had he so much time to spare? Was he so sated to overflowing in your house that he had no interest in cheap harlots? Content as he is with anything, would he have raised his eyes on his own to freeborn ladies and virgins and candidates too for an honor? I declare I shall never believe that his slavery with you was so prosperous that he had impulses to illicit lusts. This I say: the parasite only wants to rape this lady.[5] Come now, <if> you please, I will add something else: whence came the gang that stormed us, so mighty, so extravagant a commotion in the house, and finally where is he going to get the money to pay what is owing under law? If the counter-theory is unbelievable, for certain nothing now remains except that he did it for you.

But let us analyze this part too. He suborned the rapist. For he had a motive: the maidens were in competition for the same honor, my daughter could not be eliminated any-

---

[5] But would never do it (on his own). *Vult* is a vivid present, *solvet* below a vivid future.

14 Si incerta populi iudicia, non professae palam sententiae
essent, dicerem tanti tibi fuisse vel securitatem vel indignationem. Nemo est tam arrogans sui aestimator ut ac-
cessurus ad comitia et periculum subiturus[21] humanitatis
15 non malit sine adversario esse. Haec de incertis iudiciis dicerem; quid si [ad securitates et indignationes][22] accedit
metus? Manifestum erat non futuram sacerdotem filiam
tuam. Forte argumentis hoc colligo, longa difficilique con-
16 iectura probandum puto? Locutus est populus. Si alia
quaecumque mihi fama defendenda foret, dicerem tamen,
iudices, rem esse miraculo similem quod, cum pauci ad vos
testes producuntur, fidei vestrae iurique iurando[23] satis
idonei auctores habentur, quotiens vero civitatis universae
consensus et omnes qui intra hanc sedem sunt unum ali-
17 quid certumque dixerint, rumor vocatur. In aliis fortasse
falli ista possunt: utique verum dicit fama quae de se loquitur. Quis enim loquebatur? Populus. De qua re? Quam
facturus erat populus. Cum de comitiis consentiunt rumo-
res, de se quisque dicit 'haec fiet'; hoc est dicere 'hanc
faciam.' Non est ista fama: comitia sunt.
18   Neque est quod mirari, dives, aut indignari velis in comitiis plus saepe pauperes posse; non omnia possunt opes
vestrae, neque in cunctis quae humanam continent vitam

21 *Sch.*: sorti- A
22 *Wi.*
23 *Sch.*: iurisque –di A

---

6 In return for his money the rich man would not have to worry
about the election and his outrage at the challenge of the poor
man's daughter would be appeased.
7 Of defeat.

how else. If the decision of the people had been in doubt and their votes not openly professed, I should say that your peace of mind, or your outrage, would have been worth the price.[6] No one is so arrogant in his self-esteem that when he is about to go to the hustings and take a risk[7] common to all men[8] he would not rather be unopposed. I should say that much about uncertain decisions: what if there is fear[9] too? It was clear that your daughter would not be priestess. Perhaps I gather this by items of evidence, think to prove it by lengthy, difficult process of inference? Why, the people spoke! If I had to defend some other rumor, never mind what, I should still say, gentlemen, that it is well-nigh miraculous that when a few witnesses are brought before you their authority is held sufficient to satisfy the requirements of your good faith and oath, but when it is a consensus of the entire community and all who live in this habitation have said one sure thing, it is called a rumor. Perhaps such indications can be belied in other contexts, but a report which talks of itself speaks true. For who was talking? The people. What about? Whom the people was going to elect. When rumors about elections agree, each man says, "she will win;" that is to say, "I shall vote for her." That's not report: it's election.

And you should not choose to be surprised, rich man, or outraged that in elections poor men often have a bigger say. The wealth of you and your kind is not all-powerful; money is not mistress of everything that makes up human

8 Wi. compares 335.11 *solet fieri, humanum est*. His defense of *sortiturus* does not convince.

9 The rich man was not just normally concerned about the result, he had every reason to fear that his daughter would lose.

domina pecunia est. Latius possidebitis et numerosiores
familias vestras ignorabitis, magnam partem civitatis occu-
pabunt domus vestrae, ingens pondus ⟨auri atque⟩[24] ar-
genti praestringet oculos. Sed haec intra privatum valent:
cum in publicum veneritis et in campum, spectabitur inno-
19 centia, fides. Forsitan gratiae quoque non parum nobis adfert ipsa tenuitas ubi tabellam pauperes ferunt; tum subit
tacita quemque cogitatio superbiae vestrae, tum omnium
quas singulis facitis iniuriarum. Ac tamen in ceteris, petentes magistratus dico atque provincias, possitis tribus emere, dispersa pecunia parare gratiam; ubi vero de sacerdotio
quaeritur et iudicium religio agit, illam populus spectat,
illam intuetur quae semper futura sit virgo, quae a cultu
templorum, a sacris non recessura. Non vereor ne ista
videar praesentis gratia iudicii dicere: sacerdotium filiae
meae ante rumorem speravi.

20   Sed cur ego diutius circa causas maleficii istius etiam[25]
morabor[26]? Confessus est. An diutius quaeri potest an maleficium sit eius ⟨qui⟩[27] poenam solvat, praemium operae
non clam neque secreto (quamquam ista quoque profecto
facta sunt) sed palam apud magistratus in medio foro nu-
21 meret? Vidimus decem milia quae parasito donasti. Interrogo quare; non est istud propter longae servitutis officia,

[24] SB[4] (cf. Verg. Aen. 1.359, TLL II.521.71–522.28)
[25] vett.: et Aβ
[26] Hå.[1], Watt[2]: morbi Aβ
[27] e. q. coni. Ri.: cuius Aβ

---

[10] Lit "tribes" (electoral districts) as in the Roman *comitia
tributa*.

life. Your estate will grow wider, you won't know your households as they multiply, your houses will occupy a large part of the community, a huge mass of ⟨gold and⟩ silver will dazzle our eyes. But all this carries weight only in a private context; when you come into the public, into the campus, regard will be had to innocence and good faith. Perhaps our very meagerness brings us no little favor when poor men cast their votes. Then it is that the silent thought of your haughtiness comes into each man's mind, the thought of all the wrongs you people do to individuals. Even so, in other matters, when you are seeking magistracies and provinces I mean, you might buy the voters[10] and get popularity by scattering money. But when a priesthood is in question and religion makes the decision, the people has in view a woman, looks at a woman, who is always going to be a virgin, who will not leave the temple worship, the rites. I am not afraid of appearing to say this for the sake of the present trial; I hoped for the priesthood for my daughter before the rumor.

But why shall I linger longer over the reasons for his wrongdoing? He has confessed. Or can there be any further question whether the wrongdoing lies with a man ⟨who⟩ pays the penalty, counts out the reward[11] for services rendered, not in secret, in privacy (though no doubt there has been that too), but openly before magistrates in the middle of the Forum? We saw the ten thousand that you gave the parasite. I ask why? It was not on account of services rendered during a long slavery, it was not ⟨a con-

[11] The ten thousand with which he paid the penalty, not properly the reward. That would be paid to the parasite in private.

non ‹solacium›[28] illarum quibus gratiam meruit contume-
liarum: decem ‹milia›[29] dedisti quod rapuisset. Nisi debe-
res, summa indignatione etiam vindicare volueras; nam
qui candidatam sacerdotii rapuit, nocuerat exemplo et tibi.

22   (Igitur et inscriptum maleficium est adversus eum ‹qui
agit et eius›[30] cum quo agitur, et maleficium non solum
confessum sed etiam grave. Ex his apparet: et ex persona
parasiti, qui numquam ad tantam peccandi audaciam pro-
cessisset sua sponte, et ex persona divitis et ex causis et ex
numeratione pecuniae, ex eventu denique.)

Quid impulerit, quid[31] coegerit superest ut ostendam.
‹Attendite iam›[32] non quid parasitus acceperit sed quid
dives ipse. Quaeritis quid iste decem milibus emerit? Videte filiam contra sacerdotem, videte vittas, videte honores.

23   Fortasse ego superbe faciam atque arroganter qui tamquam privatam iniuriam, tamquam maleficium adversus
me commissum persequar. Quota enim ego sum portio
istius indignationis? Perdidi sine dubio honorem, pretio-
sissimum pauperum censum; perdidi virginitatem filiae
meae, et cui modo sacerdotium sperabam difficile inven-
turus sum etiam maritum: sed populus perdidit arbitrium
dandi honoris, sed sacerdotem creavit quam paulo ante[33]
24   noluit. Ite nunc et excludite campo divites et corrumpi

---

28 *SB*[1], *Hå*.[2]   29 *Sch.* (*lac. in* A)   30 *Ri., auct. Ro.*
31 quid . . . quid *SB*[3]: quis . . . quis Aβ
32 *SB*[1] (*cf. SB*[2])   33 p. a. *hic Bu.: post* sed Aβ

---

12 For *solacium* thus in the jurists see *OLD solacium* 2; also
252.21; 344.11; 329.11; 383.1; Calp. Fl. 22.1 fin, 24.19; and often
in *Decl. Mai.* 11.

solation[12] > for those indignities with which he won favor:
you gave him ten <thousand> for committing rape. Unless
you owed it, you would even have wanted to punish him in
high indignation. For the man who raped a candidate for
the priesthood had injured you too by the example.

(So[13] we have unwritten wrongdoing against the person
<prosecuting by the person under prosecution>, wrong-
doing not only confessed but grave. It is evident from the
following: from the nature of the parasite, who would
never have gone to such a length of original audacity on his
own, and from the persona of the rich man, and from the
motives, and from the payment of the money, and finally
from the outcome.)

It remains for me to show what pushed him, what drove
him. <Look now> not <at> what the parasite got but what
the rich man himself got. Do you gentlemen ask what he
bought with his ten thousand? Look at his daughter opposite, the priestess, look at the fillets, look at the honors.

Perhaps I am acting haughtily and arrogantly when I
proceed against it as a private injury, a wrongdoing committed against myself. For how small a part am I of this
outrage! Doubtless I have lost an honor, the poor man's
most precious fortune; I have lost my daughter's virginity
and for her for whom I was lately hoping a priestly office I
shall be hard to put to it even to find a husband. But the
people has lost its free choice in the bestowal of an honor, it
has elected a priestess whom a little earlier it did not want
to elect. Do what you will, exclude rich men from the cam-

13 Wi. (after Ritter) thinks the passage in parenthesis belongs
in a *sermo*.

sacra vetate, de ambitu leges conscribite: comitia nostra
decem milibus rapta sunt atque translata. Quam sanctum
istud sacerdotium fore putatis quod stupro debetur?

253

Tyrannicida volens dedi

In duabus civitatibus vicinis tyranni erant. In altera cum
quidam tyrannum occidisset, alter vicinae civitatis tyrannus petît eum in deditionem et bellum minatus est nisi
darent. Fert ipse rogationem ut dedatur.

1
DECLAMATIO

Ut meo nomine sum vobis, Quirites, obligatus quod quamquam necessarium et ad salutem pertinens civitatis remedium praesentis timoris respectu tamen mei praetermisis-
tis, ita ipsius rei publicae nomine irascor neminem extitisse
priorem qui pro salute communi me offendere auderet.
2 Neque id satis est, sed invenio qui adulentur et ne a me
quidem latam hanc rogationem existiment respectu mei
recipiendam. Cum quibus mihi consistere fortius atque
etiam, si ita res exigat, acerbius necesse est, cum in id
quoque periculum venire intellegam rogationem[1] meam,
an hoc velim.
3 Satis erat mihi dicere: rogationem fero utilem civitati.
Ista enim speciosa dictu et vana quadam imagine honesti

[1] *Aer.*: opt- Aβ

---

[1] See crit. note. *Optionem* will have its origin in a recollection
of the choice of rewards offered to tyrannicides (cf. 345), which
has no relevance here.

pus, forbid that our religious institutions be corrupted, draft laws against bribery: our elections have been raped and transferred for ten thousand. How sanctified do you suppose a priesthood will be that is owed to illicit sex?

253

Tyrannicide willing to be surrendered

There were tyrants in two neighboring communities. When somebody killed the tyrant in one, the other tyrant of the neighboring community demanded his surrender and threatened war unless they gave him up. He himself proposes a bill for his surrender.

DECLAMATION

I am obliged to you, citizens, for having forgone out of regard for myself a remedy for the present alarm, necessary though it is and pertinent to the welfare of the community. At the same time I am angry on behalf of the commonwealth itself that no one before me has appeared with the courage to do me a disservice for the sake of the common welfare. And that is not enough: I find adulators who judge that this bill, even though proposed by myself, ought not to be adopted out of regard for me. It is necessary for me to take issue with them rather strongly, and even, if the occasion demands, rather harshly, since I realize that my bill[1] is actually endangered by doubts about whether this is what I want.

It were sufficient for me to say: "The bill I am proposing is expedient for the community." These fine-sounding notions, wrapped up in a vain semblance of the moral ideal,

83

circumdata non respiciunt praesentes necessitates; si tantas vires haberet civitas ut bella suscipere, ut frangere impetus tyranni posset, non tam diu servissemus, non illum
4 cruentissimum dominum unus ex insidiis occidisset. Atque ego, etiamsi plurimum esse virium[2] in hac civitate spectarem, bene tamen redimi capite unius civis pacem putarem. Facile est ista in contionibus et conciliis[3] despicere dicendo: iam si exercitus hostium intra fines nostros fuerit, si ardere villas, si frugifera succidi, si fugam rusticorum in urbem, si compulsa intra muros pecora viderimus, si moenia oppugnabuntur, si turres quatientur, si ad dilectum ab amplexu matrum iuvenes rapientur, quam sero
5 paenitebit tam caro uni pepercisse! Et si quid tamen deforme habitura civitas fuit dedito (ut subinde dicitis) tyrannicida, id omne mea rogatione detractum est; omni pudore liberati estis: invitum non dedidissetis.[4] Quod ad vos pertinet, bellum suscipere maluistis. Sed hoc est praecipue quare ego hanc ferre debeam rogationem. Ego pro civitate tam grata, pro populo tali, non subibo qualecumque periculum?

6 Sed non solum rei publicae verum etiam mea interest hanc recipi rogationem. Quem vultis enim ponite eventum: periculum mihi mortis est. Quid? Ego non satis vixi? Non enim annorum numero nec spatio aetatis terminari certum est fortium virorum vitam, sed laude et fama et
7 perpetuae posteritatis immortalitate. Ita dii faciant ut magnum exemplum posteritati etiam poena dare possim. Satis videbitur mihi omnia facere Fortuna ut tyrannicidium meum maius sit.

[2] D²: civium Aβ   [3] *Gron.*: consi- Aβ
[4] *Pith.*: dediss- Aβ

pay no regard to present necessities. If the community had strength enough to take on wars and break the tyrant's onslaught, we should not have been so long enslaved and our bloody master would not have been killed by an individual from ambush. And for my part, even if I saw a great deal of strength in this community, I should think peace well worth the life of a single member. It is easy to speak contemptuously of such an attitude in popular assemblies and gatherings. But let an enemy army be inside our borders, let us see our houses on fire, our crops cut down, the flight of country folk into the city, flocks driven inside the city walls, let our battlements be assaulted, turrets shaken, young men snatched from their mothers' arms to join the levy: how late will come regret for sparing one man at such a cost! And if all the same the surrender of a tyrannicide was going to damage the community's image, as you people keep saying, all that has been obviated by my bill. You are freed from all embarrassment. You would not have surrendered me against my will. So far as you are concerned, you preferred to take on a war. But this is the main reason why I thought to sponsor this bill. For so grateful a community, for such a people, shall I not take any risk?

But it is not only in the interest of the commonwealth that my bill be passed, it is mine too. Imagine whatever outcome you like. I risk death. Well, have I not lived long enough? Sure it is that the life of a brave man is not bounded by a number of years, a life-span, but by glory and fame and the immortality conferred by all posterity. May the gods grant that even by my punishment I may be able to give posterity a fine example! I shall think Fortune does all I can ask of her to make my tyrannicide gain in glory.

Sed illud interim vereor, ne tyrannus ex me petat famam lenitatis. Habet enim apud malos quoque multum
auctoritatis virtus, et forsitan hoc ille ambitiose faciet, ut
8 potestate contentus sit. Quidquid est, videat me et illa civitas vicina: multum illis servientibus prodero. Videant quo
vultu tyrannum feram, quam interritus tribunali eius ad-
sistam, quam me nihil minae, nihil supplicia ipsa moveant.
Potest fieri ut exhortetur illos hic animus meus, haec mea
9 mens. Vobis quidem custodire pacem, reddere quietem
maius ipso tyrannicidio puto. Nam si bellum imminet, si
periculum universa civitas habet, quod illum cuius nomine
mihi gratias agitis occidi maximam vobis iniuriam feci.

254

Exul accusator et sententiae pares

Exul qui secretum ad rem publicam pertinens indicare
voluerit habeat in civitatem redeundi potestatem, et si indicaverit maneat in civitate. Exul dixit se habere quod de
adfectata tyrannide diceret. Venit in civitatem. Postulavit
reum. Is aequis sententiis absolutus est. ‹Exul se in exilium rediturum pronuntiavit.›[1] Fert quidam rogationem
ut maneat. ‹Praescribitur.›[2] CD.

1   SERMO

Potest venire in dubium quo genere divisionis uti nos in
hac controversia oporteat. Videtur enim quaedam posse

[1] *SB*[3]
[2] *SB*[4]

---

[1] How divide our discourse.

But I sometimes fear that the tyrant will use me to get a reputation for lenity. Virtue has much authority even among scoundrels, and perhaps to gain approval he will be content with the power. In any event, let that neighboring community too look at me: I shall do much for them in their slavery. Let them see my face as I brave the tyrant, how undaunted I stand before his tribunal, how no threats, no actual cruelties have any effect upon me. It is possible that this courage of mine, this attitude, will urge them on. As for you, to safeguard peace, to restore tranquillity I judge to be a greater benefaction than the slaying of the tyrant. For if war looms, if the entire community is in peril, my killing of him on whose account you thank me was the worst injury I could have done you.

254

Exile accuser and equal votes

Let an exile who wishes to give secret information pertaining to the commonwealth have the power to return to the community and, if he gives such, let him remain in the community. An exile said he had something to say about a plot to set up a tyranny. He came to the community. He charged a man. The man was acquitted on a tied vote. ‹The exile declared that he would go back into exile.› Somebody proposes a bill requiring that he stay. ‹A demurrer is entered.› Speech in opposition.

DISCUSSION

A question may arise, what sort of division we should make in this controversy.[1] For it seems that the defendant's

dicere etiam citra rogationem advocatus huius exulis per quae ius manendi vindicet. Utrum ergo haec quae citra rogationem quoque pro illo futura sunt dicemus ante principium, an statim rogationem? Species eo ducit ut, quoniam et praecedant et leviora videantur, [et][3] prima sint. Sed ratio diversum mihi suadere videtur, ideo quod necessaria nobis quaestio superabit, an haec rogatio contra legem feratur: in cuius parte sint necesse est illa quaecumque dicturi sumus—an videatur hic etiam [alia][4] lege remanere potuisse, an rogationem ferre oporteat ad singulos pertinentem, an contra legem, an haec rogatio contra legem sit, an meruerit ille remanere.

2

3

DECLAMATIO

Si aut minus verecundus esset is quem rogatione mea retinere in civitate constitui aut iudicia felicius expertus, nihil contione, nihil conscripto meo, nihil denique opera rogationis opus esset. Primum[5] igitur carere [hunc][6] invidia vel propter hoc possum, Quirites: nemo enim crediderit me rogatum ab eo ad vos processisse qui ipse ut remaneat non laborat. Verum ille quidem multas, atque utinam minus potentes, huius propositi sui causas habeat: ego praeter cetera propter hoc quoque eum existimo esse retinendum, quod manifestum fecit ad indicium tyrannidis adfectatae venisse, non remanendi cupiditate. Quod nisi vetustissi-

4

---

³ *Ri.*   ⁴ *SB²*
⁵ *Pith.*: -ma Aβ
⁶ A¹: hac A²β: hanc D: *del. SB³*

---

² Not advocate. The exile is not on trial. But see Wi.
³ Antedating the bill.

backer[2] can bring arguments to assert his right to stay even irrespective of the bill. Shall we then make points which are to count in his favor even irrespective of the bill before our opening or come immediately to the bill? Appearance makes for their coming first, since they are prior[3] and seem of less weight. But reason seems to me to advise the contrary, because we shall necessarily be left with the question whether this bill is proposed illegally. Whatever we are going to say must come in that sector, as: does it appear that he could have stayed even under the law?[4] Is it right to propose a bill pertaining to individuals? Is it illegal? Is this bill illegal? Did he deserve to stay?

DECLAMATION[5]

If the person whom I have determined to keep in the community were less modest or had had better luck with trials, there would have been no need for me to make a speech or a draft[6] or indeed to do any work on a bill. First then, citizens, I can be exempt from hostile criticism just because nobody would believe that I was asked to come before you by a man who himself does not care about staying. But let him have many reasons (and I could wish they were of lesser weight) for the course he proposes. I for my part aside from anything else think he should be kept because he has made it clear that he came to give information about a plot to set up a tyranny, not from a desire to remain. Had

---

4 I.e. irrespective of the bill. Being a legal point, this is best left to be taken later on along with other legal points. *Lege* may mean "legally" or refer to the law in the theme (SB[2]).

5 Addressed to an assembly of citizens.

6 Of the bill surely, not "deposition" (Wi.).

mum ius, Quirites, eos qui secreta ad rem publicam perti-
nentia indicassent remanere in civitate iussisset, forsitan
dicendum mihi necessario existimarem qua gratia hic
pressus, quibus inimicitiis in exilium esset actus. Sed quid
5   necesse est repetere haec quae videtis? Et quod ad animum quidem illius pertinet, satis vobis est, ut existimo,
probatus, quod quamquam damnatus, quamquam in exilium actus, rei publicae tamen non potuit irasci: indicium
professus est. Viderimus an verum; interim tamen nihil
eum finxisse manifestum est quod persuaderi tam multis
6   utique potuerit. Causam qua condicione dixerit damnatus,
exul, contra potentem, contra gratiosum, quid necesse est
diu dicere, quando is exitus iudicii fuit ut non plures sententiae pro adversario fuerint? Non enim causa victus est
sed legibus, sed publica humanitate; quae quidem ipsa me
in hoc exhortata est, ut rogationem ad vos de retinendo
cive ferrem in civitate tam misericorde.
7   Negant rogationem esse recipiendam quae ad singulos
homines pertineat. Ego porro hoc in eo iure quod perpetuum et in omnia tempora scribitur existimo esse servandum. Potest enim dici mihi: 'in honorem hominis unius
obligas tempora futura, et omnes eadem necessitate con-
8   stringes.' At[7] quotiens ad praesens tantummodo tempus
rogatio fertur, ne ferri quidem nisi de singulis potest. Quod
si hanc tollimus consuetudinem, nec duces ad exercitus
deligemus[8] nec provincias decernemus nec imperia pro-
rogabimus: omnia enim ista rogationibus ad singulos per-
tinentibus consummantur.

[7] *Aer.*: itaque A: ita β
[8] *Wi.* (deleg- *Sch.*): ducemus Aβ

not a very ancient law, citizens, enacted that persons having given secret information pertaining to the commonwealth should remain in the community, perhaps I should think it necessary for me to speak of the influences and enmities which weighed him down and drove him into exile. But what need is there to repeat these things that are in front of your eyes? As for his disposition, I think he is sufficiently approved by you, in that, although found guilty, although driven into exile, yet he could not be angry with the commonwealth: he offered information. Whether true, we shall consider later. Meanwhile it is clear that he did not make anything up, since so many gave it absolute credence. At what a disadvantage he spoke—a man convicted, an exile, against a powerful and influential individual—no need to speak at length, since the result of the trial was that there was no majority of votes for his opponent. He was not defeated because of his case but because of the laws[7] and the humanity of the public—which itself urged me to propose to you a bill for keeping a citizen in so tender-hearted a community.

They say that a bill pertaining to individuals should not be passed. I do think that this is to be observed in the case of a law in perpetuity, written for all time. For I can be told: "You are binding times to come in honor of one individual and you will constrain everyone by the same compulsion." But when a bill is proposed only with a view to the present time, it cannot even be proposed except about individuals. If we abolish this practice, we shall not choose leaders for armies or decree provinces or prolong terms of command. For all these are finalized by bills pertaining to individuals.

7 Under which equal voting counted as acquittal.

9   'At enim contra legem rogatio est.' Si confiterer, dicerem tamen non fere rogationis esse causam ubi lex est.
Quid enim necesse est convocari tribus, contrahi populum, si idem effici iure vetere et iam olim constituto potest? Igitur si rogatio supervacua ubi lex [non][9] est, non
10   fere poterit ferri nisi contra alicuius legis voluntatem. Et
hoc tamen apud quos dicit? Video enim praescriptione
me[10] excludi posse iudicio; et[11] in rebus parvis ac peculiari-
bus[12] ista iudex recipiat. Ceterum quidem quotiens de iure
populi agitur apud populum, cui mutare, cui obrogare, cui
ferre quas velit leges, accipere quas velit rogationes liceat,
numquam se ipse deminuet.

11   Quomodo tamen rogatio ista contra legem est [contra
commodum suum contraque eam][13] quae hunc in exilium
misit? Non iure novo sed vetere atque olim constituto
reversus est; manere etiam citra hanc rogationem potest.

    De quo priusquam loquar, necessario illud quod ab
adversariis frequentissime obiectum est depellendum vi-
12   detur. 'Cur enim,' inquiunt, 'si remanere suo iure poterat,
expectavit rogationem?' Ut verecundia ei adeo nihil apud
vos prosit ut etiam [in causa][14] plurimum noceat, ante omnia non miror hominem iudicia totiens infeliciter ex-
pertum, tot in civitate inimicos habentem, nihil temptasse

9 *Sch.*
10 -tione (*Aer.*) me *Obr.*: -onem Aβ
11 Aβ: ut B: *del. Wi.*
12 *SB*[1]: periculosis Aβ
13 *SB*[3], *auct. Ro., Wi.*
14 *del. coni. SB*[3]

It may be argued that this bill is illegal. If I were to admit that, I should say nevertheless that in general there is no need for a bill where there is a law. For why is it necessary that the tribes be convened, the people assembled, if the same result can be achieved by an ancient law long since constituted? So if a bill is superfluous where there is a law, it will not in general be possible for one to be proposed which will not contravene the purpose of some law or other. And yet before whom is the objector talking? For I realize that I can be excluded from a trial by a demurrer, and in matters small and peculiar let a judge entertain such objections. But when the rights of the people are at issue before the people, which has the right to change and contradict and pass what laws it pleases and to accept what bills it pleases, it will never diminish itself.

Yet how does this bill contravene the law which sent this man into exile? He did not return under a new law but under an old one long since constituted. He can remain even irrespective of this bill.[8]

Before I speak to that point, I think I am compelled to rebut an objection very frequently raised by my opponents. "Why," they say, "if he could stay by his own right, did he wait for a bill?"[9] Suppose his modesty does him no good with you, suppose it even does his case a lot of harm, to begin with I am not surprised that a man who has so often had unfortunate experiences in trials and has so many enemies in the community did not attempt anything pri-

[8] Provided his information is *bona fide* (s.16). Therefore the bill is not against the law.

[9] The exile's announcement of his intention to leave will have come after the bill was proposed.

privatim. Litigavit innocens reus: damnatus est. Detulit
adfectatae tyrannidis reum (ut pars iudicum putat) manifestum: impedimento publicae humanitatis victus est.
Hodie citra[15] rogationem, citra ius vestrum, citra[16] potes-
13 tatem populi pugnabit? Ille tamen mihi alias et, ut dixi,
graviores in exilium abeundi causas videtur habuisse.
Absolutus est quidem reus, sed innocentem se esse accusatori nondum persuasit. Ego vero non miror quod hic timet
adhuc civitati, quod velut impendentem quandam omnibus nobis ruinam suffugere et evitare quod praevidit periculum cupit. Sed tanto magis retinendus est.
14   Putemus alioqui citra rogationem talem institutam esse
legem qualis esset si hunc[17] in civitate remanere vellet.
Lex quid dicet[18]? 'Qui secretum ad rem publicam pertinens indicaverit[19] habeat remanendi potestatem.' Nemo
15 dubitabit an indicaverit. Verba igitur legis pro nobis omnia; sed ad interpretationem voluntatis vocamur. Nec enim
secretum[20] putant esse nisi quod certum ac probatum sit;
negant indicari nisi id de quo non dubitetur. Ego autem
existimo legum latori non defuisse eloquendi facultatem
ut, ⟨si⟩ approbatis demum iis quae detulisset remanere in

[15] *Aer.*: contra Aβ
[16] citra . . . citra *coni. Wi.*: contra . . . contra Aβ
[17] *SB1, coni. Wi.*: hic Aβ
[18] *SB1*: dicit Aβ
[19] *SB3*: -are voluerit (*cf. thema*) Aβ
[20] *Ranc.*: scriptum Aβ

[10] At the trial which sent him into exile. His innocence is assumed *extra thema*.

[11] After these experiences.

vately. He went to law an innocent[10] defendant; he was found guilty. He charged a man clearly guilty of plotting to set up a tyranny (so half the jury thinks): he lost because public humanity stood in his way. Today[11] is he to fight[12] without a bill, without the law you make, without the people's power? But as I have said,[13] I think he had weightier reasons to go back into exile. The defendant was acquitted, it is true, but he has not yet persuaded his accuser of his innocence. For my part I am not surprised that he is still afraid for this community and that he wants to flee from the avalanche, so to speak, that hangs over us all and avoid the peril he foresaw. But that is all the more reason for keeping him.

On another tack, let us suppose, irrespective of this bill, that a law had been established such as it would be if its purpose was that this man remain in the community. What will the law say? "Let him who shall give secret information pertaining to the commonwealth have the power to remain."[14] Nobody will doubt that he has informed. Therefore the words of the law are all in our favor. But we are challenged to interpret its intention. For they do not think anything secret unless it is certain and proved; they deny that information is given except what is not in doubt. But I conceive that our lawgiver did not lack the faculty of expression; so that <if> he had wished an exile to remain in

[12] "Against the influence of a budding tyrant" (Wi). Or to assert his right to stay? There seems to be a suggestion that, if the bill goes through, the exile will reconsider.   [13] S.4 init.

[14] Such a law would only reiterate what the old law says: i.e. the exile's right to stay is already statutory. Wi. saw the problem but not the answer.

civitate exulem vellet, id ipsum plane aperteque diceret.[21]
16 Nunc[22] contentum puto esse legum latorem voluntatem
eius intueri.[23] Satis est igitur ut nihil finxerit, nihil cupiditate revertendi mentitus sit, nihil denique ideo fecerit ut
remaneret. Vos quid dicitis? Mentitum eum vultis? Inter-
rogemus partem iudicum. Non accuso nunc reum: evasit,
17 absolutus est; habet beneficium legis. Illud tantum[24] contentus sum dicere, fuisse aliqua quibus index moveretur:
illa quae moverunt iudicum partem, illa quae tot tristes
sententias effecerunt. Iam ergo animum dignum habeo
emendatione fortunae: cum adfectari tyrannidem putaret
(sic enim loquamur), non dissimulavit, non ultionem putavit, non, cum ipse patriam perdidisset, invidit, sed venit in
civitatem, et suscepit gravissimum laborem et novas inimicitias et recentem aemulationem. Non excepit divitem ab
indice Fortuna.
18   Haec ego dicerem etiamsi victus iudicio esset. Nunc
fortiter hoc possum contendere, quod ‹frustra›[25] fuisse
dicitis eum causa inferiorem. Quid est igitur? Lex iubet
eos absolvi qui pares sententias tulerint. Imputabitis istud
publicae misericordiae, imputabitis humanitati. Non ego
arguo hanc legem, sed dico esse communem. Eodem enim
tempore non id modo quaesitum est, an adfectatae tyrannidis reum damnari oporteret, sed illud etiam, an hunc
19 remanere in civitate oporteret. Quod si pares sententiae
periculo prosunt, pro utroque sunt. An vero adfectatae

---

[21] ut ‹si› . . . diceret *Ro., Ri., auct. Gron.*: ut . . . dicere Aβ
[22] *Sch.*: non Aβ   [23] *Hå.2, duce Aer.*: retinuit Aβ
[24] *Ro.*: tamen Aβ   [25] *Hå.2*

the community only after his information has been approved, he would have said so plainly and openly. As it is, I think the lawgiver was content to look at the intention. So it is enough that he did not invent anything, did not lie from a desire to return, did nothing in fine in order to remain. What do you say? Do you hold that he lied? Let us ask half the jury. I am not now accusing the defendant. He got off, he was acquitted, he has the benefit of the law. I am content to say only this, that there were some things that moved the informer, those things that moved half the jury, those things that resulted in so many votes of guilty. So I hold his spirit deserving of an amendment in his fortune. When he thought there was a plot to set up a tyranny (so let us say), he did not keep quiet, did not think it a revenge, did not hold a grudge because he himself had lost his country, but came to the community and took on a very heavy task and new enmities and fresh rivalry. Fortune[15] did not exempt the rich man from an informer.

I should have said all this even if he had been worsted in the trial. As it is I can vigorously contend that <it does you no good> to say that he lost his case. So what is the fact? The law orders that defendants who get half the votes are acquitted. You will set that to the score of public compassion, the score of humanity. I am not finding fault with this law, but I say it cuts both ways. For the issue was not only whether the defendant should be convicted of plotting to set up a tyranny but also at the same time whether this man ought to remain in the community. If equal votes favor the endangered,[16] they are in favor of both. Or should a man

15 I.e. their respective situations: one a wealthy, powerful citizen, the other an exile.   16 Lit, "the danger."

tyrannidis reus absolvatur quoniam non plures pro accusa-
tore quam pro reo sententiae fuerunt, hic qui †periculi qui
exilii† vel eandem[26] vel etiam graviorem poenam experire-
tur, non eandem experietur legis humanitatem?

(Haec de iure, haec de rogatione. Illa iam de aequitate.)

Dignum esse existimo qui maneat in civitate. Pericula
nostra ‹propulsare›[27] temptavit; servitutem rei publicae
discutere, quantum in ipso erat, voluit. Nescio an plus debeamus si ad indicium non certis argumentis perductus sit.

21 Nam si manifesta detulisset, si ea de quibus dubitare nemo
nostrum posset, crederetur cupiditate manendi in civitate
fecisse. Solam pietatem in causa indicii habuit qui incer-
tam[28] detulit litem, et litem iniusta condicione: ex altera
parte solus et exul, damnatus, ex altera parte homo potens,
gratiosus. Omnia ista diligenter perpendite: intellegetis
non esse sententias pares. Quid est igitur? [cur][29] ⟦Ego
etiam pro ipso qui absolutus est reo existimo esse manere
hunc in civitate.⟧

22 Illud dicere pro re publica satis erat: habemus in civitate custodem, inquirit adhuc. Forsitan omnia iam videre
non potuit exul, non omnia iam[30] clara perspicere. Hoc
visum iri ‹puto›[31] pro opinione eius qui absolutus est: non
timebitur quamdiu hic fuerit in civitate. Immo hercule si
mentitus est, si fictum detulit crimen, satis alioqui daturus

---

[26] periculi ‹in partem veniat› (*melius* venit SB[3]) qui vel
eandem SB[1]   [27] SB[2]   [28] *Ri.*: in urbem Aβ
[29] *Sch., Gron.*   [30] SB[1]: tam Aβ   [31] visum (*Ro.*) i.
p. *Wi.*: vis viri A: visuri β

---

[17] The declaimer assumes, contrary to his showing in s.15f.,
that if the jury had found the information to be false, the informer

charged with plotting to set up a tyranny be acquitted because the prosecution did not get more votes than the defense, and shall not he that <shared> the danger, that would have met with the same or even heavier punishment,[17] meet with the same legal humanity?

(So much for the law, so much for the bill. Now for equity.)

I think he deserves to stay in the community. He tried <to ward off> our dangers. He wanted, so far as lay in him, to shake off slavery from the commonwealth. I rather think we should owe him all the more if he were led to inform by evidence less than certain. For if he had informed of manifest facts, such as none of us could possibly doubt, he would be believed to have acted out of desire to stay in the community. But only patriotism could have motivated him to inform bringing a doubtful action and one in which he was at a disadvantage: on the one hand he alone, an exile, found guilty, and on the other a man of power and influence. Think all that over carefully: you will realize that the votes were *not* equal. What is one to say then? ⟦I think it is even in the interest of the defendant himself who was acquitted that this man stay in the community.⟧

On behalf of the commonwealth it would have been enough to say this: we have a watchman in the community, he is still investigating. Perhaps as an exile he could not see everything clearly. This, <I think,> will appear advantageous to the reputation of the person acquitted; he will not be feared as long as this man is in the community. Or rather, upon my word, if he[18] lied, if the charges were

---

would have been penalized.   [18] The exile.

est poenarum inter inimicos potentes et inimicos gratio-
sos.

23   SERMO

Totam autem existimo commodiorem esse partem diver-
sam; suadeo iis qui dicturi sunt in illam potius incumbant.

255

Transfugae excludendi

Inter duas civitates bellum erat. In alteram multi transfugae veniebant. Fert quidam legem ne recipiantur.

1   SERMO

Proxime ad suasorias accedit hoc genus: nam et suasoria-
rum [et]¹ legis suasio et dissuasio est. Ergo dicet is qui
legem fert non esse honestum recipere transfugas, nihil
prodesse, forsitan ⟨etiam obesse⟩,² ad finem belli. Summum: illud propter quod lex fertur periculosum esse.

2   DECLAMATIO

Etiamsi non esset in eo statu bellum ut honesta cogitare
vacaret, vel cum periculo tamen optima et ad famam itura
fecisse fortasse honestius foret quam ut obstare utilitas videretur. Nunc minus laudis, nimio³ plus tamen securitatis
est honesta facere.

¹ *Ri.*   ² *SB*¹, *Watt*¹   ³ *Hå.*²: immo AC(BD)

---

¹ Speeches of persuasion or advice in imaginary historical contexts.

² *Honesta* may combine what is morally right with what looks
well, but *honestius* below is confined to the latter.

trumped up, he will be sufficiently punished anyway, living among powerful enemies, influential enemies.

DISCUSSION

I think the whole opposition case is the easier. I recommend intending speakers to put their efforts that way rather than the other.

255

Deserters to be excluded

There was war between two communities. Many deserters used to come to one of them. Somebody proposes a law that they not be received.

DISCUSSION

This type comes very close to Suasoriae;[1] for the persuasion or dissuasion of a law belongs to Suasoriae also. So the proposer of the law will say that to receive deserters is discreditable, that it does no good, perhaps <actually does harm>, as regards the end of the war. Finally: the practice on account of which the law is proposed is dangerous.

DECLAMATION

Even if the war were not in a state that allowed us to think of appearances,[2] yet to have done even with risk what is best and conducive to reputation might look so well that expediency should not seem to stand in the way. As it is, doing the right thing brings less credit but a great deal more security.[3]

[3] With the war going well it is easier, and so less laudable, to take the high moral line (*honesta facere*). See crit. note.

3   Nemo igitur dubitaverit turpissimos esse qui transfugerint. Spectemus enim rem ipsam, neque eo decipiamur
quod utile videtur, ⟨neque quod⟩[4] hostis ⟨est⟩[5] qui facit
aliter constituamus quam ut intellegamus potuisse hoc
et nostros facere. Numquam prodest malum exemplum;
etiamsi in praesentia[6] occasione quadam delectat, in futu-
4   rum tamen altius nocet. Proximos existimo esse eos trans-
fugis a quibus transfugae recipiantur. Hoc natura simile
est, facere scelus et probare. An si quis nostrum transfugis-
set, non ipsum modo pessimum civem et omnibus suppliciis dignum iudicaretis, sed infamia etiam qui receperunt,
et velut auctores scelerum, velut magistros turpitudinis
†colligeritis†[7]: idem non reflectemus in nos?
5   Tandem utilitate ducti in auxiliis habituri sumus quos
recipiemus? Fingamus eam civitatis esse fortunam ut auxiliis opus sit: hos in auxiliis? Scilicet qui, cum ex altera parte
intueremur patriam et memoriam pueritiae et necessitu-
dines omnes, ad Fortunam tamen inclinaverunt, pleniore[8]
pro nobis sacramento, fortiore animo stabunt. Adeo facilius est in istis scelus deprehendere quam paenitentiam?
6   Inutile ergo militum genus, nobis minime necessarium.
Quippe etiam hi qui recipiendos esse transfugas hoc ⟨di-
cunt⟩,[9] in superiore esse loco nostram civitatem. Neque enim amore nostri sed metu imminentis fortunae
7   transfugiunt. An facilius deposituros propositum bellandi

4 SB1   5 SB4   6 Hå.2: -ti Aβ
7 A(B): -retis CD: sugillaretis Wi.
8 coni. SB3: pron- Aβ
9 Aer.

4 Translating Wi.'s conjecture.

So nobody would doubt that deserters are loathsome. For let us look at the thing itself and not be deceived by the appearance of expediency, and let us <not> decide <because it is> an enemy who does it without realizing that our own folk could have done the same. A bad example is never to the good; even if it pleases, offering some advantage in the present, in the future it does deeper harm. I think those who receive deserters are next door to deserters. Commission of a crime and approval of it are similar by nature. If one of ours had deserted, you would not only judge the man himself a thoroughly bad citizen deserving of every punishment but those also who received him as deserving of infamy, and you would censure[4] them as instigators of crime, as teachers of dishonor. Shall we not turn the same back upon ourselves?

Led by expediency, are we finally going to have those we receive among our auxiliaries? Suppose the community was in such a condition as to need auxiliaries: shall we take these among them? I suppose that those who bent Fortune's way, although they saw their country and the memory of their boyhood and all their personal ties on the other side, will stand for us with an ampler[5] oath and a braver spirit? Are they so much more easily found perpetrating a crime than repenting it? So this is a useless sort of soldier, one we are very far from needing. For even those who <say> deserters ought to be received are saying that our community has the upper hand; for they don't desert for love of us but from fear of imminent fortune. Or do we think that our enemies will more easily give up their war

5 The oath means more; cf. 271.13 *minore sacramento*. *Pronus* and *plenus* are easily confused.

hostes putamus si plures transfugerint? Minime: nam hi
qui bellum gerere contra nos non audent, si locum in civitate nostra non habuerint, saepe deponendi belli auctores
erunt. Nunc in privatum sibi singuli consulunt. ‹Non›[10]
est magnum in singulis momentum; at[11] si praeclusa haec
fuerit spes, quod singuli faciunt universi suadebunt.

8   Haec dicerem etiamsi nihil ex istis metus esset; nunc
vero non possum non confiteri sollicitudinem meam. Quotiens oculos circumtuli et singulas castrorum metior partes, non aliter quam si vallum hostis invaserit alienos habitus, aliena arma video; versantur inter domos nostras, inter
templa, inter muros, in mediis rei publicae visceribus. An
aliquid mali velint facere postea videro; interim, possunt.

9   Ego istud credidi scelus cum a singulis factum[12] est; cum a
paucis, spes est; cum a plurimis, iam consensus.[13] Novum
hercule genus artis. Supervacuum est cuniculos fodere
et per occultos specus ingenti labore exhaustis terris in
mediam subito emergere civitatem, supervacuum est re-
dimere proditorem et scelus pecunia pacisci: videntes
palam, immo gaudentes etiam accepimus intra viscera
10 hostem. Vos aestimabitis an suspectum debeatis habere
quod ad tantum numerum per singulos pervenerunt:
nemo illos recepisset si universi venissent. Omnesne hi
desperaverunt? Omnesne ‹sibi›[14] consulere ac prospicere
voluerunt? Adeone facilius est transfugere quam cedere[15]? Omnes hi reliquerunt in civitate coniuges in ludi-

10 *SB*[1]
11 *SB*[1]: ac Aβ
12 factum *noluit* Wi.: spes Aβ
13 *SB*[2]: -nsi Aβ   14 *Sch.*
15 *SB*[2]: cad- Aβ

policy if more desert? Not at all. For if those who don't
have courage to wage war against us find no place in our
community, they will often advocate giving up the war. As
it is, they are privately taking counsel for their individual
selves. There is <no> great dynamic in individuals; but if
this hope[6] is cut off, all will advocate what individuals are
doing.[7]

I should say all this even if there were no danger from
these people. But as it is, I cannot help confessing my anxiety. Whenever I cast my eyes around and measure particular parts of our encampment, I see alien dress, alien arms,
just as though the enemy had invaded our rampart. They
come and go in our houses, our temples, our walls, right in
the very heart of the commonwealth. Whether they want
to do some harm I shall consider later; meanwhile, they
have the power. Done by individuals I considered that a
crime; done by a few, it's a hope; done by a large number it
becomes a conspiracy. Upon my word, it's a new sort of tac-
tic. No need to dig tunnels and excavate earth with enor-
mous labor so as to emerge all of a sudden through hidden
passages into the middle of the community, no need to buy
a traitor and barter money for crime: openly, open-eyed, or
rather gleefully, we have taken the enemy into our vitals.
You will judge whether their coming through in such numbers one by one ought to make you suspicious: no one
would have let them in if they had come all together. Did
they all despair? Did they all choose to take counsel <for
themselves> and look ahead? Is it so much easier to desert
than just to go away? Did they all leave wives in their com-

6 Of going over to the winning side individually.
7 Giving up the war.

brium atque contumeliam eorum qui se a scelere maximo
11 ulcisci velint? Manifestiorem quandam coniecturam[16] capere possumus: num minus animi sine his, num minus per-
tinaciae desertis? Age sane, hoc non cogitatis, quod nec
custodiunt nec reprehendunt, nec portas praecludere nec
publica retinere cura tanti putant? Miratur aliquis timere
me hostes quod isti transfugiunt? Illi me non timent. Ca-
veamus, obsecro, dum plures sumus.

256

Furiosus trium filiorum pater

Qui tres filios habebat duos per furorem occidit. A tertio
sanatus abdicat eum.

1   DECLAMATIO

Poteram, etiamsi non irascerer, abdicare tamquam bonus
pater. Omnia de fortuna mea timeo, omnia de tam fragili
ac tam mutabili mente, et propter hoc dimittendus mihi a
2 domo filius erat, ne incideret in meum furorem. Sed quatenus et causas quoque abdicationis interrogor, id est cogit
me frequentius malorum meorum meminisse, quamquam
inter praecipua propter quae abdicem hoc est, quod mihi
ista narranda sunt, dicam tamen.
3   Imputo filio meo orbitatem. Respondebit: 'non ego occidi.' Scio; mea manu factum est, ipse ego pater qui genue-

---

[16] *Sch.*: -ore quadam (quandam A1?) –ura Aβ

---

[8] Instead of "us," "in the interests of rhetoric" (Wi.).

munity to be mocked and insulted by people wishing to take revenge for a heinous crime? We can draw plainer inference: without them is there less courage, less pertinacity in the deserted? Come now, doesn't it make you think, the fact that they don't keep them under surveillance or blame them or think it worth while to close the gates in advance or keep them back by public precaution? Is it surprising that I fear the enemy because these folk are deserting? They don't fear *me*.[8] I beg you, let us guard ourselves while we are in the majority.

256

Mad father of three sons

A father of three sons killed two of them in madness. Cured by the third, he disowns him.

DECLAMATION

Even if I were not angry, I could be disowning him as a good father. All ways I am afraid of my fortune, likewise of my mind, so fragile and changeable, and for this reason I had to send my son from my house for fear he might happen upon my madness. But since I am asked about the reasons for my action, since, that is, he forces me to remember often my misfortunes,[1] I shall speak, even though the necessity of telling the story is one of the principal reasons why I disown him.

I hold my son responsible for my bereavement. He will answer: "I did not kill them." I know. The hand was mine, I

---

[1] *Id est . . . meminisse* perhaps to be deleted ("surely a gloss" Wi.).

ram, qui educaveram, per viscera liberorum ferrum exegi.
Credo enim tibi, et orbitatem tamen tibi imputo, tibi. Aes-
timo illam ex die mei doloris. Quaedam ignorare simile
non passi est: tunc liberos perdidi cum perdidisse me sen-
4 si. Esto, gravem sine dubio manibus ⟨mihi⟩[1] meis iniuriam
Fortuna fecerat; posuerat tamen huius rei in ipso animo
remedium illo tempore quo furere et agi dementia videbar. Frequentius in ea cogitatione eram ut crederem esse
cum liberis omnibus. Abstulisti mihi ignorantiam malorum. Quanto miserabilior fui ex die tuae sanitatis! Furio-
sum me non sic cecidi; tum lacerare vestes, tum verberare
5 vultus meos coepi. Omnia igitur haec non in aliam vim
accipi debent quam si filios meos ipse occidisses, quam si
ipse abstulisses. Unde tantum boni ut reddere possis illam
valetudinem, illum furorem?

6   Quod unum possum praestare infelicissimis illis iuveni-
bus meis praestabo: ne quis eorum morte gaudeat, ne cui
prosit quod filios meos occidi.

257

Nuptiae inter inimicorum filios

Qui habebat filium et divitem inimicum, captus a piratis,
scripsit filio de redemptione. Ille cum pecuniam non haberet, offerente divite filiam suam, duxit eam in matrimonium et ⟨soceri⟩[1] pecunia redemit patrem. Reversus ille
imperat ut dimittat. Nolentem abdicat.

256: [1] SB4
257: [1] SB1

---

[2] I.e. of his awareness that he had killed his sons.

drove the knife through my children's vitals, I that begot and reared them. I believe you, and yet I hold you, yes you, responsible for my bereavement. I estimate it from the day of my grief.[2] To be ignorant of some things is like never having suffered them. I lost my sons when I realized that I had lost them. Yes, Fortune had certainly inflicted a great injury <upon me> by my hands; but she had placed a remedy for this in my very mind during the period when I seemed mad, driven by dementia. Quite often my thoughts were such that I believed myself with all my children. You took my ignorance of my misfortune away from me. How much more pitiable I was from the day of sanity, your gift! When I was mad, I did not strike myself so. It was then that I began to tear my clothes and beat my face. All this then ought not to be taken otherwise than as if you yourself had killed my sons, as if you yourself had robbed me of them. Ah, what a blessing it would be if you could give me back that sickness, that madness!

The only thing I can do for these unhappy young men of mine, do I will. Nobody shall be glad of their death, nobody shall profit from my having killed my sons.

257

Marriage between the children of enemies

A man who had a son and a rich man for an enemy was captured by pirates. He wrote to his son about ransom. Since the son had no money, when the rich man offered his daughter, he married her and ransomed his father with <his father-in-law's> money. His father returns and orders him to divorce her. When he refuses, his father disowns him.

1

Si ab alio redemptus esset pater ⟨et⟩[2] statim ut redisset a
gravissima fortuna [et][2] abdicare me instituisset, dicerem
tamen: 'Quid intra tam breve tempus commisi? Quid tam
scelerate a me factum est ut ira patris praecederet ipsam
gratulationem?' Nunc certum habeo indigna quaedam ex-
2 pectare vos facinora, cum abdicetur filius qui redemit. Est
sine dubio istud non meum beneficium, et omne redempti
patris munus ad socerum redit. Ego tamen navigavi, ego
periculosa maria ingressus sum ut redimerem patrem,
quemadmodum ipsum dicere audistis; quaedam etiam
non patiendo[3] passus sum. Quae ei ratio abdicationis est?
3   'Non obsequeris' inquit 'mihi.' Si hoc ad abdicandum
satis esset, supervacua erant omnino iudicia ipsa. Cur enim
nobis defensionis potestatem dedistis si nihil nostris con-
siliis libertatis relictum est? Servi mehercule quaedam liberius ex bona mente faciunt, et aliquando indicium fidei
4 putant pretio empta mancipia non paruisse. Filios vero
quis dubitavit umquam esse plerumque suae potestatis?
Ut ea praeteream quae sub tam bono patre ne argumenti
quidem causa referenda sunt, nec dicam 'non coges templa incendere, non coges operibus publicis manus adferre': leviora certe nostrae †mediocritatis†[4] esse manifestum est, ut sententiam iudices dicere ⟨quam⟩[5] velimus, ut

----

2 *Pith.*   3 *SB*[1]: facienda A*β*: patienda *Aer.*
4 auctoritatis *Ro.*: volunta- *SB*[3]
5 *Watt*[1], *Wi., auct. Ro.*

----

[1] The possibility of an offense committed before the father's
return is ignored.

DECLAMATION

If my father had been ransomed by somebody else ⟨and⟩ as soon as he had returned from his calamities had set about disowning me, I should have said none the less: "What have I done wrong in so short a time? What action of mine was so criminal that my father's anger came before I could congratulate him?"[1] As it is, I am sure you are expecting some shocking misbehaviors, seeing a son disowned by the father he ransomed. Doubtless that is no benefaction of mine, the whole gift—a father ransomed—belongs to my father-in-law. All the same, I made the voyage, entered dangerous seas to ransom my father, as you have heard him say himself. Some things I suffered[2] even without suffering them. What reason has he for disowning?

"You don't obey me," he says. If this were sufficient cause to disown, the trials themselves would be altogether superfluous. For why did you give us the license to defend ourselves if no freedom to make up our own minds is left us? Slaves, upon my word, take some actions quite freely, intending well, and sometimes people think disobedience in chattels bought for a price a sign of loyalty. But as for sons, who ever doubted that for the most part they are in their own control? Suppose I pass over doings which under so good a father ought not to be mentioned even for argument's sake, suppose I don't say that you won't force me to set fire to temples or vandalize public works: lighter matters are clearly our responsibility: as jurors we vote ⟨as⟩ we

---

[2] In imagination. *Etiam non patienda*, "not even to be suffered," is hopelessly limp and leaves curiosity as referring to actual sufferings.

testimonium non ad arbitrium parentum reddere, ⟨ut⟩[6]
5 amico[7] suadere quod animus dictaverit. Quod si licet aliquando etiam contra patris voluntatem ea quae alioqui re-
prehensionem non merentur filio facere, nusquam tamen
libertas tam necessaria quam in matrimonio est. Et hoc dicerem si quaereretur hoc iudicio an mihi aliqua ducenda
esset: ego eligam cum qua victurus sum, ego comitem
laborum, sollicitudinum, curarum ipse perpendam. Quis
6 enim amare alieno animo potest? Nunc vero firmius hoc
esse atque facilius coepit: uxorem iam duxi (non dico
quare) meo impulsu, mea voluntate. Eripuerat enim te
mihi Fortuna dederatque mihi illam miseram libertatem.
Repudium igitur imperas et copulatos iam diu diducis animos. Neque enim hoc tu spectaveris, quod cum uxore mea
non diu vixi. Sine dubio secundum nuptias profectus sum,
continuo me peregrinatio excepit; sed[8] vel hoc ipso iniquius est repudiari eam quae certe non potuit offendere.
7   Descendamus sane ad hanc quoque necessitatem, ut
imperante patre etiam repudium filius debeat pati: quid de
ipsa quam repudiari vis querar? Sane pater fuerit inimicus:
cur haec nurus esse desinat quam nihil peccasse tu quoque
confiteris qui expellis? Negat idoneam esse matrimonio
meo locupletem. Quam vereor ne cui videatur pater sic
8 inimicus diviti esse coepisse! Non enim fortuna in utram-
libet partem intuenda est. An vero apud me noceat puellae
quod dives est cum apud patrem illius non nocuerit mihi
quod pauper sum? 'Dives est.' Numquid ergo hoc dicere

---

6 *Watt*[2]   7 *Opitz*: immo Aβ
8 *Wi.*: et Aβ

---

[3] Our attitude to fortune (rich and poor) should be consistent.

please, as witnesses we do not give evidence at our father's discretion, we advise a friend as our mind dictates. But if a son be allowed at times to act in things not otherwise blameworthy even against his father's wishes, yet in nothing is freedom so necessary as in marriage. And I should say this even if the question at this trial was whether I should take some woman as my wife: *I* shall choose my life-partner, *I* shall form my opinion of the companion of my labors, anxieties, and cares. For who can love with another man's heart? But as it is, the thing gets firmer and easier. I have already married a wife (never mind why) of my own impulse, my own volition. For Fortune had taken you from me and given me that miserable freedom. So you command divorce and part hearts already long linked—for do not look to the fact that I did not live long with my wife. No doubt I set out after the marriage, foreign travel took me immediately. That very circumstance makes it the more unfair that a wife should be divorced who assuredly could not have done anything to offend.

Well, let us get down to this compulsion even: at his father's command a son ought to suffer even a divorce. What complaint am I to make of the lady herself whom you want me to divorce? Granted that her father was your enemy: why should she cease to be your daughter-in-law, when even you that drive her out admit that she did nothing wrong? He says a wealthy woman is no match for me. I am very much afraid that someone may think this was how my father became an enemy to the rich man. We mustn't look at fortune this way or that as we choose[3]: or should the fact that she is rich prejudice me against the girl when the fact that I am poor did not prejudice her father against me? "She's rich." So can you say: "She will be haughty and put

113

potes: 'superbior erit et fastidiet'? Securus sis, pater: petiti
9 sumus, empti sumus. 'At inimicus' inquit 'fuit.' Volo adhuc
sic loqui tamquam odia utraque parte durent. Non oportet
immortales esse inimicitias, et ita demum tutum perpe-
tuumque ‹poterit›[9] esse humanum genus si amor ac fides
nullam habuerint oblivionem, ea rursus ‹in›[10] quae aliquo
10 incommodo commutantur brevi morte deficiant. Sed non
est diu mihi in hac parte commorandum, quae certe satis
potens apud divitem fuerat. Inimici nomen habuerit aliquando (nec quaero quam immerito, nec quaero quam
iniuste), modo redire in gratiam cum eo potuerim. Sed hoc
solum reprehendit, quod se absente omiserim cum divite
inimicitias. Ita, opinor: feci hoc contemptu patris, feci vili-
11 tate. Restitui nos in integrum putate, iudices. Captus est
pater meus a piratis, vincla et ultimos metus patitur et ea
quibus gravius id tantum est quod imminet. Hoc scio, hoc
ipsius epistulis cognovi; hinc redimi potest. Duram putate
condicionem poni: nonne subeunda est? Si piratae hoc
mihi pollicerentur, ut vicarias pro patre manus acciperent,
non recusarem catenas. Si obligarer faenore, aes alienum
12 tamen non timuissem ut redimerem patrem. Duxi puellam
honestam, locupletem. Ego tamen (si ulla mihi dicenti
fides est) non hoc in ista condicione spectavi. Ille me movit, ut beneficiis ‹non›[11] vinceremur. Sed neque in me ille
probavit aliud quam pietatem. Vidit fletus meos, vidit totius animi atque etiam corporis defectionem. Sic homini
inter principes nostrae civitatis numerando coepi bona
esse condicio.

---

[9] Wi. (*post* tutum *Leo*) [10] *SB*3 [11] *SB*4

---

[4] See *HSCP* 80 (1976), 202.

on airs"? Don't worry, father: I was wooed, I was bought. "But he was my enemy," he says. So far I choose to speak as though hate lasts on both sides. But enmities should not be immortal, and the human race <can> be safe and perpetual only if love and loyalty are unforgettable while on the other hand those feelings <into> which by some misadventure they are changed quickly die and fade away. But I need not dwell on this topic[4] for long; it had certainly been effective enough with the rich man. Granted that he had the name of "enemy" at one time (and I don't enquire how undeservedly, how unfairly), provided that I was able to become friends with him again. But my father blames me only for this, that in his absence I discontinued our feud with the rich man. I suppose I did that in contempt of my father, holding him cheap! Gentlemen, imagine that we go back to where we were before this happened. My father has been captured by pirates, he suffers bonds and ultimate terrors, and present pains only exceeded by what threatens. This I know, this I learned from his own letters, from this he can be ransomed. Suppose the terms are harsh: ought I not to accept them? Suppose the pirates had promised to take me as my father's substitute, I should not have refused the chains. If it had meant getting tied up in a loan, I should not have been afraid of debt in order to ransom my father. I married a respectable, rich girl. However, if my words get any credence, that was not what I thought of in that marriage. *He* moved me; I did <not> want us to be outdone in kindnesses. But he too approved nothing else in me but my filial devotion. He saw my tears, the failing of my whole mind and body. That was how I became a good match in the eyes of a man to be counted among the leaders of our community.

13   Itaque intellego mihi, iudices, non in hoc tantum laborandum, ut iram patris mitigem, ut leniam; illud est partium mearum, illud vobis adhibitis rogo, in gratiam velit
redire iam cum propinquo meo, cum redemptore suo.
Non enim iactabo meam pietatem: illius opus est quod re-
demi.

258

Fortis contumax patri forti

Si duo aut plures fortiter fecerint, de praemio armis contendant. Vir fortis optet quod volet. Pater et filius fortiter
fecerunt. Petît pater a filio ut cederet sibi praemio; non impetravit. Cessit ipse et abdicat.

1   DECLAMATIO

Etiamsi dissimulari posset quae causa [patri][1] fuisset, ipsum tamen hoc abdicatione dignum erat, aliquid ⟨paren-
ti⟩[2] petenti negasse. Quantum enim mihi praestare poterat
ut paria redderet? Non iam imputo illa vulgaria, lucem et
ius libertatis et usum vitae. Hoc, hoc imputo, quod fortiter
fecisti. Robur istud corporis [mei][3] meum est; animus iste
ad contemnenda pericula paratus ex meo fluxit. Ego te diu
praeceptis feci virum fortem, proxime quidem etiam ex-
2   emplo. Quantumcumque sit istud quod peto, non indicare
satis est? Non desiderium pervenire in notitiam tuam suf-

---

[1] *SB*3   [2] *SB*4   [3] *SB*2: tui *Gron.*

---

[5] *Propinquus* is normally a blood relation, though the plural
can include others. The singular, of a relative by marriage (*affinis*),
is at least unusual.

So I understand, gentlemen, that I ought not only to strive to mitigate my father's anger, soften him, but that it is in my role (and I ask this invoking your support) that he be willing to be friends again with my relative[5] and his ransomer. For I shall make no boast of my filial behavior: it was *his* doing that I ransomed.

258

Hero defies hero father

If two or more become heroes, let them contend in arms for the reward. Let the hero opt for what he wants. A father and son become heroes. The father asked his son to yield the reward to him; he was refused. He yielded himself, and disowns.

DECLAMATION

Even if it were possible for the reason[1] to be concealed, the refusal of a parent's request in itself deserved disowning. For how much could[2] he render me so as to make me an equal return? I am not now debiting you with things commonly brought up—the daylight, the right of freedom, the use of life: I debit you with this very fact that you became a hero. This bodily strength of yours is mine. This courage ready to despise danger flowed from mine. For a long while I made a hero of you by precept, most recently by example also. However much I ask of you, is it not enough to name it? Is it not enough for a desire to come to your no-

---

[1] For the disownment.
[2] "Logic might suggest rather *debebat*" (Wi.). Perhaps a contamination: "how much is due" and "how could he repay?"

ficit nisi preces adhibuero, nisi auctoritatem paternam summisero? Multum peccaveras etiamsi praestitisses.

3 Nunc vero quid a te petieram? Ut mihi praemio cede-rés. ⟨Non impetravi.⟩[4] Non dico quid fuerit secuturum. Sane ita sit constituta lex ut in iudicio contendamus, ut ci-tra periculum feratur de nostra virtute sententia: non erat

4 aequum cedere te, ut non dicam patri, seni? Tibi appro-bandae virtutis multa tempora supersunt, tu sperare id quod hodie cesseris potes: mihi indulsit Fortuna hunc su-premum honorem. Inter extraneos quoque et alienos est aliquod privilegium aetatis. Honores prior peterem, ad si-gnandum advocatus prior ⟨signarem, sententiam prior⟩[5] rogarer. In his etiam minimis observationibus inhumane non cederes ⟨honorem sedis⟩,[6] honorem lateris.

5 Age vero, non praeter hoc etiam dignior praemio fuit virtus mea? Non est tam admirabile cum fortiter facit iuve-nis. Hoc aetas postulat, hoc robur iuventae poscit; paene turpe est non fecisse. Hoc est honore dignius, vicisse annos et ultra aetatem durantes agere virtutes. Eo tempore forti-ter feci quo cogi non possem ut militarem. Utrum tandem vis magnum esse quod ego feci an minus esse quod tu fecisti?

6 Videamus nunc quis[7] fuerit secuturus exitus si in ista contentione praemii idem animi ego quoque habuissem.

[4] *SB*[2]
[5] *lac. sic suppl. Ri.*
[6] *SB*[1]
[7] *SB*[3]: ẹquis A: h(a)ec qui β

---

[3] *Privilegium* in the declamations is a law (here unwritten) granting a special right to a particular group.

tice, without my adding entreaties, without my lowering paternal authority? You would have much offended, even if you had done what I asked.

But as it is, what had I asked of you? To yield the reward to me. <I was refused.> I don't speak of what was to follow. Let us suppose the law was so framed that we contend in court and a verdict about our valor be given with no danger: would it not have been fair for you to yield, I don't say to your father, but to an old man? You have plenty of time left in which to approve your valor, you can hope for what you yield today. Me Fortune has indulged with this final honor. Even among outsiders and strangers age has some privilege.[3] I would have stood for office before you; if called in for my signature, <I would have signed before you>; I would have been asked <to speak in the senate> before you. Even in these minor observances it would have been uncivilized of you not to yield, as preference <in seating>, in walking.[4]

But come, besides this, was not my valor more deserving of the reward? When a young man becomes a hero, it is not so much to be wondered at. His age demands it, the strength of youth demands it. It is almost a disgrace not to have done it. This is more worthy of honor, to have conquered one's years and practiced virtues enduring beyond their age. I became a hero at a time when I could not have been compelled to serve. Which do you prefer? That what I did was big or that what you did was not so big?

Let us see now what would have been the outcome if I too had been of the same mind as you in the strife over the

[4] The older man would walk between two companions or on the inside of one (Wi. cites Ov. *Fasti.* 5.67f.).

Armis contendendum erat et laetissimo alioqui domus
nostrae proventu gravissimum vulnus[8] et crimen inureba-
tur. Iam video[9] quare non cesseris: hoc tibi praemio maius
videbatur, committi cum patre et parricidium facere iure;
hoc profecto etiam in acie [facere][10] cogitasti et, cum imi-
tareris[11] virtutem meam, non optandi ius sed pugnandi
7   videbas. Ergo,[12] quantum in te, in medio foro et universa spectante civitate filii manu trucidatus sum vel, quod
est gravius, occidi. Tu perseverasti cum me cupere sic videres. Etiamnum interrogo, staturusne contra fueris. Dic
utrum.[13] Nam si ‹non›[14] fuisti perseveraturus, vide an gravius etiam crimen sit patri negasse quod praestare poteras.

8   Habe ergo praemium istud, quantumcumque in eo honoris est; sed contentus esto rem appellasse publicam: discede de domo mea. Non iam ultionis gratia facio, sed etiam
securitatis: insomnes noctes ago et ad omnes terreor stre-
pitus. [Nulla mihi secura nox est.][15] Habeo in domo filium
9   qui me potuit occidere. Nam praemii quidem gratia strin-
xisses ferrum contra patrem et in conspectu civitatis popu-
lique parricidium fecisses; ut heres citius fias, ut bona mea
occupes, homo tam cupidus non audebis parricidium facere secretum?

10   Non ignoro omnium fere qui abdicantur hunc esse morem, ut acta iam causa ad preces convertantur et mitigare
patres rogando velint; hocine tu concipis animo posse fieri,
ut exores?

8 *Obr.*: funus Aβ   9 *Obr.*: -es Aβ   10 *Sch.*
11 A: -aris β   12 *Watt*[2]: ego Aβ
13 *Obr.*: dicturum Aβ   14 *Ri.*   15 *ita secl.* SB[3]

5 Instead of settling the matter within the family.

award. We would have had to contend in arms and a terrible wound and crime would have been branded upon this otherwise most happy advancement of our house. Now I see why you did not yield. It meant more to you than the reward to duel with your father and commit parricide under the law. Even in battle you doubtless thought of this, and when you were imitating my valor, you had in view not the right of option but the right of combat. Thus, so far as lay in you, I was slaughtered, in the middle of the Forum with the whole community looking on, by my son's hand; or, what is worse, I was the killer, you kept going when you saw how my heart was set on it. I still ask you, were you going to stand up against me? Tell me, yes or no. If you were ⟨not⟩ going to keep on, ask yourself whether it is not an even greater offence to have denied your father what you could have granted.

Well then, keep that reward, whatever honor it carries, but let it be enough for you to have called in the commonwealth.[5] Leave my house. I am not doing it just for revenge now, but also for security. My nights are sleepless and I am afraid at every sound. ⟦No night is free of fear for me.⟧ I have a son in my house who could have killed me. For the sake of a reward you would have drawn your sword against your father and committed parricide in the sight of the community and people. To inherit sooner, to seize upon my property, will so greedy a man as yourself not dare to commit parricide in secret?

I am aware that the practice of almost all who are disowned, when they have pleaded their case, is to turn to entreaties and try to soften their fathers by begging. Can you conceive that there is any possibility of your prayers prevailing with me?

259

Pauper naufragae liberator, maritus

Dives cum amico paupere et filia navigabat. Naufragium
fecit. Extulit filiam divitis pauper. Rumor erat eam nuptu-
ram cuidam nobili iuveni. Quodam tempore in domo divitis tumultus fuit; inventi sunt una pauper et puella; ab
utroque dictum est vitiatam puellam. Imperavit filiae dives
ut nuptias optaret. Educta ad magistratum optavit. Postea
comperit dives non esse vitiatam puellam. Imperat ut re-
linquat pauperem. Nolentem relinquere abdicat.

1

SERMO

In omnibus quidem abdicationis controversiis, quatenus
pro liberis dicimus, summissa debebit esse actio et satis-
factioni similis. In hac tamen controversia istud aliquanto
magis servandum est. Nam et filia est quae abdicatur, et hic
pater aliquid etiam boni et clementis viri fecit et nobis
tutissimum uti hic etiam[1] bonitate.

2

DECLAMATIO

Non ignoro, iudices, quantum causae nostrae oneris acce-
dat ex persona abdicantis, non propter illud commune,
quod pater est, sed quod pater indulgentissimus, amicus
optimus, etiam[2] quando iniuriam accepisse videtur mitis-
simus. Itaque priusquam defensionem adgredimur, in hoc

[1] *SB*[2]: hac e. Aβ: hac eius *coni. Wi.*
[2] *Wi.*: -msi (-m si) Aβ

---

[1] "An odd word in the context" (Dingel ap. Wi.), which calls for
servator, perhaps from a misapprehension that the girl has been
rescued from pirates.

259

A poor man, liberator[1] of a shipwrecked girl, husband

A rich man took ship with a poor friend and a daughter. He was shipwrecked. The poor man rescued the rich man's daughter. There was a report that she was to marry a certain young nobleman. On a day there was a commotion in the rich man's house. The poor man and the girl were found together. Both said that the girl had been violated. The rich man commanded the girl to opt for marriage. Brought before the magistrate, she opted. Later on the rich man discovered that the girl had not been violated. He commands her to leave the poor man. On her refusal to leave, he disowns her.

DISCUSSION

In all controversies concerning a disowning, when speaking for the children, our style should be restrained, like an apology. But in the present controversy this rule applies rather more than usual. For it is a daughter who is being disowned, and this father had behaved like a good, merciful man, and here too it will be safest for us to use his kindness.[2]

DECLAMATION

I am aware, gentlemen, how much the person of the disowner adds to our burden in this case; not because he is the father, as always in such cases, but because he is a very loving father, an excellent friend, most gentle even when on occasion he appears to have suffered an injury. So before I embark on the defense, I shall give my own mind the

2 Cf. s.14 *hac tanta bonitate*.

satisfaciemus animo nostro, ut gratias agamus ante omnia
filiae nomine: quam sic amavit ut eam diduci a se ne navi-
gaturus quidem voluerit, cui ad magistratus eductae prae-
standum putavit ne qua occisi hominis infamia inquinare-
tur, quam tradidit amico suo (<et>[3] quod iam dici potest)

3 optimo marito. Proximum est ab hoc ut amici quoque et, si
permittit, generi mandata perferamus. Sunt autem similia;
nam et plurimum cum eo vixit et nulla causa, nullo diduc-
tus est loco, et usque in hoc tempus in ea fuit opinione ut se

4 crederet vivere beneficio istius. Erat profecto felix domus
si in illa prima simulatione hi manere voluissent; sed, dum
hanc quoque beneficiis optimi senis referre gratiam volunt
et simpliciter fatentur omnia, inciderunt ambo in hanc
dicendae causae necessitatem, dum scilicet ambitiosus gener vult videri socero suo innocentior quam videbatur.

5   Equidem peractis gratiarum agendarum mandatis hoc
primum puto, ut isti, si permittit, gratuler. Filia eius, pro-
bissima puella ac verecundissima, nullam accepit iniuriam; amicus et gener nullum scelus fecit: nam si quid tale
cogitare et in animum inducere potuisset, illo tempore vi-
tiandi habuit occasionem quo naufragam in litus evexerat.

6   Reliqua pars actionis meae non tam ad defensionem,
iudices, spectat quam ad deprecationem. Iam[4] nulla profecto certior ratio est quam ut istum priorum temporum
admoneam.

7   Hic enim, iudices, adulescens, (quod in hoc demum
iudicio audîmus a divite dici) pauper, unam sibi domum

3 *Sch.*
4 *SB*[1]: nam Aβ

---

3 The son-in-law.

satisfaction of first of all thanking him on his daughter's behalf. He loved her so much that even with a sea voyage to
make he did not want her to be separated from him. When
she was brought before the magistrates, he thought he
should see to it that she was not tainted with the ill fame of
a man's killing. He handed her over to his friend, ⟨and⟩, as
can now be said, an excellent husband. Next after this, I
have to convey a message also from his friend and, if he
permits, son-in-law. It is similar; for he[3] had a close rela-
tionship with him and was never separated from him for
any reason or in any place, and up to the present time, as he
saw the matter, he believed that he owed him his life. It
would surely have been a happy home if they had chosen to
keep up that first deception. But wishing to repay the kindnesses of the excellent old gentleman in this way among
others, they artlessly confess everything. So both of them
have fallen into the necessity of pleading this case. The
son-in-law, one sees, sought favor and wanted to appear to
his father-in-law more innocent than he looked.

For my part, now that I have given my messages of
thanks, the first thing, I think, is for me to congratulate
that gentleman, if he permits. His daughter, a very well-
conducted and modest young lady, received no injury, his
friend and son-in-law committed no crime. For if he could
have thought of such a thing, let it enter his mind, he had
the opportunity to violate her when he carried her shipwrecked to shore.

The rest of my plea, gentlemen, looks not so much to
defense as to deprecation. Surely no line is safer than to re-
mind him of times gone by.

This young man, gentlemen, a poor man, as we have

quam coleret elegit, unum hunc cui fidem suam impende-
ret. Ac brevi moribus, sanctitate, innocentia effecit[5] ut inter omnes etiam superioris fortunae carissimus videretur.
Itaque hercule, cum peregre proficisci destinasset, quamquam navigationum pericula non ignoraret adulescens,
8   tamen secutus per maria, per tempestates. Non nimium
de Fortuna querimur: etiamsi naufragium illud multos
metus, longam vexationem, aliquod attulit detrimentum,
tamen rem difficillimam expressit, fidei experimentum. In
illa omnium trepidatione, in qua pro sua quisque salute
sollicitus nihil de proximo cogitabat, cum inter fluctus et
turbati maris minas vix evadere ⟨quisquam posset⟩[6] ac
suae quisque consulere saluti videretur, non mehercule
miror quod quamvis optimus pater filiam tamen respicere
9   non potuit. Quis enim hoc crederet posse fieri, ut non
modo saluti suae consuleret verum etiam suscepto onere
infirmitatis alienae evadere in terram et vincere imminentis fortunae metus posset? Itaque non servus ullus tam
fidelis, non libertus tam beneficio obligatus manumittentis
fuit ut hoc subire periculum posset: unus amicus (nondum
enim illud faciebat tamquam gener), accepta umeris suis
puella, per tot difficultates, per tot pericula nihil pro se
10 ipso sollicitus tulit. Iam[7] istud non humani tantum operis
sed divini cuiusdam beneficii arbitrandum est. Tu[8] hos

[5] C: f- Aβ   [6] SB4   [7] SB1: quam Aβ
[8] Wi.: tum BC: cum AD

---

[4] He had made nothing of it when he ordered the marriage, cf.
s.21 fin.

[5] A supplement seems necessary; *vix evadere* can hardly be
stretched to mean *vix futurum esse ut quisquam evaderet*.

heard the rich man say for the first time at this trial,[4] chose one house to cultivate, this one person to whom to give his loyalty. And soon by his manners, his purity of life, his blameless character, he made himself appear his dearest friend even among all of those superior to him in fortune. And so, upon my word, when the other decided to travel abroad, the young man (though he was not ignorant of the dangers of navigation) followed him none the less through seas and tempests. We don't complain too much of Fortune. That shipwreck brought much fear, protracted distress, a certain amount of loss, but it forced out something very difficult, a test of loyalty. In the universal panic, when each man was concerned for his own life without a thought for his neighbor, and amid the waves and the menaces of a sea in turmoil it seemed that hardly <anybody could> escape[5] and everyone seemed to be for himself, upon my word, I don't wonder that even the best of fathers could not pay attention to his daughter. For who would have thought it possible that <anyone>[6] should not only look to his own survival but also be able to shoulder the burden of another's weakness and escape to land and overcome fears of imminent fate?[7] So no slave was so faithful, no freedman so bound by the benefaction of his liberator that he could brave this peril. Only the friend (he was not yet acting in the role of son-in-law) took the girl over his shoulders and carried her through so many difficulties and dangers without a care for himself. This must surely be deemed some kind of divine favor, not merely the work of man. Fortune,

6 *Quisquam* supplied. I do not think it possible to understand *quis* as "who among them?"

7 Lit. "fortune."

coniunxisti copulastique,[9] Fortuna[10]!

Nihil necesse habeo diutius hoc imputare tamquam non intellectum. Non perdidit beneficium: et puella se nihil non huic debere credidit et pater ita interpretatus est munus[11] istud ut existimaret amico in se ac suos omnia licere. Rumor itaque in civitate non quibus alias solet causis exortus est, sed homines, dum indignantur nescio cui iuveni opulento[12] et nobili dari puellam, convicium moribus huius tamquam ingrati fecerunt. Intellego, iudices, quam difficili ac velut scopuloso loco versetur oratio mea. Quomodo narrem istud quod confessi sumus? Illud puto tutissimum est: rapere voluit (huic enim certe crimini ignoscis); inde tumultus, inde voces repugnantis, inde fortasse etiam nimia puellae querela, quod audaciam pro iniuria tulit, quod se raptam quoniam ille rapere voluisset proclamavit. Nec is sane negandum existimavit et, quamquam nihil acciderat tale, amico[13] suo confessus est. Illud certe manifestum est: pater filiam putavit irasci. Itaque sollicite quoque nec pro imperio tantum patris sed etiam pro auctoritate, pro sententia deprecatus est. Tum admonuit illam: 'memento hunc esse cui vitam debeas, hunc esse qui te ex periculis servaverit maris.' Quanta illa gratulatio! Quanta patris laus fuit! Quam felix domus! Nihil deerat gratulationi nostrae si raptor fuisset. His moribus suis, hac tanta bonitate meruisse visus est pater qui non

---

[9] *Obr.*: -tis culpastique Aβ   [10] *Obr.*: -n(a)e Aβ
[11] *Ri.*: maius Aβ
[12] *Gron.*: opinor Aβ: opimo B: optimo *ed. princ.*
[13] *Obr.*: animo Aβ

---

[8] "Not the usual gossipy sort" (Wi.).

you joined them, you tied them together!

I have no need to claim credit for this at length as though it had not been understood. He did not waste his good deed. The girl felt she could never repay him and her father looked upon that benefaction as entitling his friend to do with him and his whatever he wanted. So a rumor arose in the community, not for the usual reasons;[8] people were indignant that the girl should be given to some rich young nobleman or other and abused his[9] character as an ingrate. Gentlemen, I realize that my address has entered a difficult area, full of pitfalls.[10] How should I narrate what we have confessed? This, I think, is the safest way: he wanted to rape her (you[11] forgive that offense at least); hence the commotion, hence her cries as she resisted, hence perhaps also she overdid her protest, taking audacity for injury, screaming that she had been raped because he had wanted to rape her. As for him, true, he thought it better not to deny it, and though nothing of the sort had happened, he confessed to his friend. This at least is clear: the father thought his daughter was angry. Accordingly, he interceded with her, in concern, not only commanding her as a father, but giving his advice and opinion. Then he admonished her: "Remember, this is the man to whom you owe your life, who saved you from the dangers of the sea." What congratulations there were! How the father was belauded! What a happy home! Nothing was wanting to our rejoicings if there *had* been a rapist. By his behavior, his abundant kindness, this it seemed was a father who should

9 The father's.
10 Lit. "rocks" (lifted from Cic. *Div. in Caec.* 36).
11 Addressing the father.

15 falleretur: indicaverunt integritatem. Quo speraverant futurum ut magis amarentur, incidunt in offensam: nisi forte
invicem ludimur, et nos pater mutuo mendacio temptat
⟨et⟩[14] quare non omnia statim simpliciter dixerimus mina-
tur. Di faciant ut iste sit eventus qui adhuc in hac domo
omnium periculorum fuit!

16 Nunc[15] tamen, quatenus forma iudicii proponitur, agitur defendentis imitatio. Nam si te prorsus irasci existimarem, optime pater, illa dicerem: 'Filiam abdicas. Nondum
defendo factum, nihil de isto crimine loquor: ⟨filiae no-

17 men⟩[16] satis tutum esse potest apud iudices. Fulmen istud
patrum adversus ferociam adulescentiae datum est, adversus filios, qui peccare plus possunt; filia vero vix nutricum
minas tulerit vel eorum a quibus educatur tristitiam. Et ut
virgo pertineat ad patrem, tamen nupta pertinet ad maritum. Post ⟨diem⟩[17] illum quo spes liberorum inchoata est,
quo in nepotes usque cogitationem misisti, quid aliud potes exigere a filia tua quam quod placuit[18] ei cui collocata

18 est?' Si latius[19] agendum esset, illud dicerem: 'Abdicari
propter matrimonium non potest. Paulo fortior recusaret
etiam nubere nisi cui voluisset; haec subiecit in hoc se imperio tuo, ex arbitrio patris nupsit. Paulo fortius vindicari[20]
debet matrimonium iam factum. Ut etiam nuptias imperare possis, repudium imperare non potes eius ad quem
puella legibus et magistratibus et iure iurando pervenit.'

19 Verum contra haec paulo altius[21] repetit abdicationem,

---

[14] SB[1]   [15] Watt[2]: nostra Aβ
[16] coni. SB[3]   [17] Ro.
[18] anne placeat ?
[19] Aer.: l(a)et- Aβ
[20] Gron.: -re Aβ   [21] Aer.: lat- Aβ

not be deceived: they told the truth, there had been no violation. They had thought they would be loved more than ever; but they stumbled into offense. Or perhaps we are being played with in our turn and the father is testing us with a lie like our own ‹and› threatening us because we did not simply tell the whole truth in the first place. May the gods grant that this turn out as have all dangers so far in this home.

As it is, however, since we have the form of a trial to deal with, our imitation of a defense proceeds. For if I thought you were really angry, best of fathers, I should say: "You disown your daughter. I don't as yet defend what was done, I say nothing about your charge. ‹The name of daughter› can be safe enough with the jury. This thunderbolt of fathers was given against the rashness of youth, against sons, who can misbehave in a larger way. But a daughter could hardly bear her nurse's threats or the frowns of those who bring her up. And although a daughter is her father's business, a wife is her husband's. After that ‹day› on which hope of children has begun, on which you sent your thoughts ahead to grandsons, what can you demand of your daughter except that she pleased the man with whom she has been placed?" If I was to plead more at large, I should say: "Because of her marriage, she cannot be disowned. A somewhat bolder girl would have refused even to marry except a man of her choice: this one submitted herself to your command, married at her father's discretion. Matrimony already in effect should be championed a little more robustly. You may even command her to wed, but you cannot command her to divorce the man to whom she came by laws and magistrates and oath."

But against this he carries his disowning a little further

et non est contentus ea obicere propter quae iudicium est.
'Mentita est' inquit 'patri, de raptu mentita est.' Defendam
ista, iudices? [Absoluta sunt.]²² Ego vero malo esse crimen, ut patri plus debeamus.

20   Deceptus es: ita malles filiam tuam raptam esse? Volo
sic defendere puellam tamquam factum sit ipsius culpa:
ecquid ignoscis? Non est hic amor: gratus animus est. An
illa sibi ullum fideliorem fore tota vita existimaret quam
eum cui secundum te debeat plurimum? Cogita quae fuerint illa pericula ex quibus evasit, quae tempestates, qui
fluctus et naufragia et cetera quae nihil divisione egent no-
21   mina. Sed omnem hanc culpam maritus ad se trahit: 'Nihil
tantum puella cogitavit: quidquid est istud, ego feci; qualecumque istud est, meum consilium est. Tu ignosce, qui
soles.' Recedere iubes a marito tali? Qua tandem causa?
22   'Pauper est.' Non solebat hoc illi apud te nocere. '‹Nec›²³
relinquam nec dico pauperem; nam in matrimonio qui-
dem †filiae quod solebat nocere.†²⁴' Te auctore nupsit, te
hortante nupsit. Redde rationem illius sententiae: quamvis
putares turpem, tamen cogitasti quid praestitisset filiae
tuae.

23   SERMO

In summa parte declamationis utrumque producemus et
pro utroque pariter rogabimus, sed aliquanto magis pro

---

²² *SB*³   ²³ *SB*²   ²⁴ *anne* bona sunt quodam modo
communia *vel sim.*? *Cf.* 247, 7 *et* 11

---

¹² Her refusal to leave her husband.
¹³ When he forgives us again.   ¹⁴ That she planned the
alleged rape in order to marry her rescuer.

back and is not content to charge her with what occasioned the trial.[12] "She lied," says he, "to her father, lied about the rape." Shall I defend that, gentlemen? No, I would rather be charged, so that our debt to the father be the greater.[13]

You were deceived: would you so much rather your daughter *had* been raped? I want to defend the girl on the assumption that it was her fault.[14] Don't you forgive her? This isn't love, it's gratitude. Or was she to think that anyone would be more faithful to her all through life than the man to whom after yourself she owes most?[15] Think of the dangers from which she escaped, the tempests, the waves, and the shipwrecks and the rest of it that need not be detailed. But the husband takes all the blame upon himself: "The girl never thought of anything this big.[16] Whatever it is, it is my idea. Forgive me, as is your way." "Are you ordering me to leave a husband like this? For what reason, pray?" "He is poor." "That did not use to count against him with you. I shall <not> leave him nor do I call him poor. For in marriage <property is in a fashion common>."[17] She married him on your advice, at your urging. Account for that way of thinking: although you believed him disgraced, you still thought of what he had done for your daughter.

DISCUSSION

In the final part of the declamation we shall bring both of them forward and make an appeal for both equally—but

---

[15] Two excuses then: (a) it was gratitude, not love (passion), that made her want to marry him and (b) she knew she could count on him all through life. [16] *Tale* might have been expected, but he may mean that a mere girl could never have contrived anything so drastic. [17] See crit. note.

marito misero. Decet enim ‹illam›[25] illum amare. Dicat se
moriturum. †Totum est enim in eodem.†

24

DECLAMATIO

Petiturum se adfirmat quo tu[26] illum exemisti cum ad magistratus eductus est. Hic animum tuum exigit priorem,
hic illam misericordiam.

260

Pastor abdicatorum

Dives adulescens abdicatos recipiebat et de suo alebat.
Laesae rei publicae reus est.

1

SERMO

In plerisque controversiis plerumque hoc quaerere solemus, utrum ipsorum persona utamur ad dicendum an ad-
vocati, vel propter sexum, sicut ‹in›[1] feminis, vel propter
aliquam alioqui[2] vitae vel ipsius de quo quaeritur facti
deformitatem. Hic adulescens et honestus est et, cum sit
locuples quoque, nihil tam turpe commisit ut illi pro se

2 loqui fas non sit. Ego tamen existimo dandum esse advocatum: primum quod, etiamsi quid remissius ac liberalius
fecit, aetate excusari potest, non consentiunt autem haec
inter se, ut idem *[3] et tantum infirmitatis animi ut hac ex-

---

  25 *SB*[4]   26 *Obr.*: quodu A[2](β): quod tu A[1]: cum tu B
  1 *Ro.*   2 A: -que B: maliciam C: aliam D: maculam *Watt*[1]:
del. coni. idem, Wi.   3 idem ‹et tantum roboris habeat ut
pro se ipse dicere possit› *Ro., auct. Aer., Sch.*

---

18 Perhaps a marginal comment (Wi.). Inept anyway.

rather more for the unfortunate husband. For it's seemly ⟨for her⟩ to love him. Let him say that he is going to die. For everything depends on the same.[18]

DECLAMATION

He says he will seek what you saved him from[19] when he was brought before the magistrates. He demands of you your former disposition, that pity.

260

Feeder of the disowned

A rich young man was used to take in disowned persons and maintain[1] them at his own expense. He is accused of harming the commonwealth.[2]

DISCUSSION

In most controversies for the most part we ask whether we should use the person of the individuals themselves to make the speech or that of an advocate, either on account of sex, as ⟨in the case of⟩ women, or of some ugliness in the rest of life or in the act in question. This young man is of good character, and since he is also rich,[3] he has done nothing so disgraceful as to bar him from speaking on his own behalf. However, I think we should give him an advocate, first because, even if he acted rather remissly and over-generously, he can be excused by his youth; moreover, the positions are incompatible—that the same person ⟨is both tough enough to defend himself⟩ and mentally weak enough to be excused for that reason. There

---

[19] Death.   [1] Lit. "nourish."
[2] Lese-majesty.   [3] And so could afford the expense.

3 cusandus sit. Alterum illud est, quod, si defensionem ultra
excusationis terminum proferimus, laudandus est adulescens, arroganter autem faciet et tumide si coeperit se ipse
laudare, praesertim iactaturis[4] id quod facere possit a Fortuna esse. Dabimus ergo illi his causis advocatum.

4   DECLAMATIO

Non necesse erat mihi, iudices, de facti huiusce quod in
crimen vocatur ratione disserere. Scio quid advocato satis
sit. Sufficiebat hoc solum, si eximerem legi reum; et cetera
fiant fortasse pro dignitate, fiant pro conscientia, pro
laude: ad vos id unum pertinet, an legi qua cognoscitis
obligatus sit qui accusatur. Quae vobis, quo atrocior est,
hoc diligentius intuenda est. Sit tolerabile formula errare
et in petitione pecuniae non uti iure concesso: aliquis
caput hominis perperam petit, et errat[5] ut occidat?

5   Rei publicae laesae ‹hic accusatur›.[6] Quaedam sunt,
iudices, ad quorum pronuntiationem oculi sufficiant; satis
erat accusatori ostendere si quid hic laeserit: aliqua publi-
corum operum incensa vel eversa,[7] corrupta navalia, arma
usibus belli erepta, aliquid denique eorum quae publice
possidemus (ea sunt enim rei publicae) deterius huius
6 fraude atque iniuria factum.[8] Cetera habent suas leges, sua
iura, suas actiones. Si hos quos recepisse dicitur occidisset,
non tamen rei publicae laesae iure teneri videretur. Sint

    [4] *SB²:* -rus Aβ   [5] *Hå.²:* terreat Aβ
    [6] *Wi., duce Hå.²*
    [7] i. vel e. *SB⁴, duce Pith.:* in pens(a)e versa vel A(β)
    [8] *Gron.:* -ta Aβ

---

[4] Under which an action is brought.

is another point: if we carry the defense forward beyond the limit of excuse, the young man has to be praised; but if he starts praising himself, that will be arrogant and boastful behavior, especially as hearers will throw in his teeth that his ability to do what he did comes from Fortune. So for these reasons we will give him an advocate.

DECLAMATION

It was unnecessary, gentlemen, for me to discourse about the rationale of this act which is produced as a charge. I know what suffices for an advocate. It would be enough of itself if I exculpated the defendant under the law. Other things might perhaps be done for his dignity, his conscience, his credit, but all that concerns you is whether the accused is liable under the law governing your inquiry. The more drastic that law is, the more carefully you must look into it. An error in the legal formula[4] or a failure to employ a permitted right in a financial claim may be tolerated; but does anyone incorrectly attack a man's civic status and err in order to kill?

< He is accused > of harming the commonwealth. There are some things, gentlemen, in which the eyes are enough to make a pronouncement. It would have been enough for the prosecutor to show something he has harmed: some public works burned or overturned, docks damaged, weapons taken away from use in war, in short one of those items which we publicly possess (for these belong to the commonwealth) the worse for his misdoing and injury. Other things have their own laws and statutes and legal processes. If he had murdered the people whom he is said to have taken in, yet he would not appear liable under the law governing harm to the commonwealth. Suppose

137

igitur ista gravia quae obiciuntur, aliquid fecisse clementer, contra duros et asperos patres interposuisse misericordiam pro sua aetate: non hoc vidit lex quae recitata est, non voluntas eius quicumque conditor iuris istius fuit.

7   Haec ego fortius dixi, quia ⟨rem⟩[9] remissurus sum. Quid enim obicitur? 'Abdicatos recipit et sua pecunia alit.' Ut gravissime iudicemus de hoc crimine, stultitia est et supervacuas impensas facit. Quis est iste qui nobis tamquam pater irascitur? 'Patrimonium consumis et alioqui splendidas opes cotidie effundis.' Quae tandem ista inter se pugna est? Legem recitas laesae rei publicae et agis quasi abdices. Sic respondebo tamquam abdicanti. Ignosce: iuvenis est, non satis roboris, nondum satis iudicii confirmare potuit. Et tamen si faciendae sunt impensae, si perdendum aliquid, non potest honestiore via impendere. Non meretricibus donat, non in parasitos profundit, non illi magno cupiditates suae constant: sumptuosus est misericordiae.

9   Libet etiam augere crimen et si qua nesciunt accusatores indicare. Vos eum largiri tantum abdicatis putatis? Iste aliquid et mendicantibus porrigit, iste et multos, fortunae

10   iniuria lapsos, sustentat atque erigit. 'Quid faciam' inquit 'animo meo? Quotiens infelicem vidi aliquem et necessarii etiam victus egentem, lacrimas tenere non possum. Invidiam mihi facere videtur patrimonium meum; pulsant frontem meam caeduntque, etiamsi taceant, ipso habitu,

9 *SB*[2]

the acts charged against him are serious—that he showed some charity, interposed his compassion against harsh, bitter fathers, on behalf of his own generation: this was not in the purview of the law as recited, was not the intention of whoever originated that statute.

I have spoken rather forcibly because I am going to concede ⟨the fact⟩. What is he charged with? "He takes in disowned persons and maintains them with his own money." To take the worst view of this accusation, it's foolishness, he is spending money unnecessarily. Who is this who is angry with us like a father? "You are wasting your patrimony, squandering an otherwise fine fortune every day." What sort of a contradiction have we here? You recite a law governing harm to the commonwealth and you plead as though you were disowning him. I shall reply as though that was what you were doing. Forgive him. He is young, he has not been able to confirm strength enough, not yet judgment enough. And yet if money is to be spent, if anything is to be squandered, he can't spend in a more honorable way. He is not giving to prostitutes, pouring out on parasites, his own desires don't cost him much. His extravagance is on compassion.

I even have a mind to add to the charge and tell the accusers anything they don't know. Do you think he is generous only to the disowned? He also hands out something to beggars, many also who have slipped through bad luck he sustains and puts on their feet. "What am I to do with my feelings?" he says. "Every time I see somebody down on his luck, without even the necessities of life, I can't keep back my tears. My patrimony seems to bring me into discredit. They strike my face, hit me, even though they say nothing, with their very bearing, their very sadness, their

ipsa tristitia, ipso silentio; sed et rogant et provolvuntur ad genua. Nec mihi illa saltem simulata, ut plerisque, excusatio superest, ut dicam: non possum.'

11 Tu vero tanto, adulescens, fortior atque omni laude non in nostra modo tempora sed etiam in futura omnia saecula dignior! Solus mihi mortalium videris usum pecuniae intellexisse. Frustra tibi alioqui[10] Fortuna tantum patrimonium dedit et in breve humani tempus aevi veluti grande pondus imposuit. Relinquendum erat istud, et res transisset ad alios: quandoque locupletem fecisset nescio quem
12 mors liberalis. Libet vobiscum loqui nostro nomine, avari parcique, qui aliquid non fecisse sordide iam etiam scelus existimatis. Non sunt ista ferenda nobiscum, neque ad inferos servata per vitam fortuna persequitur. Tolle usum:
13 quid est pecunia? Quis igitur usus honestior? Nullus. Nec hic lege posset[11] fieri reus si hanc ipsam pecuniam, quam per tot beneficia divisit, per gulam ventremque transmitteret. Nihil obesse rei publicae videretur si vitiorum institores hos eosdem sumptus divisissent. Ego vero huic comparare ne illos quidem timeo qui aliqua in re publica opes[12] posuerunt. Haec enim muta et inhumanis tantum[13] constructa muneribus [et][14] speciem modo et brevem quendam
14 dam usum voluptatibus nostris attulerunt. At hercule referamus ad illam de qua modo locutus sum speciem: quanto pulchrius integrum populi vultum, illibatam dignitatem

---

[10] alioqui(n) D², *Gron.*: aliqua AC: -quando B
[11] *Watt*[1]: possit Aβ   [12] *SB*[2]: opera Aβ
[13] *Gron.*: tamen Aβ   [14] *Ro.*

---

[5] Like *tanto melior*: see Lewis and Short *tantum* 10.3b (not *OLD*), also *HSCP* 87 (1983), 225.

very silence; but they also beg and grovel at my knees. And I don't even have left to me, as most do, that disingenuous excuse, as to say, 'I can't.'"

No, young man, congratulations on your brave spirit![5] Well do you deserve unstinted praise, not only for our own time but for all future ages. Alone of mankind you seem to me to have understood the use of money. In vain otherwise did Fortune give you so great a patrimony, placing upon you a massive load, as it were, for the brief span of human life. You would have had to leave it and the wealth would have passed to others; some day your generous death would have made someone or other rich. You greedy misers who nowadays think an unsordid action a crime, I should like a word with you on my own account. These things can't be taken with us, fortune preserved through life does not follow us to the world below. Take away the use of it, and what is money? So what use is nobler? None. This young man could not be put on trial under the law if he had passed this very money, which he has distributed in so many acts of charity, down his throat and stomach. The commonwealth would not have been thought to take any harm if peddlers of vice had shared out these same outlays. For my part, I am not afraid to compare him with those who have put their wealth into some public work. Such edifices,[6] mute,[7] constructed only for cruel spectacles, brought nothing but a show, a brief employment for our pleasure. Ah, but let us judge that by reference to the display I have just been talking about. How much more beautiful to have preserved the face of the

6 Amphitheaters.
7 Unlike the objects of the young man's charity.

civium servasse! Si ad utilitatem: quanto melius ac maius servasse suum numerum civitati, suos ordines! An vero illos qui ingentes noxiorum familias occisuri tamen pascunt plausu fovebimus et in omnibus spectaculis adulatione multa prosequemur: hunc qui partem civium, levibus offensis miseram, sustentat ac paenitentiae suae suorumque integram servat lege etiam gravissime persequemur? Quid enim nobis tam naturale, quid ab ipsa providentia magis datum concessumque videri potest quam alere homines ac sustinere? Muta mehercule animalia, quae venire ad manum et mansuescere queunt, non humanum modo sed etiam voluptuosum est alere ac pascere. Quid de homine dicam? Quisquamne magis negotium publicum non civitatis modo sed totius rerum naturae agit quam qui animal hoc deo proximum et in contemplationem omnium quaecumque mundo contigerunt constitutum prorogat producitque? Opes suas in publico posuit quo locuplete nemo pauper est, nemo eget.

15

16

O misera tempora! hoc defendendum est? Scilicet illud honestius, liberos sublatos iamque in adulescentiam provectos pellere domo et prohibere penatibus et omissa emendandi cura sic punire ut iis succurri non liceat. 'Abdicatos in domum recipit et pascit.' Sic istud, tamquam sacrilegos, tamquam homicidas, tamquam latrones? Si tam grave crimen est aetate labi, si tam inexpiabile offendisse aliquando paternam severitatem, novas excogitate leges,

17

18

---

8 And not marred by beggary in the streets.

people intact,[8] the dignity of citizens unimpaired! If we judge by the yardstick of utility, how much better and greater to have preserved the community in its proper numbers and ranks! Or shall we caress with our applause and attend at every show with our lavish adulation those who maintain great families of criminals only to slaughter them, while at the same time we pursue with the full rigor of the law this young man, who sustains a part of our community, in misery for minor offences, keeps them intact for repentance—their own and the parents'? For what can we perceive as so natural, more granted and permitted by providence itself, than the nourishment and sustenance of human beings? Dumb animals, for heaven's sake, that can come to hand and grow tame—to raise and feed them is not only humane, it is a pleasure. What shall I say about a human being? Does anyone do more for the public business, not only of the community but of the whole Nature of Things, than he that keeps going and prolongs this living creature, closest to God, constituted for the contemplation of all that has happened to the universe. A man has put his wealth into the public if, when he is rich, nobody is poor, nobody in want.

Sorry times! Does this have to be defended? The nobler course, it would seem, is to drive from home children we have recognized, already grown to be young men, and forbid them the house, take no thought for their amendment, punish them, with nobody allowed to come to their rescue! "He takes the disowned in and feeds them." You say that as though they were temple-thieves, murderers, brigands. If a youthful slip is so grave a crime, if at some point to have offended fatherly severity is so inexpiable, think out new laws and enact some harsher punishments.

143

asperiora aliqua constituite supplicia. Hos si pascere non licet, parum est abdicare. ⟦Audite, audite, patres, quae optimum adulescentem ad misericordiam moverint, quae ad
19 liberalitatem; aliquid et discite.⟧ Nulli horum obiectum est quod venenum patri parasset, nulli quod percussorem in fata parentis sui conduxisset. Credite,[15] iudices: alioqui puto non tam levem subituros fuisse poenam sub tam asperis patribus. Quid est igitur? Amavit ille meretricem et intra concessos adulescentiae lusus, licet aliud parentibus videatur, natura tamen datos, forsitan minus tenuerit cupi-
20 ditatium frenos: en quod fames emendet! Ille ductus aequalitate cum sodalibus iniit paulo tempestiviora convivia: en quod mendicitas coerceat! Ille liberalius vixit et, quoniam[16] crimen istud hoc tempore est, aliquid fortasse donavit. Non vultis in his causis, in hac criminum summa, misereatur hominum qui dicunt: 'et tu[17] iuvenis es'?
21 At nimium diu, iudices, sic defendo optimum iuvenem tamquam istud abdicatis praestiterit. Non iam abdicatis,[18] rei publicae (fortius libet agere) imputo—et magis imputarem si tales essent quales eos accusator esse contenderet. Nihil est periculosius, iudices, in hominibus mutata subito fortuna, nihil ad vilitatem[19] sui pronius miseris deli-
22 catis. Iuvenes in magnis patrimoniis atque in summa nati dignitate, subito excussi non dico opibus sed necessariis etiam ad victum spiritumque ultimum sustinendum, non

---

[15] *Sch.*: -tis Aβ   [16] *SB²*: quomodo Aβ

[17] *Pith.*: cum A: dum β

[18] *Gron.*: nolo iam abdicare Aβ

[19] *Aer.*: util- Aβ

---

[9] Early dining being a recognized component of fast living.

If feeding these people is not permitted, disowning is not enough. ⟦Hear, hear you fathers, what considerations moved an excellent young man to compassion and generosity, and learn something.⟧ None of them is charged with preparing poison for his father or hiring an assassin to take a parent's life. Believe it, gentlemen. Otherwise I don't think they would suffer so light a punishment under parents so harsh. So what did they do? One of them fell in love with a prostitute and perhaps failed to rein his desires within the amusements permitted to youth, granted by nature though parents may say otherwise: and that is what hunger is to correct! Another, led on by comradeship of age, went to dinners with his friends a little too early in the day:[9] behold the offence which beggary is to curb! A third lived too liberally and perhaps gave something away, since that is a crime nowadays. Such being the cases, such the sum-total of crimes, will you not have him take pity on fellows who say "you are young yourself"?

But, gentlemen, I have too long been defending this excellent young man as though he did it for the disowned. Now I have a mind to talk more boldly. I debit his action, not to the disowned, but to the commonwealth—and would do so all the more if they were such as the prosecutor contended. Nothing among men is more dangerous, gentlemen, than a sudden change of fortune; nothing makes for self-contempt more than poverty after soft living. Young men born heirs to great patrimonies and in the highest station, when suddenly evicted, I won't say from wealth but from things necessary to sustain life and the final breath,[10] will not turn to everyday work, will not have

10 Even the dying need sustenance.

redibunt ad opus cotidianum, non sufficient adsiduo labo-
ri; superest ut audeant aliquid vel propter quod moriantur.

23 Tot hos quos obicitis (nam turbam quoque[20] abdicatorum
esse dixistis) emittite subito nudos, omnium egenos: ip-
sisne aliquis poterit irasci si quid fecerint, si in latrocinia se
praedasque miserint? Quantumlibet animis nostris remittamus ac totam innocentiam credamus esse persuasionis,

24 multum contra iustitiam necessitas valet. Ac si nihil adversus alios, adversus se certe multa fecissent. Ornatamne
rem publicam atque adiutam, iudices, crederetis si horum
fortissimus quisque venisset in ludum atque harenam, si
paulo mollior frons ad laqueum, ad praecipitia, ad qualem-
cumque vitae festinasset exitum? Tum civitas felix, tum
numerus iste minus invidiosus fuisset?

25 Volo, iudices, relicta iam hac quam ad rem publicam
composui defensione, transire ad eos qui praecipue irasci
videntur, patres dico ipsos qui abdicaverunt. Quibus hoc
primum, iudices, dico: quam accipitis iniuriam? Malis
vos sane filiis levastis et exonerata sunt vestra patrimonia.
Sinite illos perisse et, velut expositos in aliqua solitudine
aut in maria proiectos, nihil ad animum vestrum, nihil ad

26 cogitationes pertinere. Fortunam sibi quaerant. Quid ad
vos quid sint postquam vestri esse desierunt? Renati sunt
novumque fatum quodammodo sortiti. Num invidiam vobis faciunt? Hoc enim malebatis fortasse, ut oculis vestris
sordidati obversarentur, ut impexi squalidique incede-

---

[20] t. q. β: q. t. A

---

[11] As Socrates held.
[12] Gladiator school.

strength enough for continual labor: as an alternative they only have some act of daring, even one they may die for. All these people you charge us with (for you have said there is actually a crowd of the disowned), send them out suddenly naked, needy of everything: will anyone find it possible to be angry with these same people if they do something, embark on robberies and plunderings? However much we leave to our minds and believe that innocence is entirely a matter of how we think,[11] necessity has much power against justice. And if nothing against others, they would certainly have perpetrated much against themselves. Would you have thought the commonwealth adorned and helped, gentlemen, if the bravest among them had come to the school[12] and the arena, or if one a little less hard-faced had hurried to the noose, precipice, any and every exit from life? Would the community have been happy then, their numbers less of a reproach?

I should like now, gentlemen, to leave this defense that I have composed with reference to the commonwealth and pass to those who seem to be especially incensed: I mean the fathers themselves, the disowners. To them, gentlemen, I say first: what injury is it you suffer? You have relieved yourselves, have you not, of bad sons and your fortunes are unburdened. Let them have perished, let them have no place in your feelings or thoughts, as though they had been exposed in some wilderness or thrown into the sea. Let them seek their own fortune. What is it to you what they are after they have ceased to be yours? They have been born again, allotted a new destiny in some sort. Are they bringing you into bad odor? For perhaps you would have rather they presented themselves to your eyes wearing mourning, unkempt and squalid? For cruelty is

rent? Verecunde nomine severitatis[21] dissimulatur vestra
crudelitas; minus vos malos patres putavimus. Quod quidem animadversioni sat est, pendunt poenas magnumque
27 supplicium miseri luunt. An vos in hoc demum creditis paternam animadversionem, si esuriant, si inopia omnium
deficiant atque tabescant? Illud parum est, notari infamia?
Illud parum est, exulem esse domus suae, larum suorum?
Nunc vos putatis esse felicem quemquam horum aut
28 hilarem? Experiatur aliquis et revocet. Et haec quidem,
iudices, duris atque asperis patribus, illa melioribus[22]:
'Speravi' inquit adulescens 'aliquam impetus vestri paenitentiam, credidi futurum ut aliquando succurrerent initia
infantiae, blandimenta pueritiae. Reservavi filios iudiciis
vestris et, si quando ignosceretis, in integro habui. Vos
aestimate causas propter quas expulistis: si credetis, satis
poenarum dederunt. Ego illud praesto, illud promitto:
nihil postea turpiter fecerunt.'
29 Ne tamen nimium iactare atque imputare videatur,
illum quoque misericordiae suae ordinem confitebitur.
'Unus' inquit 'fuit primo qui sollicitaret hanc nimiam liberalitatem, aequalis alioqui[23] et in studiis comes et in lusi-
bus. Hic fecit exemplum. Ausus est rogare proximus; nec
adhuc illud onerosum patrimonio videbatur. Inde factus
est ordo; et iam legem mihi videor dixisse misericordiae.
Cui negarem? Omnes idem rogabant, omnes idem excu-
30 sabant, omnes idem pollicebantur. Ego vero,' inquit,
'quamdiu fuerit hoc patrimonium, sic ero, sic utar; et si de-
fecerint omnia, non tamen pauperem me putabo neque
egentem, sed pro illis paternis possessionibus hos osten-

[21] *Aer.*: servitutis Aβ
[22] *Hå.²*, *Wi.* (molli- *Sch.*): -ora Aβ   [23] β: aliqui A

discreetly dissembled under the name of severity. We did not think you such bad fathers. As for punishment, it is enough that they are paying their penalties, suffering grievously, poor souls, in atonement. Or do you think that fatherly chastisement consists only in hunger, in fainting and wasting away in total want? Is it not enough to bear the mark of infamy? Is it not enough to be exiled from house and hearth? Do you suppose that any one of them is happy now and cheerful? Let one of you put it to the test and call him back. This then, gentlemen, to the hard, harsh fathers. Now to the better ones: "I hoped," says our young man, "for some regret for your impulsive actions, I thought that eventually early infancy and the blandishments of boyhood would come to aid. I reserved your sons for your judgments, kept them intact for your pardon some day. It is for you to judge of the reasons why you drove them out; if you will credit it, they have been punished enough. I guarantee, I promise this: they have done nothing discreditable since."

But lest you think he is boasting and claiming too much, he will further confess to the stages of his compassion. "There was one at first," he says, "who begged for this overgenerosity, of my own age as it happened, a companion in studies and sports. He set the example. Next came another who dared to ask. It still didn't seem burdensome to my fortune. Thence began a series; and by now I feel I have given myself a law of compassion. Who was I to say no to? They all made the same plea, the same excuse, the same promise. For my part," he says, "as long as this fortune exists, so shall I be, so shall I use it. And if I am left with nothing, I shall not consider myself a needy pauper, but in place of those paternal possessions I shall show these citi-

dam cives, pro illo faenore hunc populum. Et quae tanta
patribus ira, quae tanta infelicitas nostrae civitatis, quod
rei publicae fatum, ut istud diutius aut pluribus necesse sit

31 ⟨defendere⟩[24]? Et[25] ne vobis multum videar imputare,
non sunt isti onerosi facultatibus meis, non quos ampla,
quia sic a parentibus meis constituta est, fortuna graves
sentiat. [quia][26] Vivimus parce: quantulum est enim quod
accipiunt, quantulum est quod exigunt! Vos fortasse plus
consumpseritis, patres, qui studia fovistis, qui ad hanc ae-

32 tatem usque vexistis; mihi servare cives satis est. Ac nihilo-
minus, quod in istos impendo, si creditis, ipse frugalius
vivo. Quidquid in hos confertur atque congeritur, de meo
est: detrahitur adulescentiae voluptatibus, detrahitur con-
cessis alioqui, quamdiu in his annis sumus, cupiditatibus.
Duo simul adsequor, quod et liberalius et frugalius vivo.'

261

Aequatio patrimoniorum

In qua civitate frequenter tyranni erant, fert quidam legem ut patrimonia aequentur.

1   SERMO

Haec quoque aliquotiens tractata controversia est, et per
summas digeri potest.

2   DECLAMATIO

Primum incusamus legem non satis significanter scriptam

24 *Aer.*   25 *anne* at ?   26 *Ro.*

---

13 Apparently the jury, as representing the public.

zens, in place of that interest this people. And what is this great anger among fathers, this great infelicity of our community, this fate of the commonwealth, that I must needs ‹defend› my conduct at length, in many words? And not to let it look as though I were making a heavy claim on you,[13] these people are not burdensome to my means; my ample fortune, ample because my forebears made it so, doesn't feel the weight of them. We live sparingly. How little it is that they receive, how little that they demand! Perhaps you fathers, who have cultivated your pursuits and brought them along up to your present time of life, will have consumed more: for me it is enough to have saved my fellow citizens. And nevertheless, if you believe me, I live more frugally myself because I spend money on them. Whatever is gathered and got together for them, comes from me; it is taken from the pleasures of youth, what is conceded anyway to our desires so long as we are in this time of life. I kill two birds, because I live both more generously and more frugally."

261

Equalization of properties

In a community in which there were often tyrants someone proposes a law that properties be equalized.

DISCUSSION

This controversy also has been handled a number of times and can be divided under heads.

DECLAMATION

First we criticize the law as imprecisely worded and con-

et multa obscura in se habentem. Nam hoc non satis distinxit, utrumne patrimonia nunc demum aequari oporteat, an quotiens aliquod eminebit. At[1] si vere remedium id solum pro re publica est, perpetuum esse debet, et ideo lex repudianda quia hoc non satis dispexit. ⟦Si haec vis est legis istius, ut sit de aequalitate patrimoniorum, idem census omnibus detur, omnes paene dies, omnia tempora necesse erit in hac partitione consumi, si quis frugalius[2] vixerit, si quis luxuriosius[3] vixerit.⟧

3

4 Est praeterea contra leges omnes scripta haec lex: quippe nullum ius non ita compositum est ut suum quisque habeat et alieno abstineat.

5 Sed ne servari quidem potest. Quid enim futurum est? Praetereo illud, quod aliqui negotiabuntur, aliqui acquirent, aliqui frugaliter vivent: quae ratio relinquendae hereditatis erit, quae ratio testamentorum, cum is qui creverit hereditatem continuo plus sit habiturus quam ceteri, nec[4] divisurus cum iis qui non eundem honorem supremis defuncti tabulis habuerunt?

6 His adiciamus quod etiam inutilis est, duabus praecipue[5] causis. Nam et frugalitatem eorum qui servaturi sunt imminuet et luxuriae eorum qui consumpturi sunt prospiciet: cur enim quisquam servet, tam perditurus aliena luxuria quam sua, cur enim non quisque abutatur?

7 Haec de ipsa lege dixisse satis erat, remota temporum aestimatione. Nunc videamus quid sit propter quod pona-

---

[1] *Ro.*: an Aβ
[2] *Aer.*: -lis Aβ
[3] *Aer.*: -osus Aβ
[4] *SB*[3]: et Aβ
[5] *Ro.*: pr(a)eterea Aβ

taining many obscurities. It has not made it sufficiently clear whether properties are to be equalized just for the present moment or as often as one stands out. But if that is truly the only remedy for the commonwealth, it ought to be in perpetuity and for that reason the law is to be rejected because it has not sufficiently made that discrimination. ⟦If this is the force of your law, that it be about equality of properties, that all be given the same amount, almost every day and every season will have to be spent in this apportioning, if one man lives more frugally and another more lavishly.⟧

Moreover, this law is written against all laws: for no law is composed but with the assumption that each have what is his and keep his hands from what is somebody else's.

But it isn't even practicable. For what will happen? I pass over the point that some will do business, some will make money, some will live frugally; what will be done about leaving estates, about wills, when anyone coming into an inheritance will at once have more than the rest, and is not going to share with those who did not have the same compliment[1] under the final testament of the deceased?

Let us add that the law is also inexpedient, principally for two reasons: it will diminish the frugality of prospective savers and will serve the extravagance of prospective consumers. For why should anyone save when he will lose as much by the extravagance of others as by his own? Why should not everybody splurge?

This would have been enough said about the law itself, irrespective of the times. Let us now see why it is pro-

---

[1] *Honor*, sometimes used of mention in a will.

tur. 'Frequentes tyranni sunt.' Primum, quam inicum est, ideo quod aliquos improbos habeas, exui patrimoniis paternis atque avitis eos etiam quos bonos esse cives constabit! Nam si tyrannidem timemus, erat aliquanto aequius in personas eorum qui possent rei publicae esse suspecti derigi actiones quam poenam esse publicam metus (ut
8 dicitis) publici. Adice quod ne praecipua quidem causa est adfectandae tyrannidis magnitudo facultatium. Quin ex diverso facilius aliquanto[6] occupaverint tyrannidem ii quorum fracta ratio, quorum clauda fortuna, et qui stare re
9 publica salva non possunt. Deinde adeo non inhibetis ista re tyrannidem ut, si qui in civitate nostra dementes sunt, etiam causam habituri sint adfectandae tyrannidis. Nam si qui tyrannidem occupat ut aliena bona possideat, quanto facilius ad tyrannidem perveniet ut sua vindicet, sua recipiat!

262

Maritus virginis raptor

Iniusti repudii sit actio. Qui habebat uxorem rapuit virginem. Nuptias rapta optavit. Ille repudiavit uxorem. Agit illa iniusti repudii.

1   DECLAMATIO

Lex iniusti repudii, maxime necessaria ad continenda matrimonia, [et][1] his praecipue moribus, quibus finem tantum necessitas facit,[2] super omnes leges tuenda est.

---

[6] *Sch.*: -ndo Aβ
[1] *SB*[4]   [2] *Wi.*: fecit Aβ

posed. "Tyrants come often." First, how unfair it is that because you have rascals even those who are agreed to be good citizens should be stripped of property inherited from their fathers and grandfathers! If we are afraid of tyranny, it would have been a good deal more equitable that actions be directed against the persons of those who could be suspect to the commonwealth than that there should be public penalty for, as you say, public fear. Add that largeness of means is not the principal reason for aiming at a tyranny. On the contrary, tyranny is a good deal more likely to be seized by broken men, crippled in fortune, who cannot survive in a stable commonwealth. Then, you are so far from inhibiting tyranny by this means that if there are madmen in our community they will actually have a reason for aiming at tyranny. For if a man seizes tyranny in order to get possession of other men's goods, how much more readily will he get to be a tyrant in order to protect his own or retrieve his own!

262

The husband who raped a virgin

Let there be an action for wrongful divorce. A man who had a wife raped a virgin. The victim opted for marriage. He divorced his wife. She brings action for wrongful divorce.

DECLAMATION

The law of wrongful divorce, most necessary to keep marriages together, especially in the present state of morals in which necessity makes the only limit, is to be maintained above all laws.

2   Repudiatam ab hoc uxorem esse manifestum est: reli-
cum est ut aliquid repudiatae obiciat. Ita demum enim potest esse iustum repudium si meruit id quae repudiatur.
Ne ipse quidem tam impudens est (quamquam non desit
audacia) ut crimen ullum fingat in uxorem. Necessitate
defenditur.

3   Poteram dicere ⟨aliud necessarium,⟩[3] aliud esse iustum. Nam lex iniusti repudii spectat utramque personam,
nec satis est id modo intueri, quid maritus facere debuerit,
verum id quoque intuendum est, quid pati debuerit uxor.
Quare licet tu necessario repudiaveris, haec iniuste repu-
4 diata est. Haec dicerem si non tua culpa accidisset ut repu-
diares. ⟦Sed miror si in hac civitate diligentissima iuris ulla
lex contra alteram scripta est, aut hoc prudentissimi constitutores iuris non viderunt. Quomodo necesse est quod
5 iustum non erat?⟧ 'Rapta' inquit 'nuptias meas optaverat.'
Non est hoc tale quale si diceres: tyrannus coegit, quale si
diceres: aliquis cui potestatem dederat res publica hoc iussit, senatus aut populus pertinere id ad rem publicam existimavit; ut rapta repudiare coegerit, ut cogi posses, tu fe-
6 cisti. Et ipsum hoc repudii tempus male computas. Tunc
repudiatam tu credis uxorem cum res suas sibi habere iussa est, cum egredi domo? Uxorem tunc repudiasti cum
rapuisti, cum potestatem huic legis adversus te dedisti,
cum egisti ut raptae adversus te liceret quantum adversus
7 caelibem licet. 'Rapta raptoris mortem vel nuptias optet':
hanc potestatem adversus te vitiata habuit. Ecquid intelle-

---

[3] *Aer.* (*sed post* iustum)

It is clear that this man divorced his wife. It remains for him to bring some charge against the woman he has divorced. For divorce can only be rightful if the divorcée has deserved it. The husband himself is not so impudent (though he doesn't lack audacity) as to make up any misdoing against his wife. His defense is necessity.

I could say that ‹necessity is one thing,› right another. For the law of wrongful divorce regards both parties, and it is not enough to look at what the husband ought to have done but we must also look at what the wife ought to have suffered. Therefore, although you have divorced her of necessity, she has been divorced wrongfully. This I should say if the divorce had not happened through your fault. ⟦But I am surprised if in this community, so careful of legality as it is, any law was written in conflict with any other law, or if the very wise men who constituted our legal system did not see this. How is anything necessary that was not right?⟧ "A woman was raped," he says, "and opted for marrying me." This is not like saying "The tyrant forced me" or like saying "Somebody empowered by the commonwealth gave the order, the senate or the people considered it to be in the public interest": it was *your* doing that the raped woman forced you to divorce, that you could be forced. And you are out in your reckoning as to the actual time of the divorce. Do you believe that your wife was divorced when she was told to keep her own property and leave the house? No, you divorced your wife when you committed rape, when you gave this woman the power of the law against yourself, when you acted so that she you raped had as much license against you as against a bachelor. "Let a woman raped opt for the rapist's death or marriage": that was the power the woman you violated had

157

gis iam non esse uxorem quae non obstat? Ego te adeo non
puto defendi hoc genere patrocinii posse ut, quocumque
alio modo dimisisses uxorem, meliorem tum[4] causam fuis-
8 ses habiturus. Egregia hercule defensio! Dico: 'repudiasti
uxorem pudicam, obsequentem, fidelem'; respondes mihi:
'sed rapui, sed alienam domum expugnavi.' Pessimus maritus videreris si amorem in aliquam meretricem deflexis-
ses, si ancillarum cupiditas a geniali ⟨te⟩[5] toro avocaret.
Iam tum non eras maritus cum animus tuus spectabat
9 vacantes. Et hoc si tantum libidine et cupiditate fecisses,
repudii[6] tamen causa ad te rediret. Quid si ne credibile
quidem est nisi eo pacto factum hoc esse, ut tibi raptori
ignosceretur? An vero tu in tantum periculum venisses ut
raperes maritus, ut crimini tuo hanc quoque adiceres invi-
10 diam? Nisi succurritis, iudices, inventum est iam quomodo
uxores optimas repudiare liceat. Prospicienda tantum virgo est, rapienda est. Ceterum defendemus istud, quod
nullo genere licet facere, specie necessitatis.
11   Praeter haec illud quoque, iudices, intueri oportebit,
quomodo[7] maximorum istius criminum aliqua tamen vindicta contingat.[8] Per se indignum erat raptorem impune
fecisse; indignum erat iniuste repudiatam esse uxorem.
Utrique crimini una poena erit, levis quidem. Et sane ha-

---

[4] Aβ: cum B: tamen *Ro*.   [5] *Ro*.
[6] *Gron*.: -diat(a)e Aβ   [7] *Ri*.: quo Aβ
[8] *Gron*.: -tineat Aβ

---

[1] The thought of whom didn't prevent you from doing what
you have done.

[2] Implying that the rape had been prearranged between the
rapist and his "victim" as means of getting the former's divorce.

against you. Don't you understand that she who doesn't stand in your way[1] is no longer your wife? I am so far from thinking that you can be defended by this sort of advocacy that if you had dismissed your wife in any other way you would have had a better case. An excellent defense, upon my word; I say, "You divorced a chaste, obedient, loyal wife"; you answer: "But I committed rape, I broke into another man's house." You would appear a very bad husband if you had turned your love toward some prostitute or if a passion for slave girls called <you> away from the marriage bed. You had already ceased to be a husband when your mind was on anyone available. Even if you had acted only out of lust and desire, the reason for the divorce would have been at your door. What if it is not believable that you did what you did except on the understanding that your rape would be forgiven?[2] Would you, a married man, have taken so great a risk as to commit a rape, thereby adding this discredit to your guilt?[3] Gentlemen, unless you come to the rescue, a way has been devised to divorce excellent wives legally. All it needs is to find a virgin and rape her;[4] for the rest,[5] we shall defend an act that is in no way legal by the pretence of necessity.

Apart from all this, gentlemen, it will also be your duty to ask yourselves how some punishment at least for this man's heinous offences come to pass. It would have been outrageous in itself that a rapist went scot-free; it would have been outrageous that a wife was wrongfully divorced. There will be one penalty for both offences and a light one

---

3 "Adultery as well as guilt" (Wi.). Surely the other way round —the adultery came first.

4 Overlooking a necessary element—the girl's co-operation.

5 In the further developments.

beat hoc lucrum magna nequitia, quod non fere puniri pro meritis potest: ab illa quidem rapta vindicabit[9] nos ipse.

263

Ignominiosus contra tres rogationes

Qui tribus rogationibus contradixerit nec tenuerit, ignominiosus sit. Duabus quidam rogationibus contradixit; non tenuit. Tertia rogatio ferebatur qua ignominia remittebatur notatis. Contradixit et huic; non tenuit. Dicitur ignominiosus.

1   DECLAMATIO

'Qui tribus rogationibus contradixerit nec tenuerit, ignominiosus sit.' Lex manifesta. Fortasse supervacuum ista dicere, verumtamen permittite[1]: lex [et hoc dicere][2] iusta. Quis maiore ignomia dignus est quam homo inquietus, qui publicis utilitatibus ter obstiterit, qui ne metu quidem ignominiae ad silentium compelli saltem tertio potuerit?

2   Ergo de lege dubitari nihil potest; videamus an hic in legem inciderit. Tribus rogationibus contradixit. Num fallimur numero? Num aliquid adversus istum mentimur? Non ut[3] opinor ipsum saltem dicere ausurum. Bis iam contradixerat, bis non tenuerat. Proxime dixit[4]; non tenuisse eum scimus. Ergo si et lex ignominiosum vult esse eum qui ter contradixerit nec tenuerit, et hic contradixit ter nec

---

9 *Gron.*: -avit Aβ   1 *SB²*: -ittit Aβ
2 *SB²*   3 *del. Pith.* (*vide* Wi.)
4 *Ri.*: dixerat Aβ: contrad- *Aer.*

---

6 "Envisaged as pecuniary" (Wi.).

at that.[6] Very well, let great wickedness take advantage of the impossibility as a rule of its being punished as it deserves. As for the woman he raped, he himself will avenge us upon her.[7]

263

Under stigma against three bills

Let him who has opposed three bills unsuccessfully be stigmatized. A man has opposed two bills. He failed. A third bill was going through in which stigma was lifted from those who had incurred it. He opposed this bill too; he failed. He is declared under stigma.

DECLAMATION

"Let whoso shall oppose three bills unsuccessfully be stigmatized." The law is clear. Perhaps it is superfluous to argue further, but give me leave. The law is just. Who deserves a bigger stigma than a troublesome fellow who has three times obstructed public utility, who could not be forced into silence a third time at least even by fear of stigma?

So there can be no doubt about the law. Let us see whether he falls within its scope. He opposed three bills. Am I mistaken about the number? Am I making any false statement against him? I don't think even he himself will dare to say that. He had opposed twice and failed twice. Most recently he spoke: we know he failed. So if the law says that he who opposes three times unsuccessfully be stigmatized and he has opposed three times and failed,

---

[7] He will make her a bad husband.

tenuit, quomodo non sit ignominiosus inveniri profecto
non poterit.

3   Non negat se in hanc legem incidisse; sed eadem rogatione cui contradixit solutum esse contendit: placuisse
enim publice ut omnibus ignominiosis nota remitteretur.
Non miror istum ‹frustra›[5] tam frequenter contradicere:
vim legum parum perspicit, quo pertineant rogationes aut
dissimulat aut ignorat. Ferri profecto rogatio, quotiens
poena aliqua remittitur, non potest nisi de iis qui poena
4   iam tenentur. Id vel cogitatione eius qui tulit rogationem
vel aestimatione populi vel ipsa rei natura perspiciamus. Is
qui ferebat rogationem num aliquid cogitare de eo potuit
qui non erat ignominiosus? Non, ut opinor. Neque enim
hic iam ter contradixerat rogationi, nec an tertio contradic-
turus esset divinari[6] poterat. Ergo qui ferebat rogationem
5   nihil de eo cogitavit. Populus, cum in consilium mitteretur
et miseratione hominum moveretur, de iis cogitavit qui
ignominiosi iam erant. Fortasse motus est numero, fortasse motus est personis, fortasse motus est causis. Hic
neque in numero esse poterat (nondum enim ignominiosis
accesserat), neque causa miserabilis, qui ne damnatus quidem esset, neque persona. Ergo nec qui ferebat rogatio-
6   nem nec qui accipiebant de hoc cogitaverunt. Nunc ipsam
rei naturam intueamur. Quid remitti potest nisi quod †cre-
ditur†[7]? Haec rogatio nihil aliud fuit quam ignominioso-

5 SB[2]

6 Gron.: -re Aβ

7 creditum Obr.: debetur Ro.: ‹deberi› creditur Watt[1]: prae-
cedit vel sim. Hå.[3]

---

[1] Qua ("whereby") would fit better than quotiens.

surely no reason can be found why he should not be stigmatized.

He does not deny that he has fallen within the scope of
this law. But he contends that he has been released by the
same bill that he opposed; for he says it is the public will
that all persons under stigma should have it lifted. I don't
wonder that he so often opposes ⟨and fails⟩. He has too
little perception of the meaning of laws, he either pretends
not to know or doesn't know what bills are about. Obviously a bill cannot be put through whenever[1] some penalty
is remitted except concerning persons who are already
subject to that penalty. Let us consider that as it relates to
the thought of the mover of the bill and the judgment of
the people and the very nature of the thing. Could the
mover of the bill have any thought of a person not under
stigma? I think not. For he had not already opposed a bill
three times nor could it be divined whether he was going
to oppose a third time. So the mover of the bill had no
thought of him. When the people was sent into counsel
and was moved by compassion for their fellow men, they
thought of persons already under stigma. Perhaps they
were moved by the number, perhaps by the personalities,
perhaps by the cases. He could not be in the number (for
he had not yet joined the stigmatized) nor be pitied by reason of his case, since he had not even been found guilty,
nor by reason of his personality. So neither the mover of
the bill nor those who passed it had any thought of him.
Now let us look at the very nature of the thing. What can be
remitted except what has been imposed?[2] This bill was

[2] Such is the sense required by the context, not "loaned"
(*creditum*, see crit. note).

rum in pristinum statum restitutio. Tu nondum eras in ea
fortuna ut restituendus esses. 'Sed eodem' inquis 'tempore
ego ignominiam merui quo remissa est.' Postea dicam
quam dignus ista sis ignominia; interim ista temporis com-
putatione excludo. Quamvis enim ea rogatio recepta sit cui
tu tertio contradixisti, ante tamen rogatio recepta est quam
7 tu ignominiosus esse coepisses. Lex enim quid dicit? 'Qui
rogationi ter contradixerit neque tenuerit, ignominiosus
sit.' De praeterito et de perfecto iam transactoque tempore loquitur. Cum de rogatione ageretur, contradicebas;
nondum eras ignominiosus: nondum enim rogatio erat. At
cum recepta est rogatio, tum, quia non tenueras, ignominiosus esse coepisti.

8   Illud etiam adiciendum videtur, neminem umquam
digniorem fuisse ignominia quam te. Viderimus enim
quales illae fuerint rogationes quibus antea contradixisti.
Utiles utique: receptae sunt enim et pro re publica placue-
runt. Enimvero huic aliquis rogationi contradicit tam mi-
sericordi, tam leni, quae civium numerum ampliat! Si alius
quilibet contradixisset, inhumanam rem fecisset. At tu istud contradicis, ne ignominiosi restituantur, homo intra[8]
periculum positus? Dignus es ergo ut patiaris ea quae pati
9 omnes voluisti. Nisi forte sic intellegimus istam receptam
rogationem ut nemo sit umquam omnino in civitate nostra
ignominiosus. At <si>[9] id vel populus voluisset vel ille qui
ferebat, abrogasset potius hanc legem quam novam consti-

---

8 *SB*[3]: extra Aβ
9 at si *Aer.*: an Aβ

---

3 Or "by the following calculation" (Wi.), taking *ista* prospec-
tively.

nothing but a restitution of persons under stigma to their original status. You were not yet in case to be restituted. "But," you say, "I became liable to stigma at the same time as it was lifted." Later on I shall speak of how thoroughly you deserve that stigma; meanwhile I exclude you from this calculation of time.[3] For although the bill that you opposed for the third time[4] was passed, it was passed before you fell under stigma. For what says the law? "Let whoso shall oppose a bill three times unsuccessfully be stigmatized." It speaks of time passed and perfect and already spent. When the bill was in progress, you were opposing: you were not yet under stigma, for it was not yet a bill. But when the bill was passed, *then* you came under stigma because you had failed.

I think I should add that no one ever deserved stigma more than you. For we'll see what sort of bills they were that you previously opposed. Useful, certainly; for they were passed and approved in the interest of the commonwealth. Someone actually opposes this bill: so compassionate a bill, so merciful, one that increases the number of citizens! If anyone else had opposed, it would have been an act of inhumanity. But *you* oppose restitution of persons under stigma, you, a man in danger of it! Therefore you deserve to suffer what you wanted everyone to suffer. Or do we perhaps understand that this bill was passed as enacting that nobodysoever in our community ever be under stigma? But <if> that was what the people or the mover wanted, he would rather have abrogated the existing law

---

[4] Badly phrased. The bills previously passed against his opposition obviously had different contents, presumably not relating to stigma.

10 tuisset. Rogationem apparet[10] de his tantummodo latam qui erant ignominiosi; illis remisit istam veniam. Fortasse isti placebit[11] si plures inciderint in eandem sortem, in eandem condicionem.[12]

11   Pars altera

                           DECLAMATIO

⟨Non⟩[13] idem tempus est ignominiae meae et receptae rogationis. Nam natura prius est ut ego non teneam quam ut recepta lex sit. Nam si ego tenuissem, lex recepta non esset; quoniam non tenui, recepta lex est. Igitur ignominia

12 mea praecessit tempus rogationis. Prius apud animos suos constituerunt homines non parere contradictioni meae quam rogationem receperunt. Antequam tabella referretur, antequam excuteretur numerus populi, ego iam non tenueram. ⟦Rogatio nondum erat recepta nisi posteaquam dinumeratae sunt populi sententiae.⟧

13   †Hoc† ergo[14] tenui. Atque etiamsi hoc tempus mihi non remitteret totam ignominiam, lex tamen, quae ignominiosos vacare omni nota voluerat, remiserat mihi duas illas contradictiones. Quod si duae illae recesserant,[15] quae maiorem partem ignominiae conficiunt, id quod iam me premebat remiserant. Non enim facit ignominiam tertia contradictio, sed tres.[16]

---

[10] *Opitz*: appella- Aβ   [11] *Sch.*: -bunt Aβ
[12] in e. c. *del. coni.* SB²   [13] *SB³*
[14] tunc ergo ⟨non⟩ *coni.* SB³   [15] *SB⁴*: praec- Aβ
[16] non. . . tres *huc transp.* SB⁴: *ante* quod Aβ

---

[5] Sarcastic. If he himself (having lost the case) and others to follow are stigmatized, perhaps he will come to see merit in the

than made a new one. It is evident that the bill was prepared only as applying to persons who were under stigma. To them it extended this mercy. Perhaps he will approve of it if more fall into the same fate, the same condition.[5]

The other side

DECLAMATION

The time of my stigma and the bill's passing is ‹not› the same. For my failure came by nature before the bill was passed. For if I had succeeded, the bill would not have been passed; since I failed, it was. So my stigma preceded the time of the bill. People decided in their own minds not to comply with my opposition before they passed the bill. Before the voting tablet was presented, before the people were counted, I had already failed. [[The bill had not been passed before the vote of the people had been numbered.]][6]

Then, therefore, I did ‹not› succeed (?). And even if this timing did not remit the whole of the stigma, yet the law which had wished persons under stigma to be free of any mark had remitted to me those two oppositions. But if those two, which make up the greater part of the stigma, had been subtracted, it had remitted what now lay upon me.[7] For it is not a third opposition that carries stigma, but three.

bill. Not "perhaps he will be gratified if . . ." "The same condition" is a particularly noticeable pleonasm, rivaling 280.17 fin.

[6] The bill passed when it became law, not before. But this negates what precedes, so I have double-bracketed.

[7] Because only one opposition remained and one did not carry stigma. "Now" (*iam*), i.e. after the removal of the earlier two.

264

Fraus legis Voconiae

Ne liceat mulieri nisi dimidiam partem bonorum dare.
Quidam duas mulieres dimidiis partibus instituit heredes.
Testamentum cognati arguunt.

1 DECLAMATIO

Antequam ius excutio et vim legis, quae per se satis manifesta est, intueor, primum illud apud vos dixisse contentus
sum: adsum testamento. Eventum huic legi dabit religio
vestra, et excussa parte utraque sententiam formabit. Interest tamen supremae hominis voluntati legem favere, ut,
quod de bonis suis constituit in supremis dominus, fecerit
2 iure. Nec me confundit quod ex diverso sunt propinqui.
Iactent, ut volent, sanguinis coniunctionem; ego intellego
quasdam fuisse causas propter quas is qui hos cognatos ha-
3 bebat aliis moreretur heredibus. Ac si in hac parte haberent fiduciam, arguerent testamentum tamquam impium,
tamquam inofficiosum. Nunc apparet neque de personis
earum quae heredes sunt institutae dici apud vos posse,
neque eorum qui sibi ⟨bona⟩[1] contra testamentum vindi-
cant merita proferri. Solum enim ius excipiunt et circa
legem calumniantur.

4   Quae lex tamen qualis est? 'Ne liceat mulieri plus quam
dimidiam partem bonorum suorum relinquere.' Etiamsi
forma iudicii unius est, apparet tamen duabus[2] cum here-

---

[1] SB[2]   [2] Sch., Gron.: vobis A: no- β

---

[1] I.e. nothing unfavorable.   [2] Like a hunter lying in wait
for a quarry. But *excutiunt* (Watt) is highly plausible.

264

Cheating the Voconian Law

No more than half of an estate may be bequeathed to a woman. A man named two women heirs to half shares. Relatives contest the will.

DECLAMATION

Before I analyze the law and take a look at the meaning of the statute, which is clear enough in itself, I am first content to say this in your presence: I am here for the will. Your respect for your oath will give the law its upshot and form a verdict after you have analyzed both sides. But it is important that the law favor the final wishes of a human being, so that what a proprietor has determined about his possessions in his final moments he has done legally. I am not disconcerted by the fact that relatives are on the other side. Let them brag all they like about community of blood: I understand that there were certain reasons why the gentleman who had these relatives died leaving other heirs. And if they had confidence in this angle, they would challenge the will as contrary to family loyalty and duty. As it is, we see that nothing[1] can be said before you about the persons of the ladies who were named heirs and that no merits are advanced on the part of those who claim ⟨the property⟩ for themselves against the will. They only pounce on[2] the law and make legal quibbles.

Well, but what kind of a law is it? "No more than half of a person's estate can be bequeathed to a woman." Even though we have the form of a single action, it is evident that

dibus[3] esse litem. Quaero igitur ab istis utram eligant, cum[4] qua malint consistere. Neque enim litigant de bonorum parte, sed totum arguunt testamentum.

5   Incipiamus igitur ab ea quae prior scripta est. Quid in hac parte testamenti vitiosum est? Vetatur plus quam dimidiam partem bonorum relinquere: dimidiam partem patrimonii accipit. Excutiemus postea quale sit illud quod consecutum est: interim hoc prius[5] firmum est, nec everti sequentibus potest.

6   At enim ius illa quidem[6] habuit capiendi; sed ea quae postea scripta est non habuit. Iterum interrogabo: quare? 'Quoniam plus quam dimidiam partem patrimonii relinquere feminae non potuit.' Atqui haec quoque non plus quam dimidia parte patrimonii heres instituta est. Nec video rationem cur id quod illi capere licuit huic non liceat, cum in eodem scripta sit testamento. Manifestum est nihil posse calumniae admittere verba legis ac scriptum.[7]

7   Nunc peritissimi litium homines ad interpretationem nos iuris adducunt. Non enim hanc esse legis voluntatem quae verbis ostendatur videri volunt. Quorum ego prudentiam, iudices, magnopere miror: tantum vicerunt illos maiores nostros, illos constitutores iuris, illos qui rudem civitatem legibus ac iure formarunt, ut hoc approbare

8   conentur, defuisse his sermonem, defuisse consilium. Ac priusquam rationem ipsius legis excutio, interim hoc dico, iudices, perniciosissimam esse civitati hanc legum inter-

---

[3] *Gron.*: legi- Aβ   [4] *Sch., Gron.*: in Aβ
[5] *Hå.*[2]: ius β: in A   [6] *Ro.*: q. i. Aβ
[7] *Ri.*: ac –pti Aβ: ascripta B

---

[3] And therefore both have to be tackled. I formerly double-

the dispute is with the two heirs. I ask them therefore which of the two they choose, whom they prefer as their adversary. For they are not litigating about part of the estate, they are challenging the entire will.[3]

Let us begin then with the lady who is put down first. What is wrong in this part of the will? It is forbidden to leave more than half an estate: well, she gets half the patrimony. We shall examine later what came next; meanwhile this prior item is solid and cannot be overturned by what follows.

It may be argued that *she* could inherit legally, but the lady written later could not. I shall ask once more: why so? "Because he could not leave more half the estate to a female." But she too was named heir to no more than half the estate, and I don't see any reason why what one of them could inherit the other could not, since she is named in the same will. It is clear that the words of the will, the text, cannot admit of any quibble.

Now persons highly expert in litigation bring us to the interpretation of the law. They want it to appear that the intention of the statute is not what is shown by its words. Gentlemen, I am full of admiration for their skill. They are so much superior to those ancestors of ours, the founders of our legal system, who shaped our primitive community by statute and law, that they try to prove them lacking verbally and lacking intellectually. Before I examine the purport of the law itself, this, gentlemen, I say for now: that this interpretation of laws is thoroughly pernicious to the

bracketed *quaero . . . consistere*, which may however stand as confronting the opposition with an unanswerable question: they cannot choose either one.

pretationem. Nam si apud iudicium hoc semper quaeri de
legibus oportet, quid in his iustum, quid aecum, quid con-
veniens sit civitati, supervacuum fuit scribi omnino leges.

9   Et credo fuisse tempora aliquando quae solam et nudam
iustitiae haberent aestimationem. Sed quoniam haec ingeniis in diversum trahebatur, nec umquam satis constitui
poterat quid oporteret, certa forma ad quam viveremus
instituta est. Hanc illi auctores legum verbis complexi
sunt; quam si mutare et ad utilitates suas pervertere licet,
omnis sit iuris, omnis usus eripitur. Nam quid interest
nullae sint an incertae leges?

10   Lex illa complexa est ne plus liceat quam dimidiam partem mulieri relinquere. Neutri ex his quibus adsumus plus
dimidia parte relictum esse manifestum est. Et apparet
potuisse legum latorem, [ut][8] si partem demum patrimonii
pervenire ad feminas vellet, partem utique viris relinqui,[9]
id ipsum cavere[10]; neque id magno aut difficili circuitu
effici potuit, sed vel sic scripta lege, ne plus quam dimidia

11   pars patrimonii ad feminas perveniret. Interrogo enim: si
‹quis›[11] pluribus feminis sed minores aliquanto portiones
reliquerit, quae tamen computatae et in unum contractae
plus quam semissem patrimonii efficiant, quaero an moveri lis possit. Nam si movetur lis, non hac, ut opinor, lege
litigabitur, qua plus quam dimidiam partem patrimonii
relinquere feminae non liceat, cum ex illis nulla dimidiam
partem acceperit. Sive ad totam nos vocas computatio-
nem, nihil interest quantum cuique feminae relinquatur.

8 *Ro., auct. Aer.*
9 *Ro.*: -quere Aβ
10 *Fr.*: -ret Aβ
11 *SB*3

community. For if in court there is always to be question about laws, what is just in them, what equitable, what convenable to the community, there was no need for laws to be written at all. And I do believe there were times in the past when justice rested on judgment, alone and unsupported. But men's minds pulled it this way and that, and the right course could never be adequately determined; for that reason a fixed pattern was put in place by which we were to live. Those authors of our laws embraced this pattern in words; if this may be changed and perverted to suit particular interests, there goes the whole meaning and use of law. For what does it matter whether laws are nonexistent or whether their import is doubtful?

That law embraced the provision that no more than a half be left to a woman. That no more than a half was left to either one of my clients is clear. And if the lawmaker had wished that only half an estate go to females and half be left to males in all circumstances, he could obviously have provided just that. No big, difficult roundabout was needed,[4] only a law so framed that no more than half an estate go to females. For I ask: if <somebody> bequeaths to a number of women, but somewhat lesser portions, which however when calculated and amalgamated amount to more than one half of the estate, I ask, can there be a legal challenge. For if suit be filed, it will not, as I imagine, be under this law, under which more than half the estate may not be bequeathed to a female, since none of them will get a half. But if you ask us to calculate the total, it makes no difference how much is left to each woman.[5]

---

4 *Neque . . . potuit = et potuit non* is very careless.
5 The opposition might say that this is in fact their position.

12   Quid si ne ratio quidem repugnat scripto et verbis legis istius? Quid enim putas voluisse legis latorem cum hoc ius constitueret? Ne feminae nimias opes possiderent, ne potentia earum civitas premeretur. Hoc ergo adversus singulas constituit, et ad evitandas opes feminarum satis hoc quaesitum, ne uni plus quam dimidia pars patrimonii re-
13   linqueretur. Ceterum quidem illud non caverunt leges, ne plures feminae eodem testamento scriberentur, non hercule magis quam illud, ne plures hereditates isdem feminis relinquerentur.

265

Ignominiosi pulsator in templo

Si quis in templo iniuriam fecerit, decem milia det ei cui iniuriam fecerit, decem civitati. Ignominioso ne sit actio iniuriarum. Quidam ignominiosum pulsavit in templo. Decem milia petit magistratus nomine civitatis.

1   DECLAMATIO

Si pudor commendandus est, cuius difficillima ratio est in lite pecuniaria, non nobis litigamus, ac ne rei publicae quidem et civitatis nomine avari sumus; et haec omnis actio non tam lucri gratia et acquirendae huius pecuniae constituta est quam in ultionem deorum inmortalium et templi (ut proprie dixerim) expiationem.

2   Nec minus manifestum ius est quam integer pudor. Lex

What if logic too is not at odds with the text and wording of that law? For what do you think the lawmaker intended when he laid down this statute? He did not want women to possess too much wealth, for fear the community be weighed down by their power. So he laid this down against individual women; to obviate women's wealth it was enough to provide that no more than half of an estate should be bequeathed to one of them individually. But the laws did not stipulate that no more than one woman should be written as heir in the same will, any more to be sure than that more than one legacy should not be left to the same women.

265

Beater of a person under stigma in a temple

Whoso commits injury in a temple, let him pay ten thousand to the person he has injured and ten to the community. Let a person under stigma be barred from taking action for injuries. A man beat a person under stigma in a temple. The magistrate claims ten thousand in the name of the community.

DECLAMATION

If a sense of decency is commendable, which is a very hard matter in a financial suit, we are not at law for ourselves, nor are we greedy even on behalf of the commonwealth and the community. This entire action has been set up not so much for gain, to acquire this money, as to avenge the immortal gods and for the expiation, to use the proper word, of the temple.

The law is as clear as our sense of decency is uncom-

enim palam scripta est, ut is qui in templo iniuriam fecerit decem milia det civitati. Mihi hoc satis est, qui civitatis

3 nomine litigo. Sed totam legem a nobis pars diversa legi desiderat. 'Decem milia' inquit 'ipsi qui iniuriam acceperit, decem civitati.' Et hoc excludere temptat civitatem, quod ipse qui iniuriam acceperit non habeat actionem, sane contumeliosus et pro cetera morum suorum petulantia adversus magistratum vestrum audax, qui praescribere

4 temptet civitati tamquam ignominiosae. Facile, ut opinor, constabit nihil ad nostram actionem pertinere quam legem habeat ipse qui pulsatus sit. Existimemus enim esse aliquem non ignominiosum in templo pulsatum, sed vel dedisse huius iniuriae veniam vel alio aliquo impedimento agere noluisse: num ideo ne civitas quidem ius suum tuebitur, ut omnia impune fecerit?

5 Verum ne ipse quidem adversarius tantum in exemptione[1] fiduciae habet quantum in ipsa iniuriae interpretatione. Non[2] enim iniuriam dicit[3] esse, quod ignominiosum pulsaverit cui actio non est. Ego, iudices, plurimum interesse existimo utrum quid facere liceat an vindicare non

6 liceat. Non enim continuo, si ignominioso actio non datur, licet adversus ignominiosum facere quod quisque velit. Tale est ignominiosum pulsare quale furtum sine teste facere: ut damnari quidem non possit, admittere tamen non debuerit.

7 Quin ex hoc ipso quod ignominioso actio non datur apparet esse rei publicae actionem. Quid enim lex eripuit si

---

[1] *Ro.*: exemplum A: -lo B
[2] *Aer.*: nos Aβ   [3] *Ri.*: dicimus Aβ

---

[1] The assailant.

promised. The law is written publicly, that a person committing injury in a temple pay ten thousand to the community. This is enough for me. I am bringing action on the community's behalf. But the other side wants the whole law read by us. "Ten thousand," it says, "to the person injured, ten thousand to the community." And he is trying to exclude the community on the ground that the person injured is barred from bringing action himself: quite insolently and audaciously, in line with his characteristic effrontery towards your magistrates, an attempt to bar the community as though it were under stigma. I imagine it will readily be agreed that the legal status of the person injured has nothing to do with our action. Let us suppose that a person not under stigma had been beaten in a temple, but had forgiven the injury or had not wanted to take action because of some other impediment, shall the community too on that account not maintain its right, with the result that he[1] goes scot-free after all he has done?

But my opponent himself has less confidence in the exclusion than in the actual interpretation of injury. He says it is not injury because he beat a person under stigma, who is barred from taking action. For my part, gentlemen, I think there is a great gap between what it is lawful to commit and what it is not lawful to punish. If action is not given to a person under stigma, it does not follow that everybody may do what he likes to such a person. To beat a person under stigma is like a committing a theft without a witness; he cannot be condemned, but ought not to have committed it.

Why, from the very fact that a person under stigma is not allowed to take action it is evident that the commonwealth *is* so allowed. For what did the law snatch away if

177

eius demum rei non dedit actionem quam facere licuit?
Non autem ius peccandi adversus ignominiosos dari uno et
brevi et manifesto videor argumento probaturus. Quem
pulsare licet, occidere licet. Atqui ignominiosum si quis
occiderit, caedis lege tenebitur. Quare? Quoniam actio
8 huius necessario ad alium pertinet. Apparet ergo non tibi
aliquid adversus ignominiosum licuisse, sed ignominioso
nihil pro se licere. Itaque ignominiosus non aget[4] tecum
iniuriarum, tu tamen iniuriam feceris; et hoc ad poenam
eius vitae ac turpitudinis pertinebit, quod tu non dabis
poenas peccati.

9 Haec dicerem si ubicumque pulsasses ignominiosum;
nunc, ut iniuria non sit alio[5] loco pulsasse ignominiosum,
iniuria tamen est in templo pulsare. ⟦Nam si id est utriusque nostrum confessione iniuria quod manifestum est non
esse iure factum: ut tibi ius fuerit alibi pulsandi ignominiosum (quod non esse iam docui), in templo pulsandi ius non
fuit.⟧

10 Haec ego dicerem etiamsi omnis ista ultio pertineret ad

---

[4] *Gron.*: agit Aβ   [5] D²: aliquo Aβ

---

[2] If a person under stigma could be assaulted with legal impunity there would be no purpose in a law forbidding such persons to
take action. Nobody could take action.

[3] An *ignominiosus* who had been assaulted was barred by law
from prosecuting his assailant, but the assault, as here argued, is
nonetheless a crime. Why then does somebody else not prosecute? The question is not asked in the text, but the answer would
be that a prosecution would serve no purpose since the penalty
prescribed by law, a fine payable to the victim, would be inopera-
tive (whether specifically or by implication) if the victim was un-

it barred action respecting something allowed under the law?[2] That no license is given to wrongdoing against persons under stigma I think I shall prove by a single brief, clear argument: someone whom it is lawful to beat it is lawful to kill; but if anybody kills a person under stigma, he will be liable under the law of homicide. Why? Because this person's action necessarily pertains to someone else.[3] Evidently, therefore, you were not licensed to do anything against a person under stigma; but a person under stigma has no license on his own behalf. So the person under stigma will not bring an action for injuries against you, but you will have committed injury all the same. That you will escape punishment for your wrongdoing will be part of the penalty he pays for his disreputable life.

That is what I should be saying if you had beaten a person under stigma just anywhere. As it is, even though it is not injury to have beaten a person under stigma in another place, beating in a temple is injury. [[For if both of us admit that something clearly done illegally is injury, then even though it was legal for you to beat a person under stigma somewhere else (and I have already shown that such is not the case), it was not legal to beat him in a temple.]][4]

This is what I should be saying even if that penalty per-

---

der stigma. To prove his point, the declaimer argues that the murder of an *ignominiosus* can be prosecuted (the victim being dead) and the penalty, death, imposed. In both cases the assailant has committed a crime, whether punishable or not.

4 (a) There is no such mutual *confessio*. (b) The point in *ut . . . fuit* has just been made. (c) The conclusion does not follow from the postulate.

eum qui iniuriam accepisset; nunc res duplex est, crimina
duo sunt eius qui in templo pulsaverit.[6] Quid enim lex
dicit? 'Qui in templo iniuriam fecerit, decem milia dena-
riorum det ei cui iniuriam fecerit, decem milia civitati.'
Non, si haec iuncta atque contexta sunt, continuo unius
legis habent vim et proprietatem. Id sic cognoscite: duos
actores habent, nec potest videri una lex cuius pars ad pri-
11 vatum, pars ad rem publicam pertinet. Ergo, etsi[7] iuncta
sunt ista, ut dixi, duas causas habent. Pars est legis ea[8] quae
vindicat templum. Ergo ut remittatur tibi ea quae pertinet
ad privatum, restat ea quae pertinet ad civitatem. Duae
enim sunt iniuriae in hoc tuo facto, et ideo duae poenae.

12 An vero inicum videri potest eum qui in templo pulsaverit decem milia civitati dare? Quid enim magis in ulla
re publica curari observarique oportet quam religionem?
Sane petulantia aliis locis mediocrem habeat reprehensio-
nem; in templo vero, in quo verbis parcimus, in quo animos componimus, in quo tacitam etiam mentem nostram
custodimus, pulsare velut in solitudine, velut in secreto
13 quodam, non est ferendum. Dic nunc: 'ignominiosus erat.'
Sed in templo. Captis urbibus vis hostium atque impetus[9]
religione templorum defenditur. Qui iam arma ferre non
possunt, qui salutem suam tueri fuga nequeunt, circa aras
iacent. In templo pulsasti hominem; rem petulantem

[6] *Gron.*: -satus sit Aβ   [7] *Ro.*: si Aβ
[8] *SB4*: eius Aβ   [9] atque i. *Watt2*: ac metus Aβ

[5] In this case there is only one, the prosecuting magistrate,
claiming penalty for the temple; and prosecution by the victim (or
in practice anybody else so far as concerns him; see n. 2) is legally
barred.

tained entirely to the person receiving the injury. As it is, the matter is twofold; there are two charges against a man who beats someone in a temple. For what says the law? "Whoso commits injury in a temple, let him pay ten thousand denarii to the person injured and ten thousand to the community." If these items are linked and intertwined, it does not follow that they have the force and speciality of a single law. Find that to be so thus: they have two pleaders[5] and a law of which part pertains to an individual, part to the commonwealth cannot be considered one law. So even though the two are linked, as I have said, they have two cases. There is a part of the law which protects the temple. So although that part which pertains to the individual be remitted to you, that which pertains to the community remains. For there are two injuries in what you have done and therefore two penalties.

Or can it seem unfair that a man who has beaten someone in a temple pay ten thousand to the community? For what should be more cared for and cultivated in any commonwealth than religion? Grant that aggressive behavior in other locales may be only moderately reprehended: but to beat someone in a temple, in which we are careful of our words, in which we compose our minds, in which we watch even our silent thoughts, as though it were done in a solitude, in some secret place—that is not to be borne. Tell us now: "He was under stigma." But in a temple. When cities are captured, the impetuous violence of enemies is warded off by the sanctity of temples. Those who can no longer bear arms or protect their lives by flight lie around the altar. You beat a man in a temple. You committed an act of

fecisti inter sacra, fecisti religiosissimo loco.

14   Et utcumque, temeraria licet, aliqua ratio tamen appareret facti tui si impetu lapsus esses, si ductus ira: nullam petulantiam magis odi quam quae se propter hoc exerit, quia putat licere. Est sine dubio et hoc ipsum dignum odio, persequi hominem fortasse infelicem, verecundum certe,

15 quod ⟨pulsari⟩ se passus[10] sit. Sane mereatur ille poenam ulteriorem: manibus tuis parce, parce animo tuo—aut certe relinque istius impudentiae locum.

    Respicere ad ictus tuos coegisti patres fortasse qui vota faciebant; tumultuosa lite aliqua nescio an etiam publica sacra turbasti. Quomodo enim cecidisse te existimemus, qui faciebas hoc tamquam liceret?

266

Ex proditore exule fortis

Bis de eadem re agere ne liceat. In quadam civitate proditionis damnatus missus est in exilium. Bello eadem civitate laborante revocati sunt exules. Is qui proditionis damnatus fuerat fortiter fecit. Petit ut iterum causam suam agat. Accusator praescribit quod bis de eadem re agere non liceat.

---

[10] p. se p. *SB*[1]: confessus Aβ

---

[6] The suggestion is that left alone *ignominiosus* would be sure to compound his impudence in entering the temple by further outrageous behavior, for which he would be punished. *Locum relinquere* is common in this sense (*TLL* VII.2.1597.5[2]). Not "retreat in the face of this man's impudence," or "leave the place to be polluted by this man's impudence," the two interpretations

aggression among the rites, you did it in a most sacred place.

And one way or another, what you did might make some sense, however rash, if you had erred through an impulse, led on by anger. No aggression is more odious to me that one which thrusts out because the doer thinks himself licensed. This very action too deserves hatred without doubt—to hound one perhaps unfortunate, certainly not without shame since he let himself ⟨be beaten⟩. Grant that he deserved further punishment: don't use your own hands, your own passion—or at least leave him an opportunity to display his impudence.[6]

You forced Fathers,[7] it may be, at prayer to look round[8] at your blows. You may even have disturbed public ritual by some noisy brawling. For how should we think you did the beating, when you thought you were doing something legal?

266

Hero ex-traitor

Let it not be legal to go to law twice about the same matter. In a certain community a man found guilty of treason was sent into exile. When the same community was struggling in a war, exiles were recalled. The man found guilty of treason became a hero. He asks[1] to plead his case again. His prosecutor enters a demurrer on the ground that it is illegal to go to law twice about the same matter.

suggested by Wi.   [7] Senators.   [8] A bad omen; see Wi.
  [1] By declamatory convention a "hero" is entitled to ask for any reward he chooses.

[QUINTILIAN]

1

Initia communia habet controversia: 'praemium peto lege
concessum sine exceptione.' Secuntur et illa, ut iustum
quoque sit virum fortem optare quod velit. Secunda illa
quaestio est, an contra legem optare liceat: in qua illud dicere solemus, nullum praemium posse inveniri quod non
contra legem aliquam sit, et ideo magnam esse virorum
fortium potestatem, quia supra omnia iura sit. Deinde
comparabimus etiam leges,[1] et dispiciemus utram servare

2 magis e re publica sit, si utique altera tollenda sit. Postea
veniemus ad id quoque, an utique ista praescriptio valere
debeat semper, hoc est, an etiam in publicis causis bis de
eadem re agere non liceat. In quo illud dicetur: privatis litibus, quoniam et minus momenti et plus numeri habeant,
succursum esse hac lege, publicas actiones maiores esse

3 quam ut cadant exceptione. Insequetur denique illud, ut
dicamus, etiamsi in aliis publicis causis bis de eadem re
agere non liceat, non tamen eam condicionem esse proditionis, quoniam in ceteris fortasse de poena tantum et periculo quaeratur eius qui accusatur, in causa proditionis de

4 totius civitatis discrimine litigetur. Illud ⟨quoque⟩[2] quaeramus, an ista praescriptio ad eos tantum pertineat cum
quibus agitur, patiente eo qui accusatur liceat bis agere.

5

Putemus te esse qui velis accusare, ⟨me⟩[3] reum non con-

---

[1] *Sch.*: legem Aβ   [2] *Sch.*
[3] *hic add. Ri., post* reum *Sch.*

---

[2] Their power is (and should be) great just because . . .
[3] For the defense.

At the beginning of the controversy is the common topic: "I seek my reward as allowed by law without exception." Follows the point that it is just furthermore that a hero opt for anything he wants. The second question is whether he has license to opt against the law. Here we are accustomed to say that no reward can be found which is not in conflict with some law, and that the power of heroes is great because it transcends all laws.[2] Then we shall further set the laws against each other and determine which it is more in the public interest to preserve if one of them must necessarily be invalidated. After that we shall come to another question, whether that bar should always be valid absolutely, that is, whether the provision against going to law twice about the same matter applies in public cases also. Here this will be said: in private suits, since they are of less moment and more numerous, this law is a recourse,[3] but public cases are too important to fail by exception.[4] Finally, this will follow: we shall say that even if in other public cases it is not legal to go to law twice about the same matter, this is not so in a case of treason, since in all others perhaps it is only the punishment and peril of the accused that is in question, whereas in a case of treason the litigation concerns a danger to the whole community. Let us <also> ask whether this demurrer pertains only to adversaries, and it is legal to go to law twice with the consent of the accused.

Let us suppose that you are the one who wants to prose-

---

[4] By a technicality, so to speak; see Wi.

tradicere: quis tum[4] prohiberet quo minus iterum accusa-
rer? Ergo quod tibi liceret facere me patiente, necesse erit
me optante.

6

SERMO

His excussis quaestionibus veniemus ad aequitatem. Dicemus hoc esse pro nobis, dicemus hoc esse pro re publica.

7

DECLAMATIO

Opto ut causam iterum dicam. Nec me fallit quam multa
praeteream quae mihi lege concessa sint. Sed quis tandem
me innocentem, quis dignum conversatione vestra putaret, si aliud optarem? Est pro me. Non enim et tum ideo
tantum defensus sum ut in civitate remanerem, ut essem
vobiscum, sed ut probarem me innocentem, nihil contra
8 patriam meam esse molitum. Et nunc non est satis si mihi
ignovistis, si me civem vestrum publica necessitas fecit.
Ego vero si merito damnatus sum, si quid tale quale contra
me pronuntiatum est feci, non utor isto beneficio.

9   Non sit[5] pro me; sed est pro civitate. Homicidii damnatus, etiamsi merito exulabat, si revocatus est, potest de eo
dici: 'satis dedit poenarum.' Alia scelera finem supplicio-
rum acceperint: vos proditorem in civitate sinetis esse,
cum totiens bella interveniant (non dico de extremo illo
discrimine)? †Tantine est metus quisquam?† Toto animo
adversus hostem nisi, non respicietis, non expavescetis?
Est pro re publica.

    [4] *Ranc.*: tamen Aβ   [5] *Sch.*: est Aβ

---

    [5] The recent crisis, when exiles were recalled.
    [6] Leaving out *metus*; but this can only be tentative. Deletion of
quisquam is another possibility.

cute and that <I>, the defendant, <do> not object: who would then say that I must not be prosecuted a second time? So what you would be free to do with my consent, will be necessary when I opt for it.

DISCUSSION

When these questions have been scrutinized, we shall come to equity. We shall say that this is for my good and for the good of the commonwealth.

DECLAMATION

I opt that I plead my case again. Nor am I unaware how many choices I pass by that would be legally conceded me. But who, pray, would believe me innocent and worthy to associate with you people if I opted for anything else? It is for my good. For then too I was not defended only to let me remain in the community, be with you, but to prove that I was innocent and had not plotted against my country. Now too it is not enough if you have pardoned me, if public necessity has made me your fellow citizen. No, if I was rightfully found guilty, if I did anything like the verdict against me pronounced, I do not accept your boon.

Supposing it is not for my good: but it is for the sake of the community. If a man found guilty of homicide has been recalled, even though he deserved to be in exile, it can be said of him that he has been penalized enough. Let other crimes receive an end to their punishments: but will you let a traitor be in your community when wars occur so often (I am not talking about that extremity of peril[5])? Is any man worth it?[26] Struggling with all your heart against the enemy, will you not look over your shoulder, not take fright? It is for the good of the commonwealth.

10   Sed accusatoris quid interest, aut quid est cur *[6] ini-
quiore condicione dicturus sim hodie causam quam antea
dixi? Tum detulerat eum cui nihil obici posset; hodie de-
fert damnatum. Hoc in primis mihi obiciet, quod contra
me sententias tulerint sanctissimi iudices, quod prodito-
11   rem me esse pronuntiaverint. Obiciat; et sic defendam. Et
ne quis me, iudices, sic audiat tamquam ego de his querar
qui pronuntiaverunt. Si istud invidiosum iudicibus esset,
poterat videri non immerito praemio meo aliquis obstare.
12   Sed non semper iudicum culpa erit cum innocens damnatus est[7]: aliquando testis corrumpitur, aliquando parum
diligenter causa defenditur, aliquando reo nocet et ipsa
fiducia. Vultis scire hoc non pertinere ad iudicum pudorem? Nemo contradicit nisi accusator.

267

Flens ad arcem depositor tyrannidis

Adfectatae tyrannidis sit actio. Qui tyrannidem deposuerat
sub pacto abolitionis iuxta arcem flens deprehensus est.
Adfectatae tyrannidis reus est.

1   DECLAMATIO

Non fui, iudices, dubius eo tempore quo paenitentia iuve-

---

⁶ *lac. ind. Aer.*: queratur, cum *tempt. Wi.*
⁷ *Wi.*: erit Aβ

---

[7] See crit. note.
[8] The giving of a wrong verdict. Or, as Wi., "my stand," i.e. "my

But what does it matter to the prosecutor or why <should he complain,>[7] since I shall today be pleading my case at a worse disadvantage than I pleaded it before? Then he had charged a man against whom nothing could be said: today he charges one who has been found guilty. This especially he will bring against me, that jurors of the highest character voted against me, pronounced me a traitor. Well, let him; even so I shall defend. And let no one, gentlemen, hear me under the impression that I am complaining of those who gave the verdict. If that[8] brought discredit on jurors, somebody might seem justified in objecting to my reward. But it will not always be the jury's fault when an innocent man is found guilty. Sometimes a witness is bribed, sometimes the case is sloppily defended, sometimes a defendant's confidence actually makes against him. Do you really want to be assured that this has nothing to do with the honor of the jurors? No one opposes except the prosecutor.

267

Abdicator of tyranny in tears close by the castle

Let an action lie for attempted tyranny. A man who had laid down his tyranny under a covenant of abolition was caught weeping hard by the castle. He is charged with attempted tyranny.

DECLAMATION

Gentlemen of the jury, at that time when repenting of my

criticism of the verdict." Either way he means that a new trial might be objected to as reflecting on the previous jury.

nilis temeritatis rem publicam legibus ac ⟨populi⟩[1] potes-
tati reddidi quin mihi multum vexationis, sive ab iratis sive
ab invidis, immineret. Neque enim iste accusator odio[2]
futurae tyrannidis in iudicium descendit, nec mihi ullum
imminere periculum ex eo crimine quod intentatur intel-
2   lego. Quapropter et initio actionis et per omnem oratio-
nem nihil magis faciendum mihi esse intellego quam ut
invocem publicam fidem, ut id quod remisistis, cuius oblivisci optimum putastis, non intra verba modo primumque
promissum steterit, sed penitus animis ac mente *[3] impe-
trasse videar.

3   Reliqua adeo longe a suspicione adfectatae tyrannidis
aberunt ut propius spectent ad priorum[4] temporum paenitentiam. Lacrimas quidem meas †si hic in iudicio temporibus etiam in hac pace tranquillitate degendum est† cum
sint exorandi adhuc animi multorum, sustinenda maligni-
4   tas. Haec mihi omnia arx fecit. An ego possum non flere
quotiens cogito quos habuerim parentes, quam domus
famam, quas spes adulescentiae infelici temeritate, dam-
nandis cupiditatibus everterim, ut sentio, in perpetuum?
5   Nihil est enim quod accusator meus simulatione quadam
†alte†[5] ea quae praeterierunt obliqua malignitate obicere
conetur. Ego me fecisse quod nollem et scio, iudices, et
confiteor; et quamdiu vixero, semper hoc †animo tota

---

[1] *Ranc.*
[2] *Pith.*: hodie Aβ
[3] *lac. ind. Leo*: ⟨ab⟩ animis ac mente ⟨profectum⟩ *Hå.*[2]
[4] *Pith.*: poster- Aβ
[5] alteea A: alta ea C: ad ea B: arte e(que) D: ea *SB*[1]: *anne*
simulationis quadam arte ea?

youthful rashness I handed the commonwealth back to the laws and the sovereignty ⟨of the people⟩, I had no doubt that a great deal of annoyance hung over me, whether from the angry or the malicious. For this prosecutor does not come to court in hatred of a future tyranny, nor do I believe that I am in any danger from the charge that is leveled at me. Therefore from the start of my plea and throughout my address, what I think I have to do as much as anything is to invoke public good faith. What you forgave, what you thought best forgotten, let it not stop short merely at words and the initial promise, but let it appear that you gave me something that came from the depth (?) of your hearts and minds.[1]

As for the rest, it will be found to lie far from any suspicion of plotting tyranny; rather, it will rather point to repentance for times past. My tears * * *[2] since I still have to win pardon in the minds of many and bear up against their malignity. All this the castle did to me. Or can I *not* weep whenever I think of my ancestors, of the fame of my house, of the hopes that I ruined, as I perceive, for ever by the unhappy rashness of youth and criminal ambition? For my prosecutor has no need to try to bring up the past against me under some sort of pretence,[3] in oblique malignity. I know, gentlemen, and confess that I did what I regret having done, and as long as I live this will ever stick fast in ⟨all⟩

[1] See crit. note.

[2] The sense may have been something like: "my tears are well warranted since even in this tranquil time I am here standing trial."

[3] See crit. note. The prosecutor had to disguise his real motives because of the amnesty.

6 mente†[6] inhaerebit. Neque enim illas quae me tetigerant
suspiciones pertinere ad praesentem defensionem puto,
securissima re publica, nec quid illud fuerit, an alienis
cupiditatibus obstiterim dum meas amolior.[7] Omnia ista
absoluta esse credo eo tempore quo inter me remque publicam convenit ut haec omnia memoriae exciderent, ut
non ad leges, non ad odium pertinerent; tunc certe lauda-
7 batis. Sed quemadmodum apud vos moderationis famam
consecutus sum, ita apud me ipsum haec quoque gravis
verecundia animo fuit, quod videbar hoc fecisse tamquam
8 moderator. Quid postea? Satellitesne contraxi? Aut arma
habui? Aut divisi[8] pecuniam? Aliquid inter amicos conti-
nui quod[9] obici mihi potest in futurum?—cum praesertim
adfectatio tyrannidis multa crimina <desider>et,[10] quae
non coniectura colligi oporteat verum manifesta deprehendi.[11]

9 'Apparet' inquit 'cupiditas tua: fles enim iuxta arcem.'
Si confiterer depositae potestatis illius paenitentiam, dicerem tamen aliud esse adfectare tyrannidem, aliud cupere.
Verum quid signi, quid argumenti istae lacrimae habent?
Flere miratur aliquis hominem? 'Sed iuxta arcem fles.'
Num ego possum continere lacrimas quotiens illum locum
video a quo tam libenter descendi? Illic mihi succurrit
infamata adulescentia; quotiens arcem video, succurrit:
10 inde has inimicitias. Sero me, accusatores, deprehendistis:

[6] <toto> animo, t. m. Wi.   [7] SB4: simul Aβ
[8] aut . . . aut divisi Ro.: ad . . . ante divisam Aβ
[9] SB2: quid Aβ   [10] SB2, auct. Wi. (-ret et)
[11] deprendi Wi.: -raehendit A1: -r(a)ehendat A2β

[4] What suspicions? We gather from what immediately follows

my heart and all my mind. For I do not think that those suspicions that had touched me[4] have anything to do with my
present defense, now that the commonwealth is in full
security, nor yet the question whether I blocked the ambi-
tions of others as I put away my own. I believe that all such
matters were disposed of when it was agreed between myself and the commonwealth that they should all drop out of
memory, should not pertain to the laws nor yet to odium.[5]
At the time at least you were praising me. But even as
I won with you a reputation for self-mastery, in my own
mind there was serious embarrassment, because I appeared to have done it like a ruler. What followed? Did
I gather bodyguards? Or keep weapons? Or distribute
money? Did I keep anything among my friends that can be
brought against me in the future, especially as plotting a
tyranny <calls for> many misdoings which should not be
raked up by guesswork but caught in plain view?

"Your ambition is evident," I am told. "For you shed
tears hard by the castle." If I were to admit regret for the
power I laid down, I should still say that it is one thing to
plot tyranny, another to desire it. But what indication, what
proof is there in those tears? Is anyone surprised that a human being sheds tears? "But you shed them hard by the
castle." Can I contain my tears whenever I see that place
from which I so willingly came down? There my ill-famed
youth comes to me; whenever I see the castle, comes the
thought: thence these enmities. Accusers, you have caught

that some believed he had abdicated in order to foil a plot to re-
place him.
[5] The understanding had been that there should be no legal
action or ill will arising from the tyranny.

quantum me putatis flevisse antequam descenderem? Ceterum adfectare tyrannidem sperantis est, erectioris animi sunt ista crimina, fletus remissi, fatigati. Tu id mihi criminis eius argumentum vis videri cuius desperatio est. Istius
11 enim adfectus argumentum lacrimae habent.[12] Quaero enim ex te unde istum fletum putes. Nam si adfecto, si spero, si rediturum me ad ea ex quibus invitus descenderim puto, quae causa lacrimarum est? Si vero hoc est quod animum meum torqueat, quod ex illo fastigio descenderim, quod ex aequo vivam, quomodo adfectare possum quod scio mihi non posse contingere?
12 Eodem revolvatur oratio necesse est unde coepit. Ego publicam appello fidem, quae inter piratas sacra est, quae inter armatos hostes indutias facit, quae deditarum civitatium iura conservat. Qualecumque istud est, promisistis,
13 censuistis. Ac de me quidem nihil. Mihi enim iam taedio vita est, iamque hae lacrimae cotidianae accesserunt prope ad vota mortis. Illud videte, an si aliquem †rei publicae†[13] error aut fortuna, si quem aut consilium aliquod aut temeritas miserit, detis locum paenitentiae, permittatis emendari, velitis [ne][14] meliores fieri cives.

268

Orator, medicus, philosophus

Contendunt orator, medicus, philosophus de bonis patris, qui testamento eum heredem reliquerat qui se probasset

[12] istius . . . h. *huc transp. SB²: post* descenderem (*supra*) Aβ
[13] <in> rem –am *Sch.*: <in oppressionem> rei p. *Ri.*
[14] *Pith.*

me too late. How many tears do you suppose I shed before I stepped down? For the rest, plotting tyranny implies hope; such a charge goes with a mind on the alert, weeping with one relaxed, tired. The behavior you represent as proof of that crime is despair of it. For that is the emotion that tears indicate. For I ask you, whence do you think comes this weeping? For if I am plotting, if I hope, if I think to return to something from which I stepped down reluctantly, what cause is there for tears? But if what tortures my spirit is that I stepped down from that height, that I am living on level terms, how can I be plotting something that I know cannot come my way?

My address must return to its starting point. I appeal to public good faith, which is sacred among pirates, which makes truce between enemies in arms, which conserves the rights of communities after surrender. Whatever it amounts to, you promised, you decreed. As for myself, nothing. Life is a weariness to me now, these daily tears have now come close to a prayer for death. It is for you to see to it that if error or Fortune, if some plan or rash impulse send a man against the commonwealth, you give room for repentance, allow his amendment, want citizens to become better.

268

Orator, physician, philosopher

An orator, a physician, and a philosopher dispute for their father's property, who in his will had left as his heir the one

amplius prodesse civibus.

1

DECLAMATIO

Lex contentionis et formula et omne praescriptum ex testamento patris pendet: cuius vis non est ea, ut quaeratur quae professio ex nostris speciosissima (quamquam sic quoque vincerem), sed quae civitati sit utilissima. Nihil est ergo quod ingenia iactent, nihil quod [ex][1] animo suo
2 tantum referant: quaeritur quis omnibus prosit. Sit philosophia res summa: ad paucos pertinet; sit eloquentia res admirabilis: non pluribus prodest quam nocet. Sola est medicina qua opus sit omnibus. Et patrem quoque nostrum id voluisse, ut hanc quam in contentione reliquisse videtur partem quodammodo civitati daret, manifestum
3 est. Non sibi utilissimum, non amicis utilissimum, non de patre optime meritum: proprie quid ferre ex testamento suo voluit qui fuerit utilis civitati. Ergo et aequaliter ad omnes medicina sola pertinet et nulla ⟨ars⟩[2] tam necessaria est omni generi hominum quam medicina. Reliqua conferamus.
4 Ac mihi primum agendum est cum fratre philosopho, cuius ego in hodierna contentione propositum mirari satis non possum. Nihil enim videtur habere philosophia praestantius quam quod modicis contenta est, ampliores opes non desiderat. Nam si cupiditates easdem quas ceteri ha-

---

[1] SB[4]   [2] Hå.[2], Watt[1]: res D[2]

---

[1] The theme appears to be incomplete. Only part of the estate was assigned to the winner of the dispute. The rest was presumably otherwise disposed of, perhaps to be divided equally between the three.

who should prove that he does most for his fellow citizens.[1]

The rule governing the dispute, the terms, all the preliminary framework depends on the father's will. The gist of this is not to enquire which of our professions makes the best show (though even so I should be the winner), but which is the most useful to the community. So there is no use in their boasting of their intellects or making their own minds the only criterion (?). The question is, who benefits everybody? Philosophy may be an exalted thing, but it concerns few; eloquence may be a thing to admire, but it does not help more people than it harms. Only medicine is needed by everybody. That our father too wanted to give that part which he is seen to have left in dispute in some sort to the community, is evident: not the one most useful to himself, not the one most useful to his friends, not to the one who had deserved best of his father, but the one who was useful to the community—that was the one whom he wished to get something special for himself out of his will. So only medicine pertains equally to everybody and no ‹art›[2] is so necessary to every sort of human being as medicine. Let us compare other points.

And first I must take issue with my brother the philosopher, whose purpose in the present dispute I cannot sufficiently wonder at. For there seems to be nothing so admirable in philosophy as its contentment with modest means, its lack of desire for ampler wealth. For if it has the same

---

[2] A better supplement than *res*. *Ars* is used of philosophy in s.7 and twice of medicine in 21.

5 bet, non video quid prosit. Neque me praeterit, iudices,
quam multa dici adversus hanc professionem ab iis soleant
quorum libertatem non impediunt personae. Quippe hos
illi et vanos vocant et otiosos et in ambitum ipsum contra
quem maxime disserere videntur alligatos. Mihi cum fra-
6 tre quaestio est. Haec ergo leviora dixisse satis est, philosophiam non esse necessariam. Ego enim[3] mores nasci puto
et propriam cuiusque naturae virtutem. Alia forsitan dis-
cantur, quaedam experimentis cognoscenda sunt: boni
7 mores constant voluntate. Id patere diversis utriusque partis exemplis potest. Nam et optimos viros citra philosophiam fuisse constabit et studiosos sapientiae usque ad
ultima exempla scelerum nequitiaeque venisse. Non enim,
ut opinor, ex istorum scholis abstinentiam didicere Fabricii, Curii, nec uti mortem contemnerent Decii consecuti
sunt [nec][4] vetera horum explicando monumenta. Tulit
civitas populi Romani liberatores[5] Brutos, tulit Camillos,
8 antequam ulla istius artis simulatio irreperet. Iam vero si
ex diverso intueri placeat, quis ignorat ex ipsa Socratis, quo
velut fonte omnis philosophia manasse creditur, schola
evasisse tyrannos et hostes patriae suae? Non est igitur ne-
9 cessaria philosophia. Atqui etiam[6] ut studio perveniri ad
Sapientiam possit, via tamen eius incerta[7] est. Namque ut
omnes in unum philosophos contraham, non tamen inter

---

3 *β*: autem A   4 *Gron*.   5 *Aer*.: liberiores A*β*
6 *Sch*.: enim A*β*   7 *Pith*.: certa A*β*

---

3 Literary texts on papyrus rolls. *Horum* are the philosophers.
4 L. Brutus, the first Consul. Except for the Decii the plurals
refer to individuals.
5 Critias, chief of the "Thirty Tyrants," and Alcibiades, who at

cravings as the rest of the world, I don't see what it is good for. I am not unaware, gentlemen, how many things are often said against this profession by those whose freedom of speech is not hampered by personalities. They call these folk insincere and lazy and tied to that very self-aggrandizement against which they are seen most forcibly to discourse. But this is between me and my brother. So it is enough to take the gentler line and say that philosophy is unnecessary. For I think that character is inborn and virtue belongs to every nature. Other things may perhaps be learned, other things are to be found out by experience: a good character consists in the will. This can be obvious from examples on either side. For it will be generally agreed that there have been excellent men outside of philosophy and that pursuers of wisdom have plumbed the depth of crime and worthlessness. It was not, I imagine, from these folks' schools that the Fabricii and Curii learned abstinence, nor did the Decii attain contempt of death by unrolling their ancient memorials.[3] The community bore Bruti,[4] liberators of the Roman people, bore Camilli, before any semblance of this art crept in. And if you care to look from the opposite angle, who does not know that tyrants and enemies of their country[5] came from the very school of Socrates, the fountainhead, so to speak, from which all philosophy is said to have flowed. So philosophy is unnecessary. Moreover, even though Wisdom could be attained by its pursuits, yet the way to it is uncertain. For if I were to lump all philosophers together, yet

one point went over to Sparta; not Dionysius II, for whose career as a tyrant Plato could hardly be held responsible, let alone Socrates.

eos constare potest quae potissimum secta adsciscenda[8]
nobis, quibus praeceptis parendum sit. Pugnant inter se
atque dissentiunt et perpetuam hanc per saecula litem tra-
10 hunt. Aliis summum bonum voluptas habetur; quidam id
in nuda virtute posuerunt; nonnulli miscere ista conati
sunt atque confundere, et ex bonis corporis animique et
eorum quae extra essent ad finem vitae beatae perveniri[9]
posse existimaverunt; delectavit quosdam modus omni-
11 um.[10] Iam vero quanta circa deos pugna! Quidam nihil agi
sine providentia credunt; alii curam deorum intra sidera
continent; quidam in totum deos sustulerunt; quidam,
12 dum[11] hoc erubescunt, cura vacare utique[12] dixerunt. Hi
nos ad administrationem rei publicae hortantur; illi nihil
periculosius civilibus officiis credunt. Quosdam videas
odio pecuniae ferri nudos expositosque, veluti ad provo-
candas calamitates; sunt qui voluptates non animi modo
13 sed etiam corporis inter praecipua ducant bona. Quibus
credam? Quibus accedam? Quidquid probavero, plures
negaturi sint. Nec porro quaecumque praecipiuntur *[13]
possunt. Ergo et non necessariam esse philosophiam et
difficilem electionem esse diximus; atque inter ipsos etiam
plerosque philosophos constat ‹verum›[14] vix posse per-
14 cipi. Neque ego ignoro esse quosdam qui, quamquam

    8 *Ro.*: disce- Aβ   9 CD: -ire AB
    10 *Bu.*: hominum Aβ   11 *Wi.*: cum Aβ
    12 *Pith.*: utraque Aβ   13 *lac. ind. Wi.*   14 *SB*1

---

6 The schools in mind are: Epicureans, Stoics, Peripatetics,
and again, primarily, Peripatetics (Wi). I translate as though
eorum was *eis*, which I think is what the writer intended.

7 The allusions are to the Stoics, Plato and Aristotle ("so it

there can be no agreement among them on which particular school we must adopt, which precepts we should obey. They quarrel among themselves and are at loggerheads, they carry this dispute all through the centuries. For some pleasure is the supreme good, others have placed it in naked virtue, some have tried to mingle and confuse the two, thinking that the end of a happy life can be attained from bodily and mental goods and things external.[6] Some liked moderation in all things. And again, what a battle about the gods! Some believe that nothing happens without providence; others confine the gods' care within the stars; some have got rid of the gods altogether; some, who are ashamed to go so far, said they are absolutely without care.[7] One group urge us to take part in governing the commonwealth; others believe that nothing is more dangerous that civic duties.[8] Some[9] you may see carried away by hatred of money, naked and exposed, as though to challenge calamities; there are those[10] who put pleasures not only of the mind but of the body among the chief of good things. Whom am I to believe? Whom to join? Whatever I approve, more will deny. Nor can all that is prescribed[11] <be approved>. So I have said both that philosophy is unnecessary and that choice is difficult. And even philosophers themselves mostly agree that <the truth> can hardly be perceived.[12] Nor am I ignorant that some, though they

would seem (cf. Cic. *n.d.* 1.30 and 33)" (Wi)), atheists, Epicureans.   [8] Stoics; Epicureans.

[9] Cynics.

[10] Perhaps vaguely Cyrenaics rather than Epicureans again.

[11] By a chosen school.

[12] In especial the Carneadean Academy.

nomen Sapientiae facile atque avide (ut sic dixerim) dederunt,[15] tamen idem[16] Sapientem[17] ex fabulis repetunt, et
inter eos qui studuerunt, qui elaboraverunt, nullum adhuc
15 inventum esse confitentur. Verumtamen, ut aliqua etiam
de universo loquamur, quis usus ipsorum virorum? Mili-
tiaene utiles an civilibus officiis? Quid in his deprehendas
praeter fictam frontem et perpetuum otium et quandam
ex arrogantia auctoritatem? Verum sint ista (ut dicitur)
magna: ego haec ad formam legemque paterni testamenti
voco. Quid civitati prosunt? Amputant vitia? Nimirum
nemo luxuriosus est, nemo pecuniae cupidus!

16   Haec de philosopho dixisse satis est: transeamus ad
oratorem. Quem intellego fiducia eloquentiae ad hanc
descendisse causam. Multum se valere in iudiciis putant;
rapiunt malas aliquando causas. Et sane si iustitia valeat,
17 quid ⟨opus⟩[18] est eloquentia? Quid ergo civitati conferunt?
Illa enim sane remittamus, omne circa verba studium et,
cum rerum natura beneficio suo ita homines instruxerit ut
nulla res non voce explicetur, supervacuum quendam in
18 exornando laborem. Eodem redeant omnia: quid civitati
profuisti? Advocatione tua defensus est aliquis: sed laesus
qui ex diverso erat. Eripuisti periculo reum: unde scio an
nocentem? Innocentia quidem per se valet. Damnatus est
aliquis accusante te: unde scio an eloquentiae vitium sit?
19 Quid ego de privatis loquor? Civitatium status scimus ab

---

[15] nomen . . . d.] *cf.* Watt[2], *qui* Sap. *pro* sap.
[16] *Gron.:* quidem Aβ
[17] *Aer.:* -tiam Aβ
[18] *SB*[4]

---

[13] As Hercules and Ulysses (Wi., comparing Sen. *Dial.* 2.2.1).

may have enlisted under Wisdom, so to speak, readily and avidly, yet at the same time seek the Wise Man from fable[13] and confess that no such being has yet been found among those who have studied and toiled. But all the same, to say something universally, what is the use of the men themselves? Are they useful for the military or for civic functions? What would you find in them except hypocrisy and perpetual idleness and a certain air of authority stemming from arrogance? But suppose these are great matters, as they are said to be: I summon them to comparison with the form and terms of our father's will. What do they do for the community? Do they amputate vices? No one, I suppose, is a loose-liver, no one a money-grubber!

Enough said about the philosopher; let us pass on to the orator. I realize that he has come to this trial relying on his eloquence. They think they carry a lot of weight in the courts. Sometimes they snatch up[14] bad cases. And indeed, if justice prevailed, what <need for> eloquence? So what do they bring to the community? For I won't press the point that all their effort is about words and a labor of embellishment, superfluous, seeing that the Nature of Things by her kindness has so equipped mankind that nothing exists without a word to express it. Let everything come back to the same question: what have you done for the community? Somebody has been defended by your advocacy: but his opponent has been damaged. You have snatched a defendant from peril; how do I know whether he was guilty? Innocence is strong in itself. Somebody is found guilty, you prosecuting: how do I know whether your eloquence is not to blame? Why do I speak of private individuals? We know

14 I.e. "pull out of the fire."

oratoribus esse conversos: sive illam Atheniensium civitatem, quondam late principem, intueri placeat, accisas eius
vires animadvertemus vitio contionantium; sive populi
Romani statum excutere voluerimus, nonne gravissimas
seditiones, nonne turbidissimas contiones eloquentissi-
mus quisque habuit, nonne illi Gracchi ad evertendam
20 rem publicam his veluti armis succincti accesserunt? Quid
ego dicam quantum civitati obfuerit[19] eloquentia? Sibi nocuit. Summos utriusque partis oratores videamus. Nonne
Demosthenen illum oppressum veneno suo scimus, nonne
Ciceronem in illis in quibus totiens placuerat rostris poena
sua[20] expositum?

21   Haec dixisse satis erat: nam si civitati nihil utilitatis adferunt hi cum quibus contendi, satis erat relictum esse me
solum. Aliqua tamen de medicina dicam, non mehercule
iactandi mei causa, sed commendandae artis ipsius. Cuius
auctores ante omnia accepimus deos, sive (ut maxime reor)
‹re vera dederunt›,[21] ut haec infirmitas hominum haberet
adiumenta aliqua atque solacia, sive tantum huic arti tribuere maiores ut eam vix crederent humanis potuisse
ingeniis inveniri, sive ipsa medicina per se sacrum est.
22 Contendamus sane apud securos: si quem (quod absit omnibus) subita deprehenderit valetudo, oratoremne con-
sulet? Quid nunc ego enumerem contra quot Fortunae
iniurias medicina advocetur?—illam valetudinem qua spiritus frangitur, an illam qua visus periclitatur, an illam qua

---

[19] *Sch.*: profu- Aβ   [20] parte sui *Sch.*
[21] *SB*[2]

---

[15] *Parte sui* (see crit. note), meaning head and hands, certainly
makes better sense.

204

that communities have been turned upside down by orators. If we care to look at the Athenian community, once preeminent far and wide, we shall find that its strength was crippled through the fault of public speakers. Or if we wish to examine the status of the Roman People, were not the worst seditions, the most turbulent assemblies, the work of the most eloquent among them? Girt with these arms, as it were, did not those Gracchi advance to the overthrow of the commonwealth? Why tell of damage done by eloquence to the community? It has harmed itself. Let us look at the greatest orators in both areas. Do we not know that Demosthenes was destroyed by his own poison and that Cicero was exposed by his punishment[15] on the Rostra where he had so often found favor?

What I have said would have been enough. If those with whom I have contended bring nothing useful to the community, it would have been enough that I alone am left. However, I shall say something about medicine, not, I assure you, to cry myself up but to commend the art itself. We are told that its original authors were gods,[16] whether, as I think most likely, <they really gave it,> so that mankind's infirmity should have some succor and solace, or whether our ancestors valued this art so much that they could hardly believe that it was discovered by mortal minds, or whether medicine itself is in itself a sacred thing. Let us by all means be contending before the secure: but if a sudden sickness lay hold of one of you (far be it from you all!), will he consult an orator? Why should I now enumerate how many of Fortune's injuries medicine is called in to combat—the sickness that breaks the breath, or that en-

16 Apollo and Aesculapius.

vulnera curanda sunt, an illam qua debilitati occurritur.
23 Removeam medicinam: tu, philosophe, consolaberis?
Quod hominum genus est, qui sexus, quae aetas, quae non
utilitatem ex hac[22] petat? Itaque, etiamsi medicina vinci
Fata non potuerunt, productus est tamen usque ad eam
‹aetatem›[23] pater noster qua[24] tres liberos habebat, ‹in his
et medicum›.[25]

269

Dives sub tyranno auctionatus

Depositi sit actio. Pauper et dives amici erant, pauperi duo
filii adulescentes. Cum tyrannus esse coepisset in civitate,
dives facta auctione discessit. Rumor erat pecuniam apud
pauperem esse depositam. Tyrannus accersît pauperem;
torsit ipsum, torsit et filios eius. Cum ille pernegaret penes
se esse, dimissus est. Postea tyrannus occisus est. Redît dives. Petit pecuniam, quam se deposuisse apud pauperem
dicit,[1] et duos servos, quos solos exilii comites habuerat, in
quaestionem pollicetur.

1   DECLAMATIO

Depositum peto. Scio hunc esse ordinem probationis, ut
primum ostendam ‹me›[2] habuisse pecuniam quam depo-
nerem. De hoc nemo dubitat: dives fui. Etiamsi me cupiditas amici ad duos servos redegit, aliquando tamen numera-
bar inter principes huius civitatis. Et ut sciatis pecuniam

---

22 *Aer.*: hoc Aβ   23 *Sch.*
24 *SB*[4]: qui Aβ   25 *SB*[4]
1 *Ri.*: dixit Aβ
2 *Ri.*

dangers the sight, or that involves the curing of wounds or
the counteracting of debility? Let me take medicine away:
will you console, philosopher? What sort of mankind, what
sex, what age, but seeks benefit therefrom? And so, even if
medicine could not conquer the Fates, yet our father's life
was prolonged to ⟨an age⟩ in which he had three children,
⟨including a physician⟩.[17]

269

Rich man who auctioned his property under a tyrant

Let an action lie for a deposit. A poor man and a rich man
were friends. The poor man had two young sons. When a
tyrant had arisen in the community, the rich man held an
auction and left. It was rumored that money been deposited with the poor man. The tyrant summoned the poor
man, tortured him and also tortured his sons. When he
persisted in denying that the money was in his possession,
he was let go. Later the tyrant was killed. The rich man
returned. He claims the money, which he says he had deposited with the poor man, and promises to hand over two
slaves, his only companions in exile, for torture.

DECLAMATION

I claim my deposit. I know that the sequence of proof is
that I first show that ⟨I⟩ *had* money to deposit. This no one
doubts: I was rich. Even though my friend's greed has re-
duced me to two slaves, I was once numbered among the
leading men of this community. And so you may know that

17 Some such addition, implying that the doctor had prolonged his father's life, is called for. See Wi.

non satis esse, patrimonium meum detinet, si domum, si
mancipia, si vendita esse omnia, si in pecuniam redacta
2 constabit. Superest ut deponendae pecuniae habuerim
causam. Fuisse me in metu fortunae huius quam patior
manifestum est; nihil minus fuisse rationis quam ut mecum pecuniam ferrem liquere omnibus credo. Nec illud
tantummodo dico, ne persequeretur tyrannus: ne quid iti-
neris casus auferret, ne fugientem onus ipsum gravaret.
Potestis aliquid etiam ex ipso fugae comitatu colligere: ne
servos quidem amplius quam duos duxi. Deponendi fuit
3 ratio. Proximum est ut quaeramus: apud quem deponen-
dum fuit? Apud aliquem in civitate. Quis amicior mihi? In
quo plus esse fidei existimavi? Hoc probandum diutius
4 foret nisi sciretis; constitit inter omnes. Dicat iste quam
multa volet adversus famam, dum tamen constet nihil
aliud esse istam quam consensum³ civitatis. Si ab universis
tamen ad singulos vocamur, et tyrannum testem dabo.
Illum quidem neque ego laudo; sed ipsa vitia eius, ipsa scelera facient huic rei auctoritatem: ubi pecuniam credidit
esse qui quaerebat, ‹qui adeo›⁴ non dubitavit ut torto tibi
et perneganti non crederet, ut quaestionem usque in liberos mitteret?
5   ‘Sed in tormentis’ inquit ‘perseveravi.’ Quam honeste
feceras si redderes! ‘Sed et liberi perseverarunt.’ Nam et
tu fortasse propter illos perseverasti. Neque ego dubito
quin prius istud a⁵ fide feceris. Sed te male (ut sic dixerim)
docuit patientia. Indignum putasti tam multa passum esse

---

³ *Ri.*: se- Aβ ⁴ *Wi.* (adeo *Ro.*)
⁵ a] bona *Aer., fort. recte*

---

¹ He traveled light. The imputation in s.1 is forgotten.

money is not enough, he is keeping my patrimony, if it shall be established that my house, my slaves, everything was sold and converted into cash. It remains to show that I had a reason for depositing the money. That I was in fear of this fortune which I suffer is manifest; that nothing made less sense than to take the money with me I believe is clear to everybody. I don't mean only for fear the tyrant might pursue me but for fear the chances of the journey might rob me of something or that the load itself might weigh me down as I fled. You can infer something too from the very companionship of my flight: even of slaves I took only two.[1] It made sense to deposit. Next the question: with whom was I to deposit? Someone in the community. Who was more my friend? Whose loyalty did I trust more? This would need proving at greater length if you didn't know it. It was common knowledge. Let him say as much as he likes against common report, so long as we agree that it is nothing other than the consensus of the community. But if I am challenged to come from the universal to the particular, I shall call the tyrant himself to witness. I too say no good of him; but his very crimes and vices will give him credibility in this matter. Where did he believe the money was, the man who made search, ⟨who⟩ was ⟨so⟩ certain that he didn't believe you when you persisted in denying under torture and put your sons to the torture as well?

He says, "but I held fast in the torture." How greatly would that have been to your credit, if you were returning the money! "But my children too held fast." Yes, and perhaps you held fast on their account. And I don't doubt that earlier on you acted in good faith. But endurance taught you amiss, shall I say? You thought it unfair that you had

propter alienam pecuniam. Illud certe manifestum est, hinc tibi venire fiduciam negandi, quod negasti.

6 Si tortus non esses, mihi illa sufficerent: pecuniam habui, deponere debui, apud neminem alium deponere illam debui, sciunt servi mei. Mutasti animum post istud tormentum.[6] Si tamen tibi magnum videtur in tormentis esse

7 momentum, et isti torqueantur.[7] Rem quidem facio miseram: do in quaestionem (iam dices mihi) servos—sed qui propter hoc servi sunt, ut torqueantur; alioqui non eram tam ingratus ut in hoc nomine adhuc eos detinerem qui

8 mecum soli fuissent. Sustinebitis igitur tormenta, fidelissimi comites, sustinebitis quaestionem, optime meriti. Sed ignoscite. Facilius est egestatem ferre in hac natis. Me onerat maiorum meorum dignitas, onerat prioris consuetudo vitae, onerat etiam fama; et omnino de innocentia mea quaeritur.

9 Indebitam pecuniam ab amico peto, et hunc potissimum quem calumniarer elegi, quam[8] si defodi,[9] si abscondi, [cum][10] si hic vere pauper est, ne damnato quidem sim recepturus? Rem incredibilem, et in qua me dementiae

10 crimine damnari necesse est! Ante omnia perdidisse me omnem pecuniam dico ne dives esse possim, ideo demum

[6] β: instrumentum A   [7] *Ri.*: -erentur Aβ
[8] *SB*[1]: cum Aβ   [9] *Ri., auct. Gron.*: eff- Aβ
[10] *SB*[1]

---

[2] So stated in s.5. I now doubt the need to double-bracket with Wi. Under the torture the poor man had denied that he had the money, falsely, but he later claimed that the denial was true, thus (as far as that went) supporting the reliability of statement under torture.

suffered so much because of another man's money. This at least is clear, that your denial then gives you confidence to deny now.

If you had not been tortured, that would be enough for me: I had money, I had to deposit, there was nobody else with whom I could well leave it, my slaves know. You changed your mind after the torture.[2] But if you think torture carries great weight, let them be tortured too. To be sure, it's a sorry thing I am doing. I give slaves (as you will presently tell me)[3] for torture, but they are slaves just for that purpose. Otherwise I was not so ungrateful that I would have still kept them under that name, the only ones who had been with me. So you will sustain the pains, my most faithful companions, you will sustain the torture, most deserving. But forgive me. Poverty is easier to bear for those born in it.[4] I am burdened by the prestige of my forebears, by my former lifestyle, even by common report; and, all told, my innocence is in question.[5]

Am I claiming money that is not owed to me from a friend and have I chosen this one in particular for a false accusation? If I had buried the money, hidden it away, even if he is found guilty I could not recover it, if he is truly a poor man. Unbelievable! I must needs be convicted on a charge of dementia! To begin with, do I say that I have lost all my money in order to lose the possibility of becoming

---

[3] Only slaves, as opposed to the freeborn sons (cf. s.14). Reply: those slaves would have been free by now if I had not needed them to testify under torture.   [4] An excuse for putting them through the ordeal: "you can bear our present straits more easily than I" (Wi.).   [5] *Quaeritur* implies torture if slaves are involved (cf. "put to the question").

mentior ut mihi cum duobus servis tortis, si tamen quaestioni superfuerint, vivendum sit, qualis in exilio fui, qualis cum tyrannum fugerem, si minus, soli[11]? Ego si calumnior amicum meum, graviorem poenam ferre non possum: perdo quidquid peto. Et quam causam irascendi tibi habui? Quid tantum mali fecisti mihi ut ego non sim tormentis istis[12] contentus?

11   Scio dici simile aliquid etiam ex parte diversa: quem sibi usum fore pecuniae [dicet][13]? Ante omnia hoc dissimile est, quod pauperi alioqui et duorum liberorum patri (quae res acerbiorem paupertatem facit) tamen secreta

12   pecunia et abdita adfert securitatem. Nam ut possessiones non pares, ut familiam non emas, non laxiore habites domo, adversus Fortunam tamen tutus es: tibi pecunia hoc praestat, ut sis pauper securus. Adice illud, quod tu de longioribus temporibus cogitas.

13   In summa, si vincis, aliquam tamen potes spectare rationem; ego cur litigem quid est? Ut aliquid auferam? Quid habes nisi depositum? Ego me, iudices, hanc pecuniam perdidisse scio. Nam ut damnetis, quomodo[14] manum[15] mittam? Perseverabit enim in ista simulatione homo quem nec tormenta vicerunt. Omnis litis huiusce causa mihi in hoc est, ut defendam pudorem meum.

14   Tu tamen inveni ubi abdiderim.[16] Nescis? Quaere! Hi servi a me non recesserunt, hi conscii sunt omnium, hi

---

[11] si minus, soli *huc transp. SB*[1]: *post* sit Aβ
[12] *Aer.:* istius Aβ   [13] *Hå.*[2]   [14] *Hå.*[3]: quo Aβ
[15] *Aer.:* -u Aβ: -us *Pith.*   [16] *Wi.:* perdid- Aβ

---

[6] Having made the accusation he would not dare to dig up the money, neither could he get it from a genuinely poor man.

rich?[6] Am I lying just in order to live with two tortured slaves, if indeed they survive the torture, as I did in exile, as I did when I was escaping the tyrant, or if not so, then alone? If I am accusing my friend falsely, I can pay no heavier penalty: I lose whatever I claim. And what reason did I have for being angry with you? What harm did you ever do me so serious that I am not content with your torments?

I know that the other side has a somewhat similar point: what use will he have for the money? To begin with, this is not similar, because to a poor man anyway and the father of two children (something that exacerbates poverty) money hidden away secretly at least brings security. You may not acquire possessions, you may not buy slaves or live in a larger house, but at least you are safe against fortune; the money lets you be a poor man who does not have to worry. Add that you think about times long ahead.[7]

In fine,[8] you can at least see some sense in it, if you win; but why should *I* go to law? To get something from you? What do you have other than the deposit? I know, gentlemen, that I have lost this money. For even if you find him guilty, how am I going to put my hands on it? He will persist in his pretense—a man who did not yield even to torture. My whole reason for this suit is to defend my honor.[9]

But you now, find where I have hidden it. Don't you know? Search. These slaves did not leave me, they know all

---

[7] The reference is to the sons, who will enjoy the money later (Håkanson).   [8] *In summa*, introducing a final touch, as regularly in these texts; not "in sum."

[9] To show by the evidence of the slaves that he is telling the truth.

mihi irasci possunt si tormentis sine causa offeruntur. 'Non est tamen aequum comparari fidem tormentorum. Ex altera parte liberi et ingenui torti sunt, ex altera parte servi.'

15 Non facit status[17] pertinaciam, sed causa mentiendi. Ergo quomodo ego dico: 'perseverasti ut pecuniam lucrifaceres; spectasti sequentia tempora, spectasti lucrum', sic tu dic: servi mei quid spectaturi sunt, quid ex hoc consequemur?

16 Et vos quidem tyrannus (ut parcissime loquar) dimisit; tu arbitrio tuo torque. Quidquid passus es, quidquid adicere inveniendae veritatis gratia potes, adhibe. Dum spiritus erit, dum loqui poterunt, quaere [an negent][18]; et si perseveraverint, aude dicere homines in tormentis solere mentiri.

270

Rapta ex duabus geminis

Qui causa mortis fuerit, capite puniatur. Ex duabus geminis adulescens alteram rapuit. Ea se suspendit. Pater alteram eduxit ad magistratus et praecepit illi ut mortem raptoris optaret. Adulescens putavit eam esse quam rapuerat. Duci eum iussit magistratus. Postea compertum est quid accidisset. Accusatur pater quod causa mortis fuerit.

1

SERMO

Facilis et in promptu ratio est huic seni quod pertinet ad

17 *Gron.*: ista res Aβ
18 *SB¹*

---

10 Implying that the torture was not as severe as it might have been.

there is to know, they are liable to be angry with me if they are given up for torture for no reason. "Oh but the reliability of the tortures cannot fairly be compared. On one side free men, freeborn, were tortured, on the other slaves." Status does not make pertinacity, but a reason for lying does. So I say, "You held fast in order to snaffle the money; your motive was time to come, profit." Likewise you tell me: what motive will my slaves have, what will they get out of this? And the tyrant to say the least[10] let you go, whereas you—torture all you want. Bring to bear whatever you suffered, whatever you can add, for the sake of finding the truth. While there's breath, while they can speak, lay it on. And if they persist, dare to say that men under torture often lie.[11]

270

Raped girl, one of twins

Let him who is the cause of a death receive capital punishment. A young man raped a girl, one of twins. She hanged herself. The father brought the other before the magistrates and instructed her to opt for the rapist's death. The young man thought that she was the one he had raped. The magistrate ordered him to be executed. Later it came out what had happened. The father is accused of having been the cause of a death.

DISCUSSION

This old man has an easy and obvious case so far as emotion

---

11 That would be to admit that he and his children may have lied.

adfectum [paenitentiae],[1] quod pertinet ad aequitatem.
Nisi tamen etiam iure defenditur, verendum erit ne illum
flentes[2] iudices damnent. Diligenter ergo pugnare circa le-
2 gem debebimus. Et sane asperiores in controversia partes
fortasse recte declamatores relinquant: divisio paene hoc
proprium habet, ostendere ossa et nervos controversiae,
et, secundum[3] meum quidem iudicium, idem praestare
declamatio debet. Nam sine his de quibus locutus sum
caro ipsa per se quid sit intellegitis. Sed in declamatione
vestienda sunt haec, ut ex illis ‹externis decorem, ex his›[4]
3 interioribus vires habeat.[5] Finiamus ergo necesse est quid
sit causa mortis. Tota enim lis et omne discrimen controversiae in hoc positum est. Nam si ad finitionem partis adversae accedimus, ut causa mortis sit qui attulerit causam
alicui moriendi, per quem factum sit ut aliquis moreretur,
nullo modo defendere nos possumus. Neque enim dubita-
bitur quin per hunc factum sit ut ille moreretur, qui filiam
ad magistratum produxit,[6] qui praecepit ut mortem rapto-
4 ris optaret. Nos ergo causam id esse mortis dicemus quod
nullis extra accidentibus causis mortem homini adferat,
quod solum mortem homini attulerit. Deinde dicemus, si
accedendum sit finitioni partis adversae, frequenter etiam
5 honestissima in hanc calumniam cadere posse. Subiunge-
mus quaestionem an possit quisquam accusari quod causa
mortis fuerit in eo qui iure sit occisus. Sequitur quaestio an

---

[1] *Ri.*
[2] *SB*[1], *Hå.*[2], *Wi* (*coni.*): -em Aβ
[3] et s. *Pith.*: s. et Aβ
[4] *SB*[3]
[5] *Leo*: -ant Aβ
[6] *Sch.*: perd- Aβ

and equity are concerned. But unless he is also defended on legal grounds, there will be a risk that the jury may convict him with tears in their eyes. So we shall need to put up a strenuous fight on the legal issue. And to be sure declaimers may leave aside the tougher points in this controversy, perhaps rightly; but it is almost the specialty of division to show the bones and sinews of the controversy, and in my judgment at least, declamation should provide the same. For without what I have spoken of, you perceive what the flesh amounts to by itself. But in a declamation these[1] have to be clothed, so that it has ⟨grace⟩ from the ⟨external items⟩ and strength ⟨from these⟩ internal ones. So we must define what is a cause of death. For the whole suit and the entire crux of the controversy is located in this. For if we assent to the definition of the other side, that one who has brought to another a cause of dying, one through whose act somebody has died, is a cause of a death, there is no way we can defend ourselves. For it will not be doubted that it was our man's action that brought about the other's death: he brought his daughter before the magistrate, he told her to opt for the death of the rapist. So *we* shall say that a cause of a death is what brings death to a human being without any additional extraneous causes, what by itself brings death to a human being. Then we shall say that if the other side's definition were to be accepted, even perfectly proper actions would often fall under this false charge. We shall subjoin the question whether anyone can be accused of having been cause of a death in the case of one who has been put to death legally. Follows the ques-

---

[1] The bones and sinews.

hic iure sit occisus. Post haec licebit nobis dicere illa quae
sola dicuntur.

6 DECLAMATIO

'Qui causa mortis fuerit, capite puniatur.' Satis ostendit
ipsa poena eum demum teneri hac lege qui idem commiserit quod si occidisset. Neque enim gravius quicquam
adversus eum qui sua manu interfecerit constituere potuit
legum lator quam adversus eum qui causam praestitisset.
Ergo [et][7] similitudine poenae etiam crimen par exigere
7 debetis. Hoc quo pertinet? Ne existimetis veram illam esse
finitionem qua pars diversa complectitur, ut per quem-
cumque steterit uti homo occidatur, is continuo causa
mortis fuisse videatur. Alioqui ista ratione et ille qui nocentem accusavit causa mortis fuit, et ille qui testimonium in
reum dixit, etiamsi verum id fuit, causa tamen mortis haberi potest, et ille qui adulteros marito prodidit [causa
mortis haberi potest][8] et ille qui sceleratum produxit in
8 publicum. Cur igitur hi accusari ista lege non possunt?
Quoniam non per ipsos tantum stetit, quoniam iure perie-
9 runt ii quibus mors allata est. Sed hanc partem reserve-
mus. Interim videamus quid sit causa mortis. Nos id dicimus causam esse mortis quod homini mortem attulerit
solum, quod[9] nullis extra accidentibus causis noxium fuerit, quo homo periturus fuerit etiamsi nil ipse fecisset.
10 Id quod dicimus tale est? Intuendae sunt res ipsae quae

[7] *Ri.*
[8] *SB*[2]
[9] *Ri.*: q. s. ACD: quod B

[2] By declaimers (s.2 init.).

tion whether this person was put to death legally. After that
we shall be free to say those things that are the only things
said.[2]

"Let him who has been the cause of a death receive capital
punishment." The punishment itself is enough to show
that this law applies only to a person who has committed
the same thing as if he had killed. For the lawgiver could
not have laid down a harsher penalty against one who had
slaughtered with his own hand than he did against one
who had supplied a cause. So from the similarity of the
punishment you should require a similar crime also. To
what purpose is this? So that you don't think the definition
with which the other side embraces the matter to be true,
namely that whoever has brought about the killing of a
human being is automatically regarded as the cause of a
death. Otherwise by your argument the accuser of a guilty
man was the cause of his death, and one who gave evidence
against a defendant, even though it was the truth, can none
the less be considered the cause of his death, and one
who has revealed adulterers to a husband, and one who
has brought a criminal into public view. Why then cannot
these be accused under this law? Because they themselves
were not the sole cause, since those who were put to death
perished legally. But let us keep this part till later. Meanwhile, let us see what a cause of death is. We say that a
cause of a death is what has brought death to a human being by itself, what has brought harm without any additional
extraneous causes, something by which a human being
would have perished even if he himself had done nothing.

Is what we are talking about such? The items them-

in crimen deducuntur. Produxi filiam ad magistratum: quid hoc ad inferendam per se pertinet mortem? Praecepi ut mortem optaret. Detrahe quod ille raptor est, detrahe quod [et][10] lex raptorem interfici iubet, detrahe quod filia mortem raptoris optavit: ipsum quod ego feci mortem homini adferre non potuit. Non possum ergo videri causa

11 mortis homini fuisse. Quid feci? Quod innoxium erat si nihil ille fecisset. Fingite enim haec accidere potuisse: produxi filiam, optare mortem iussi; ignoret sane quae sit ad magistratus educta. Si potest dicere: 'nihil tale admisi', nihil nocuerint ea quae ego feci. Quid ergo illi causa mortis

12 fuit? Quod rapuit, quod lex mortem constituit. Et hoc paene adversariorum confessione manifestum est: non agunt cum ea quae optavit. Neque ego sum tam durus ac demens ut pro salute mea filiam[11] periculo meo opponam; sed uti mihi hoc argumento licet, quoniam et illa tuta est. Eadem enim quae dicuntur a me ab illa dicerentur: 'optavi mortem; num tamen hoc nocuisset si adversus alium fecis-

13 sem?' Quemlibet apprehendi ex turba circumstantium credite; huius mortem optavit: num occidetur? Non, ut opinor. Non ergo ipsa optio[12] in causa mortis est, sed id propter quod optio valet. Tuta est hac defensione filia mea,

14 et (ut dixi) sententia quoque accusatorum secura. Quid mihi accedit[13] supra haec? Unum adhuc patrocinium: non enim hoc tantum dico: 'si ille non rapuisset, causa mortis non fuissem', sed illud etiam: 'si filia mihi non paruisset, causa mortis non fuissem.'

10 *Wi.*   11 mea f. *SB*[1]: f. meam Aβ
12 *Aer.*: opinio Aβ 13 *Sch.*: accidit Aβ

---

3 Add "or married to the victim"?

selves on which the charge is based must be examined. I brought my daughter before the magistrate. What does this by itself have to do with bringing death? I told her to opt for death. Take away the fact that he was a rapist, that the law requires a rapist to be killed,[3] that the girl opted for death: what I did in itself could not bring death to a human being. What did I do? Something harmless, if he had done nothing. For imagine that the following could have happened: I have brought my daughter forward, I have commanded her to opt for death; let us assume he does not know who the girl brought before the magistrate really is: if he can say "I did no such thing," what I did will have done no hurt. So what was the cause of death for him? That he committed rape, that the law lays down death. And this is clear almost by the admission of my opponents: they are not going to law with the girl who opted. Not that I am so cruel and crazy as to put my daughter in my danger to save myself, but I may use this argument since she too is safe. For the same things that are said by me would be said by her: "I opted for death; but would this have hurt if I had done it against anyone else?" Imagine that somebody in the crowd of bystanders is arrested; she opts for his death: will he be killed? I don't think so. So the option itself is not a cause of death, but that on account of which the option has force. My daughter is safe with this defense and by the prosecution's own admission, as I have said, secure. What additional point do I have besides all this? One further plea: not only do I say, "If he had not committed rape, I would not have been a cause of death," but this too: "If my daughter had not obeyed me, I would not have been a cause of death."

15   Haec, si non iure occisus esset, si errore tantum perisset, dicerem; nunc illud utique inter me et partem diver-
sam conveniat necesse est, non posse eum accusari qui
[unus vel][14] attulerit mortem nocenti si erit unus ex iis de
quibus paulo ante loquebamur, vel accusator vel testis vel
16 iudex vel index. Videamus igitur an iure raptor sit occisus,
et sic agamus tamquam adhuc vivat, tamquam adhuc de eo
quaeratur, an occidi raptorem oporteat. Non educo alteram filiam ad magistratus, nihil ut optet praecipio. Filia
mea vitiata est, ob hoc perît. Dico raptorem occidi opor-
17 tere. Nec statim nitor illa aequitate, ut dicam quam[15] iustum sit eum qui intulerit iniuriam interfici cum perierit illa
quae accepit; de iure ipso loquor. Lege comprehensum est
18 ut rapta raptoris mortem vel nuptias optet. Ut opinor, una
causa legis huius fuit ut de raptore secundum voluntatem
raptae constitueretur. Alioqui multa accidere possunt
propter quae rapta non optet. Fingamus vitiatam esse eam
quae loqui non possit: num impune iniuriam fecerit quoniam miserae fecit? Nutum nempe eius aut vultum aut
aliquod signum animi intueri oporteret. 'At id non est optio, nec satis verba legis explebuntur.' Occideretur tamen
19 raptor si id velle raptam intellegeremus. Fingamus valetudinem consecutam raptae, ut educi ad magistratus non
posset. Deerit aliquid legi, vindicari tamen eam tanto magis oportet quod credibile erit etiam ipsam valetudinem ex
20 iniuria natam. Quod si non utique (ut ex his manifestum

---

[14] Wi. (vel *del. Sch.*)   [15] *Ri.*: quod Aβ

---

[4] S.7.

[5] *Alioqui* apparently = "apart from what actually happened."

All this I should have said if he had not been put to death legally, if he had perished only by mistake. As it is, it must necessarily be agreed between me and the other side that no one bringing death to a guilty man can be accused if he is one of those of whom I was speaking a little while ago:[4] accuser or witness or juror or informer. So let us see whether the rapist was put to death legally; and let us pretend that he is still alive, that we are still asking a question about him: ought a rapist to be put to death? I do not bring my other daughter before the magistrates, I do not tell her what to choose. My daughter was violated, for that reason she perished. I say that the rapist should be put to death. And I am not yet relying on equity, so as to say how just it is that he who did the injury should be killed since she who received it has perished: I am speaking about the law itself. It is included in the law that a raped woman opt for the death of the rapist or marriage. As I suppose, the only object of this law was that a decision about the rapist be made according to the wish of the victim. Anyway,[5] many things may happen to prevent the victim from opting. Let us imagine that a woman who is unable to speak is violated: will he have done an injury with impunity because he has done it to an unfortunate? I suppose one should look at her nod or expression or some other sign of her mind. "But that is not option, the words of the law will not be sufficiently implemented." All the same, the rapist would be put to death if we understood that this was the victim's wish. Let us imagine that the victim fell ill so that she could not be brought before the magistrates. The law will not be fully satisfied, but she ought to be avenged all the more because it will be credible that this very illness arose from the injury. But if, as is clear from all this, it is not absolutely re-

223

est) vocem raptae exigi oportet sed solam voluntatem, videamus iam[16] an quae rapta est mori raptorem voluerit. Plusne vobis videretur, iudices, si apud magistratum locuta esset quam quod ad magistratum venire non ausa est, quod oculos suos ostendere circumstantibus, ostendere luci non
21 potuit, ipsa[17] sua manu vitam misera finivit[18]? Da vires: occidet prius quae propter hanc iniuriam perit. Dubium est scilicet quid factura fuerit si vixisset? Raptorem ergo
22 perire oportuit. Iam fortiter dico: quid interest quo modo perierit? Cur ergo, si hoc modo poterat occidi, falso alteram filiam eduxi? <Si>[19] dicerem: 'luctus confuderat', si dicerem[20]: 'dolor suadebat', ignosceretis tamen; nunc mihi necessarium consilium praesens iniuria dedit. Duas filias habueram, rapta erat altera, perierat. Munienda domus fuit, et voce potissimum alterius virginis soror vindicanda, ne quis dubitaret quid factura esset <in>[21] iniuria sua.
23   Partis quidem adversae impudentiam mirari satis non possum. Causam mortis esse existimant eum propter quem <quis>[22] perierit, cum eum cui causa mortis fuerit occidi oportere constet, et raptorem perisse indignantur, cum certum sit filiam meam propter raptorem perisse. [Hoc isti causam mortis vocant.][23] Cur ergo occisum vindicari oportet quem certum esset, si viveret, occidi opor-
24 tere? Et haec omnia quae pro causa mea dixi, quibus collegi me non esse obligatum huic legi, non temporis causa nec

---

16 *Ro.*: tamen Aβ: autem D   17 CD: ipsi AB
18 *Ri., auct. Sch.*: pun- A²CD: puniunt A¹B
19 *Delrio*   20 *Sch., Gron.*: liceret Aβ
21 *Aer.*   22 *Ri.*   23 *del. SB³, auct. Wi.*

---

6 By assuming that this was what the dead girl wished.

quired that an utterance be elicited from the victim but
only her wish, let us see now whether the raped girl wished
her rapist to die. Would you think it of more weight, gentlemen, that she had spoken before a magistrate than the
fact that she did not have the courage to come before a
magistrate, that she could not show her eyes to bystanders
or to the light of day, that the unfortunate girl ended her
life by her own hand? Give her the strength: she will kill
before she perishes on account of this injury. Is there any
doubt, I ask you, what she would have done if she had
lived? So it was right that the rapist perish. I say now
boldly: what does it matter how he perished? So if he could
be killed this way,[6] why did I falsely bring out my other
daughter? <If> I were to say that my mourning had confused me or that my grief induced me, you would forgive
me even so. As it is, present injury gave me necessary
counsel. I had had two daughters; one of them was raped,
she had perished. My house needed protection, and it was
right that the other girl's voice should avenge her sister, so
that nobody have any doubt what she could have done
<about> her own injury.

I cannot wonder enough at the impudence of the other
side. They think the cause of death to be the person because of whom <somebody> has perished, although it is
agreed that the person for whom he was a cause of death
was rightfully killed; and they are indignant that the rapist
has perished, although it is certain that my daughter perished on account of the rapist. [This they call cause of his
death.] Why then ought the person killed to be avenged
when it is certain that, if he were alive, he ought to be
killed? And that all that that I have said in my defense,
showing that I was not liable under this law, is not con-

praesentis periculi fingere me vel ex eo manifestum est,
quod raptorem aliter occidi: nam si id esset causa mortis
quod isti videri volunt, hac lege me ulcisci potuissem.

25   Iamdiu me, iudices, circa iura morari scio longeque re-
cessisse a paternis adfectibus. Ergo ego in ultionem filiae
meae nihil feci nisi quod licuit? Adii magistratus, fortiorem puellae vocem imperavi, quia tutum erat? Ego vero
totos in medium profero adfectus: nec mihi in cogitatione
tum lex fuit, nec iura respexi, sed quae proxima vindi-
candae infelicis filiae via occurrit, hac[24] intendi, hanc secu-
26   tus sum. Bene cessit quod et licuit. Age, si non habuissem
quam educerem ad magistratus, cuius vice me ulciscerer,
non in publico, non in foro his me senilibus manibus vindi-
cassem? Tu, Fortuna, facies quod occurrerit; iam non po-
27   tes efficere ut paeniteat. Filiam perdidi: scio hoc minimum
esse malorum meorum. Sunt qui gravissimum existimant
unicos perdere, et quotiens non habeant ad quod solacium
respiciant calamitatis,[25] videtur sine medicina dolor. Hoc
gravius est, iudices, perdere alteram ex geminis. Cotidie
mihi occurrit imago funeris mei. Quo magis placet filiae
verecundia, quo magis probitas, hoc validius subeunt cogi-
28   tationes: talem miser perdidi. Si tamen hoc vulnus intulis-
set Fortuna, si casus, communi ‹me›[26] mortalitatis condicione solarer. Nunc miser filiam quo modo perdidi? Ante
omnia nec virginem nec nuptam. Qualis ego infelix vultus

---

[24] *SB*[1]: hanc A*β*   [25] -ates *Ro.*
[26] *Wi.* (*post* solarer *habet β*)

---

[7] To opt for death.   [8] *Quotiens* seems to be arbitrarily
used instead of *quia* or *quatenus*. For another odd use see 262.2
fin.   [9] By the rapist.

cocted by me for the occasion, because of my present danger, is clear from the very fact that I killed the rapist in
another way; for if cause of death meant what they wish it
to be thought to mean, I could have avenged myself by this
law.

I know, gentlemen, that I have been dwelling all this
while on legalities and have gone back a long way from my
feelings as a father. So did I do nothing but what was legal
to avenge my daughter? Did I go to the magistrates, did I
command the girl to say the bolder thing[7] because it was
safe? No, I will come out with all my feelings: at that point
the law was not in my thoughts, I had no regard for legalities, but went by the nearest way to avenge my unhappy
daughter that offered and followed it. It was lucky that it
was my right. Come, if I had not had someone to bring before the magistrates by whose substitution I could avenge
myself, should I not have done so in public, in the Forum,
with these aged hands? Fortune, you will do what comes;
you cannot now make me sorry. I lost a daughter. I know
that this is the least of my misfortunes. Some hold that to
lose only sons is the worst, and since[8] they can look to no
solace of their calamity, their grief seems to have no medicine. But this is worse, gentlemen, to lose one of twin
daughters. Every day the image of my bereavement comes
before me. The more my daughter's modesty and goodness
please me, the more powerfully the thoughts come upon
me: alas, such was she I lost. But if Fortune had brought
this stroke upon me, or chance, I should console <myself>
with the common condition of humanity. As it is, how, alas,
did I lose my daughter? To begin with, she was neither virgin nor married. Wretch that I am, how bruised and torn[9]

caesos alioqui laceratosque ac laqueo tumentes pater vidi!
Qui me motus,[27] qui intus aestus agitant! Quae fuit vere-
29 cundia illa quae ultionem expectare non potuit! Horret
animus recordari, refugium cogitationes. Misera quid passa est! Nec sane in causa raptus amor fuit, non propositum
matrimonii, non cupiditas nuptiarum. Nihil horum cogitavit qui nescît quam rapuisset.

271

Ter fortis contra tertium fortem

Pauper et dives inimici erant; pauperi unus filius, diviti
tres. Fortiter pugnaverunt pauperis filius et unus ex divitis
filiis. E lege fortes armis contenderunt. Occisus est divitis
filius. Iterum alter divitis filius cum filio pauperis fortiter
fecit et de praemio dimicans occisus est. Tertio bello is
quoque[1] qui residuus erat divitis filius fortiter fecit, et
idem ille pauperis filius. Dives prohibet filium pugnare.
Non parentem abdicat.

1 SERMO

Prima illa communis omnibus fere ex abdicatione penden-
tibus controversiis quaestio, an utique necesse sit facere
filio quidquid pater iusserit: in his tamen controversiis
2 quibus de praesenti agitur, non de praeterito. Duo enim
genera scitis esse abdicationum: aut obicitur quare fecerit
filius aliquid aut obicitur quare non faciat. Asperius est

[27] *Hå*.[2]: metus Aβ   [1] *Ro*.: b. q. is Aβ: q. b. is D

---

[1] Disobedience in the past might still raise the same question,
if it were ground for disownment.

anyway, and swollen by the noose did I see her face, I, her father! What emotions, what inner surgings, agitate me! How ashamed she was! She could not wait for her vengeance! My mind shudders to remember, my thoughts recoil. Poor girl, how she suffered! To be sure, love did not cause the rape, nor intention of matrimony, nor desire for marriage: the man who did not know whom he had raped had no thought of these.

271

Three times a hero against third hero

A poor man and a rich man were enemies. The poor man's son became a hero as did one of the rich man's sons. Under the law the heroes contended in arms. The rich man's son was killed. Again, another son of the rich man became a hero, as did the poor man's son, and was killed fighting about the reward. In a third war the rich man's remaining son also became a hero, as did the same son of the poor man. The rich man forbids his son to fight. When he disobeys, he disowns him.

DISCUSSION

The first question is common to pretty well all controversies dependent on a disowning: whether a son must in all circumstances do what his father orders him—that is in those controversies that are about the present, not the past.[1] For you know that there are two kinds of disownings: either the complaint is about why he did something or it's about why he is not doing something. The harsher sort of

illud genus abdicationum, in quo iam praeterît crimen nec
emendationem recipit. In hoc lenius versantur patres et
filii paulo liberius, in quo est emendationi locus.

3   DECLAMATIO

Ergo non omnia necesse est facere liberis quaecumque
patres imperant. Multa sunt quae fieri non possunt; et ideo
iudicium constitutum est adversus abdicantes quoniam recipiebat natura ut etiam patres aliquando aut errarent aut
iniuste imperarent.

4   SERMO[2]

Illis argumentis adiuvari solet haec quaestio:

5   [DECLAMATIO][3]

Si imperes filio ut ‹iudex›[4] sententiam dicat contra quam
existimat, si testimonium iubeas dici eius rei quam ignorat,
si sententiam in senatu *[5] Haec magis civilia et in medio
posita. ‹Illa› si[6] ex nostra libertate argumenta repetenda
sunt, si Capitolium me incendere iubeas, arcem occupare,
licet dicere: haec sunt quae fieri non oportet.

6   [SERMO][7]

Secundo loco quaerimus an abdicari possit[8] propter id
quod facere vult e lege.

7   DECLAMATIO

Postea videbimus ius istud utrum tale sit ut permittat mihi
pugnare an tale ut iubeat etiam. Interim, etsi utor mea

---

[2] *om.* β   [3] A: sermo β: *del.* SB³   [4] *Leo*
[5] *lac. ind.* SB³, contra ipsius iudicium *vel sim. add. coni.* SB²
[6] ‹illa› si SB²: illa *coni.* Wi.   [7] SB³
[8] *Ri.:* -set Aβ

disownings is that in which the offence is already past and
does not admit of amendment. In the kind where there is a
possibility of amendment fathers take a gentler line and
sons a little more free-spoken one.

DECLAMATION[2]

So children are not bound to do everything their father orders. There are many things that cannot be done; and judicial proceedings against disowners were constituted just
because nature allowed that even fathers sometimes either
erred or ordered unjustly.

DISCUSSION

This question can be supported by the following arguments: if you were to order your son ⟨as a juror⟩ to give a
verdict contrary to his opinion or command that he bear
witness about something of which he is ignorant or give his
opinion in the senate ⟨contrary to his own judgment⟩.
These examples are more from public life, there for the
taking. If ⟨those others⟩ derived from our freedom are to
be recalled,[3] if you were to order me to set fire to the
Capitol, seize the castle, it is permissible to say: these are
things that ought not to be done.

In the second place we ask whether he can be disowned
for something he can do legally.

DECLAMATION

We shall see later on whether that law is such that it allows
me to fight or such that it even orders me. Meanwhile,

---

2 The first three declamations are excerpts.

3 See SB[2]; but I now think the text can stand (with *illa*) without
rewriting.

potestate, non debeo tamen incidere in poenam huius of-
fensionis.

8

SERMO

Tertio loco quaerimus illud, an pugnare viris fortibus
etiam necesse sit. Haec quoque quaestio in multis controversiis tractata est. Secundum nos erit scriptum legis.

9

DECLAMATIO

'Si plures fortiter fecerint, de praemio armis contendant.'
Iubemur pugnare; cogimur, etiam si ego noluero. Hoc
unum acturi sumus, ut me adversarius timere putet. 'At
enim de praemio iubet contendere; et si praemium remittitur, non est necessaria pugna.' At id ipsum lex complexa
est, ne praemium remittatur, cum de praemio contendere
armis iubet.

10

SERMO

Post haec dicemus domui[9] etiam honestam esse hanc
contentionem; adiuvabimus propositionem nostram ipsius
patris iudicio.

11

DECLAMATIO

Primo filio pugnare permisisti. Iterum, quamvis experimentum triste, quod nunc maxime mihi opponis, iam
haberes, pugnare tamen permisisti. Quid est cur de me
pessime sentias?

12   Omnis abdicationis causa ex timore tuo pendet. Et
est quidem istud inconsultum et sibi repugnans, abdicari
filium indulgentia patris et aliquem carere liberis orbitatis
metu. Verum hanc quoque detrahere tibi sollicitudinem
volo.

[9] *Sch.*: domi Aβ

232

even if I am using my own discretion, I ought not to incur the punishment of this offence.

DISCUSSION

The third question we ask is whether it is actually necessary for heroes to fight. This question also has been handled in many controversies. The letter of the law will be in our favor.

DECLAMATION

"If more than one become heroes, let them contend in arms for the reward." We are ordered to fight, we are compelled, even if I don't want to. All we shall be doing is to make my adversary think I am afraid. "But it orders you to contend for the reward, and if the reward is waived, no fight is necessary." Ah, but the law itself has covered that very point, that the reward *not* be waived, when it orders us to contend in arms for the reward.

DISCUSSION

After this we shall say that this fight is actually to our credit; we shall support our proposition by the judgment of our father himself.

DECLAMATION

The first time you allowed your son to fight. A second time, although you already had a sad experience (which you urge against me at this moment), you nonetheless gave permission to fight. Why do you think so poorly of me?

The whole reason for your disowning depends on your fear. And it is hasty and self-contradictory that a son be disowned because his father loves him and that anyone should be without children out of fear of bereavement. But I want to relieve you of this anxiety too.

⟦Erat illud quod a bono fratre[10] et a pio dici posset: etiamsi periculosum sit, tanti est mihi. Non tam me ducit gloria militaris, nec fama victoriae: vindicandi mihi fratres

13 sunt. An ego, qui paulo ante arma (ignoscat patria, ignoscant leges!) minore sacramento tuli et contra hostes sine respectu mei sanguinisque pugnavi, ubi mihi vindicandi sunt fratres, et duo fratres, non pugnabo? Non vel discrimen vitae subibo?⟧[11]

14 Ego accederem tuo consilio si timerem. Sed multa sunt quae me faciant fortiorem. Ante omnia adversarius iam fatigatus est: cogita quotiens pugnaverit. Non dico quid fecerint hostes: non †inde†[12] ceciderunt fratres mei. Fortiorem me faciet melior conscientia, fortiorem faciet et causa pugnae. Ille pro praemio pugnaturus est, quod iam bis ac-

15 cepit; ego pugnaturus sum pro fratribus, pro pietate. Fortiorem me faciet et Fortuna: solet fatigari, solet, posteaquam nimium indulsit, in fine deficere. Facit me fortiorem etiam usus quidam[13]: pugnantem illum saepius vidi. Scio quid maximum fratrem meum fefellerit, quomodo is qui secundo loco pugnabat deceptus sit.

16 Illud autem plus quam verecundum et erubescendum nobis est: pauper pugnare filium suum non vetat. Quantum tu adicis illi animi quod times! Sed forsitan et incautiorem illum faciat haec ipsa fiducia. Illud scio, favebit pugnanti mihi populus; scio futurum ut dii immortales

17 stent pro mea parte. Non solus mihi stare videbor: habebo

[10] *Hå*.²: pa- A*β*
[11] *ita secl. SB*³ *a Wi. monitus, fort. post* 15 *ponendum*
[12] timide *Hå*.², *alii alia*
[13] *Aer*.: -dem A*β*

⟦This is what could be said by a good and loving brother: Even if it be dangerous, it is worth it for me. I am not so much motivated by military glory or the fame of victory: I have to avenge my brothers. Or shall I, who a little while ago bore arms under a lesser[4] oath (my country and the laws forgive me!) and fought against the enemy without regard for myself and my blood, now when I have brothers to avenge, and two brothers—shall I not fight? Shall I not even risk my life?⟧

I should follow your counsel if I were afraid. But there are many things to make me braver. To begin with, my adversary is tired; think how often he has fought. I won't speak of what the enemy did: my brothers fell in no craven fashion.[5] My better conscience will make me braver, so will my reason for fighting. He will fight for the reward, which he has already received twice: I shall fight for my brothers, for the family. Fortune too will make me braver; she is apt to flag and fail at the finish after she has been overindulgent. Experience of a sort too makes me braver: I have often seen him fighting. I know what misled my eldest brother, how he that fought in the second place was taken in.

And what is more than shameful, something for us to blush for, is this: the poor man does not forbid his son to fight. How much extra courage do you give him by your fear! But perhaps this very confidence makes him more careless. One thing I know, the people will be on my side as I fight. I know that the immortal gods stand with me. I shall not feel that I stand alone; the spirits of my brothers will be

4 I.e. less compelling, cf. 255.5.
5 Translating *non timide*.

235

in commilitio fratrum meorum animas. Si quid est in animo praesagii, si quid in mente, ipsa spe praecipio[14] victoriam, neque aliunde haec pertinacia venit. Non precibus
18 tuis, non minis terreor. Alioqui quid agis abdicando me nisi
ut non pugnem incolumi rerum mearum statu? Cogitabo
de victoria, cogitabo de vindicta. Si vero cum hac me infamia dimittis, iam nunc dico: arma dimittam.

272

Orbata proditrix

Qui consilia publica enuntiaverit, capite puniatur. Ad colli-
gendum filii corpus nocte processit mater. Comprehensa
ab hostibus et torta indicavit auxilia venire; quibus oppressis de vinculis effugit et nuntiavit cuniculum agi. Oppressis
hostibus rea est quod consilia publica enuntiaverit. CD.

1
SERMO

Potentior[1] in hac causa controversia quam lis est. Lis enim
circa unum factum versatur. In qua illae sunt quaestiones:
an hoc enuntiare sit; an etiamsi hoc est enuntiare, quisquis
enuntiavit puniendus sit; an haec punienda quod enuntia-
2 verit. Cetera vero controversiae maiorem cumulum habent: occisum praesidium et oppressus hostis et filius ille
et hac causa egressa portas. Haec themata tractanda sunt

---

[14] *SB*[3]: conc- Aβ   [1] *SB*[2]: potior Aβ

---

[6] I.e. "I shall let my opponent kill me."   [1] "A *controversia* may consist entirely of a *lis*, the point(s) in dispute, but the
lis may be accompanied by other elements which are not disputed" (SB[2]), but which make a powerful impression on the jury.

my comrades. If there is any presage in my mind, in my thoughts, hope itself makes me anticipate victory, from no other source comes this pertinacity. I am not alarmed by your pleas or your threats. After all, what do you accomplish by disowning me except that I shall not fight as a citizen in good standing? I shall think of victory, I shall think of revenge. But if you send me away with this disgrace, I say it here and now: I shall drop my weapons.[6]

272

The bereaved traitress

Let him who gives away public counsels be capitally punished. A mother went out at night to gather up her son's body. Seized by the enemy and tortured, she told them that help was on its way. When this was crushed, she escaped from her bonds and reported that a tunnel was in progress. After the enemy has been crushed, she is accused of giving away public counsels. Speech in rebuttal.

DISCUSSION

In this case the controversy counts for more than the point at issue.[1] For the point at issue is about one act only. In this one the questions are as follows: is this "giving away"? Even if it is "giving away," should anybody who has "given away" be punished? Should this woman be punished because she has "given away"? The other elements in the controversy are more cumulative: the slaughter of the reinforcement, the crushing of the enemy, the son, the woman going outside the gates on his account. All these

omnia; sed curae habendum ut suo quidque loco tractetur.

3   DECLAMATIO

'Qui publica consilia enuntiaverit, capite puniatur.' Possum mirari, iudices, hac lege ream esse feminam; neque ⟨id⟩[2] ideo dico quoniam non etiam gravius puniendum[3] sit si mentem prodendae rei publicae, perdendae civitatis in hoc sexu deprehenderimus, sed publica consilia quomodo 4 in feminam ceciderint invenire non possum. Quam quidem ego postea adfectus necessitate merito defendam; interim defendere verbis legis volo.

Nam ut confiterer sic enuntiari consilia, satis poterat tamen vindictae in eam expensum videri per tormenta. Deinde nec consilia enuntiasse videtur, quae nobis rursus quid hostis ageret nuntiavit. Quid enim dicitur fecisse? Indicasse venire auxilia. Hoc neque nostrae civitatis est consilium neque ullius alterius iam tantum consilium. 5 Enuntiare vero aliud esse quam confiteri nemo adeo ignarus est loquendi ut nesciat. Enuntiatio voluntatem habet et animum non coactum, confessio expressam dolore multo necessitatem. Sed intellego non eam esse personam de qua loquimur ut satis sit eximere eam accusationi.

6   Volo ire per singula, cum tamen illud prius interrogavero vos, iudices, an eadem ira eademque poena dignos putetis eos quos Fortuna, quos vis, quos dolor coegerit confiteri aliquid et eos quos odium rei publicae, spes praedae, amor

---

[2] *Gron., auct. Pith.*   [3] *Ro.*: -da Aβ

---

[2] Not a *legal* argument.

[3] But an action.

[4] Mere exculpation is not enough. She needs pity and credit.

themes are to be dealt with, but care must be taken that
each is dealt with in its proper place.

"Let whoso gives away public counsels be capitally punished." I can marvel, gentlemen, that a defendant under
this law is a female; and I do not say ⟨so⟩ because an even
more severe punishment is not appropriate if we discover
in this sex a will to betray the commonwealth, to ruin
the community, but I cannot imagine how public counsels
came to the knowledge of a woman. I shall later defend
her with good cause on the plea of emotional constraint.
Meanwhile I want to defend her by the words of the law.

For even though I admitted that "counsels are given
away" in this fashion, sufficient punishment might seem to
have been meted out to her through the torture.[2] Next, a
woman who reported to us in turn what the enemy was up
to does not appear to have "given away counsels." For what
is she said to have done? Told them that help was on the
way. This is not a "counsel" of our community neither is it
any longer a counsel merely of any other.[3] But that "giving
away" is not the same as confessing, nobody is so linguisti-
cally uninformed as to be ignorant. "Giving away" implies
intention and a mind not coerced, confession is necessity
imposed by much pain. But I realize that the persona of
the woman of whom we speak is such that more is needed
than to free her of the charge.[4]

I want to go through the points one by one; but first let
me ask you, gentlemen, whether you think that they whom
Fortune, violence, pain have forced to confess something
deserve the same anger and the same punishment as those
whom hatred of the commonwealth, hope of plunder, or

hostis in hanc egerit proditionem. Quod si nullo modo
apud quemquam bonorum virorum potest videri simile,
iam et quemadmodum in hostes inciderit videbimus et
7 quanta necessitate confessa sit. Ac satis erat primum illud
dicere: quae filium in proelium misit, cuius partus et sanguis in proelio stetit, cuius filius, dum nihil carius habet patria, dum propulsare hostem vel virtute[4] sua vel sanguine
vel postremo corpore ipso morari studet, spiritum pro nobis in certamine amisit, ita profecto institutus, ita a matre
dimissus, hanc accusari aequum est, cuius[5] misereri satis
8 non possumus? Nocte egressa est. Quis hunc in matre
[quis][6] miratur adfectum tamquam novum? Ego vero plura confitebor, et quae forsitan plane admiratione [eius][7]
digna sint. Noctem illam tenebrasque non timuit, horri-
dam ipsius loci in quo pugnatum erat imaginem tulit. Haec
per sanguinem humanum et per fracta tela et per mixta
virorum equorumque corpora quaesivit filium suum, et,
ne in totum nulla sua culpa incidisse in hostes videatur,
9 planxit et deos invocavit. Neminem puto hactenus irasci
calamitatibus. Cetera iam imputari ipsi non possunt. Hostibus confessa est, nondum dico torta—illud satis est dicere: femina. Si mehercule primae tantum minae ac timor
ille exercitus qui modo feliciter pugnaverat confudisset
feminam orbam, stupentem malis, erat tamen res digna
10 venia: confessa est cum torqueretur. Ubi tantum robur
animi, ubi tam firmam solidamque mentem quae non do-

---

4 *SB*[1]: vel morte Aβ: virtute *Leo*
5 *Gron.*: cui AB: cum CD   6 *Ro.*   7 *del. coni. Wi.*

---

5 Recalling the Spartan mother who told her son to come back
from battle with his shield or upon it.

love of the enemy has driven into this betrayal. If there can be no manner of similarity here in the view of any decent man, we shall now see how she fell into the enemy's hands and under how great a compulsion she confessed. And it would have been enough to say this first: she sent her son into battle, her child and blood stood in battle, holding nothing dearer than his country, as he strove to repel the enemy by his courage or his blood, or finally to hold them up with his very body, lost his life fighting for us, so trained we may be sure, so taken leave of by his mother.[5] Is it fair that she be accused, a woman whom we cannot pity enough? She went out by night. Who wonders at this emotion in a mother, as though it was a novelty? But I will confess more, things worthy perhaps of outright admiration. She was not afraid of that night and darkness, she endured the horrid spectacle of the very battlefield. Through human blood and broken weapons and mingled bodies of men and horses she sought her son and, lest it seem that she fell into the enemy's hands through absolutely no fault of her own,[6] she wailed and called upon the gods. I think nobody so far is angry at her misfortunes. The rest cannot be laid to her account. She confessed to the enemies—I won't say under torture: enough to say, a woman. Upon my word, if at first the threats only, the fear of a recently victorious army, had confounded her, a woman bereaved and stupefied by her calamities, the thing would still have merited forgiveness: but she confessed under torture. Where will you find such strength of soul, so firm and solid a mind,

6 An ironic admission, see SB[2].

lore vincatur, non ignibus cedat, non verberibus ingemis-
cat? Hanc vero satis fortiter ac supra sexum suum fecisse
11 credo quod nihil dixit antequam torqueretur. In his tamen
necessitatibus, in his malis num demonstravit aditus quibus in urbem venire possent, num proposita nostra, num
occultam civitatis voluntatem patefecit? Cum torqueretur,
minata est.

12 'At oppressa sunt auxilia a sociis missa.' Si damna bello-
rum deflere hic, iudices, vacat, plura perdidimus; et acie in
illa[8] quae circa filium miserae huius iacet tot fortissimi
cives nostri ceciderunt. Si vero lex ista belli est, si nulla
umquam tam incruenta victoria contigit quae non haberet
aliquam tristitiae recordationem, pensavimus omnia ista
victoria †recuso†[9] ut possit videri secundis ominibus et
quadam providentia pro nobis deorum immortalium fac-
13 tum ut haec caperetur. Intrassent civitatem hostes; nobis
et somno sepultis et securis[10] ab omni cogitatione bello-
rum totus subito in visceribus ipsius urbis hostilis[11] appa-
ruisset exercitus, nec prius decessisset[12] quam incenderet,
opprimeret, diriperet.

14 Hic, si placet, feminae animum et in amorem patriae
adsumptas culpate vires. Discussit vincula illa; quae (ut
parcissime dicam) hostis imposuerat, femina, anus, torta
rupit. Quaeritis quo animo fecerit? Cogitate quid passura
15 fuerit deprehensa: torta est antequam offenderet. Iterum
ingressa nocturnum iter, non confusa tenebris, non pericu-

8 *SB3*: aciem illam A*β*   9 secuta *Ri.*
10 *Aer.*: -itate A*β*   11 *Gron.*: -tis A*β*
12 *SB3*: desi(i)sset A*β*

7 "By announcing the approach of help" (Wi.).

as not to be overcome by pain, not to yield to fire, not to groan under the lash? I believe that she behaved bravely enough and beyond her sex in that she said nothing before she was tortured. Yet in these constraints, in these distresses, did she show the approaches by which they could get into the city, did she lay open our plans, the hidden intentions of the community? Under torture she threatened.[7]

"But the help sent by our allies was crushed." If time serves here to bewail our losses in the war, gentlemen, we have lost more than that; so many of our bravest citizens also fell in the ranks that lie around that unfortunate woman's son. But if that is the law of war and no victory was ever so bloodless but that it held some recollection of sadness, we have balanced all that with the victory that followed,[8] so that her capture may seem to have occurred under favorable omens and a providence of the immortal gods on our behalf. The enemy would have got inside the community; the whole hostile army would have suddenly appeared in the vitals of the city itself as we slept deep, free of any thought of wars, and would not have left before they had burned and overturned and plundered.

Here, if you will, find fault with the woman's courage and the strength she put into her love of country. She shook off her bonds; the bonds that the enemy had laid upon her (to use the mildest of words), she broke them, a woman, an old woman, tortured. Do you ask how courageously? Consider what she would have suffered had she been caught—she was tortured before she did anything to annoy them. Again she embarked on the nighttime jour-

8 Translating *secuta*.

lo, vicit cursu aetatem, sexum, infirmitatem. Secuti cives quidquid dixerat, quidquid fecerat mater. Salus ergo civitatis et victoria qua nunc gaudemus huic debentur. Hoc est enuntiare?

273

Debitor adulter

Maritus deprehensi adulteri bona possideat. Adversus sponsorem sit actio quae adversus debitorem. Quod debitor non solverit, sponsor solvat. Quidam debitorem suum in adulterio deprehendit. Bona omnia ex lege occupavit. Petit debitum ab sponsore. Ille CD.

1   SERMO

Priusquam venimus ad causam, praeparare debebimus animum iudicis pro ipsa persona sponsoris.

2   DECLAMATIO

Petitur a nobis pecunia quam non accepimus, non consumpsimus, non in ullum rerum nostrarum usum convertimus. Etiam cum istud periculum est sponsoris, miserabile est: bonitate labitur, humanitate conturbat. Hoc quo pertinet? Non ut extorqueam vobis, iudices, religionem, sed ut intellegatis, quod profecto cognoscitis, non esse exigendum a sponsore creditum nisi iure summo.

3   De quo priusquam loquor, etiamnum ea quae humanitatis et consuetudinis gratia dici solent non omitto. Debitorem appellasti? Cum ipso cui dederas pecuniam egisti?

---

9 She will have led them to the tunnel.

ney; the darkness, the danger did not confuse her. By her courage she triumphed over age, sex, infirmity. Her countrymen followed whatever the mother said, whatever she did.[9] So the survival of the community, the victory in which we now rejoice, are due to her. Is this "giving away"?

273

Debtor adulterer

Let the husband take possession of the goods of a caught adulterer. Let action which lies against a debtor lie against a sponsor. What the debtor does not pay, let the sponsor pay. A man caught his debtor in adultery. He seized all his property under the law. He claims the debt from the sponsor. The sponsor rebuts.

DISCUSSION

Before we come to the case, we shall need to prepare the judge's mind in favor of the actual persona of the sponsor.

DECLAMATION

Money is claimed from us which we did not receive, did not spend, did not convert into any use pertaining to our affairs. Even when this is the risk a sponsor takes, it deserves pity; kindness is his undoing, humanity bankrupts him. Why do I say so? Not, gentlemen, to twist your oath away from you, but so that you realize, what of course you know, that a loan should not be exacted from a sponsor without the most compelling legal right.

Before I speak of that, once again I shall not omit what is usually said for the sake of humanity and custom. Did you call upon the debtor? Did you broach it with the man

Non enim aliter salvo pudore ad sponsorem venit creditor
4 quam si recipere a debitore non possit. Inhumane exigis,
iniuste petis. Pecuniam quam credideras recepisti; nihil
mea interest qua via. Quidquid est istud quod a te ad debitorem tuum pervenit, penes te est. Sponsor porro in hoc
accipitur, ne creditor in damno sit. Vis scire quam sponsorem appellare non possis? Debitorem appellare non potes.
5 Et quoniam confitendum est eandem esse causam meam
quam debitoris, nec tu aliud videri vis, volo sic agere tamquam petas a debitore, semota illa ratione, quod honestior
persona sponsoris est, detracto eo quod debitor adulter
6 est, quod deprehensus est, quod punitus est. Fingamus
ergo petere te a debitore cuius nos sponsores sumus. Respondere pro debitore tuo volo. 'Recepisti omnia; quaecumque possedi ad te transierunt. In his quae possedi erat
debitum tuum. Totum habes; immo plus habes.'
7   Adversum haec quid respondes? 'Lege mihi bona debitoris tradita sunt, quoniam eum in adulterio deprehendi.'
Non facimus legi isti[1] controversiam. Quid tamen continet? Ut ad te bona debitoris pertineant. Bona porro quae
sunt? Ut opinor, ea quae detractis alienis deprehensi[2] sunt.
8 Finge alium creditorem fuisse eius quem tu deprehendisti. Num dubium est quin, quamvis ad te bona pertinerent
adulteri, recepturus tamen suum creditor fuerit? Ponamus
nunc[3] debitorem sine sponsore. Rationem, ut opinor, de-
posceres[4]: detracto aere alieno omni, detractis oneribus
bonorum, quod residuum ex patrimonio fuisset, id tibi lex

---

[1] *Fr.*: istam Aβ   [2] *Fornerius*: -sa Aβ
[3] *Ri.*: enim n. A: enim β   [4] *coni. Wi.*: deponeres Aβ

---

[1] In adultery. See crit. note and cf. *huic deprehenso* in s.9.

to whom you had given the money? For in decency a creditor does not come to a sponsor except if he cannot recover from the debtor. Your exaction is inhuman, your claim is unjust. You have recovered the money you loaned; how is not my concern. Whatever it was that came from you to your debtor, you have it. A sponsor, moreover, is accepted so that the creditor shall not be out of pocket. Would you like to know how impossible it is for you to call upon the sponsor? You can't call upon the debtor. And since it must be admitted that my case is the same as the debtor's and you do not wish it to appear otherwise, I want to deal with you as though you were claiming from the debtor, never mind that the sponsor's persona is more respectable, leaving aside that the debtor is an adulterer, that he has been caught and punished. Let us imagine then that you are claiming from the debtor whose sponsor I am. I want to reply on behalf of your debtor: "You have recovered everything. All that I possessed was transferred to you. Among my possessions was what was owed you. You have it all; or rather, more than all."

What is your answer to this? "The debtor's property was handed over to me by law because I caught him in adultery." We are not challenging that law. But what is its content? That the debtor's property belongs to you. And what property is that? As I suppose, the property of the person caught[1] after subtracting what belongs to other people. Suppose the person you caught had another creditor: is there any doubt that the creditor would have recovered his money, although the adulterer's money belonged to you? Let us now suppose the debtor without any sponsor: I suppose you would ask for an accounting: after all debt had been deducted, all burdens on the estate, the law would

concederet. Quem igitur calculum cum alio posuisti, po-
nas necesse est tecum. Nam patrimonii in alium transituri
ea ratio est, ut primum credito satisfiat. Partem tamquam
9 debitor solvis,[5] partem tamquam creditor accipis. Etiam-
nunc fingamus alios creditores et nihil in patrimonio quod
supersit. Id ut manifestius atque apertius dicam, sint possessiones huic deprehenso, sint mancipia, supellex, sit aes
alienum cui aeri alieno non sufficiant ea quae in patrimonio sunt. Occupabis mancipia, occupabis supellectilem?
Creditores inanes excuties atque dimittes? Non potest hoc
10 aecum videri tibimet ipsi faeneranti. Omnia igitur ea quae
apparerent in creditum et in aes alienum transissent; tu,
quamvis legem haberes qua tibi adulteri bona deberentur,
nihil tamen ex eius adulteri bonis qui nihil haberet recepis-
ses. Sic ergo tecum debitor tuus loquitur: 'Bona mea, id
est, quod liberum in patrimonio meo est et quod proprie
meum, ad te transire debet lege. Prius solvo; et quid inter-
11 est ego solvam an tu auferas?' Non debet ergo tibi is cui
pecuniam credidisti, multo minus ego qui profecto solutus
sum si alter iam solvit. Quid enim alioqui facere me vis?
Integro statu debitoris [mei][6] si a me petere maluisses, ad
debitorem reverterer. Si debitor decessisset et bona eius
ad heredem pervenissent, ad heredem redirem,[7] id est,
bona persequerer patrimonii[8] < eius >[9] pro quo ego spopondi. Idem esset[10] reus a quo fui repetiturus si quid tamquam

---

[5] C: solvit Aβ   [6] SB[4] (*anne* tui ?)   [7] *Ri.*: -irent . . .
redissem (-et C) Aβ   [8] *fort. delendum* SB[4]   [9] SB[3]
[10] *Sch.*: es Aβ: esses *Gron.*

---

[2] In my hypothesis.
[3] Cf. s.10 *in creditum et in aes alienum.*

allow you the residue of the property. So you must make the same reckoning with yourself as you have made[2] with another. For of an estate which is to pass to another owner, it is required that first satisfaction be given to money owed.[3] You pay part as debtor, you recover part as creditor. Once again, let us imagine other creditors and nothing left in the estate. To put it more clearly and plainly, suppose the person caught has possessions such as slaves and furniture, and debt, which debt the contents of the estate would be insufficient to pay off. Will you seize the slaves and the furniture? As for the creditors, will you shake them off and send them away empty? You yourself, the usurer, cannot think that fair. So all visible items would have been transferred to loan and debt. As for you, although you had the law under which the property of the adulterer was owed to you, you would have got nothing from the property of an adulterer who had nothing. So your debtor speaks to you as follows: "My property, that is, what is unencumbered in my estate and properly mine, should pass to you under the law. First, I pay—and what is the difference whether I pay or you take?" Wherefore the man to whom you lent money doesn't owe you, much less do I, who am surely freed of obligation if someone else has already paid. For what after all do you want me to do? If you had preferred to claim from me, when the debtor's status was unimpaired, I should have gone back to the debtor. If the debtor had deceased and his property had passed to an heir, I should have gone to the heir, that is, I should have claimed the property appertaining to the estate <of the person> for whom I went sponsor. The same person would have been sued from whom I would have reclaimed anything I had paid as spon-

12   sponsor solvissem. Nunc ad te transît patrimonium, coepisti vicem habere heredis. Quid enim interest iure testamenti a defuncto veniat ad te hereditas an lege a vivente?
Si patrimonium mihi persequi licet, ad te redeam necesse
est. Ita istud quod accipere non potes, si posses accipere,
solveres.

13   SERMO

Haec de iure; illa iam de circumscriptione huius sponsoris.

14   DECLAMATIO

Ego fortiter spopondi sine periculo pro eo homine qui
bona habebat. Tu quousque avaritiam perduxisti? Parum
est faenerare civibus? Sine aliqua tua fraude factum videbitur ut qui aliena pecunia utebatur incideret in hoc potissimum adulterium? Sed inciderit sane (neque enim mihi
causa pro illo hodie dicenda est): quod protulisti habes, et
plus quam protulisti habes. Est quod in rationes tuas tamquam creditor referas; est quod in lucrum tamquam maritus referas.

                        274

                 Tyrannus fulminatus

Quo quis loco fulmine ictus fuerit, eodem sepeliatur. Ty-

---

   4 Enough of it to cover his responsibility as sponsor. He seems
to be envisaging the situation as it would be if he lost the case. It
would be paradoxical, with the sponsor calling on the debtor's
quasi-heir, who would be none other than the creditor. But this is
hypothesis; actually he has received nothing from the sponsor, nor
will.   5 "No apparent risk" (Wi.).

sor. As it is, the estate has passed to you, you are now in lieu
of an heir. For what difference does it make whether it
comes to you as an inheritance by testamentary right from
him defunct or by law from him still living? If I am entitled
to claim the estate,[4] I must necessarily go back to you. So
what you cannot receive, that, if you could receive it, you
would pay.

DISCUSSION

This as to the law. What follows concerns the sharp practice against this sponsor.

DECLAMATION

I boldly went sponsor at no risk[5] for a man of property.
How far have you pushed your greed? Is it not enough that
you lent money at usury to citizens? Shall it be thought that
a man living on someone else's money fell into this particular adultery without some chicanery on your part?[6] But
supposing he did (for I do not have to plead on his behalf
today): you have what you advanced, and more than you
advanced. You have something to put into your accounts as
creditor; you have something to put in under "windfall" as
husband.[7]

274

The tyrant struck by lightning

In whatever place a man be struck by lightning, in the same
let him be buried. Let the body of a tyrant be cast outside

---

[6] A dark hint that the adultery was part of a scheme by the husband to get money out of the sponsor.

[7] The debtor's property apart from what he owed.

ranni corpus extra fines abiciatur. Tyrannus in foro fulmi-
natus est. Quaeritur an eodem loco sepeliatur.

1   SERMO

In legum comparatione multa quaeri possunt, sed varie in
quaque controversia. Interim quaeri solet an privata altera, altera publica sit, et utrum militaris altera, altera pertinens ad civilia officia. Hic omnia fere cetera paria sunt;
utra utilior et magis necessaria civitati sit quaerendum est.

2   DECLAMATIO

Nondum rem comparo. Interim utrum magis necessarium
putatis esse, servari eam legem quae ad sepulturam alicuius pertineat an eam quae ad poenam tyranni? Si in totum lex altera tollenda sit, nec ad praesens modo tempus
sed in universum, sine utra tandem facilius civitas stabit?
3   Fulmine icti ut eodem loco sepeliantur quo sunt percussi
ad quam tandem civitatis pertinet utilitatem? At hercule ut
insepultus abiciatur tyrannus ad vindictam, ad securitatem
4   pertinet. Non satis putaverunt maiores eas poenas adversus tyrannum constituere quas possit excipere in vita. Multos magis tangit sepultura; ad cogitationem post se futurorum plerique gravius moventur. Vultis scire? Propter hoc
litigatur. Est ergo ⟨haec⟩[1] utilior.
5   Quid si de eo quaerimus hodie ad quem leges, nisi in
poenam eius scriptae, non pertinent? Exuit se tyrannus

1 *SB*[3]

the borders. A tyrant was struck by lightning in the Forum. The question is whether he should be buried in the same place.

DISCUSSION

In a comparison of laws many questions can be raised, but they vary from one controversy to another. Sometimes it is a question whether one law is private and the other public, and whether one is military and the other pertaining to civil duties. In this case pretty well everything else is equal: the question should be which is more useful and necessary to the community.

DECLAMATION

I am not yet comparing the circumstances. Meanwhile, which do you think the more necessary, that the law which pertains to someone's burial be observed or the one pertaining to the punishment of a tyrant? If one or the other law should be totally abolished and not only for the present but altogether, which will the community more easily stand without? That persons struck by lightning be buried in the same place where they were hit, to what utility of the community does that, I ask, pertain? But that a tyrant be cast out unburied pertains, upon my word, to vengeance, to security. Our ancestors thought it not enough to lay down punishments against a tyrant which he might receive in his lifetime. With many people burial goes deeper, most are more heavily affected by the thought of what comes after them. Would you like to know? This is the reason for our litigation. So <this law> is the more useful.

What if we are asking today about a person to whom the laws, except those written for his punishment, do not apply? The tyrant strips himself and raises himself; by plac-

et erigit; supra leges ⟨se⟩[2] ponendo extra illas se posuit.
Hominem occidere non licet, tyrannum licet. Expugnare
domum fas non est: arcem expugnabit optimus quisque.
Insidiatus civi, etiamsi non effecerit scelus, poenas tamen
legibus solvet: at qui hoc idem adversus tyrannum fecerit,
6 etiamsi deprehensus fuerit, laudabitur. Lex [praecipue][3]
ista ad eos pertinet qui alioqui sepeliendi sunt, idque verbis legis ipsis manifestum est. 'Quo quis loco fulmine ictus
fuerit, eo sepeliatur': apparet non de sepultura quaeri sed
de loco sepulturae. Magis aliquanto esse contraria lex
⟨ista⟩[4] huic videretur si ita scripta esset ut fulmine icti
sepelirentur; tum enim ipsa sepultura illis adsignari videretur, nunc tantum locus. Et porro cui sepultura non dari
debet, adsignari locus debet?

7 Sed tyrannus fulmine ictus est (non dico quo loco, nec
adhuc ad tractatum huius invidiae accedo): hoc illi proderit? Si nobis libertatem humanae manus et mortalia
consilia attulissent, traheretur publicis manibus corpus
extra fines et unusquisque vexatione eius ludibrioque gau-
deret, nemo non suam manum esse quae traheret, suas
vires putaret; quoniam scelera eius atque flagitia ab ipsis
diis immortalibus condemnata sunt, quoniam patientiam
nostram ac servitutem numina non tulerunt, continget illi
8 honor? Hoc enim voluit ille qui fulmen vibravit? Hoc cogitavit cum illud noxium caput sacris flammis petivit? Parum

² *Aer.*   ³ *SB*¹   ⁴ *coni. Ro.*

---

¹ *Constitui* ("the ordinance") rather than *quaeri* would be the
logical word.

² *Invidia* is the sentiment of outrage provoked by the death of
the tyrant in the Forum of all places; cf. s.9.

ing ⟨himself⟩ above the laws he placed himself outside them. Killing a human being is forbidden: killing a tyrant is allowed. It is unlawful to break into a house: the best among us will break into a castle. A plotter against a citizen will pay a penalty to the laws even if he has not effected the crime: but whoever does this same against a tyrant will be praised, even if he is caught first. Your law applies to persons who ought in general to be buried, and that is clear from the very words of the law: "In whatsoever place a man be struck by lightning, in that let him be buried." It is plain that the question[1] is not about burial but the place of burial. ⟨Your⟩ law would seem somewhat more in conflict with this one if it had stated that persons struck by lightning are to be buried. For then it would seem that they are assigned burial itself; as it is, merely the place. And indeed, ought a place to be assigned to someone who should not be given burial?

But the tyrant has been struck by lightning (I don't say in what place, nor do I come as yet to deal with the outrage[2] involved in that). Shall this work to his advantage? If human hands and mortal counsels had brought us freedom, the corpse would have been publicly dragged outside our borders and each one of us would have enjoyed harassing and mocking it, nobody but would have thought the hand that dragged his own, the strength his own: seeing that his crimes and outrages have been condemned by the immortal gods themselves, seeing that the deities did not tolerate our patience and servitude, shall he be accorded honor? Was that what he who hurled the bolt desired? Was that in his mind when he attacked that accursed creature with his sacred flames? Was it not enough that the tyrant

erat sepeliri tyrannum nisi in foro etiam sepeliretur? Quo-
nam fato ego nostram civitatem, iudices, laborasse in illo
homine crediderim si, praeter ea quae adversus nos singulos universosque fecit, partem speciosissimam civitatis et
celeberrimam nobis ablaturus est?

9   Si mehercule aliqui liberalis civis, immo si optime meritus in foro fulmine esset ictus, dicerem tamen excipienda
quaedam. Neque enim[5] omnes casus providere legum latores potuerunt; nec templa excepta sunt. Forum, quod
mihi templum quoddam Pacis videtur, in quo iura exer-
centur, propter quod leges valent, bustis occupabimus,
infaustis cineribus polluemus? Totum hercule potius relin-
quamus tyranni sepulchro; mutemus locum iudiciorum.

10   Pars altera

SERMO

Ut sepeliatur superstitione sola effici potest: ut in comparatione legum illud potentissime dicamus, eam legem magis esse servandam quae deorum gratia scripta sit quam
quae hominum: adversus tyranni ultionem hominibus tantum esse scriptam, et scriptam levissimam partem ultionis;
hoc vero quod constitutum est, ut quo quisque loco fulmine ictus esset eodem sepeliretur, religionis esse.

11   DECLAMATIO

Neque hoc propter personam neque in honorem alicuius
scripsisse potest legum lator videri, sed in reverentiam

---

[5] n. enim *Hå.*²: immo n. Aβ

be buried if he was not also buried in the Forum? Under what fate, gentlemen, should I believe our community labored in relation to this man if, beyond what he did to us individually and collectively, he is to rob us of the most handsome and frequented part of the community?

Upon my word, if some munificent, or rather excellently deserving, citizen had been struck by lightning in the Forum, I should say all the same that some exceptions should be made. For our lawgivers could not provide for all contingencies; even temples were not excepted. The Forum, which I think of as a temple of Peace, in which the laws are put into operation, because of which they are in force—shall we occupy it with tombs, pollute it with sinister ashes? Rather, I tell you, let us abandon it wholly to the tyrant's sepulcher. Let us change the locality of the law-courts.

The other side

DISCUSSION

Religious scruple alone can determine that he be buried. So in a comparison of the laws let it be our most effective argument that the law to be observed is that which was written for the gods' sake rather than that written for men's; the one regarding vengeance against the tyrant was written only for men and only the lightest part of vengeance written: whereas the ordinance that anyone struck by lightning be buried in the same place belongs to religion.

DECLAMATION

The lawgiver cannot be thought to have so written because of some person or in somebody's honor, but in reverence of

deorum. Fas non est visum movere[6] ictum illum: quomodo
sederant flammae, ita concremandum corpus universum
putaverunt. Existimans locum illum corpori datum? Ful-
12 mini datus est. 'At tyrannus fulmine percussus est.' Hoc
magis omnia religiose et cum cura deorum facere debemus. 'Sed in foro sepelietur tyrannus.' Qua[7] magis? Mihi
inter cetera etiam hoc quoque provisum esse †facto† a diis
immortalibus videtur, quod illi loco destinatus est: nemo
inire forum nostrum poterit[8] quin videat illud sepulchrum.
13 Protinus enim sequatur cogitatio necesse est: tyrannus fuit
ille, et ob hoc[9] fulmine ictus est, et poenas diis immortalibus dedit. Quotiens noxios cruci figimus, celeberrimae eliguntur viae, ubi plurimi intueri, plurimi commoveri hoc
metu possint. Omnis enim poena non tam ad delictum pertinet quam ad exemplum.

275

Heres ob adulterum fratrem

Qui ob adulterium pecuniam acceperit, ignominiosus sit.
Maior frater minorem in adulterio deprehendit. Pro ⟨eo⟩[1]
rogante patre et abdicationem eius promittente, dimisit.
Abdicatus est adulter. Mortuo patre inventus heres qui de-
prehenderat. Ignominiosus dicitur.

1 DECLAMATIO

'Qui pecuniam ob adulterium acceperit, ignominiosus sit.'

6 *Hå.*[2]: visubmoveri (*ex* –re) A: vi submovere *vel sim.* β
7 *SB*[2]: quam Aβ   8 *Ro.*: -est Aβ
9 ob hoc *hic SB*[4]: *ante* poenas Aβ
1 *Pith.*

the gods. It appeared irreligious to move the man struck; they thought that the entire corpse should be cremated just as the flames had settled. Do you suppose that this place was given to the corpse? It was given to the bolt. "But the tyrant was hit by the lightning." All the more ought we to do everything religiously, with thought for the gods. "But the tyrant will be buried in the Forum." Where better? This too among other things seems to me to have been by providence of the immortal gods, that he was destined to that place. No one will be able to enter our Forum without seeing that sepulcher. For the thought necessarily follows: he was a tyrant and he was struck by lightning on that account[3] and paid a penalty to the immortal gods. When we crucify criminals the most frequented roads are chosen, where the greatest number of people can look and be seized by this fear. For every punishment has less to do with the offence than with the example.

275

Heir on account of an adulterous brother

Let whoso takes money on account of adultery be under stigma. An elder brother caught a younger in adultery. When his father pleaded for ⟨him⟩ and promised to disown him, he let him go. The adulterer was disowned. At the father's death, the catcher was found heir. He is put under stigma.

DECLAMATION

"Let whoso takes money on account of adultery be under

---

[3] See crit. note.

Hanc legem adversus eos primum constitutam esse dico
qui pecuniam acceperunt ut adulterium committeretur,
ideoque ignominiam adiunctam quod viderentur rem fecisse lenonis. Verum etiamsi ii quoque tenentur qui in poenam commissi adulterii pecuniam acceperint, is tenetur
qui pecuniam accepit. In mea causa utrum contendis?
Pecuniam me accepisse cum dimitterem non probabis.
Alioqui si hoc putares[2] esse pecuniam accipere, abdicari
fratrem, statim detulisses. Postea videbo qua causa dimissus sit; interim nego hoc esse pecuniam accipere. Sine dubio est tam manifestum ut nulla interpretatione egeat quid
sit accipere pecuniam. Ego tamen non sum contentus hac
defensione, nisi illud probavero, ne spem quidem pecuniae oblatam. Quid enim mihi pollicitus est pater? Si dimisissem, futurum ut abdicaret fratrem meum. Heredem
testamento etiam eum quem abdicasset quis vetabat ‹in-
stitui, vel›[3] substitui in locum abdicati alium heredem?
Non possum ergo videri propter pecuniam dimisisse,
etiamsi propter hoc tantum dimisissem; nunc vero quam
multa fuerunt propter quae dimitterem! Si hoc tantum me
movit, quod frater erat, erat tamen satis plena defensio:
‹accedit›[4] et quod minor frater et quod sub ‹bono›[4] patre
frater, ut etiamsi ipsi non parcerem, tamen et patris et mea
5 causa non debuerim occidere. Nunc vero quis dubitet exorari me debuisse cum pater peteret? Putemus nihil patrem
esse pollicitum, nullam mihi ultionem praestitisse, quis
non impium me, quis non sceleratum putaret si non impe-

---

[2] *Ri.*: -ris Aβ   [3] *Pith.*   [4] *Hå.*²

[1] Ineptly or perversely for "even if I had no other assignable
reason."

stigma." I maintain that this law was first enacted against persons taking money in promotion of an adultery and that a stigma was added because they were thought to be doing the job of a pimp. But even though persons receiving money as penalty for adultery committed also fall under this law, only one who *has* taken money falls under it. In my case which do you contend? You will not show that I took money when I let him go. Or if you thought that "take money" meant your brother's disowning, you would have brought your charge straight away. I shall see later on for what reasons he was let go; meanwhile, I deny that this is to take money. Beyond question, what it is to take money is so clear that it needs no interpretation. However, I am not content with this defense unless I show that not even a prospect of money was held out. For what did my father promise me? That if I let my brother go, he would disown him. Who was to stop him ⟨making⟩ even a son he had disowned his testamentary heir ⟨or⟩ substituting another heir in place of the disowned? So I cannot be thought to have let him go because of money, even if I had let him go only for that reason.[1] But in fact how many reasons I had for letting him go! If the fact that he was my brother was my only motive, that would be a sufficiently complete defense— and that he was my younger brother and under a ⟨good⟩ father, so that even if I were not sparing[2] himself I ought not to have killed him for my father's sake and my own. As it is, who would doubt that I was right to be prevailed upon when my father was begging? Let us suppose my father had promised nothing, granted me no vengeance, who would not have thought me undutiful, who would not have

---

[2] *Parcere vellem*, "willing to spare," would be more accurate.

trasset? Nunc vero promisit ultionem pleniorem, integris
inviolatisque manibus meis, et ipse pater severus: neque
enim est quod putetis defuisse ei gravitatem, defuisse ad
vindictam animum: abdicavit; et non fecisse hoc eum tem-
6 poris causa manifestum testamento fuit. Ergo nec pecuniam mihi pollicitus est pater, et ego alias causas dimittendi habui quam pecuniam, et ille non abdicatus est[5] ut ego
lucrum facerem. Nec enim persuaderi cuiquam potest
eum qui abdicatus sit haec passum esse causa mea.

Quanto plenior mihi vindicta contigit! Brevis enim
poena mortis est; nunc diu eget, diu male audit.[6]

276

Bona raptoris qui se suspendit

Rapta raptoris mortem aut bona optet. Raptor se suspendit. Rapta optat bona.

1 DECLAMATIO
'Rapta raptoris mortem vel bona optet.' Raptam hanc esse
pro qua loquor constat; ab eo raptam esse cuius bona optat
non negatur; lege datam esse potestatem utrum vellet[1]
convenit inter nos. Quid est igitur quod obstet?
2 Negant dandam esse optionem puellae quoniam perie-

---

[5] *SB*[1]: a. est non Aβ
[6] *SB*[3]: audiet Aβ
[1] v. <optandi> *tempt. Wi.*

---

[3] *Lucrum facere* = make a profit as a by-product of some other
activity.

thought me criminal, if I had refused him? As it was, he promised a fuller vengeance, leaving my hands clean and untainted, himself too a strict father; for you should not think he lacked gravity, did not have the spirit to punish. He disowned, and that he did not do this for the occasion his will made clear. So my father did not promise me money and I had other reasons than money for letting him go and he was not disowned for me to make an incidental profit.[3] For nobody can be persuaded that the person disowned suffered all this on my account.

How much more ample a vengeance has come my way! The punishment of death is brief; as it is, he is long in want, long in bad odor.[4]

276

Property of a rapist who hanged himself

Let a raped woman opt for the rapist's death or property. A rapist hanged himself. The raped woman opts for property.

DECLAMATION

Let a raped woman opt for the rapist's death or property.[1] That this girl, my client, was raped is agreed. That she was raped by the man for whose property she opts is not denied. That the law gave her power to opt for whichever she wished is common ground between us. So what is there to stand in the way?

They say that the girl should not be given the option

---

[4] Another non-pecuniary motive: disowning was a worse punishment than death.

[1] Instead of the usual alternative of marriage.

rit raptor. Id nulla lege exceptum, nullo scripto verbo cautum est. Interpretatione igitur [temporis][2] nituntur. Videamus haec qualis sit. 'Lex' inquit 'quae optare vel mortem vel bona permittit hoc satis significat, ex duobus optandum esse. Quoniam igitur iam alterum optari non potest, ne
3 optioni quidem locus est.' ‹Si›[3] hanc legis vim esse concederemus[4] ut[5] ex duobus esset optio [eligenda][6] puellae, duo tamen haec esse contenderem, natura et vi. Neque enim si raptor nobis subductus est, mors ipsa nihil est. Sed quomodo non satis est unum superesse, cum etiamsi duo essent non potuerit optari nisi unum?
4 ⟦Et haec duo ita demum potenter a parte diversa proponerentur si essent iuncta. Nunc vero discreta sunt ipsa legis scriptura: 'mortem vel nuptias': ita duo; simplicia, singula sunt [tamen].[7]⟧[8] Praeterea ‹si›[9] lex ita scripta esset[10] ut eligi iuberet, posset opponi [vel][11] electioni si ex pluri-
5 bus non esset; nunc optio potest esse etiam singulorum. Et illud, iudices, ante omnia intueri vos oportet: si quid ex lege inclinandum sit, spectate[12] ut quam minimum ex eadem pereat. Adversarius enim queritur aliquam verbi interpretationem perire, nos totam legem, totum ius. Tolerabilis enim esset mihi cum adversariis contentio si quae-

---

2 *SB*[4]: optionis *Pith.*: legis *coni. Ro.*   3 *Aer.*
4 *Aer.*: contend- β: condend- A   5 *Ri.*: si Aβ
6 *SB*[3]   7 *SB*[3]   8 *ita secl. SB*[4]   9 *Ro.*
10 *Ro.*: est Aβ   11 *coni. Wi.*   12 *Wi.*: -are Aβ

---

2 See crit. note.

3 Arguing (as Wi.) that the other side's contention could be valid only if they produced a law that read *mortem et bona*. But

because the rapist has perished. No law makes that exception, no written word provides it. So they rely on interpretation.[2] Let us see what sort of interpretation. "The law," he says, "that allows an option between property and death sufficiently signifies that the option is between two alternatives. Since then one of them cannot now be opted for, neither can there be any room for an option." <If> we conceded that this is the meaning of the law, so that the girl's option lay between two alternatives, I should argue nevertheless that these *are* two, by nature and meaning. For if the rapist has been withdrawn from us, it does not follow that death itself is nothing. But how is it not enough that one remains, since even if there were two, it would only be possible to choose one?

⟦And these two would be validly put forward by the other side only if they were joint. But as it is, they are separated by the very text of the law: "death or marriage": so they are two; simple, individual.[3] ⟧ Moreover, <if> the law were so written as to require a *choice*, a choice could be opposed if it was not from more than one; as it is, *option* even of individual items is possible.[4] And you should look at this, gentlemen, to start with: if anything in the law is to be bent, see to it that as little as possible of it be lost. For our opponent complains that some interpretation of the wording is lost, we complain that whole statute, the whole legal right, is lost. For my contention with the opposition would be tol-

then there would be no choice. *Nuptiae*, the normal formula, substituted for *bona*, is further reason for suspecting the passage.

[4] Another futility. He makes a distinction between *electio*, choice from a plurality of items, and *optio*, which etymologically might mean merely "desire"—but never does.

reretur an hoc optare puella deberet; nunc id agunt ut nihil
optet, et nova quadam ac perversa actione nituntur, ut
bona raptoris optare puella non debeat quia optare nil
aliud potest quam bona.

6   'At non est aequum et mortem raptoris contingere et
bona.' Sed hoc eo pertinet ut si mortem optavit optare non
debeat bona. Ita demum enim et mortem ei contigisse raptoris dicemus et bona. Aequum est etiam[13] interpellari
posse optionem [etiam][14] facto ipsius, alieno vero iniquissimum. Quare si per hanc stetisset[15] ut raptor periret
(quamquam possem dicere: 'illud non optavit, et legi non
est satisfactum'), haberet tamen aliquam rationem saltem
falsa eius calumnia. Nunc quid fecit puella ut raptor more-
7 retur? Itaque huic non tantum in hoc labor est, ut bona
raptoris accipiat, sed in illo maior aliquanto, ut vobis
approbet quid optatura fuerit si viveret. Duas enim sine
dubio poenas adversus raptorem lex constituit, †alteram
tamen mitem; nec semper hac cogitata et publicata crudeli
illi et sanguinariae tenetur.†[16] Hodieque alioqui nonne
merito a vobis, merito a civitate reprehenderetur si aliud
non optando hoc ostenderet [et][17] fecisse raptorem quod
ipsa esset optatura?

8   Hinc transeunt ad coniecturam, et suspicari vos volunt
ea quae probare non possunt. 'Non enim' inquiunt 'est
credibile periturum fuisse raptorem nisi hoc optaturam

---

[13] *Wi.*: enim Aβ   [14] *Ri.*

[15] *Aer.*: testis sed Aβ   [16] alteram <saevam, alteram> [ta-
men] mitem, nec semper haec lenis et moderata . . . anteponitur
(antefertur *Watt*[1]) *tempt. SB*[1]

[17] *Morawski*

erable if the question were whether the girl should have made *this* option. As it is, they are out to stop any option, and they rely on a novel and perverse plea, that the girl ought not to opt for the rapist's property because she cannot opt for anything except the property.

"Well, but it is unfair that she should get the rapist's death *and* his property." But that is to say that if she opted for death she ought not to opt for the property. For if we say that she got both the rapist's death and his property, it amounts to just that.[5] It is fair also that the option can be blocked by an act of her own, but most unfair that this happen by the act of another. So if it had been her doing that the rapist perished, although I could say "she made no option and the law has not been satisfied," his false quibble would still have made some sense at least. As it is, what did the girl do to cause the rapist's death? So she is not so much concerned to take the rapist's property, she is somewhat more concerned to show you what she would have opted for if he had been alive. For the law unquestionably established two penalties against the rapist, one ⟨cruel, the other merciful⟩, and the lenient and moderate penalty is not always preferred to that cruel and sanguinary one. Today anyway would she not deservedly be blamed by you and by the community if by not opting for something else she had shown that the rapist had done what she herself had been going to opt for?

From this point they pass on to guesswork and want you to suspect what they are unable to prove. "For," they say, "it is not credible that the rapist would have perished if he had not known that the girl would opt for this." To start with,

[5] And is therefore nugatory, since she had not so opted.

scisset puellam.' Ante omnia, cum dicitur scisse, illud os-
9 tenditur, posse probari quomodo scierit. Quaero enim a
vobis ipsis adversariis quomodo colligatis scisse eum, quomodo[18] liqueat hoc vobis. Si quid est, adferte et ad iudicem. Unum argumentum est ipsum quod perierit. Hoc
etiamsi mortis fecit metu, potuit tamen naturaliter fuisse
timidus, ‹potuit›[19] etiam nullo accepto signo propter quod
vitam desperaret confusione tamen et proprio animi sui
10 perisse motu. Nunc vero credibile non est quemquam perire mortis metu. Quid enim timuit ulterius? Quare etiam
credibilius videtur mihi idcirco perisse eum quod optaturam puellam bona existimaret. Sunt enim plerique qui
mortem potiorem quam egestatem putent, quibus delicate
educatis (ex deliciis enim haec licentia facta est) intolerabi-
lis videatur nuda illa vita et omnibus quibuscumque antea
abundaverunt destituta. Hoc igitur est credibilius; et hoc
puella voluit et in hoc perseverat.
11   Et certe nulli tolerabile aut aequum videri potest ‹ut›[20]
in gravissima iniuria, qua virginitatem perdidit, qua florem
aetatis amisit, qua prima illa gratia apud maritum futura
praerepta est, neque mortem optaverit neque bona accipiat.

277

Praegnas adultera

Supplicia praegnatium in diem partus differantur. Prae-

---

[18] *SB*[1]: cum non Aβ
[19] *SB*[1]   [20] *Gron.*

---

[6] Alluding to the rape.

when he is said to have known, it is implied that it can be proved *how* he knew. For I ask you yourselves, my opponents, how you infer that he knew, how this is clear to you. If you have something, bring it to the jury too. Your only proof is the fact itself, that he perished. Even if he did it out of fear of death, ⟨he may⟩ have been timid by nature, he⟨may have⟩ perished even though he had been given no indication to make him despair of life, out of confusion and a spontaneous motion of his mind. But in reality, it is not credible that anyone perishes because of fear of death. For what more did he fear? Therefore I find it actually more credible that he perished because he thought the girl would opt for the property. For there are many who think death preferable to poverty. After a pampered upbringing (for much licentiousness[6] is a product of pampering), the bare life before them, destitute of all they previously had in plenty, would seem intolerable. This therefore is more credible; and this is what the girl wanted[7] and in this she perseveres.

And certainly nobody can find it tolerable or fair ⟨that⟩ after a most grievous injury, by which she forfeited her virginity, lost the flower of her youth, was robbed of what would have been that first charm in her husband's eyes, she has neither opted for death nor gets the property.

277

The pregnant adulteress

Let punishments of pregnant women be deferred until the

---

[7] Not that he kill himself, for that would undermine her case, but that he lose his property.

gnatem in adulterio deprehensam occidit maritus. Reus
est caedis. CD.

1 ### DECLAMATIO

Cum reus agar caedis, nihil fortius confiteor quam a me
occisos homines, et, si quid numerus quoque adicere invidiae potest, tres.[1] Verum istud non potest videri saevitia,
non crudelitas, quae per leges venit. Occidere adulterum
licet cum adultera. Ex alia parte nascitur origo huius calumniae.

2 'Praegnatem' inquit 'occidisti, et supplicia praegnatium
lex differre in diem partus iubet.' Ut confiterer hoc esse
supplicium atque eo nomine appellandum, fortiter tamen
dicerem leges omnes quaecumque de suppliciis scriptae
sunt ad eos pertinere qui damnati sunt, qui in iudicio convicti, qui per ministeria publica et carnificum manus occi-
3 duntur. Nam et ceterorum supplicia ante iudicium non
solent esse et non nisi per magistratus exiguntur, non nisi
certa lege ordinantur[2]: hoc ius scriptum est mariti dolori,
hoc ius ille conditor conscriptorque legis huius noluit[3] esse
privatum. ⟦Non magis ergo tempus aut diem praestituit[4]
adulterae quam manum carnificis, quam sententiam iudi-

---

[1] *SB*[4] (*i.e.* III): duos Aβ
[2] *Wi.*: -ationum Aβ
[3] *SB*[4]: voluit Aβ
[4] *Ro.*: -uisset Aβ

---

[1] His wife, her lover, and the fetus. As Wi. says, *duos* is an anti-
climax (*homines* could not cover less). See crit. note and on 382.5.
[2] He has just said that no such laws exist. A superficial reading
of ss.2–6 leaves apparently hopeless confusion. But the basis of

day of delivery. A husband killed a pregnant woman taken in adultery. He is charged with murder. He rebuts.

DECLAMATION

Charged as I am with murder, I make no confession more boldly than that human beings were killed by me, and if the number can add anything to the odium, three.[1] But what comes through the laws cannot seem savagery or cruelty. It is permitted to kill an adulterer along with an adulteress. The origin of this false charge arises from another quarter.

He says: "You killed a pregnant woman and the law requires that punishment of pregnant women be deferred until the day of delivery." Though I were to admit that this is a punishment, to be called by that name, I should still say boldly that all laws whatsoever written about punishments pertain to persons convicted, found guilty in court, who are put to death by public servants and the hands of executioners. Punishments of other persons are not usually carried out before trial, nor unless ordered by magistrates, unless arranged under a definite law.[2] *This* statute was written for a husband's distress,[3] *this* statute the author and drafter of this law did not wish to be private. ⟦For that reason he did not specify in advance a time or day for the adulteress any more than the executioner's hand, the

the argument is sound, namely that the law applies only to an adulteress judicially condemned, not to one summarily (and legally) dispatched by her husband *in flagrante delicto*: not therefore to this case. *Noluit* for *voluit* in s.3 is crucial.

[3] By preserving the child (cf. s.8 init.), which might after all be the husband's.

4 cis, quam imperium magistratus.]]⁵ Quid si ne differri quidem hoc supplicium potest? Non enim dubium est quin
lex de iis loquatur qui quando sint in rei publicae potestate.
Damnatus aliquis custodia publica continetur, carcere
continetur; potest de hoc supplicium sumere magistratus
cum voluerit. Adultera dimissa non redit in manum mariti.

5 Nec hoc tantum in lege est, ut adulterae supplicium differri non possit, sed illud etiam, ut non tantum adulterae
pereant. Nam lex, cum occidere mihi adulterum cum adultera permittat, manifeste illud ostendit, non posse eos
diversis temporibus occidi, ac, si alteri remittatur supplicium, impunitatem etiam alteri dandam. Ergo non solum
praegnatis supplicium, ut etiam sic loquamur, sed etiam
adulteri non differendum tantum sed tollendum omnino

6 fuisset. Quid⁶ si ‹ne›⁷ hoc quidem supplicium appellari
convenit? Habent enim omnia haec nomina suam proprietatem. Non semper homo ‹merito occisus›⁸ supplicio adfectus dici potest; non ubicumque poenam habes⁹ etiam
supplicium est. Nomen hoc est publicae animadversionis,
nomen exactae per magistratus poenae.

7 ‘Indignum fuit occidere eam quae praegnas facta est.’
Nondum dico quantum gravius peccaverit; interim, cuius
misereretur? Infantis ex adultero fortasse concepti? Et, iudices, interrogo vos cuius rei gratia legem cavisse existimetis

---

⁵ *ita secl. SB*⁴   ⁶ *Sch.*: quod Aβ
⁷ *Sch.*   ⁸ *Ri.*
⁹ *Ri.*: -ent Aβ

---

⁴ On the contrary it had to be and was specified: *in diem
partus*. But the regular accompaniments of a trial had no place in

juror's vote, the magistrate's command.[4]]] What if this punishment actually cannot be deferred? For the law unquestionably speaks of those who are at a given time[5] in the power of the commonwealth. A man convicted is held in public custody, in jail; the magistrate can exact punishment on him when he wishes. But an adulteress discharged does not return into her husband's control. Nor does the law only provide that the punishment of an adulteress cannot be deferred, but it also provides that adulteresses are not the only ones to perish. For when the law permits me to kill an adulterer along with an adulteress, it clearly indicates that they cannot be killed at different times and that if the punishment is remitted to one of them, the other too is to be given immunity. So not only the pregnant woman's punishment, to continue to use this term, but that of the adulterer also would have to have been not only deferred but eliminated altogether. What if this too is <not> properly to be called a punishment? All these names have their own proper function. A man <deservedly killed> cannot always be said to have undergone punishment. A punishment is not always found wherever you have a penalty. It is the name given to public chastisement, to penalty exacted by magistrates.

"To kill a woman who had become pregnant was unseemly." I won't say at this point how much the graver was her offence. Meanwhile, whom does he pity? The infant, perhaps conceived from the adulterer? And, gentlemen, I ask you for what reason you think the law protected one

the text of the law. I take the sentence double-bracketed to be a misguided attempt to provide some rationale for *voluit*.

[5] *Quando* after *qui* = *quandoque*, "at any time."

illi[10] qui erat conceptus a nocente femina. Non est credibile legem prospexisse ei cui rerum natura datura fortasse
non erat lucem, qui an nasci posset dubium fuit, qui etiam
8 odium ex ea quae conceperat merebatur. Quare ergo
scripta lex est? Pro patribus, qui nihil fecerunt. Indignum
enim visum est, etiamsi mortem meruisset mater, auferri
filium innocenti patri. Si ergo[11] lex pro me scripta erat, non
potest videri contra me valere. In hac vero ne illius quidem, quicumque futurus fuit, movere vos miseratio potest.
Quis enim illum agnosceret, quis educeret, cum manifestum esset ex crimine, ex flagitiis, ex ea re quae morte puni-
9 tur esse conceptum? Ipsam vero adulteram adeo oportuit
occidi ut nulli umquam irasci magis leges debuerint. Ultra
commune flagitium est praegnas adultera. Aliqua hoc tempore, quo salvo pudore a marito secubaret, cum adultero
volutata est? Et cum animalibus mutis etiam, quorum libido ratione ⟨non⟩[12] continetur, haec tamen sit natura ut
posteaquam conceperint omnem refugiant venerem, ma-
trona ne pudore quidem partus, ut vos dicitis, iam instantis
moveri potuit ut pudicitiam, si non marito, at futuro certe
10 filio praestaret? Illa igitur prior damnavit ventrem suum.
Victurus autem fuit ille si ego adulteram non occidissem?
Non novimus hos mores turpissimarum feminarum, ut
oderint puerperia, ut filios velut indices aetatis suae abo-
minentur?

[10] *Ro.*: illius Aβ   [11] si ergo *Ri.*: dixero Aβ   [12] *ed. Leid.*

---

[6] *Secubaret* should be *secubare debebat*. Directly expressed,
the sense is *quo salvo pudore cum marito concumbere non posset*,
"when she could not sleep with her husband without violating
modesty."

who had been conceived by a guilty woman? It is not credible that the law looked out for a being to whom the Nature of Things was not perhaps about to give the light of day, who might or might not be born, who even deserved to be hated on account of her who had conceived him. So why was the law written? For the fathers, who have done nothing. For it appeared unseemly that a son should be taken from an innocent father, even though the mother had deserved death. So if the law was written on my behalf, it cannot be thought to operate against me. But in this woman's case pity for him, whatever was to become of him, cannot move you. For who would acknowledge him, who raise him, when it was clear that he had been conceived in crime, in outrage, in something punishable by death? As for the adulteress herself, she was so deserving of death that no laws should ever have been more wroth with anybody. A pregnant adulteress goes beyond the common run of outrage. Did a woman, at a time when she would be sleeping apart from her husband, keeping her modesty,[6] wallow with an adulterer? It is the nature even of dumb animals, although their lust is <not> restrained by reason, to eschew all sex after they have conceived: could not a married woman be moved by modesty in respect to her delivery, which you say was already imminent, to keep chaste, if not for her husband, at least for her future son? So she condemned her womb beforehand. But would he have lived if I had not killed the adulteress? Do we not know the modern ways of degraded women, how they hate giving birth and abominate their children as evidence of their age?

278

Expositor petens cum forti decem milia

Viri fortis pater decem milia accipiat. Is qui videbatur
filium habere decem milia cum ille fortiter fecisset accepit.
Postea iuvenem pater naturalis agnovit, solutis alimentis
recepit. Petit decem milia.

1   DECLAMATIO

Decem milia a me petis. Quo iure? Qua causa? Credidisti,
an deposuisti, an ex alicuius rei venditione pretium ad te
pertinet? Nihil horum: nullus inter nos contractus fuit nisi
quod mihi nuper aliquid debuisti. Legem adfers qua patri
viri fortis decem milia dari oportet; cuius quidem summae
si non praestetur fides, petitio (ut opinor) a re publica est.
2 Nam ut iam constet uter accipere debuerit, illud tamen
respondeas mihi velim, quis dare debuerit; si patri debetur, debet res publica. Viderimus an ego a civitate recte ac-
ceperim: tu non potes accipere nisi a civitate. At ego accepi
id quod tibi debebatur. Puta me in praesentia confiteri: re-
petet fortasse qui dedit; interim tibi non alius debet[1] quam
qui mihi dedit.
3   Sed volo nunc agere etiam rei publicae causam, et sic
respondere tibi tamquam istud a magistratibus petas. Non
est tempus hoc actionis istius. Quando enim filius tuus
fortiter fecit? Multum iam transisse tempus ante hanc
actionem confiteberis. Interrogabo ubi fueris. Etiamsi te

---

[1] *Sch.*: debuit Aβ

---

[1] Referring to the *alimenta* payment.

278

An exposer claiming ten thousand with a hero

Let the father of a hero receive ten thousand. A man who appeared to have a son received ten thousand after the same had become a hero. Later the natural father recognized the young man and took him back after payment of upbringing costs. He claims the ten thousand.

DECLAMATION

You claim ten thousand from me. By what right? For what reason? Did you lend it or deposit it or does it belong to you as price for the sale of some article? None of these. There was no contract between us except that latterly you owed me something.[1] You produce a law under which ten thousand is to be given to the father of a hero. If the obligation in respect of that sum is not discharged, it can be claimed, as I suppose, from the commonwealth. For although it be now agreed which of us ought to have received the money, I should like you to answer me, who ought to have given it? If it is owing to the father, the commonwealth owes it. We shall consider later on whether I properly received it from the community: you cannot receive it except from the community. But you say I received what was owing to you. Suppose I admit that for the present. Perhaps the giver will reclaim it. Meanwhile, nobody owes you except whoever gave it to me.

But I want now to plead the commonwealth's case too and reply to you as though you were claiming that money from the magistrates. This is not the time for your action. For when did your son become a hero? You will admit that much time had elapsed prior to this action. I shall ask

peregrinatio detinuit, etiamsi absentia in causa fuit quo
minus acciperes, dicam tamen pleraque iura tempore cir-
4 cumscribi. Si vero et in civitate fuisti et praesens eras cum
honoraretur filius, ut nunc res est, tuus, interrogo cur non
petieris. Nam ut non acceperis sufficit hoc, quod non petisti. Non eras illo tempore pater, quia nesciebas te esse.
Non debebatur igitur tibi eo tempore quo res publica
debuit.

5   Illud quoque interrogo, quomodo factum sit ut ego
acciperem. Pater viri fortis eram. Quorum utrumque bre-
viter ostendere iudici necessarium est, et me tum patrem
fuisse cum decem milia debebantur patri viri fortis et te
non fuisse ideoque te non accepisse. Patres enim non tantum natura et illo initio continentur; satis est plerumque ad
6 hoc ius videri. Num[2] dubium est quin, si intestatus deces-
sissem antequam tu agnosceres, aditurus ille hereditatem
quasi filius fuerit? Num dubium est quin, si honores peterem, profuturus mihi tamquam filius fuerit? Num dubium
est quin, si (quod longe ab eius animo et moribus abest)
‹me›[3] pulsasset [patrem],[3] non iniuriarum tantum lege te-
neretur, si occidisset, non caedis tantum lege poenas daret? Quod si haec omnia in confesso sunt, ne magistratus
quidem erraverunt eo tempore quo decem milia dederunt
7 mihi. Si intestatus tu decessisses, ad alios quoslibet tua

---

2 D: non Aβ   3 SB[4]

---

2 No need here for rewriting or *obeli*. *Illo initio* refers to im-
pregnation; "for *illo* as a sort of verbal nudge see my note on Cic.
Fam. 15.6.1 *illud . . . iudicium*" (SB[2]). This is common in the Declamations, e.g. 279.7 *antiquo illo errore*.
      3 As a "hero."

where you were. Even if a sojourn abroad detained you, even if absence were the reason why you did not receive the award, I shall say that many legal rights are limited by time. But if you were in the community and present when your son (as matters now stand) was honored, I ask why you did not claim. As for why you did not receive, it is enough to say: because you did not claim. You were not the father at that time because you did not know that you were. So the money was not owed to you at the time when the commonwealth owed it.

I also ask how it came about that I received the reward. I was the hero's father. I must briefly show two things to the judge, both that I was the father at the time when the ten thousand was owing to the hero's father and that you were not, and for that reason did not receive it. For paternity is not solely determined by nature and that first[2] step; appearance is often enough to establish this legal status. Is there any doubt that if I had died intestate before you recognized him, he would have entered upon the inheritance as though he was my son? Is there any doubt that if I were a candidate for office, he would have counted in my favor[3] as though he were my son? Is there any doubt that if he had beaten <me >[4] (something very far from his mind and manners), he would not have fallen merely under the law of injuries, or that if he had killed me, he would not have been punished merely under the law of murder[5]? But if all this is admitted, then the magistrates too made no mistake when they gave the ten thousand to me. If you had died intestate, your inheritance would have gone to others, no matter

---

4 Taking *patrem* as an addition replacing *me* fallen out.
5 But under the relevant special laws (cf. 358 and 372).

pertineret hereditas. Vis scire quam pater non fueris? Recipere illum nisi solutis alimentis non potuisti. Lex tibi
dicit: 'alienus est, et tibi ut pater esse incipias emendus.'
Iam illa profecto citra interrogationem sunt, cuius tulerit
nomen, in cuius censum delatus sit.

8 Nimium diu de re iudicata. Reliquum est ut intueamur
uter nostrum hac pecunia dignior esse videatur. Et ut bre-
viter dicam, tu exposuisti, ego sustuli. Scio te coepturum
altius, ut dicas: 'genui.' Hoc est quare tibi debeamus irasci:
quantum ad te pertinet, non habet res publica virum fortem; aut illum ferae laceraverunt aut aves diripuerunt aut
aliquis (quod multo sit indignius) sustulit leno aut lanista.

9 Ex meis ille beneficiis natus est. Intuendum nobis etiam illud praecipue est, quae causa constituendae legis huius
fuerit, aut unde ortum sit ut non contenta civitas fuerit
praemium ipsi viro forti dedisse, sed etiam patrem huius
honorandum censuerit. Ideone honoratum putamus patrem quod genuerit? An ideo magis praemio dignum civitas existimavit quod educasset, quod impensas fecisset?

10 Vis scire quam hoc verum sit? Pecunia honoravit. Si quid
pietatis est quod imputare nos rei publicae praeter alimenta possumus, illud est: 'sic educavi, talia praecepi, sic for-
mavi mores.' Non est satis hoc indignum, quod talem tibi

11 filium feci? Sed haec utcumque videri possint tolerabilia:
illo tempore quo pugnabat filius noster (vindicabo enim
mihi semper hoc nomen, neque a beneficiis meis appella-

---

6 "By the state at the time of the original payment" (Wi.).

whom. Would you like to know how definitely you were *not* his father? You could not get him back unless you paid for his upbringing. The law says to you: "He is not yours, you must buy him back to begin to be his father." There are other things of course not in question: whose name he bears, in whose census returns he was entered.

I have spent too long on something already determined.[6] It remains to take a look at which of us seems more deserving of this money. And to put it briefly: you exposed him, I picked him up. I know you will begin from further back and say: "I begot him." That is why we ought to be angry with you. So far as you are concerned, the commonwealth does not have its hero: either wild beasts tore him or birds pulled him apart or, what would be more shameful, some pimp or gladiator-trainer picked him up. He was born free from what I did for him. We should also pay special attention to the reason why this law was enacted, how it came about that the community was not content to give a reward to the hero himself but decided that his father too should be honored. Do we suppose that the father was honored because he begot him? Or did not rather the community think him worthy of the reward because he had brought him up, spent money on him? Would you like to know how true that is? It honored him with money. If there is something in the way of paternal feeling besides nourishment for which we can claim credit with the commonwealth, it's this: I brought him up *so*, my precepts were such and such, I formed his character in such and such a way. Is it not iniquitous enough that I made such a son for *you*? But all this may seem somehow or other tolerable: but at the time when our son (for I shall always claim this name for myself and the title will never depart from my

tio ista discedet), qualis uterque nostrum fuit? Non ego
sollicitus de muris pependi? Non ego omnes excepi ab acie
redeuntes? Non nuntios sollicitus captavi? At tu securus
eras, tamquam id quod volueras cum exponeres contigis-
12 set. Age, redeuntis vulnera quis religavit, sanguinem quis
abluit? Ad templa quis duxit? Quis gratulatus est? Scie-
basne iam tum esse officium tuum, an confiteris ad te haec
non pertinuisse? Dissimules licet, et videatur alioqui hoc
contra causam meam: sciebas, et illum esse apud me passus es.

13   Haec decem milia agnovisti. Non te moverunt tituli
adulescentis, non illa gloria de eximia virtute quam ego
praeceperam. Hac fiducia alimenta solvisti; computas mecum, ut solus omnium mortalium et expositum receperis
et lucrum feceris.

279

Dives speciosi adulter

Adulterum aut occidere aut accepta pecunia dimittere liceat. Dives pauperem, speciosi patrem, de stupro filii appellavit; ille tacuit. Iterum adiecta pecunia appellavit; ille
tacuit. Tertio appellatus uxorem filio dedit. Puer divitem
cum uxore sua deprehensum accepta pecunia dimisit.
Abdicatur a patre.

---

7 To have nothing more to do with him.
8 If he knew but did nothing, that would suggest that he was
not mainly interested in the money; but on the whole deliberate
non-recognition would count against him.   9 You *were* only
interested in the money and publicly recognized the son later on
in order to get it—implying earlier knowledge of paternity.

benefactions) was fighting, how did each of us behave? Did I not lean anxiously over the walls? Did I not catch all of them as they returned from the battle? Did I not eagerly try to get hold of the messengers? But *you* were not worrying; it was as though you had what you wanted[7] when you exposed him. Come, who bound up his wounds when he returned, who washed away the blood? Who brought him to the temple? Who gave thanks? Did you know even then that it was *your* duty, or do you admit that all this had nothing to do with you? You may pretend otherwise, and from another point of view this may seem to make against my case[8]: you knew, and you let him be with me.

You recognized this ten thousand.[9] You did not care about the young man's distinctions or about the glory of exceptional bravery that I had already taken for myself. This was what emboldened you to pay the upbringing charges. You make up your account with me, and you become the only man alive to have got back the child you exposed and made money on it.

279

A rich man cuckolds a handsome youth

Let it be lawful either to kill an adulterer or to take money and let him go. A rich man solicited a poor man, father of a handsome boy, about sex with his son. The poor man said nothing. He solicited the poor man a second time, adding money. The other said nothing. Solicited a third time, he gave a wife to his son. The boy caught the rich man with his wife and let him go after taking money. He is disowned by his father.

1

Priusquam venio ad aestimationem criminis et propriam iudicii huiusce summam, necesse habeo id dicere quod in oculos uniuscuiusque vestrum, iudices, incurrit: abdicatur puer. Nolite illum aestimare ex hoc quod maritus est; in quo illud praecipue, iudices, vereor, ne apud animos vestros suspectus sit impudentiae ac videatur intra hos annos nimium cito virum egisse: uxorem pater impuberi dedit.

2 Quid igitur haec aetas committere potuit tanta animadversione dignum? Lex abdicationis adversus ferociam iuvenum constituta est. Haec vero infirmitas adeo nocentis nomen non recipit ut vix recipiat innocentis.

3 Si tamen perseveras abdicare tamquam iuvenem, superest ut ego quoque tamquam iuvenem defendam. Vultis igitur, iudices, dicam illa omnibus fere abdicationum iudiciis vulgata pro liberis: 'non ego luxuriatus sum, non ego meretricem amavi, non paterna bona vitiis consumpsi'? Sed si hoc proposuero, respondebitur (potest enim): 'adulteros' inquit 'non occidisti.'

4 Dicamus et tamquam pro marito. Non habes ius abdicandi propter hoc quod lex huic permisit. Vereor ne risum mereatur haec defensio mea, tamquam hic utrumlibet potuerit. Sed potuerit sane. Marito vel occidere adulterum vel accepta pecunia dimittere licet. Non potes propter id 5 irasci quod iura huic permiserunt. Loquatur maritus cum animo suo, loquatur cum adfectu suo, cum propria animi sui natura. Si propter hoc licet abdicare, istud quod fecit maritus non licet. Alioqui enim tolerabilius et certe huma-

---

[1] Apparently implying "that is the only possible answer" (*quid enim potest?*). *Inquit* (not translated) would be better away.

Before I come to consider the charge and the special sum and substance of this trial, I must needs say what meets the eyes of each one of you, gentlemen of the jury: a boy is disowned. Do not judge him from the fact that he is a husband. In that respect, my principal fear, gentlemen, is that in your minds you may suspect him of impudence and think that at his age he played the grown man too soon. The father gave him a wife when he was not into puberty. So what could anyone of his age do to deserve so severe a punishment? The law on disowning was established against the unruliness of young men. But the weakness we have here is so far from allowing the name of guilty that it hardly allows the name of innocent.

If, however, you are determined to disown him as though he was a young man, I too have no alternative but to defend him as though he was a young man. Do you then wish me, gentlemen, to make the pleas commonly used on behalf of children in pretty well all disownment trials: "I have not lived loosely, I have not had an affair with a prostitute, I have not wasted my father's goods on vices"? But if I put this forward, the answer will be (for it can only be): "You did not kill the adulterers."[1]

Let me also speak as though on behalf of a husband. You have no right to disown on account of this act that the law permitted him. I am afraid that this defense of mine may deserve to be laughed at: as though he had a choice! But suppose he did. A husband may either kill an adulterer or take money and let him go. You cannot be angry because of something that the law permitted him. Let a husband consult his own mind, consult his own feelings, the particular nature of his mind. If it is lawful to disown for this, then what the husband did is not lawful. From another

nius erat arbitrium vel occidendi adulteri vel accepta pecunia dimittendi transferri ad patres, quoniam certe levius
est vetare aliqua quam punire.

6   Sic defenderetur si iure tecum ageret. Ipsius vero facti
vel hoc modo rationem facile reddidissem: non est istud
turpe quod lex permittit. ⟦'Accepta pecunia dimisisti.' Nisi

7   oporteret, nec liceret.⟧[1] An vero parum sancti illi videntur
fuisse maiores, illi constitutores iuris, qui civitates adhuc
velut antiquo illo errore confusas ad certam vivendi formam redegerunt? Illis non est visum nefas accipere pecuniam, sed et hanc poenam[2] animadversionis ∗ putaverunt,
sicut pleraque delicta ⟨multa⟩[3] puniuntur: neque enim

8   semper usque ad mortem pervenitur.[4] Credo autem illum,
quisquis fuit legis huiusce constitutor, illa intra se cogitasse, non omnium animos maritorum durare ad sanguinem, esse quosdam mitiores qui ne conspicere quidem
cruorem sufficerent. Multi se a gladiatorum vulneribus
avertunt, et quamquam[5] nemo dubitet et illud spectaculum in parte esse poenarum, tamen nequissimorum quo-

9   que hominum suprema pericula habent suam gratiam. De
spectaculo loquor: cogitaverunt quanto esset difficilius
⟨privatim⟩[6] occidere, ac scierunt futurum ut, si unam hanc

---

[1] *ita secl. SB*[3]

[2] p. ⟨satis⟩ *Hå.*[2], *sed plura excidisse videntur, velut* animadv.
(*loco gravioris concedendam esse⟩ SB*[2]

[3] *SB*[2]   [4] *Ro.:* -iunt Aβ

[5] *Pith.:* tam- Aβ   [6] *SB*[4]

---

[2] The lawgiver would not have introduced this questionable

angle, it would be more tolerable and certainly more humane that the choice between killing an adulterer and taking money and letting him go were transferred to fathers, since it is certainly less drastic to forbid something than to punish it.

That is how he could be defended if he were at issue with you on the law. As for the act itself, I could easily have made a case thus: what the law permits is not dishonorable. ⟦You took money and let him go. If that were not the right course, it would not be permitted.[2] ⟧ Or do you think those forebears of ours were too little scrupulous, those enactors of law, who brought communities still as it were in the confusion of the old-time error into a fixed pattern of living? They did not think it a sin to take money, but that this penalty too should be allowed instead of a heavier punishment (?), just as many offences are punished ⟨by a fine⟩, for it does not always come to death. And I believe that whoever laid down this law thought to himself that not all husbands have a stomach tough enough for bloodshed, that some are of milder temper, lacking the strength even to look at blood. Many turn away from gladiators' wounds and though nobody doubts that the spectacle is part of the punishment, yet the final perils of even the worst offenders have their appeal.[3] I speak of a spectacle: they considered how much more difficult it was to kill ⟨in private⟩,[4] and they knew that if they had laid down this one penalty,

and unconventional alternative if he had not actually preferred it. But this is an interruption.

[3] They can arouse pity. *Habent misericordiam* (Watt) is rather to be understood, as it was by Håkanson, than substituted.

[4] Requisite for sense. Other words (e.g. *domi*) are possible.

mortis poenam contra adulteros constituissent, saepius impune committeretur adulterium. Constituerunt ergo poenam et secundam; prospexerunt infirmioribus, prospexerunt lenioribus. Forsitan cogitaverunt et illud, non omnibus futuras esse vires. Ita temperaverunt severitatem ut vindicaret se quomodo quisque posset.

10   Dixi tamquam pro iuvene, dixi tamquam pro marito; dicendum est tamquam pro impubere. Non mehercule satis constituere apud animum meum possum an huic adulteros

11   licuerit occidere. Quo enim tandem modo defenderetur filius tuus si quis extitisset qui diceret: 'occidisti homines nondum maritus: neque enim vis ista nominis huiusce appellatione prima consistit, nec satis est maritum tantum osculo putari', postea nudari filium atque in conspectu iudicum constitui coegisset, atque interrogaret an ille ma-

12   ritus esset qui fieri pater non posset? Ac si tantum illi tamquam adultero irascereris, satis erat hoc dicere pro filio tuo: 'Puto, nondum habebat mariti dolorem. Ad vulnera adulteri et caedem et tristissimum occidendi hominis ministerium magno quodam impetu et (ut sic dixerim) furore

13   opus est. Nec miror eos concitari qui veterem matrimonii consuetudinem, qui pudorem cubiculi, qui spem liberorum expugnatam esse credunt, qui illos occultos atque inenarrabiles patiuntur aestus: non potest uxorem suam sic odisse qui adhuc amare non potuit.'

14   Verum illi quoque parti respondendum est qua vindicandam priorem iniuriam fuisse dicit: de qua hodie dum

---

    5 And not because of earlier solicitations. The failure to deal with these himself is developed in ss.14–18.   6 Hate an adulterer. The wife's role is played down throughout; cf. s.16 fin.

death, against adulterers, adultery would more often be committed with impunity. So they laid down a second penalty; they had regard for the weaker brethren, the more lenient. Perhaps they reflected also that not all would have the strength. They tempered severity so that each avenged himself according to his capability.

I have spoken as though for a young man, I have spoken as though for a husband; I must speak as for one not into puberty. Upon my word, I cannot quite settle in my mind whether it was lawful for him to kill the adulterers. For how would your son have been defended if someone had come along to say: "You killed human beings when you were not yet a husband; for the meaning of this name does not consist in the initial appellation, and it is not enough to be reckoned a husband merely for a kiss." Next he would have had your son stripped naked and set in sight of the jury, and have asked whether one who could not become a father was a husband. And if you were angry with that man simply as an adulterer,[5] it would be enough to say this on behalf of your son: "I think he didn't yet feel a husband's pain. To wound and kill an adulterer, to take on the grisly job of killing a human being, requires a mighty impulse and, if you will, madness. I don't wonder that people get excited who believe that inveterate habit of matrimony, modesty of the bedroom, hope of children have been outraged, who suffer that hideous, indescribable turmoil: but one who could not yet love his wife cannot hate so."[6]

But I must also reply to the part[7] in which he says that the previous injury should have been avenged. On that he had much to say today in the course of his disowning, vehe-

_____

[7] Of the poor man's case.

abdicat multa vehementer graviterque dixit, cum fieret
tacebat. Non existimo adeo inimicum filio suo patrem,
quamvis abdicet, ut aliquid turpiter suspicetur praeter id
maledictum quod ipse audivit, quod intra verba constitit.
15 Maximo atque admirabili potius experimento gravitatem
huius pueri severitatemque, iudices, colligetis,[7] quia is qui
tantum nefas concupierat ipsum puerum appellare non
ausus est. Facilius illi fuit loqui cum hoc patre, hoc severo,
et loqui non semel et pecuniam polliceri et adicere pre-
16 tium. Tum iste tamen non adiit magistratus, non vocifera-
tione saltem invidiam facere apud populum conatus est:
tanto facilius est exigere magnum animum quam praestare. Si hominem occidere facile est, tum feriri oportuit
cum de stupro filii tui loquebatur, cum tuarum id partium,
tui animi, tuarum etiam virium fuit. Nam fingamus sane istud matrimonium fuisse: quis tamen omnium mortalium
hoc exigat, ut fortius uxor quam filius vindicetur?
17 Sic ego hunc defenderem, iudices, si occidere noluis-
set. Rursus mihi ad id redeundum est ex quo defensionem
huius ingressus sum. Ecquid vos cogitatis aetatem, ecquid
videtis annos, ecquid semoto illo nuptiarum mimo atque inani tantummodo nomine virum esse aestimatis[8] et
18 dignum qui abdicetur quod hominem non occiderit? Itane
tu pater bonus es, qui caritate filii neglecta imitatus es pue-

7 *Watt*[2]: dilig- Aβ
8 *SB*[3] (puta- *SB*[1]): cogita- Aβ

---

8 The report of the rich man's proposition, as Wi. explains. But
no such report is mentioned either in the theme or the declamation. Has it disappeared? *Maledictum* could hardly mean the
proposition itself.

mently and impressively; but when it was going on he kept
mum. I do not think the father is so hostile to his son, although he is disowning him, as to suspect anything shameful, apart from that slander[8] which he hears himself, which
went no further than words. Rather, gentlemen, you will
deduce this boy's gravity and purity from a significant and
remarkable test, in that the man who had set his fancy[9] on
such a villainy did not dare to approach the boy himself. It
was easier for him to talk to his father, this austere gentleman, and to talk to him more than once, and to promise
money, and to add a price. At the time, however, this gentleman did not go to the magistrates, did not try at least to
create a public scandal by an outcry: so much easier is it to
demand great courage than to show it. If it is easy to kill a
human being, he should have been struck when he talked
about corrupting your son, when that was what your role,
your courage, even your strength made appropriate. For
let us suppose it was a marriage, who in the world would
demand that a wife be avenged[10] more boldly than a son?

That is how I should defend him, gentlemen, if he had
refused to kill. I must go back again to the starting point of
my defense of him. Don't you think of his age, don't you see
how young he is? Don't you put aside that charade of marriage, an empty name and nothing more? Do you judge
him as a man, deserving to be disowned because he did not
kill a human being? Good father are you? Regardless of

---

[9] For this well-established though insufficiently recognized
sense of *concupisco* see my note on Cic. *Epist. ad Oct.* 4 in *Cicero,
Letters to Quintus etc.* (Loeb), p. 348.

[10] Not "punished" (nonsense in this context). It actually seems
to be implied that the wife was a victim. See n.3 above.

ri infirmitatem adversus eum qui de stupro filii tui te appellare ausus est, quem punire etiamsi tibi moriendum esset debuisti: tu huic irasceris qui ex duobus adulteris nulli eorum par erat, qui certe praestitit tibi quantum plurimum potuit? Diu moratus est, detinuit; dum pecunia adfertur, dum expeditur,[9] dum numeratur, fuerat tuae curae, tuae severitatis intervenire et aliquid facere fortius. Ego Fortunae agendas esse gratias puto quod emissus dicitur qui potuit erumpere.

19

280

Raptor reversus

Rapta raptoris aut mortem optet aut nuptias. Quidam rapuit et profugit. Raptam pater alii collocavit. Rediit postea qui rapuerat. Vult illum ad magistratus educere pater. Patitur ille se educi; rapta tacet; maritus contradicit.

1

SERMO

Actionem oportet esse summissam et blandam. Nam primum omnium dicendum est ei adversus socerum; deinde ita dicendum est ut sciamus hoc agere eum, ut socer sit; praeterea causa illius nihil habet firmius quam ‹si›[1] sit alienus.[2] Etiam sollicitudo quodammodo temperanda est,

---

[9] *Watt*[2]: repetitur Aβ: perspicitur *SB*[2]
[1] *Aer.*   [2] *SB*[1]: -na Aβ

---

[11] Cf. s.16. You behaved as weakly as the boy—whose display of weakness, however, was subsequent to the rich man's solicitation.   [12] *Neutri* would be correct. He could not kill the lover or play husband to the wife.

love for your son, you imitated the boy's weakness[11] in dealing with the man who dared to approach you about corrupting your son, whom you ought to have punished even if you had to die for it. Are you angry with him, who of two adulterers was no match for either,[12] who certainly did all he could for you? He took a long while, kept them there. While the money was being brought, got out,[13] counted, it had been for your care, your strictness to intervene and do something more drastic. I think we should thank Fortune that he was let go, as it's said: he could have broken out!

280

Rapist returned

Let a raped woman opt either for death of the rapist or marriage. A man committed rape and fled. The father married the raped girl to somebody else. The rapist later returned. The father wants to bring him up before the magistrates. He allows himself to be brought up; the raped girl[1] says nothing. The husband opposes.

DISCUSSION

The style should be restrained and conciliatory. For, first of all, he has to plead against his father-in-law. Then he has to plead in such a way that we know he is out to keep him as his father-in-law. Moreover, the strongest thing in *his* case is <that> he[2] should be estranged. Also the husband's anxi-

---

[13] Or, reading *perspicitur*, "inspected" (for weight and metal content).   [1] She is not present at the hearing; see s.16.

[2] The father. A display of hostility towards his father-in-law, whose real object, as hinted throughout, is to get rid of him, would be counterproductive. But this is problematical (see Wi.).

ut neque desperare neque securus esse videatur.

2   Sed modus et color declamationis sic ducendus est, quaestiones illae erunt: an educi rapta nisi protinus possit; an, etiam si tempore interposito potest, possit tamen post nuptias; an, quia ante educi non potuit raptor, nunc educi debeat; quo animo pater educere ad magistratus velit; an patiente eo qui educendus est contradicere liceat, an aequum sit; quo animo hic contradicat.[3]

3   Scio posse quaeri an illa quaestio quae ad personam pertinet [et][4] in prima parte ponenda sit, ⟨non⟩ qua[5] a me supra constituta est. Ego aliquid in hoc ordinem[6] etiam thematis[7] spectavi: quo ⟨ultimo⟩[8] loco ponitur illud, quod tacente raptore hic loquatur †quid velit†. Spectavi[9] et illud, quod adfectibus qui secuturi sunt magis haec quaestio quam ulla alia coniuncta est.

4   DECLAMATIO

Si contradiceret ipse qui rapuit, id est, si timeret, sic pro se ageret: educere tibi ad magistratus raptorem non licet nisi statim. Quare? Quoniam omnium vel poenarum vel praemiorum tempus aut constitutum est aut praesens. Quotiens finitur dies, expectandus, quotiens vero non differtur,

---

[3] *Sch.*: educat Aβ   [4] *Aer.*
[5] sit, ⟨non⟩ qua *Ro.*: est quae Aβ   [6] *ed. princ.*: -e Aβ
[7] *Ro.*: -te Aβ   [8] *Ro.*   [9] *Obr.*: -ari A: -are β

---

[3] The father's motive.

[4] See crit. note.

[5] I leave the enigmatic *quid velit?* untranslated ("the despairing cry of a baffled reader?" Wi.).

[6] He is not speaking because he knows that the girl will not

ety should be somewhat tempered, so that he does not seem either despairing or at ease.

But the moderation and tone of the declamation is to be conducted so. The questions will be as follows: can the raped girl be brought up if it is not done at once? Even if it can be done after an interval of time, can it be done after a wedding? Since the rapist could not be brought up earlier, ought he to be brought up now? What is the father's motive for wanting to bring him up before the magistrates? Is there freedom to oppose when the person to be brought up acquiesces? Is it fair? With what motive does he oppose?

I know that it can be asked whether the question pertaining to the persona[3] should be in the first part rather than as I have placed it above.[4] In this matter I paid some attention to the order of the theme, in which the fact that he is speaking while the rapist says nothing is placed ⟨last⟩.[5] I also had regard to the fact that this question more than any other is connected with the emotions that are to follow.

DECLAMATION

If the rapist himself were opposing, that is, if he were afraid,[6] he would speak thus on his own behalf: you are not allowed to bring a rapist before the magistrates unless it is done at once. Why? Because the time for all punishments or rewards is either specified or it is the present.[7] When a day is definitely set, it must be waited for, but when there is

---

choose death. The implication, pivotal throughout, is that the father and the rapist are in collusion; cf. s.11.

[7] A questionable doctrine; see Wi.

praesens est. Itaque sicut, ‹si›[10] dies finiatur, nihil ultra
eum iuris futurum est, ita die non praefinito proximum
5 esse manifestum est, nihil ultra proximum ius sit.[11] Id porro quod in quolibet iure alio manifestum foret in hac lege
apertius est. Quid enim dicit? 'Rapta raptoris mortem vel
nuptias optet.' Neutra res est quam differri oporteat: sive
is est raptor qui poenam mereatur, non meretur advocatio-
nem, sive ignoscitur raptori, non debent habere moram
nuptiae ut[12] inchoatae.

6 Si tantum non statim educeres, haec fortiter dicerentur; nunc educere vis post nuptias. Utrum igitur iure prius
an aequitate consistes? Ius ipsa legis positione manifestum
est. Nam cum raptam educi in hoc iubeat, ut mortem vel
nuptias optet, manifesto ostendit eam educi oportere cui
7 utrumque liberum sit. Praeterea iam ne raptae quidem
nomen habere potest quae nupta est. Sicuti nomen pupil-
lorum legitimo tempore finitur, sicut orbam nemo post
nuptias dixerit, sicuti virginis appellationem nox illa mari-
talis aufert, ita ne rapta quidem dici potest quae maritum
habere coepit. Licet igitur raptae permissum sit quocumque tempore optare, nuptae optare permissum non est.
8 Haec ex lege manifesta sunt, illa ex aequitate. Ante omnia
non tam duram esse lex voluit condicionem ut semper raptor puniretur: ideo et misericordiae locum fecit. Et †idcir-
co†[13] iam non ad ipsum tantummodo qui rapuit sed etiam

---

[10] *Aer.*   [11] nihil . . . sit *del. Wi.*   [12] *SB*[2]: vel Aβ
[13] id *coni. Wi.*: id, credo *Watt*[2]

---

[8] See crit. note.

[9] A married woman cannot opt for marriage to her rapist without destroying her existing marriage; so the rapist does not have

no deferment, it is now. So just as, ⟨if⟩ a day is set in advance, there will be no right beyond that day, so if a day is not set in advance, it is clear that the next is meant, nothing is lawful beyond the next.[8] Furthermore, what would be clear in the case of any other law is more plain in this one. For what does it say? "Let a raped woman opt for either the death of the rapist or marriage." Neither one is something that should be deferred. If the rapist is a man deserving death, he does not deserve an adjournment, whereas if the rapist is pardoned, the wedding, as having begun already, ought not to be delayed.

I should have said this boldly if you had brought him up *almost* at once. As it is, you want to bring him up after the wedding. So will you take your stand on law or on equity? The law is clear from the very framing of the statute. For when it prescribes that a raped woman be brought up in order that she opt for death or marriage, it clearly shows the woman brought up be free to opt either way. Moreover, a married woman can no longer even be called a raped woman. Just as the name of war ends at the legal time, just as no one would refer to a woman as an orphan after her marriage, just as the wedding night cancels the appellation of virgin, so also a woman who has begun to have a husband cannot be called raped. So suppose a raped woman may be allowed to opt at any time, a married woman is not allowed to opt. That is clear from the law, this from equity: to start with, the law did not wish the terms to be so harsh as to mean that a rapist should always be punished; and so it left room for mercy.[9] And that now applies not only to

the fair chance that the lawgiver wanted for him (this, of course, ignores the suspected collusion).

ad eum qui duxit[14] pertinet, qui certe nihil peccavit, qui certe manere potuit.

9   Hoc loco mihi illud opponitur, non potuisse ante educi eum. Quasi vero intersit causae qua ratione ius interierit! Profugerat' inquit 'raptor.' Scio quid facillimum sit dicere: persecutus esset, inquisisset; si verus hic dolor, si vera indignatio erat, non omisisset. Non hoc illi profuit, quod profugit, sed illud, quod redire permisisti. Fortasse enim contentus fueras hac ipsa poena exilii, satis vindicatum te

10   credideras. Ne illud quidem verendum, ne raptoribus exemplum profugiendi permittamus si optari adversus eos amplius non potuerit. Satis enim magnum supplicium hoc est et certum. Nam is qui permanserit, sperare et nuptias poterit, etiamsi mortem timebit; ei vero qui profugerit exilium sine dubitatione erit patiendum.

11   Haec diceret ipse, quae nunc ego dico quoniam ille non dicit et obstare nihil hoc loco putat ius. Si non possem reddere rationem, iudices, quantum mea interesset id quod vindico, illud tamen responderem: 'Pro iure loqui nemini non licet. Conveniat inter vos fortasse (hoc est quod me sollicitissimum facit): loquar tamen pro lege, loquar pro

12   aequitate.' Quid si vero hoc, ut paulo ante dixi, aliquanto

---

14 *Ri.*: ed- Aβ; eam d- *Sch.*

---

10 The law should not ignore the husband, who has done nothing wrong. Why should his marriage be jeopardized? The point of *qui . . . potuit* eludes me.

11 You let him come back instead of hauling him back.

12 No need to worry about giving future rapists an easy way out.

13 He wants the option because he and the father are in collu-

the rapist himself but also to the person who married, who certainly did nothing wrong, who certainly could stay at home.[10]

At this point I encounter the objection that he could not have been brought up earlier. As though it mattered to the case *why* the right lapsed: "The rapist had fled," he says. I know the easiest answer: he should have pursued him, sought him out: if this distress, this indignation had been genuine, he would not have let the thing go. The rapist did not benefit by his flight but by your permission to return.[11] For perhaps you had been content with this very punishment of exile, believed yourself sufficiently avenged. Nor need we be afraid of allowing rapists the example of flight if subsequent option against them not be possible. For this punishment is great enough and certain. For somebody who remains will still be able to hope for marriage even though he fears death, but a fugitive will certainly have to suffer exile.[12]

All this he could have said himself; I say it now since he does not and thinks that the right is not against him at this point.[13] If I could not explain to you, gentlemen, how important my claim is to me, I should still reply: "Nobody is forbidden to speak on behalf of the law. Perhaps the two of you have an understanding (that is what worries me most): nevertheless, I shall speak for law, I shall speak for equity." But what if this, as I said just now,[14] concerns me rather

---

sion. Wi. secludes *nihil hoc loco* and thinks "the seducer keeps quiet because he thinks the law is against him." Just the reverse: see s.4 init. *Ius* in the passage may be taken as the right of option rather than the law, making no odds to the sense.

[14] See s.8 fin.

magis ad me quam ad raptorem pertinet? Periclitor enim
nuptiis, periclitor matrimonio, non una nocte cognito, nec
propter errorem fortasse nec propter iniuriam, sed delec-
to, sed probato, sed impetrato.

13   Temptat me adversus haec socer spe fallere, et non
palam ostendit quid sit optatura.[15] Ita blanditur tamen
†actioni†.[16] Libenter, iudices, credo: remansura est in meo
matrimonio. <Sed>[17] misereor raptoris, neque ego primus
coepi. Misereor: erravit fortasse. Ut scelus commiserit homo, dum periclitatur etiam imago poenae me confundit.
Hoc cum mihi accidat, quid accidere potest puellae? Neque ego tamen illum defendo. Fecit enim rem improbam,
14   fecit rem inconsultam. ⟦Sed exulavit, sed afuit.⟧ Haec si
confiderem, illud vero ad metus pertinet. Et tamen non
ego de uxore diffido, non de animo illius dubito: alioqui
minus sollicitus essem. Scio meruisse me ut amarer, scio
obsecutum, scio omnia maritalia officia plena indulgentia
consecutum. Illud dubito, quid[18] possit cum educta fuerit
ad magistratus, cum ille periturus iacuerit ad pedes, cum
15   produxerit propinquos, cum amicos. Quare alius dicat uxori meae: 'amo et ideo rapui'? Quare sit qui contra me dicat,
<dicat>[19]: 'miserere'[20]? Timeo favorem illum populi, mise-
ricordiam civitatis. Quid autem fieri iniquius potest quam

[15] *Ro.*: -rus Aβ
[16] adfectui *SB*[1]   [17] *SB*[3]
[18] *Sch.*: qui AB   [19] *SB*[4]
[20] *Obr.*: miser(a)e *vel sim.* Aβ

[15] A possibility in the rapist's case; cf. s.13 *erravit fortasse*.
[16] By the bride's father, who is now plotting to undo it.
[17] See crit. note.

than the rapist? For my wedding, my marriage is at risk, a marriage not known for a single night, not the result of error,[15] it may be, or injury, but chosen, approved, granted.[16]

In face of all this my father-in-law tries to deceive me with hope and does not show publicly what she is going to opt for.[17] Thus in spite of all he flatters my affection (?). I gladly believe it, gentlemen; she will remain married to me. <But> I am sorry for the rapist and I am not the first to be.[18] I am sorry for him. Perhaps he made a mistake. If the man did commit a crime, in his hour of danger the very imagination of his punishment confounds me. Since that happens to me, what can happen to the girl? Not that I am defending him. He did a bad thing, an ill-advised thing. ⟦But he went into exile, he was absent.⟧ If I were confident about the one, the other relates to my fears.[19] Still, I am not mistrustful about my wife, I don't doubt her feelings; otherwise I should be less worried.[20] I know that I deserved to be loved, I know that I deferred to her, I know that I fulfilled all maritial duties in complete fondness. What I am doubtful about is what she may be capable of when she is brought before the magistrates, when the doomed man lies at her feet, when he produces his kinsfolk and friends. Why should another man say to my wife: "I love you and that is why I raped you?" Why should there be someone to speak against me <and say>: "Have pity." I am afraid of public sentiment, the compassion of the community. And what can be more unfair than that my wife be

---

18 A dig at his father-in-law. In what follows the speaker affects to hope, though with misgivings, that his wife will opt for death.

19 *Haec* is the rapist's misconduct, *illud* the pity he may excite.

20 Her kind nature may make her compassionate.

abduci mihi uxorem propter quam aliquando raptor ausus
sit reverti? Qui ipse satis indicavit[21] non esse legi locum,
quod reversus est. Confundit me maxime spes illius: cum
timeret profugit; at nunc educi se patitur.

16   Silentium quidem uxoris meae ego vero neque suspectum habeo neque timeo: decet hoc matronalem pudorem;
et si educta ad magistratus fuerit, hoc illam maxime factu-
17   ram arbitror, ut taceat. Quare, socer, tu opta. Si hoc quae-
sisti educendo raptorem ad magistratus, ut confunderes,
ut terreres, ut te metu illius vindicares, intellectum arti-
ficium tuum est: non timet. Tuere nuptias quas iunxisti,
tuere matrimonium quod copulasti; istum raptorem puta
abesse.

281

Abdicandus cum gladio

Qui abdicatur contradixit. Inter moras iudicii stricto gladio
occurrit in solitudine patri; rogavit ut sibi abdicationem
remitteret et coegit iurare. Iuravit ille et accusat filium
parricidii.

1   SERMO

Narratione praeparandum est ut, quoniam nulla certa causa est abdicationis, videatur pater parricidii suspicione

[21] Showing what a treasure she is.
[22] He knew that the option would be a farce.
[23] Just rhetoric? Or could the magistrate(s) let the father de-

taken away from me for whose sake the rapist has at last ventured to return?[21] He himself by returning has sufficiently signified that there is no place for the law.[22] Most of all I am confounded by his hope. When he was afraid, he fled, but now he lets himself be brought up.

As for my wife's silence, no, I neither suspect nor fear it. It is becoming to her modesty as a married lady. And if she is brought up before the magistrates, I think she will take very good care to say nothing. Therefore, father-in-law, do you make the option.[23] If your object in bringing the rapist before the magistrates was to confound him, terrify him, avenge yourself by his fear, your trick has been fathomed: he is not afraid.[24] Protect the match you made, the marriage you joined. Think of that rapist as absent.

281

Disowned-to-be with a sword

A person who is being disowned has pleaded to the contrary. During the delays of the trial, sword in hand he met his father in a lonely place. He asked him to remit the disowning and forced him to swear an oath. The other swore and accuses the son of parricide.

DISCUSSION

In the narrative we must lay a foundation, so that, since there is no certain reason for the disowning, the father may seem to have acted out of a suspicion of parricide and to

cide if the victim refused to opt? The suggestion is premature anyway. [24] If you were playing a trick, forget it and opt for death in earnest.

fecisse et has insidias praevidisse. Quaestiones illae sunt:
an ad legem parricidii satis sit probare hoc [in][1] reo propositum fuisse; an hoc propositum huic fuerit.

2

Primum hoc mihi responde, an occisuri habitu fueris. Non
enim tibi proderit dixisse: 'non feci.' Numquam mens exitu
aestimanda est. Nam et qui impetum in patrem stricto gladio fecisset retentus diceret: 'non occidi'; si venenum para-
tum deprehendissem, diceres: 'non occidi.' Quin etiam, si
permittitur ista defensio, et ille potest dicere se non occidisse qui percussorem summiserit.

3   Satis ergo est probare animum parricidae. Superest ut
cogitetis an hic animum habuerit. Si occultius esset coniectura ducenda, dicerem turpem adulescentem, dicerem: 'abdicatus est: et si innocens, magis poterit irasci.'
Sed quid causam infirmo dicendo? In aliqua vos positos
specula putate illa quae facta sunt videre. Abdicatus in
solitudine est: locus oportunus insidiis. Habet gladium:
instrumentum parricidii. Accedit ad patrem manuque
sublata 'rogo' dicit: <rogat dico?>[2] immo iubet; non sunt
4 enim preces ubi negandi libertas non est. Utriusque intuemini animum, et, si videtur, prius meum. Occisurum te
non dubitavi ideoque ille severus negare non potui. Reliqua a vestris animis interrogate, is qui armatus rogat quid
facturus sit si non impetraverit. Duo sunt, opinor, inter
quae quaestio interposita videatur: hic si non impetrasset
aut occisurus fuerat aut moriturus. Non dico utrum credi-

[1] *Ro.*   [2] *SB³, auct. Sch.*

[1] The declamation does not take up this suggestion.

have foreseen this ambush.[1] The questions are as follows: as regards the law of parricide, is it sufficient to prove that this was the defendant's intention? Was it his intention?

DECLAMATION

First answer me this, was your get-up that of a man about to kill? It will do you no good to say, "I didn't do it." Intention is never to be judged by outcome. Even somebody who ran at his father with drawn sword and was restrained could say: "I didn't kill him." If I had caught poison prepared, you would say: "I didn't kill him." Indeed, if this defense is allowed, even someone who has hired an assassin can say that he didn't commit murder.

It is enough therefore to prove parricidal mind. It remains for you to consider whether this man had such a mind. If an inference had to be made clandestinely, I should say the young man was infamous, I should say, "He was disowned, and if he was innocent, he will have the more reason to be angry." But why weaken my case by talking? Imagine that you are on a watchtower, looking at what took place. The disowned son is in a lonely spot, the spot is opportune for an ambush. He has a sword, instrument of parricide. He goes up to his father and raises his hand, says, "I ask." "Ask," do I say? Rather, he orders; for there are no pleas where there is no freedom to refuse. Look at the minds of each of us, and, if you will, mine first. I did not doubt that you were going to kill me and therefore I, the stern father, could not say no. For the rest, question your own minds, what an armed man who is asking will do if he is refused. There are two possibilities, I think, between which the question seems to lie: if he had not gained his point, he would have either killed or died. I don't say which

305

5　bilius sit, utrum facilius. Exorare me volueras? Quanto
oportunius alibi rogasses, alio tempore, cum primum abdicatus es, adhibitis propinquis, amicis! Quid facit ad preces
solitudo? Ista instrumenta sunt parricidii, haec occasio,
hic locus, hoc tempus. Si abdicarem te, moriturus fuisti?
Reum parricidii ago. Quid superest igitur nisi ut vindicatu-
rus fueris eam quam iniuriam vocabas?

6　　'Non' inquit 'occidi.' Hoc quidem [in][3] genere nemo
non defendi potest cui voluntas parricidii obicitur. 'Non'
inquit 'occidi.' ⟨Quid⟩[4] si dicerem: 'Facilius[5] putasti, scelera propius admota plus habent horroris,' si dicerem:
'Obstitit tibi vis numinum et tacita quaedam illius solitudi-
nis religio'? Nunc vero manifestum est cur non occideris:
distulisti hunc animum dum heres fieres.

282

Tyrannicida veste muliebri

Tyrannicidae praemium. Tyrannus cum in arcem duci iussisset cuiusdam sororem, frater habitu sororis ascendit et
occidit tyrannum. Eodem habitu magistratus illi praemii
nomine statuam collocavit. Iniuriarum reus est.

3 *Gron.*
4 *Ro.*
5 *SB*[3]: diffic- A*β*

---

2 The fact that he is still alive and facing a capital charge shows
that he was not about to kill himself.

is the more credible, the easier. You had wanted to win my pardon? How much more opportunely you could have asked me somewhere else, at another time, when you were first disowned, with kinsfolk and friends called in! How is solitude good for pleas? Those are the instruments of parricide, this the opportunity, this the place, this the time. If I disowned you, were you going to die? I am accusing you of parricide.[2] What is left then but that you were going to avenge this injury, as you called it?

"I did not kill," he says. Nobody who is charged with will to commit parricide but can be defended in this way. "I did not kill," he says. <What> if I were to say: "It was not as easy as you thought. Crimes are more horrible when they come close up"? Or if I were to say, "A supernatural force stopped you, a silent awfulness of that lonely place"? But as it is, it's clear why you didn't kill me: you put off that intention until you should become my heir."[3]

282

A tyrannicide in woman's clothing

<Let there be> a reward for a tyrannicide. When a tyrant ordered that somebody's sister be brought to the castle, the brother went up in his sister's clothes and killed the tyrant. By way of reward the magistrate put up a statue to him dressed in the same clothes. He is accused of injuries.

[3] A sudden switch: he bethinks him that as soon as the son gets himself reestablished as son and heir he will kill for the inheritance—instead of killing now. Even so, he *had* intended parricide.

1
DECLAMATIO

Animus ‹nos› liberavit[1] nec interest quo habitu statua po-
natur. Varia gentibus consuetudo est, et hoc tibi honestius
erat: inter multos tyrannicidas notabilis eris in eadem
veste[2] in qua pro sorore venisti. Bella quoque insidias
habent. Statua ergo tua non transibitur; habitus faciet ut
2 interrogent transcurrentes. Iam illa tempora cogita quibus
senex aliquis narrabit fuisse te qui inexpugnabilem arcem
intrares pro sorore, puerum adhuc fecisse fortiter. Debes
igitur mihi beneficium quod tyrannicidium tuum semper
monstrabitur.

283

Cynicus diserti filius

Disertus Cynicum filium abdicat. CD.

1
DECLAMATIO

In quacumque parte non parentem iuste abdicarem; ideo
enim vos sustulimus ut nobis obsequamini, et certe nullus
excusatius a patre non probabitur quam qui non probat
patrem. Scilicet nos stulti qui forum ‹celebramus, qui›[1]
rei publicae dignitatem tuemur. Discede ab insipiente, ab
insano.

2   Sed non necesse habeo, iudices, diu commendare vobis
officia civilia, in quibus iam diu satisfeci; omnis mihi actio

[1] n. l. *SB*[1]: liber est A*β*
[2] *Gron.*: re A*β*
[1] *SB*[3] (qui *Aer.*)

---

[1] Removed the tyrant.

The mind gave us freedom,[1] and it doesn't matter in what clothes the statue was put up. Peoples have different customs; and this did you more honor. Among many tyrannicides you will be conspicuous in the same dress in which you came instead of your sister. Wars too have their tricks. So your statue will not be passed by; the dress will make people hurrying by ask questions. Think of the time when some old man will tell how it was you entered the impenetrable castle instead of your sister, that still a boy you became a hero. Therefore you owe me a favor because your slaying of the tyrant will always be pointed out.

283

Cynic son of orator

A pleader disowns his son, a Cynic. He opposes.

I might justly have disowned a disobedient son, in any context. For we acknowledged you sons so that you should obey us, and assuredly nobody will be disapproved of by his father with better excuse that one who disapproves of his father. No doubt we that <frequent> the Forum and maintain the dignity of the commonwealth are fools. Leave the idiot, the madman.[1]

But I have no need, gentlemen, to commend public duties to you at length, in which I have long given you satisfaction. My entire plea is located in examining my son's

---

283: [1] "All but the Wise Man are fools (or madmen)," said the Stoics.

in dispicienda vita filii posita est. Videte, ut alia taceam, habitum ipsum. Ceteros enim quos abdicant patres sine narratione culpae abdicare non possunt: in hoc filio satis est ad odium habitum ostendere. Quis est iste filii habitus, quae sordes? Quid mihi hanc invidiam facis, ut, cum habeas patrem, cibum ab aliis petas? Adversus fortunam te

3 exerces? Quid enim accidere gravius potest? Frigus, famem pateris ne quando accidant, et ideo aliquid pateris ne quando patiendum sit? Vos vero novo genere ambitus adorationem miseria captatis. Inde illa impudentia, quod verecundiam inter crimina ponitis et appellationem quoque

4 pessimam indidistis.[2] Omnis vero philosophiae tractatus alienus moribus nostrae civitatis est. Tamen utique placuerit: nonne aliae sectae iustiores? Attenderes physicis, quaereres utrumne ignis esset initium rerum an vero minutis editus et mobilibus[3] elementis, perpetuus hic mundus an mortalis esset. Viderint alii: ego in te hanc patientiam squaloris[4] ferre non possum. In alias te spes sustuli; de dignitate tua cogitabam.

5 Quod si abdicationem ferre non potes, si carere hereditate malum iudicas, deprehensus es: damno pecuniae moveris et detrimento famae, et homo qui has ipsas opes cotidie incusas tamen concupiscis. Indignus[5] es igitur. Verum fateamur ea quae sentimus, nec nos extra rerum natu-

2 p. i. *SB*[1]: passim nuper dedistis Aβ: *alii alia*
3 *Wi.*: mirab- Aβ
4 *SB*[1]: corpo- Aβ
5 *SB*[1]: dignus Aβ

life. To say nothing of other matters, just look at his get-up. In general, fathers cannot disown those they disown without detailing the misbehavior. In the case of this son I only have to point to the look of him to arouse disgust. What is this get-up of my son's, this filth? Why are you embarrassing me by begging food from other people when you have a father? Are you training yourself against Fortune? What worse can happen? Do you suffer cold and hunger for fear they may happen some day? Do you suffer something for fear that it may some day have to be suffered? But you and your like have a new style of self-promotion: you seek veneration by misery. Hence that shamelessness—you count modesty a crime and have taken to yourselves the most opprobrious of names.[2] But all philosophy-mongering is alien to the manners of our community. But suppose you just have to go in for it: are not other systems more legitimate? You could have listened to the natural philosophers, asked whether fire was the primal element or produced from minute and mobile atoms, whether this universe is perpetual or mortal. Others may do as they choose; I cannot put up with this tolerance of squalor in you. I acknowledged you as my son for other hopes. I was thinking of your dignity.[3]

But if you can't put up with being disowned, if you think forfeiture of inheritance is an evil, then you have been found out: you are affected by loss of money and damage to reputation. A man who every day girds against this very affluence, you want it all the same. So you don't deserve it. But let us admit what we feel; let vanity not put us outside

[2] Cynic (κυνικός from κύων, dog).
[3] When I disowned you.

ram ambitus ponat. Cuius enim est hominis pugnare cum
moribus et damnare se?

284

Adulter sacerdos

Sacerdos unius supplicio liberandi habeat potestatem.
Adulteros liceat occidere. Quidam sacerdotem deprehendit in adulterio et eum sibi ex lege impunitatem petentem
occidit. Reus est caedis.

1   SERMO

An sacerdos adhuc fuerit deprehensus, id est, an eo mo-
mento quo deprehensus est perdiderit ius sacerdotis; an, si
adhuc sacerdos erat, potuerit se postulare in hoc crimine;
an optare[1] usquam nisi in publico possit.

2   DECLAMATIO

Quod mihi sufficit, adulterum deprehendi. Neque enim
ulla excipitur persona et turpius est adulterium in sacerdote. 'Legem' inquit 'habuit.' Hoc tale est quale si ignosci
sibi velit dux proditor, vitiator pupillae tutor. Sed finge me
ex suspicione egisse cum illo adulterii: nempe damnatus
3 caruisset sacerdotio. Adice quod lex potestatem servandi
concedit alterius. Scriptum est ut qui civem servaverit ho-
noretur: numquid potest praemium accipere qui se serva-
4 verit? Aut iniuriarum damnari qui se pulsaverit? Praeterea
lex adulterii prior est quam sacerdotis. Sacerdos enim optat in publico: quod si adulter[2] tetigerit, evasit. Quid quod

---

¹ *Aer.:* occidi Aβ   ² *Sch.:* -rum Aβ

---

¹ Lit, "demand himself" as the recipient of immunity.

the Nature of Things. What kind of man fights with convention and condemns himself?

284

The adulterer-priest

Let a priest have power to release one person from punishment. Let it be lawful to kill adulterers. A man caught a priest in adultery and when he claimed immunity for himself under the law, killed him. He is charged with murder.

DISCUSSION

Was the person caught still a priest, that is, at the moment he was caught, did he lose his rights as a priest? If he was still a priest, could he ask for himself[1] in this offence? Can he exercise his option anywhere but in public?

DECLAMATION

I caught an adulterer, which is enough for me. For no persona is excepted, and adultery is more disgraceful in a priest. "He had a law," says the prosecutor. That is like a general turned traitor or a guardian who abuses his female ward asking to be let off. But imagine I went to law with him from suspicion of adultery; if he had been found guilty, I suppose he would have forfeited his priesthood. Add that the law grants power to save somebody else. It is written that he who saves the life of a citizen be honored; can someone who saves his own life receive the reward? Or can someone who beats himself be found guilty of injury? Furthermore, the law of adultery has priority over the priest's law; for the priest opts in public, and if the adul-

ille pro duobus petebat? Nam adultera sine adultero non poterat occidi: et tunc utique caedem commisissem.

285

Imperator exulis filius

Praemium victor imperator accipiat. Imperator, cuius pater in exilio quinquennii erat, vicit. Aliud praemium petit. Reversus pater post quinquennium abdicat.

1   SERMO

Pater hic et honestus et miser est, ut qui ⟨exul⟩[1] filium imperatorem habeat. Quaestio, an quinquennii illius quo pater exulavit filio sit ratio reddenda. Colorate: 'Adfert quidem iste tale patrocinium, ut me neget exulem fuisse. Sed timuit ne si ego essem revocatus transferretur imperium.'

286

Adulter fratris ex sponso

Abdicare et recusare liceat. Rapta raptoris aut mortem optet aut nuptias. Peregrinantis quidam fratris sponsam rapuit. Puella deprecante patre raptoris nuptias optavit.

[1] *Pith.*

---

[2] To the Forum. The adulterer had to be killed where he was caught.   [3] In killing the woman alone (Wi.).

285: [1] Other than his father's return (Wi.).

[2] At least not in the full sense. His banishment (for involuntary homicide?) was temporary and he was guilty of no crime.

terer gets that far,[2] he has escaped. Besides, he was claiming for two; for the adulteress could not be killed without the adulterer; then[3] I should indeed have committed
murder.

285

General, exile's son

Let a victorious general receive a reward. A general whose
father was in five-year exile won a victory. He asked for
another[1] reward. The father returns after five years and
disowns.

DISCUSSION

This father is both in good repute and in distress; ⟨an exile,⟩ he has a general for a son. Question: is the son ac-
countable for the five years in which his father was in exile?
Use the color: "By way of defense he argues that I was not
an exile.[2] But he was afraid that if I had been recalled, the
command would be transferred."

286

The adulterer of his ex-fiancé brother[1]

Let it be legal to disown and to challenge.[2] Let a raped
woman opt for the rapist's death or marriage. A man raped
the fiancée of his brother who was absent abroad. The girl's
father interceding, she chose marriage. The young man

286: [1] Cf 266, title.
[2] Lit "refuse" (to accept disownment).

[QUINTILIAN]

Iuvenis reversum fratrem et in adulterio deprehensum, cum pro illo pater deprecaretur, occidit. Abdicatur.

1
SERMO

An omnia quae adversus voluntatem patrum admissa sunt debeant abdicatione puniri; an propter id debeat abdicari quod lege fecerit.

2
DECLAMATIO

Feliciores patres sic irasci solent: 'nihil non facere debuisti secundum meam voluntatem: obicio tibi munus lucis.' Iactat se potestas illa patrum etiam in magistratus, etiam in victores. Non exigo tamen ut facias quod iubeo: peto ut fa-
3 cias quod rogaverim. 'Lex est quae permittat adulterum cum adultera occidere.' Non dicit tamquam patri 'oportuit facere', sed 'licuit mihi' tamquam alieno: quod si certe non sufficeret ad abdicationem, multum proficeret ista defensio.[1]

4   Sic agam hoc tamquam caedis causam? Quod si facerem, ignosceretur mihi. Maior sit eorum libertas qui matrimonia ⟨ipsi⟩[2] iunxerunt, qui per vota ⟨eo⟩[2] venerunt: vos vero qui nuptias facitis in poenam, ad quos uxores per lictorem deducuntur, id vindicare non potestis quod sic
5 impetratis. Sed ut omnia praetermittam, nihil praeter animum patris aestimare debuisti. Ceteris forsitan defendi legibus possis: ea quae ad patris te obligavit voluntatem

---

[1] lex . . . defensio *sic ordinavit* SB[1]: quod si . . . defensio: non dicit . . . alieno. lex est . . . occidere Aβ
[2] SB[3]

---

[3] This should be in the theme.

316

caught his brother, who had returned, in adultery and killed him, though their father interceded on his behalf. He is disowned.

DISCUSSION

Should everything done against a father's will be punished by disowning? Should he be disowned for what he did legally?

DECLAMATION

More fortunate fathers customarily get angry as follows: "There is nothing you ought not to have done according to my wish: I bring against you the gift of daylight." That parental power flaunts itself even against magistrates, even against victors. I do not demand, however, that you do as I order: I ask that you do as I have requested. "There is a law permitting to kill an adulterer with an adulteress."[3] He does not say, as though talking to a father, "it was my duty to kill," but as though talking to an outsider, "it was my right to kill." That, as a defense, would serve him well—but that it certainly is adequate cause for disowning.

Shall I handle this as a case of murder? If I were to do so, I should be pardoned. Let those have greater freedom who ⟨of themselves⟩ entered into matrimony, who came ⟨to it⟩ through their prayers:[4] but you people who make wedding a punishment, to whom wives are escorted by a lictor, you cannot avenge what is granted to you in such a fashion. But to leave aside all else, you ought to have thought of nothing except your father's sentiments. Perhaps you could be defended by other laws, but you cannot be divested of what bound you to your father's will. I dis-

---

4 Not marriage vows; there would be vows in any marriage.

exui non potes. Abdico te vel quod unicum vel quod alterum perdidi.

6 Eligat ipse qualem sortiri velit patrem, mitem an fortem: det mores, dum custodiat quos dederit. Cum adulteros occideris, necesse habes severum patrem sortiri. Abdico raptorem; necdum dico cuius, hoc certe dico: rapuisti virginem, pacis faciem turbasti, fecisti propter quod

7 iuste occidi posses. Adisti me praeterea, et propter te sollicitus fui; quod erat gravissimum, necesse habui rogare. Si rapuisti fratris tui sponsam, non sufficit severitas; non sum iracundus: non est haec vulgaris libido, sed incestum. Tu expugnare absentem fratrem ausus es, et fecisti ut videretur puella parum pudice fecisse.

8 Quid respondes? Quid dicis[3]? Solent ista sic defendi: 'iuvenis erravi, et amore lapsus sum.' Vis igitur ignoscam? Nihil est gratius[4] impositam severitatem personae detrahi. Do vitiis veniam, habes patrem lenem, mitem, sceleribus ignosco: redde rationem nunc cur[5] tu occideris fratrem.

9 Quod tantum scelus inveniri potest quod parricidio vindicandum sit? Ubi sunt illa praecepta quibus monebam ut concordes essetis[6] fratres? Parum est dicere, voluisti occi-

---

[3] *Aer.*: dices Aβ
[4] *Obr.*: gravius Aβ
[5] *SB*[2]: c. n. Aβ
[6] *Sch., Gron.*: essent Aβ

---

[5] A puzzle rather than an epigram. Did the survivor cease to exist as son at the moment of killing? If so the dead son was *unicus*. If not, he was *alter* ("one of two"). But the terms might also apply to the survivor, also now lost: he was *alter* until the killing and, after the killing, *unicus* until disowned.

own you because I lost my only son or else my other son.[5]

Let him choose for himself what sort of father he would wish to be allotted, gentle or strong; let him select the character, so long as he abides by his selection. Since you killed the adulterer, you must needs be allotted a strict father. I disown a rapist; I don't yet say of whom,[6] I do say this at least: "You raped a virgin, you troubled the face of peace, you did something for which you might justly have been put to death." You came to me, furthermore, and I was anxious for you; I found it necessary to beg—a very hard thing indeed. If you raped your brother's fiancée, strictness is not enough. I am not *angry*:[7] this is not ordinary lust, it is incest. You dared to storm[8] your absent brother and make the girl seem to have done something less than chaste.

What is your answer? What do you say? Such behavior is usually defended thus: "A young man, I erred and love made me slip." Do you want my forgiveness? Nothing goes down better than when the label of strictness is removed from a persona. I pardon your vices, you have a gentle, lenient father. I forgive your crimes. Tell me now why you killed your brother. What crime can be found so heinous that it has to be avenged by parricide?[9] Where are those precepts with which I admonished you to be brothers in harmony? It's not enough to say you wished to kill him: you

---

[6] I.e., his brother's fiancée.

[7] But appalled (see SB[2]). *Iracundus* effectively = *iratus* as in 301.1; cf. *TLL* VII.2.370.60f.

[8] With rape associations; cf. 262.8, *alienam domum expugnavi* et sim.

[9] Includes murder of a near relation.

dere: potuisti. Non deriguit[7] mens? Non soluta dextera est? Non obstipuisti propius scelere admoto?

10   Sed qua causa occidisti? 'Violaverat matrimonium.' Adice 'frater.' Non continget[8] tibi sic agere quasi marito. Tu enim profecto nocens, qui sponsam abduxisti sic amantem. Nunc intellego quantam iniuriam fecerim puellae quae coacta est te habere maritum cum altero carere non posset. Acrius incalescunt ignes legitimi, utique cum inciderunt in rudes animos. Deprehendisti in adulterio? Si ullus in te pudor est, *[9]: maritus fuerat, si per te licuisset.

287

Fortis filius proditionis rei

Proditionis reus citatus est qui duos filios habebat, ex quibus alter fortiter fecit, alter deseruit. Petit pater a filio ut abolitionem iudicii peteret. Ille fratris vitam petît et adfuit patri. Absolutus pater abdicat filium. Ille CD.

1   SERMO

An quidquid pater voluit filio facere necesse sit; an viro forti; an abdicari propter praemium possit.

2   DECLAMATIO

Duo haec, ut opinor, obicis mihi, pater: et quod desertoris vitam optaverim et quod abolitionem iudicii non optaverim. Optavi vitam: puta nocentem, sed fratris. Alieni quo-

---

[7] Wi.: dir- Aβ   [8] Ro.: -eret Aβ   [9] lac. ind. SB[3]
(averte oculos vel abi suppl. SB[1]: parce coni. Wi.)

---

[10] Could bring yourself to kill him.
[11] See crit. note.   [1] In court.

could[10] kill him. Did not your mind freeze? Your hand lose its muscle? Were you not struck dazed when the crime came close?

But why did you kill him? "He had violated my marriage." Add: "He, my brother." You won't be allowed to speak as a husband. For surely you are guilty of leading away so loving a fiancée. Now I understand what an injury I did to the girl by making her have you as a husband when she couldn't do without the other. Legitimate fires burn hotter, especially when they get into tender minds. Did you catch him in adultery? If you have any shame, <spare him>[11]: he would have been her husband if you had let him.

287

Hero son of man on trial for treason

A man who had two sons was indicted on a charge of treason. One of them became a hero, the other deserted. The father petitioned his son to ask for the trial to be quashed. The latter asked for his brother's life and appeared[1] for his father. The father was acquitted; he disowns his son. The latter opposes.

DISCUSSION

Must a son do whatever his father wishes? Must a hero? Can a man be disowned because of a reward?

DECLAMATION

As I suppose, you have these two charges against me, father: that I opted for the life of a deserter and that I did not opt for the quashing of the trial. I opted for a life: guilty if you like, but a brother's. I would have been sorry even for a

que iuvenis, aequalis mei, misertus fuissem; subisset illa cogitatio: 'Infelices huius parentes!' ⟦Non tam reprehen-
3   sione dignus est desertor quam laude vir fortis.⟧[1] Post hoc obicis mihi quod de innocentia tua nihil timui. Sciebam quomodo vixisses, quomodo causam tuam egissem: ego enim domum nostram in acie defendi. Accedit quod qui semel delatus est reus non potest absolvi nisi accusetur; omnes dixissent: 'causae patris diffidit[2] vir fortis.' Nihil [aliud][3] egissem quidem. Et quid futurum erat si impetrassem? Non absolvereris; si non impetrassem, damnareris.
4   Adfui tibi; non imputo: neque enim tu ideo absolutus es— vicit causa, vicit innocentia. Ego nihil imputo nisi quod bene speravi de causa tua.

Ecquid igitur, pater, gratularis tibi? Omnes salvi sumus. Nam de fratre noli desperare: saepe rediere virtutes. Iam domi habet exemplum. In periculo mortis fuit; scit quale sit deserere, quale fortiter facere. Denuntio tibi, frater, tollas istam ignominiam. ⟨Non tam reprehensione dignus est desertor quam laude vir fortis.⟩[4]

288

Tyrannicida filiorum duorum

Qui duos filios tyrannos occiderat, petit praemii nomine ut tertius in exilium proficiscatur.

[1] *ad finem transp.* SB[1] (*cf.* SB[2])
[2] *Sch., Gron.*: -disset Aβ   [3] SB[1]
[4] *vide n.* 1

---

[2] See s.4 fin.   [3] Because the *optio* would have been taken as an admission of guilt.   [4] See s.2 fin.

young man to whom I was not related, of my own age. I would have reflected: "How sad for his parents!" [[A deserter does not deserve blame as much as a hero deserves praise.[2]]] Then you lay it up to my charge that I had no misgivings about your innocence. I knew what kind of life you had led, how I had pleaded your cause; for I defended our family in the battle. A further point: a defendant once charged cannot be acquitted unless he is prosecuted. Everyone would have said, "the hero had no faith in his father's case." I should have done no good. And what would have been the result if I had got what I asked? You would not have been acquitted. If I had not, you would have been found guilty.[3] I appeared for you. I don't ask you to be grateful, you were not acquitted on that account: your case won, your innocence won. I don't ask you to be grateful for anything except that I was optimistic about your case.

So, father, don't you congratulate yourself? All of us are saved. For don't despair about my brother; virtues often come back. He now has an example at home. He was in danger of death; he knows what it is to desert, what it is to be a hero. I enjoin upon you, brother, wipe out that stigma. A deserter does not deserve blame so much as a hero deserves praise.[4]

288

The tyrannicide who killed two sons

The killer of two tyrants, his sons, asks as a reward that the third go into exile.[1]

1 Presumably the son opposes.

[QUINTILIAN]

1
SERMO

Indubitate pater hic timet ne et ille tyrannus fiat; sed non debet illum facere suspectum, alioqui reus erit. Non mittetur autem in exilium suspectus.

'Tyrannicida optet quod volet.' Prima illa communia: nihil excipi. Illud proprium, plus deberi huic tyrannicidae, qui senex duos et filios occiderit. Invidiosum itaque erat si quid petisset pertinens ad gratulationem.

2
DECLAMATIO

Tyrannos genui: nunc opto ut filius exulet. Quod mihi et citra praemium licebat, hoc et pro praemio peto et pro ipso iuvene. Nihil dico de fato domus nostrae, non persequor rationem quoque metus mei; illud interim contentus sum dicere: 'Supervacui sunt metus, nihil imminet. Sed expectat ista plerumque sapientia gravior: quid tu accidere cre-
3
dis illis qui liberos habent, quid maritis?' Pater timeo, seu[1] rationem metus habent sive (ut maxime vereor) fatum istud est domus nostrae. Ignosces enim quod filios meos ultra mortem persequor: nihil de illo timui qui primus tyrannus fuit; isdem praeceptis erat educatus quibus tu. Illo occiso timere non debui ne quis ex vobis idem cogitaret. Occupavit tamen arcem alter, non in totum sua culpa: difficile fuit obstare illis qui convenerant ⟨a⟩[2] tyranno pri-

---

[1] *Ri.*: sed A: sive *Aer.*   [2] *Hå.*[2]

---

[2] But executed. No need for Schulting's *nisi* (before *suspectus*) or any double brackets (SB[3]).   [3] Should be in the theme.

[4] The greater his desert, the more need to avoid *invidia*—a rather flimsy point.   [5] To send him into exile in exercise of *patria potestas*. So why not have taken that course?

DISCUSSION

Unquestionably this father is afraid that he too will turn out a tyrant, but he ought not to throw suspicion on him; otherwise he will be brought to trial. He will not be sent into exile[2] if he is suspected.

"Let the tyrannicide opt for what he wants."[3] First, the common topic: that no exception is made. Particular to this case is the point that this tyrannicide is more deserving in that he is an old man and has killed two, and them his sons. It would therefore have been invidious if he had asked for anything savoring of self-congratulation.[4]

DECLAMATION

I begot tyrants: now I opt that my son be exiled. That[5] was open to me even apart from the reward, but I ask it both as my reward and for the young man's sake. I say nothing about our family fate, I don't enter into the reason for my fear, I am content to say for the time being: "Fears are uncalled-for, there is nothing impending. But sometimes a weightier wisdom foresees such eventualities: how do you think it is with parents and husbands?"[6] I am afraid as a father, whether my apprehensions are well-founded or (as I fear most of all) it is the fate of our family. You will forgive me if I pursue my sons beyond death: I had no fears about the son who was the first tyrant; he was brought up on the same precepts as you. When he was killed, it was not incumbent on me to fear lest one of you should get the same idea. Yet the second seized the castle, not altogether by his own fault; it was difficult to resist those who flocked to him

---

[6] In fear for their children and wives under a new tyrant.

4   ore velut ad heredem. Non potes tutus esse in ea civitate in qua timeris. Nihil cogitasti: timeo dum innocens es. Vereor ne si quis te occiderit videatur tyrannicidium fecisse.

289

Amator filiae

Qui causa mortis fuerit, capite puniatur. Speciosam quidam filiam de amore confessus amico dedit servandam, et rogavit ne sibi redderetur petenti. Post tempus petît. Non accepit. Suspendit se. Accusatur amicus quod causa mortis fuerit.

1   **SERMO**

Custodienda est amici persona, ut, quamquam de re nefaria, non tamen sine respectu amici loquatur, et actione tota misereatur illius, illud vero quod perît laudet, et magis desperatione eum fecisse dicat quam cogitatione turpissimi amoris.

2   **DECLAMATIO**

Antequam dico quo crimine reus sim, dicendum est cui dicar fuisse causa mortis. Periit amicus meus. Non esse hoc vulgare nomen ipse monstravit. Hunc igitur occidisse dicor, nulla lucri spe (nam filiam relinquebat), nulla offensa (nam et illam mihi credidit, et ego nihil feci extra praeceptum). Quidquid est igitur quod obicitur mihi, ex bona mente proficiscitur. Videamus tamen an, ubi animus accu-

‹from› the previous tyrant as to the heir. You cannot be safe in a community where you are feared. You had no such idea: I fear you, in your innocence, I am afraid that whoever kills you will be thought to have done a tyrannicide.

289

The lover of his daughter

Let whoso has caused a death be capitally punished. The father of a beautiful daughter gave her into the custody of a friend, confessing his love, and asked that she not be returned to him at his request. After a while he requested. He did not get her. He hanged himself. The friend is accused as having caused his death.

DISCUSSION

The persona of the friend is to be guarded, so that he does not speak of the friend without respect, although he is talking about something nefarious, and throughout the plea he is sorry for him, but commends his death, saying that he did it out of desperation rather than thinking about a disgraceful passion.

DECLAMATION

Before I speak of the charge on which I have been accused, I must speak about the person whose death I am said to have caused. My friend has died. He himself showed that this is not just an ordinary name. So I am said to have killed him, not in any hope of gain (for he left a daughter), not for any offence (for he entrusted her to me and I did nothing that I had not been told to do). So whatever is charged against me, it comes from a good intention. But let us see

327

sari non debet, ius haereat.

3   Quaeritur quis[1] sit causa mortis. Accusator dicit: per quem factum sit ut aliquis moreretur ⟦si quis quod natura mortiferum sit adversus aliquem fecerit⟧. Quae si sequenda definitio est, accusabitur et ille qui alicui suaserit peregrinationem, deinde is aut naufragio perierit aut latrocinio, ipsi convicti infamabuntur ex quibus cruditas et interitus. Nihil igitur hic factum est quod omnibus mortiferum. Nam sicut telum omnibus mortiferum est, ita causa mortis est quae occidit omnes. Detrahe huic amorem: nihil erit propter quod moriatur.

4   Volo tamen causam facere difficiliorem. Non deposuerit apud me filiam, nihil praeceperit; tamquam melior amicus defendere filiam in qua pater furebat volui: non enim amor erat qui sic stimulabat. Abduxi, custodivi, ⟦nonne recipere non debuit qui periit quod non recepit?⟧ non reddidi. Duxisset in ius, per iudicem peteret. Hoc si fecisset,

5 mea laus erat. Sed libenter cedo: ipse fecit rem admirabilem, fecit ut in laudem verteret hoc ipsum, quod turpiter amabat. Quem tum enim illi animum fuisse putatis cum in illo furore tenuit tamen adfectum patris? Perduxit ad ami-

6 cum, deposuit. 'At enim petivit postea.' Si animum illius metiri velimus, intellegemus non fuisse petiturum nisi quod sciebat me non[2] redditurum: secutus est illum impetum animi sui. 'At enim petiit.[3]' Adice receptam[4] sanita-

---

[1] *Fr.*: qui A: quid β

[2] D: *om.* Aβ

[3] *Aer.*: prodiit Aβ

[4] SB[3], *auct.* Wi. (-ta): precetera A: pro c- β

whether the law applies where the heart cannot be accused.

The question is, who is a cause of death? The prosecutor says: someone through whom it came about that somebody died [if someone commit against a person something
that naturally entails death]. If that definition is to be followed, someone who persuades a person to travel abroad
will be accused if that person then perishes in a shipwreck
or a robbery; even social contacts will be defamed when
they result in a death from indigestion. So nothing has
been done in these cases that entails death universally. For
just as a weapon entails death for everyone, so a cause of
death is one that kills everybody. Take away love from this
man: there will be nothing from which he dies.

However, I wish to make the case more difficult. Suppose he did not leave his daughter with me, gave me no instructions; as a good friend, I wanted to defend a daughter
whose father was insane about her; for it was not love
which so goaded him. I took her away, guarded her.
[Surely he who died because he did not get her back ought
not to have got her back.] I did not return her. He might
have taken me to court, claimed her through a judge. If
he had done that, I should have been commended. But I
willingly yield: he himself did a remarkable thing, he converted his most disgraceful passion into a source of praise.
For how do you think he felt when, mad as he was, he
nonetheless retained fatherly affection? He brought her to
his friend, placed her in his care. "Ah, but he asked for her
back later on." If we were to wish to measure his heart, we
shall realize that he would not have asked except that he
knew I should not return her. He followed the impulse of
his heart. "But he did ask." Add that he had recovered his

tem,[5] et non accepisset.[6] Ne peteret, ⟨sic⟩[7] deposuerat.

7   Haec satis plena defensio esset si qua ego divinatione colligere potuissem utique periturum si non reddidissem: decepit me quod ante fortius tulerat. Neque enim ego hoc dico, redditurum me fuisse si periturum patrem scissem: optime partes amici custodissem si non reddidissem.

290

Abdicans reductum ob furorem

Luxuriosus abdicatus furere coepit. Reductus a patre, sanatus abdicatur.

1   DECLAMATIO

Si conscius mihi, iudices, ullius culpae essem propter quam iterum abdicarer, scitis mihi non defuisse tacendi verecundiam. Sed facile fuit prius silentium, primum quod sperabam fore exorabilem patrem, deinde quod certum erat propter quod abdicarer. Nunc intellego in multas me mitti posse suspiciones, cum expellar ab optimo patre; nec mihi ullo modo poterat ignosci si offendissem statim ⟨sanatus⟩.[1] Tota igitur actione hoc mihi optinendum[2] est, nihil me fecisse.

2   Nec mihi, iudices, in animo est excusare vitam priorem, nec ut me dicam numquam dignum fuisse abdicatione, sed ut me postea nil[3] fecisse abdicatum. Illa ⟨non⟩[4] narrabo, quam indulgens mihi ab aetate prima fuerit pater, quod fortasse etiam corruperit mores meos, nec illud: ⟨hic⟩[5] er-

---

[5] A: sanitate β, Wi.   [6] Wi.: -perat sed Aβ   [7] SB[3]

[1] SB[2]   [2] Bu.: obi(i)cie- Aβ

[3] p. n. SB[1]: putem (-en A) diu Aβ   [4] Pith.   [5] SB[3]

sanity; still he would not have got her. He had placed her with me ‹in such a fashion› that he would not ask for her.

This would have been a complete enough defense if I could somehow have divined that he was sure to die if I did not return her. His earlier fortitude deceived me. Not that I am saying that I should have returned her if I had known her father would die. I should have best observed the role of a friend by not returning her.

290

Disowner of a son brought back by reason of insanity

A loose-living son when disowned went mad. Brought back by his father and cured, he is disowned.

DECLAMATION

If I was conscious, gentlemen of the jury, of having committed any fault for which I should be disowned a second time, you know I should not have lacked modesty to be silent. But my former silence was easy, first because I hoped my father would relent, next because the reason why I was disowned was not in doubt. Now I realize that I may be subject to many suspicions, since I am expelled by an excellent father. Nor was there any way I could be forgiven if I had offended immediately ‹after I was cured›. So in my entire plea I have to establish that I have done nothing.

I have no intention, gentlemen, of excusing my former life or of saying that I never deserved to be disowned. I say that having been disowned I did nothing afterwards. I will ‹not› recount how indulgent my father was to me from my earliest days, which perhaps may even have corrupted my morals, nor say that ‹this› was youthful error, the nature of

3   ror adulescentiae, haec[6] aetatis natura. Luxuriosum putate fuisse: ego tamen insanus ⟨non⟩[7] eram, et defendendus quidem si contradixissem. Sed perseveraturum patrem negabant propinqui: sic factum est ut dolorem silentio premerem, qui clusus atque intra cogitationes receptus

4   abstulit mentem. Ceterum tamen, si verum velimus loqui, meritus[8] fui.[9] Quas hic ego patri gratias agam? Reduxit me non sentientem; adhibuit curam, laborem. Miserum me! sanatus sum. Sacra maiorum, deos penates [non][10] sentiens tenui, nemo ⟨non⟩[11] gratulatus est amicorum: nunc expellor resipiscens. Felices qui possunt omni vita sua parentibus dicere: 'quid feci?' Dicam tamen: 'Quid postea feci? Si luxuria intolerabile malum, ignovisti.'

5   'Ego' inquit 'te quoniam demens eras reduxi.' Ubi estis qui me putabatis infelicem? Ego vero dementiae gratias ago: non quidem sollicitudinem patris sensi, sed nec abdicationem. Quid mihi cum tam veloci remedio? Pater optime, fallit ista velox medicina. Ego scio quos animi aestus intus feram. Crede, pater, iam aliquas similes iterum[12] imagines video. Redditur[13] dementiae prior causa. Quare mihi, si non ad praesens tempus, ad futurum tamen rogandus es. Succurre, qui soles.

---

   [6] *Sch.*: nec Aβ

   [7] *Sch.*

   [8] *SB²*: muntus *ex* –u A: motus β

   [9] *Sch.*: fuit Aβ

   [10] *SB¹*, *Wi.*

   [11] *Fr.*

   [12] *SB¹*: rerum Aβ

   [13] *SB¹*: redit igitur (*ex* itur A) Aβ: redit iterum *Sch.*: redit *Wi.*

that age. Suppose I did live loosely: still I was ⟨not⟩ insane, and if I had challenged, I had a defense. But my relations told me that my father would not persist. That was how I came to suppress my sorrow in silence; shut in and become part of my inmost thoughts, it took away my mind. But all the same, to tell the truth, I had deserved it. How shall I thank my father here? He brought me back without my knowing it, used care and effort. Woe is me, I was cured. I had the rites of my ancestors, my household gods, and knew it. None of my friends ⟨but⟩ congratulated me. Now, myself again, I am expelled. Fortunate are those who can say to their parents throughout their lives: "What have I done?" But I will say: "What have I done since? If loose living is intolerable wickedness, you pardoned it."

"I brought you back," he says, "because you were demented." Where are you all that thought me unfortunate? But I thank my dementia. I did not feel my father's solicitude, it is true, but neither did I feel the disowning. What did I want with so rapid a remedy? Excellent father, that rapid cure of yours deceives. I know what bitter mental turmoil I endure within. Believe me, father, I now see again certain similar visions. The former cause of my madness[1] is back again. So I must beg you, if not for the present time, yet for the future: help me, as you always do.

[1] His disownment.

291

Adulter uxoris qua cesserat fratri

Qui duos filios habebat uni uxorem dedit. Altero aegro-
tante et dicentibus medicis animi esse languorem, intravit
stricto gladio minatus se moriturum pater nisi causam in-
dicasset. Confesso amari a se fratris uxorem, frater petente
patre cessit. Ille in adulterio eam cum priore marito deprehensos[1] occidit. Abdicatur.

1   DECLAMATIO

Ingressurus actionem interrogo qualem patrem velis: gravem et severum an facilem et ignoscentem. Non dubito
quin adulescens vindicato modo matrimonio malit me severe agere. Talis igitur pater obicit tibi quod in amorem
incideris cuiusquam: non est istud nisi lascivientis animi.
2 Quid[2] si haec quam adamasti nupta est? Tu alienam matro-
nam aliter quam leges permittunt aspexisti? Adiciamus
huc 'fratris uxorem.' Intellego me, iudices, fictae huic personae sufficere non posse, itaque tacebo: duc, duc,[3] te
sequor. Paulo ante dicebas: 'corrumpere fratris uxorem
ausus est, istud incestum est.'

3   Sed forsitan dicet: 'amavi adulescens eam quae domi
erat, cuius conversatio continua etiam invitos ad se oculos
poterat deflectere.' Ignoscamus amori: obicio igitur tibi
occisos a te homines ex eadem causa qua tu amasti. Nullus
est tam vilis hominis sanguis ut non manus inquinet.
Deinde hanc ego severitatem aliis permiserim: tu qui[4] et

---

[1] SB[1], *coll. Liv.* 45.28.11, *K.–S.* I.289: -nsam Aβ
[2] SB[3]: iam Aβ
[3] *Ro.*: dic dic Aβ
[4] *Ro.*: quod Aβ

291[1]

Adulterer of a wife he had surrendered to his brother

A man who had two sons gave one of them a wife. When the other fell ill and the doctors said the sickness was fatal, the father came in sword in hand, threatening to die unless he told the reason. When he confessed that he was in love with his brother's wife, the brother gave her to him at his father's instance. Finding her in adultery with her former husband, he killed them. He is disowned.

DECLAMATION

I start my plea with a question: what kind of father do you want? Stern and strict or easygoing and forgiving? I don't doubt that the young man, having just avenged his marriage, prefers me to take a strict line. Such a father then charges you with falling in love with someone. That only comes of a lustful mind. What if this woman you love is married? Did you look at another man's wife otherwise than as the law allows? Let us add, "your brother's wife." I realize, gentlemen of the jury, that I cannot live up to this fictive persona. So I shall be silent. You take the lead, you: I'll follow you. You were saying a little while ago: "He dared to corrupt his brother's wife, that's incest."

But maybe he'll say: "A young man, I fell in love with a girl who was in the house, whose constant company could turn even unwilling eyes upon her." Let us pardon love. So I charge you with killing human beings for the same reason as caused *your* love. No human blood is so cheap that it doesn't stain the hand. Next, I could allow such severity

[1] Cf. 286.

4
ipse amasti, nonne tibi cum deprehendisses imaginem
cernere visus es tui casus? Quid diutius differo dolorem?
Fratrem occidisti. Scio, iudices, quorundam scelerum eam
esse magnitudinem ut augeri verbis non possint. Fratrem
tuum occidisti, servatorem tuum, qui ut tu viveres matrimonium solvit: et, quod gravius est, non longe erat; in eadem domo futurus tradidit tibi uxorem qua carere non

5
poterat. Et hoc adulterium vocas? Ita est adulter ille, et tu
maritus? Istud ego adulterium quondam manu mea iunxi,
ipse auspices adhibui, optavi longam concordiam. Maiores
habet vires ignis qui legitimis facibus accenditur. Non est
tam facile desinere quam cedere. Nunc intellego, iuvenis,

6
quantum mihi praestiteris: amabas. Coibant ergo furtim et
flentes, ut satisfacerent invicem. Ita tu cum hoc videres
non erubuisti? Non deprehendi visus es quasi adulter?
Non mehercules ferrem te tantum querentem. Vides
enim, liberorum causa amabas, matrimonium cogitaveras:
adulteros tu dices iacentes in geniali toro? Duri mehercule
viderentur si cito oblivisci coniugii potuissent. Occisus est
iuvenis dum rem facit boni mariti.

7
Non erubescam, iudices, post gravissimum dolorem
descendere in hanc quoque causae partem, ut obiciam
quod uxorem occideris bene meritam, quam sic amasti. Sic
de innocentia miserorum ago tamquam hic de capite quae-

---

2 *Vides enim*, introducing an ironical statement as in 351.9 init.
and *Decl. Mai.* 5.10 (p. 95.17).

3 As he had formerly been. Actually, both brothers were pas-
sionately in love.

4 Since I am merely disowning you.

in others: but you, who yourself loved, when you caught them, did you not feel you were looking at the picture of your own experience? Why do I put off the pain any longer? You killed your brother. I know, gentlemen, that there are some crimes so heinous that words cannot en-large them. You killed your brother, your rescuer, who dissolved his marriage so that you might live. And, what weighs more heavily, he was not far away; he was going to be in the same house and he handed over to you a wife whom he could not do without. And you call this adultery? Is he an adulterer so and are you a husband? I once joined that adultery with my own hands, myself called in the soothsayers, prayed that they would live long in harmony. The fire that is kindled with lawful torches burns stronger. It is not so easy to stop as it is to yield. Now I understand, young man, how much you did for me: you were in love. So they met in secret and in tears, for their mutual satisfac-tion. When you saw it thus, did you not blush? Did you not feel as though you were caught in adultery? Upon my word, I would find you intolerable if you were merely complaining. For you see:[2] you were in love because you wanted children, you had matrimony in mind! Will you call them adulterers as they lie on the conjugal couch? Upon my word, they would appear insensitive if they had been able to forget about their marriage so soon. The young man was killed while he was doing the job of a good husband.[3]

I shall not be ashamed, gentlemen, after this terrible blow to come down to another part of the case and charge you with killing a wife who deserved well, whom you loved so dearly. I am arguing about the innocence of the un-happy pair as though this were a capital case. As it is,[4] my

ratur. Nunc[5] sufficit dolori meo quod mihi filium abstulisti, qui tibi adsedi, qui ad languentem cum gladio sollicitus intravi. Ego eosdem cibos eadem mensa qua tu capere non possum, nec illam manum videre quae fumare mihi adhuc

8 filii mei sanguine videtur. Semper mihi armatus videris, numquam solus occurris: it ante oculos laceratus filius, hunc iuxta nurus optima, nurus obsequentissima. Clamare videntur: 'Tu nos occidisti, tu qui nos iniuria prius distraxisti. Quid necesse erat solvere matrimonium? Obreptum est credulitati tuae: non amabat qui potuit occidere.'

292

Laqueus Olynthii speciosi

Victis Olynthiis cum ab Atheniensibus publice dividerentur hospitia, specioso puero quidam optulit hospitium. Ille se postero die suspendit. Accusatur hospes quod causa mortis fuerit.

1   SERMO

Duplex quaestio est, iuris et facti. Nam etiamsi vis illata est, quaeritur an causa mortis sit. Sequens potentior,[1] an propter vim perierit. Circa ius illud est, ut finitione tractetur. Is enim causa mortis argui debet qui mortem intulit. Cum vero quis sua manu perierit, non debet hoc reus tantum fecisse, ut quis mori velit, sed ut necesse habeat.

---

5 *SB*[2]: non Aβ   1 SB[2] (*cf.* 272.1): potior Aβ

---

1 By Philip of Macedon in 348 B.C. The inhabitants were enslaved but many found refuge in Athens. See my note on Stat. *Theb.* 12.510 (Loeb).

indignation is sufficiently justified by the fact that you have taken my son away from me—me, who sat beside you, and came into your sickroom with a sword, in anxiety. I cannot take the same food at the same table with you, not look upon the hand that still seems to me to be steaming with my son's blood. I always see you as armed, you never come before me alone. Before my eyes goes my lacerated son, and beside him my excellent daughter-in-law, my most obedient daughter-in-law. They seem to cry out: "You killed us, you that wrongfully parted us before. What need to dissolve the marriage? Your credulity was imposed upon. The man who could kill did not love."

292

The noose of the beautiful Olynthian

After the Olynthians had been conquered,[1] the Athenians publicly assigned them billets. A person offered lodging to a beautiful boy. The next day he hanged himself. The host is accused as a cause of death.

DISCUSSION

The question is twofold, of law and fact. For even if violence was offered, there is a question whether it was the cause of death. The second[2] has more weight: did he die because of the violence? That is about law, to be handled by definition. For he should be accused as cause of death who inflicted death. But when someone has died by his own hand, the defendant should not only have made him want to die, but made it necessary for him.

[2] Cf. *OLD sequens* 1b; the first question (was violence offered?) being of fact.

2

DECLAMATIO

Vim dicor attulisse. Quis queritur, quae proclamatio?
Impunitum reliquit eum propter quem moriebatur? Si
erubuit indicare, multis tamen aliis generibus queri potuit:
'propter hospitem morior.' Nec credibile est eum peper-
3 cisse hospiti qui sibi non pepercit. Sed suspicionibus agitur: 'formoso' inquit 'hospitium pollicitus es.' Viderint isti
qui prodigis omnes oculis intuentur: mihi tempore illo nullus Olynthius formosus visus est. Scilicet enim sollicitabar
lacrimis, squalore. Male sentitis de puero qui adversa fortiter tulit. 'Cur tamen optulisti?' Atheniensis sum. Adsi-
gnentur fortasse invitis civibus qui cum liberis, qui cum
coniugibus veniunt, qui secum habent comitatum: misera-
4 bilior est puer solus. 'At cur eadem nocte ‹se›[2] suspendit?'
Utrum hoc re admirabile videtur an persona an tempore?
Miratur aliquis Olynthium potuisse hoc Athenis? Illud
5 enim est tempus doloris. Saepe ad retinendam vitam prosunt ipsa pericula: redit metus posteaquam desivit instare
hostis; tunc cogitatio Fortunae, tunc vacat dicere: 'est iam
qui sepeliat.' Ipsa mehercules officia admonere illum potuerunt fortunae prioris: patuit quidem domus, sed non

---

[2] *Ri.*

---

[3] "A possible suicide note" (Wi.).

[4] *Prodigis*, probably corrupt; see SB[1] (*profugis*, "wandering,"
and *protervis*, "wanton," suggested); *profligatis* Watt[2].

[5] *Scilicet . . . squalore*: so advanced by the prosecution and re-
butted by the speaker. But why the suggestion? Because, "they"
hint, the boy's wretched state favored the defendant's designs—he
would be easy prey. But in fact the boy was brave. As Wi. tenta-

I am said to have offered violence. Who complains, where is the outcry? Did he leave the person responsible for his death unpunished? If he was ashamed to lay information, there were many other ways he could have complained: "I am dying because of my host."[3] Nor is it credible that one who did not spare himself spared his host. But suspicions are brought into play: "You promised lodging," says the prosecutor, "to a beauty." Let that concern those who look at everybody with lavish[4] eyes: to me at that time no Olynthian seemed beautiful. I suppose I was solicited with tears and squalor.[5] You people have a poor opinion of the boy: he bore his troubles bravely. "But why did you offer?" I am an Athenian.[6] Those who come with children and wives and have companions with them are perhaps assigned to unwilling citizens. A boy by himself is more pitiable.[7] "But why did he hang himself the same night?" What is surprising about that—the act, the persona, or the time? Does anybody wonder that an Olynthian could do that in Athens? For that is the time for grief.[8] Often danger itself keeps us holding on to life. Fear returns after the enemy is no longer upon us; then comes the thought of Fortune, then there is time to say: "Now I have someone to bury me." Upon my word, his very duties could have reminded him of his former fortune. The house was large, but not his. Slave boys welcomed him, but they belonged to a

---

tively perceives, the boy's bold front would make him an unlikely choice "on the assumption that brave boys are not $\pi\alpha\theta\iota\kappa o\iota$."

6 "Athens was traditionally hospitable to exiles" (Wi).

7 I was so sorry for him that I took him in without waiting for a city order.   8 When the danger is past.

sua; excepere servuli, sed alieni. Forsitan et illa cogitaverit: 'semper ergo alieno munere vivendum est.'

6   Interim sive illud Olynthi[3] fatum fuit sive impatientia ipsius, nullius maior iniuria est quam mea. Perdidi beneficium, et adhuc suspectus sum. Habiturum me putabam qui veniret in locum liberorum.

293

Tyrannis victae civitatis

Viro forti praemium. Quidam fortiter fecit. Petit praemio tyrannidem victae civitatis.

1   DECLAMATIO

Omnia danda esse viris fortibus dico: nec immerito danda, utique ex victis. Non aerarium inquieto, non sacerdotium rapio: peto ut sint hostes in mea potestate. Ac primum omnium interrogo: quis est iste qui prohibet? Iuste peterem etiam eversionem hostium: ac tum nescio quis iste non ste-
2   tit in acie, illi si vicissent, tyrannide se vindicarent. Sic agere volo tamquam futurus crudelis: meruerunt. Vindicari potestis sine invidia: de me querantur, cui aliquid iam irascuntur. Tyrannidem imponere volo. Asperiora narrabo: plurimos ex illa civitate manu hac occidi. Sed numquid vobis videor avarus, libidinosus? Aliter crevi. Eadem ergo ratione hoc peto qua fortiter feci. Sic praesidia imponemus: tamdiu tyrannus ero quamdiu poterunt rebellare.

---

[3] B(C): -ii AD (*cf. SB*[1])

---

[1] A not very relevant slur, obelized by Wi. and SB[1].

stranger. Perhaps too he thought: "So I shall always live by a stranger's bounty."

Meanwhile, whether it was the fate of Olynthus or his own hasty temper, nobody is more injured than I. I lost my good deed and am under suspicion as well. I thought I would have someone to take the place of children.

293

Tyranny over a conquered community

Let there be a reward for a hero. A man becomes a hero. As reward he asks to be tyrant of the defeated community.

DECLAMATION

I say that all things should be given to heroes, given not undeservedly, at any rate when they come from the defeated. I am not disturbing the treasury. I am not snatching at a priesthood: I ask that enemies be in my power. And first of all, a question: who is this individual who says nay? I would have had a right to ask that our enemies be destroyed. And this I-don't-know-who, he took no part in the battle at the time.[1] If they had won, they would have avenged themselves with a tyranny. I want to put the case as one who will be cruel; they have deserved it. You can take your revenge without any odium; let them complain about me—they already have a grudge against me—I want to impose a tyranny. Worse still: I have killed a great many from that community with this hand. But do I seem to you greedy or libidinous? I was not brought up that way. So I ask this for the same reason that I became a hero. This is how we shall set a garrison on them: I shall be tyrant as long as they are able to make war again.

294

Dives proditionis reus vir fortis

Dives proditionis accusatus fortiter fecit. Petit praemii nomine accusatoris mortem. Ille non recusat, sed postulat ut
ante peragatur iudicium.

1
SERMO

Accusator sic agere debet ut manifestum sit illum tantum
rei publicae causa postulare: non quia non sit illud verum,
ut si damnaverit vivat, sed quia facilius[1] impetraturus est si
intellectus fuerit nullo iure adiuvari posse.

2
DECLAMATIO

Si te proditorem postea dixissem quam tu mortem meam
optasses, viderer tamen et <rei publicae>[2] rem utilem
postulare et non contra legem tuam desiderare. Quid enim
optasti? Mortem accusatoris: de qua lis non est. Nihil est
quod <ad>[3] praemium confugias, nihil est quod utaris legis
tuae potestate: non recuso quo minus accipias quidquid
3 optasti. Nihil petisti praeter mortem: si exigis ut accusator
statim occidatur, alterum praemium petis. At haec voluntas fuit tuae petitionis. Nihil interest, si illam qui dabant
praemium ignoraverunt; et ideo tibi nemo contradixit
quod videbaris[4] purgasse contumeliam tuam: nihil tibi lex

---

[1] SB[1]: diffic- Aβ
[2] SB[4] (rei p.)
[3] Aer.
[4] Ri.: -atur A(β)

---

[1] If he is to die whatever the verdict.

294

Rich man, charged with treason, hero

A rich man accused of treason became a hero. As reward he asks for the death of his accuser, who does not object but asks that the trial be gone through first.

DISCUSSION

The prosecutor should plead so that it be clear that he makes that petition only for the sake of the commonwealth. Not that it is not fair that if he convicts, he should live, but because he will more easily gain his point if it be understood that no law can help him.[1]

DECLAMATION

If I had called you a traitor *after* you opted for my death, I should still appear to be asking something useful <to the commonwealth> and not to be out for anything against your law. For what did you opt for? Your accuser's death. About that we have no quarrel. You don't have to run to your reward, you don't have to use the power of your law. I am not objecting to your getting whatever you opt for. You asked for nothing but death: if you demand that your accuser be put to death immediately, you are asking for a second reward. But this, you say, was the intention of your petition. That makes no difference if those who granted the reward did not know; and the reason why nobody gainsaid it is that you seemed to have cleared[2] the insult levelled against you. The law would have done you no good if

---

[2] By his "heroism." They thought the trial would be a formality (cf. s.6). In the unexpected event of the "hero" being convicted, the reward (death of his accuser) would still be operative (s.1).

profuisset si abolitionem petisses. Nunc duo vindicas praemia, ut nec causam dicas et hominem occidas.

4   Ergo non utique comprehensum in praemio est statim
occidere, et quotiens nullum praefinitum est tempus incipit esse in potestate dantis; si abolitionem petis, alterum
5   praemium est. Et cuius tandem iudicii petis abolitionem?
Non privata disceptatio venit in quaestionem, non pecuniae lis (quamquam tunc quoque leges commendarem et
morem iudiciorum): ne agaris reus postulas. Ad summam
rem publicam pertinet. Dico proditum populum, dico
tempus constitutum. Quantulum est ut neges? Si maxime
festinas, apud hos ipsos agi iam potuit, eadem hac mora
6   qua reicimur⁵ potuit pronuntiari. Nihil est quod timeas, si
innocens es. Accessit tibi magna pars patrocinii: fortiter
fecisti. Super illam potentiam divitiarum venit nova gratia.
Nec potuisti magis experiri quantam tibi gratiam fecerit
ista militia: mortem accusatoris accipere potuisti. Quid est
istud, quod non putas eadem gratia impetrari posse tuam
salutem?

7   SERMO

In summa parte paene irate dicit hic accusator. Nam subinde interponit: 'si vultis, si vestra interest; quid ad me, qui
periturus sum?'

⁵ *Ro.*: -mus A(β)

---

³ If the "hero" had shown lack of confidence in his innocence
by asking for the case to be quashed, he would have been refused
(cf. SB²) and his option invalidated (cf 371.3).

you had asked for the trial to be quashed.[3] As it is, you are claiming two rewards, not to stand trial and to kill a man.

So immediate killing is not necessarily involved in the reward, and whenever no time is previously defined it begins to be at the discretion of the granter; if you are asking that the trial be quashed, that is a second reward. And what sort of trial is it that you want quashed? We are not talking about a private ruling, not about a dispute over money (though even then I should put in a word for the laws and judicial custom): you are asking not to be put on trial. It affects the commonwealth in the highest degree. I say that the people were betrayed, that a time was fixed. All you have to do is to deny the charge. If you are in such a hurry, the case could have been already conducted before these gentlemen here, a verdict could have been pronounced in this same period in which we stand adjourned. You have nothing to be afraid of if you are innocent. And there is a big additional factor working for you: you became a hero. A new source of favor comes your way over and above the power of your wealth. You could not have more effectively tested how much favor your soldiering was for you: you were able to get your opponent's death. How comes it that you don't think your own life can be granted you by the same favor?

DISCUSSION

In the final section this prosecutor speaks almost angrily. He keeps putting in "if you gentlemen wish, if it is in your interest; what does it matter to me? I am going to die."

9

DECLAMATIO[6]

Vos suadeo caveatis, et suadeo permittatis dum volo: merueratis enim ne vellem. Caputne meum tam cito donastis? Tam facile innocens occisus est in ea civitate in qua sibi
putat aliquis tam facile posse contingere ne reus fiat? Quid
est ergo? Nondum omnes exuimus adfectus; faciam vobis
10 hanc invidiam, ut sciatis a vobis occidi bonum civem. Neque enim quisquam expetet[7] ut hoc iudicio dicam quomodo prodiderit, quo pretio, quo tempore, quo loco. Si
vultis haec audire, date diem; si ne hoc quidem impetro,
non meruistis. Et hoc me mea causa non facere cui non
possit esse manifestum? Expediebat alioqui mihi vivere,
expediebat suspenso ac sollicito transigere haec tempora?
Fortius est quod differo mortem quam quod mori non
recuso.

295

Demens ex vinculis fortis

Dementiae damnatus a filio et alligatus ruptis vinculis fortiter fecit. Praemio petît restitutionem. Quam cum filio
contradicente accepisset, abdicat filium.

1

SERMO

Filius optabit ut pater sanus sit; dicet id genus furoris
fuisse ut intermissionem haberet.

2

DECLAMATIO

Coeperam gratulari: ecce iterum sollicitor; iam irascitur

[6] *Ro.: post* interponit (*supra*) Aβ
[7] A: expectet β

DECLAMATION

I advise you[4] to take care and I advise you to permit me,[5] while I still want to. For it would have served you right if I had not wanted. Did you donate my life so fast? Was it so easy to kill an innocent man in a community in which someone thinks he can so easily get out of standing trial? So what? I have not entirely discarded all feelings. I shall embarrass you so far as to let you know that you are killing a good citizen. For nobody will demand of me to say in this trial how he betrayed, for what price, at what time, in what place. If you want to hear all this, give me a day; if you don't give me that much, you haven't deserved it. And it is clear to everyone, isn't it, that I am not doing this for my own sake. Was it in my interest anyhow to live, to pass this period in suspense and anxiety? It is a braver thing that I defer death than that I don't object to dying.

295

A madman, from chains a hero

One convicted of dementia by his son and tied up broke his chains and became a hero. For reward he asked restitution. He got it against his son's opposition and disowns the son.

DISCUSSION

The son will pray that his father be sane; he will say that the madness was of the kind that has intermissions.

DECLAMATION

I began to rejoice. Behold, I am in trouble again! Now my

4 The jury.   5 To go to court.

pater. Quod ad me pertinet, non alia ratione contradico quam ne pater domi sine custode sit. Non aliter itaque hanc causam agam quam proxime egi, etiamsi in illa nocuit moderatio.[1]

3   Diu ego tuli valetudinem patris, donec tam manifesta esset ut damnarem etiam invitus. Tradita est curatio mihi. Quam diligenter hoc egerim aestimate: videtur nunc[2] esse sanatus. Nec illud argumentum sanitatis est, quod rupit vincula: saepe faciebat hoc ipsum. Quod in hostes impetum fecit, quod praemium petît, ago gratias Fortunae: visus est sanus.

4   Quid obicis? 'Egisti' inquit 'mecum dementiae.' Si non tenuissem, tamen licuerat: datum est hoc ius contra patrem. Legum lator prospexit senectuti: ideo medicinam filiis imperavit. Cum vero sanaverim, ⟨quid quereris⟩[3]? Poteram videri impius nisi detulissem: non est indulgentia permittere sibi furorem. Sed alligavi. Hoc si inicum esset,

5   non liceret. Deinde obicies quod non custodivi. Testor deos, non recessi a custodia donec me bellum avocavit. At contradixi praemio tuo. Hoc simile est ei quod defendi. Sed[4] non dicam: 'recentia tua fecerunt merita ut optineres: an debueris, apparebit'; non desinam optare ut hanc causae meae partem malam facias.[5] Duret ista animi tui quies: scias quibus irascaris, scias quos ames.

---

[1] *Ro.*: anter- A(β)
[2] *nescioquis*: hoc Aβ: hic D
[3] *SB*[2]   [4] *Ro.*: et Aβ
[5] *Gron.*: -iam A *sub lin.*, β

---

[1] Had him declared insane.
[2] With *poteram . . . furorem* (s.4 fin.).

father is angry. As for me, I don't oppose for any reason other than that I don't want my father at home without someone to watch him. So I shall not handle this case any differently from the way I handled the other day, even though my moderation in that one did me harm.

For a long while I put up with my father's ailment, until it became so obvious that I convicted him,[1] albeit unwillingly. His treatment was handed over to me. How conscientiously I went to work you may judge. He seems to be sane again now. It is no proof of sanity that he broke his chains; he often used to do that very thing. For that he charged the enemy, for that he asked a reward, I give thanks to Fortune. He seemed sane.

What do you have against me? He says, "You went to court to have me declared insane." Suppose I had not succeeded, still I was entitled; this legal right is given against a father. The lawgiver looked out for old age; that is why he ordered the sons to undertake the treatment. But since I made him sane, <why are you complaining>? I might have been thought undutiful if I had not taken proceedings. Leaving madness to itself is not love. But I had him tied up: if that was wrong, it would not be permitted. Then you will lay to my charge that I did not keep him guarded. I call the gods to witness, I never stopped guarding him until the war called me away. But I opposed your reward: that's like what I just answered.[2] But I won't say: "Your recent services got you your point; whether you should have got it remains to be seen." No, I shall not cease to hope that you make this part of my case bad. May this mental composure of yours be lasting. May you know whom to be angry with and whom to love.

296

Exul, tace

Exulem intra fines deprehensum liceat occidere. Imprudentis caedis damnatus ex lege in exilium quinquennii[1] missus est. Intra fines a fratre ad cenam vocatus cum parasito fratris litem fratre iam dormiente conseruit, et a parasito clamante 'exul, tace' ex lege interfectus est. Quo comperto parasitum abiecit adulescens. A patre abdicatur.

1   DECLAMATIO

Obicimus adulescenti ante omnia quod parasitum habuerit. Abdicationi hoc satis erat, ut si quid pater nolit, numquam emendet. Quare nihil est quod dicas mihi 'numquam istud obiecisti.' Quid enim hoc colligis aliud quam ut te abdicet indulgens pater? Quid enim est parasitus nisi comes vitiorum, turpissimi cuiusque facti laudator? Unum tamen videbatur esse solacium, quod eiusmodi vita ad homicidium usque non perveniret.

2   Obicio tibi quod fratrem intra fines invitasti. Fuerit quantalibet causa convivii, melius [ea][2] certe ipse ad fratrem isses. Iam et[3] hoc ipsum inter causas abdicationis: obici tibi potest quod tam impius es ut[4] fratrem post illam miseram fortunam non videris nisi ad te discumbentem.[5]

3 Nam illi ignosci potest vel cum periculo venienti: tibi vero quis ignoscat qui, cum sine periculo ad illum ire posses, in

---

1 *SB*[2]: -nium Aβ
2 *Lat.*
3 i. et (*vel* est) *SB*[1]: manet Aβ
4 *Ro.*: quod A, C (*ante* post): *om.* BD
5 *Watt*[1]: descentem A: descenden-β

296

Exile, hold your tongue!

Let it be lawful to kill an exile caught inside the borders. A man found guilty of involuntary homicide was sent into five-year exile under the law. Invited by his brother to dinner inside the borders, he struck up a quarrel with his brother's parasite when his brother had already fallen asleep and was killed by the parasite (calling out, "Exile, hold your tongue!") under the law. When the young man heard of it, he threw the parasite out. His father disowns him.

DECLAMATION

First we tax the young man with having had a parasite. It was ground enough to disown him that he never corrects anything a father disapproves of. So it does you no good to say to me: "You never taxed me with that." For what do you argue therefore except that you are disowned by an indulgent father? For what is a parasite but a companion in vice, an encomiast of every shameful act? The one consolation seemed to be that such a life was not yet getting to the point of murder.

I tax you with having invited your brother inside the borders. However important the reason for the dinner may have been, you would certainly have done better to go yourself to your brother. And this is itself one more reason for the disowning: you are to be taxed with being so lacking in family feeling that you never saw your brother after that misfortune of his except when he dined at your house. As for him, he can be pardoned for coming over even at risk: but who would pardon you? You could have gone to him at

id discrimen adduxeris fratrem tuum ut eum etiam parasitus posset occidere?

4 Obicio tibi quod adhibueris cenae tertium. Si hoc furtum pietatis est, opus est secreto. Obicio quod parasitum potissimum adhibueris: hoc enim vacabat misero, hoc exuli, cenare[6] cum parasito?

5 Cetera iam intellego non pertinere ad abdicationem. Altiora sunt crimina et suis legibus digna, at[7] tamen debent
6 ideo lucrifieri quod in patrem ‹non›[8] inciderunt. Obicio tibi occidendi fratris consilium. Si accusator essem, si te in culleum peterem, illa dixissem: Persona crimini idonea est: habes parasitum; et causa occidendi manifesta est: coheres es fratris. Occasio adiuvit consilium: intra fines occidi potest. Minister non defuit: parasitus in tua potestate
7 est. Cetera vero cui non [etiam][9] manifesta sint? Parasitus sine tua voluntate conviciari fratri tuo auderet? Homo in adulationem natus, homo cuius famem tantum tu propitius differebas, non fecisset utique quo te putaret offendi. Dormis (hoc tibi in praesentia credatur): non putabat tibi posse nuntiari? Et tamen incredibile est te dormisse hoc tempore, hoc loco: convivium erat. Et quale convivium! Frater
8 invitatus. Ita ille conviciari ausus fuisset si te amantem fratris vidisset? Credo parasitum etiam insultasse fortunae filii mei. 'Tace,' dixit 'exul' parasitus, homo (puto) qui con-

---

6 *Sch., Gron.*: -abat Aβ   7 *SB4*: non Aβ
8 *SB4*   9 *SB3*

---

[1] Inviting the exile over to dinner was inviting him to break the law.   [2] Directly. The young man's former dissolute life is irrelevant to the disownment because his father had let it go unpunished (s.1) and kept clear of involvement.

no risk, and you brought your brother into such a dangerous situation that even a parasite was able to kill him.

I tax you in that you brought a third party to the dinner.
If this underhand proceeding[1] stems from family affection,
it should have been secret. I tax you in that you brought a
parasite of all people: did the unfortunate man, the exile,
have time for dining with a parasite?

As to other matters, I realize that they are irrelevant to
the present disowning. There are charges of earlier date,
deserving of their own laws; but you should get away with
them because they did <not> fall in your father's way.[2] I tax
you with a plan to murder your brother. If I were prosecuting, if I were asking the sack[3] for you, this is what I should
have said: "The persona fits the crime. You have a parasite." And the motive for the murder is clear; you are co-
heir with your brother. Opportunity aided the plan: he can
be killed inside the borders. An agent was not lacking: the
parasite is in your power. As for other things, who cannot see them? Would the parasite have dared insult your
brother if you had not willed him? A man born to flatter,
whose starvation only your godlike favor deferred, would
never have done anything he thought might offend you.
You're asleep (let's believe you on that for the present): did
he think it could not be reported to you? And yet it's unbelievable that you were asleep at that time, in that place: it
was a dinner. And what sort of a dinner? Your brother was a
guest. Would he have dared such abuse if he had seen you
an affectionate brother? I believe that the parasite even insulted my son's condition. "Hold your tongue, exile!" said

[3] In which parricides were drowned.

355

tumeliam non ferebat, 'tace, exul.' Parum enim eum graviter torquebat sola fortuna, parum enim graviter irascebatur errori, nisi etiam parasitus obiecisset! Non fecisset hoc
9 ergo te invito. Puta tamen cadere hanc in animum parasiti indignationem: illud certe in casum non cadit, quod gladius in triclinio fuerit. Multa quae singula accidere possunt, universa extra casum sunt. *[10] ut conviciari ⟨ei⟩[11] incipiat cuius occidendi ius habuerit. Adice his ut tu dormias cum fratrem invitaveris, ⟦ut visurus fratrem post longum tempus nihil sis locutus⟧ praesertim nondum exacta nocte,
10 cum adhuc vigilaret ille miser exul. Et fortasse accidere somnus hic potuerit inter plures: tres estis, et omnis sermo in angusto est. Incredibilius hoc faciet ortum inter fratrem tuum parasitumque iurgium: ad latus tuum iacet ille qui clamat 'exul, tace.' Quomodo fieri potest ut ne ipsius quidem caedis tumultu excitatus sis, [fieri non potest][12] ut gladium frater tuus non viderit, non te excitaverit cum periclitaretur?
11 His omnibus manifestum est hoc tantum quaesitum patrocinio[13] esse, quod parasitum in praesentia dimisisti. Glorieris enim licet quod non tecum interfectorem fratris habeas: itane hoc tandem satis fuit, dimittere impunitum, dimittere inviolatum? Magni adfectus iura non spectant. Sed ne dimisisti quidem bona fide. Nam et sustineri absens
12 potest. Nec dubito quin expectetur mors mea. Ut vero[14] non solum iustae sed etiam miserabiles causae abdicatio-

10 *lac. ind.* Wi.   11 *Sch.*   12 *Wi.*
13 *Gron.:* -ium Aβ: in –ium Wi.   14 *Ro.:* ergo Aβ

---

4 The brother's killing was legal, so that the parasite could not legally be punished by anything worse than dismissal.

the parasite, a man I suppose who was not by way of toler-
ating disrespect: "Hold your tongue, exile!" His condition
alone was not torture enough, he was not angry enough at
his mistake, without a parasite to throw it in his teeth! That
he would not have done, therefore, against your wish. But
suppose such an outrage suited the parasite's mentality:
this at least does not suit chance, that there was a sword in
the dining room. Many things that can just happen individually are beyond chance when taken together. * that he
starts insulting <somebody> whom he could legally kill.
Add that you go to sleep when you have your brother as
your guest, ⟦that you were about to see your brother after a
long time and said nothing,⟧ especially with the night not
over, when that poor exile was still awake. And this sleep
could perhaps have happened in a large company, but
there are three of you and all the talk is tête-à-tête. To
make this more incredible, a brawl started between your
brother and the parasite. The man who cries "Exile, hold
your tongue" is beside you. How can it be that you were not
aroused even by the noise of the murder itself, that your
brother did not see the sword, did not arouse you in his
danger?

From all this it is clear that your dismissal of the parasite for the time being was merely a way of bolstering your
case: you can boast that you don't have your brother's mur-
derer in your company. Was this really enough, to dismiss
him unpunished, unharmed? Great affections don't regard
the laws.[4] But even the dismissal was not in good faith. He
can be supported even in his absence, and I make no doubt
that you are waiting for me to die. But to show that my reasons for disowning you are not only just but pitiable, I lost a

nis sint, filium perdidi eo tempore quo miser erat. Non licuit saltem in patria, non in domo sua extremum illi spiritum effundere; sed, quod est contumeliosissimum, manibus parasiti et impune occisus est, quem indignum erat impune saltem male audisse.

297

Meretrix ab amatore forti caecata

Qui excaecaverit aliquem, aut talionem praebeat aut excaecati dux sit. Meretricis amator fortiter fecit. Occurrentem sibi meretricem excaecavit. Petit illa ut eodem duce utatur; recusat ille et offert talionem.

1 DECLAMATIO

Si quis, iudices, lege adversus eos qui excaecaverunt ita composita ut aut talionem patiantur aut aliquatenus solacium iniuriae praestent, litem esse audiat, altera parte similem fortunam exigente, altera mitiorem partem legis amplectente, profecto existimet hanc mulierem id postulare ut excaecetur is qui sibi oculos eruit, illum autem virum fortem fiducia meritorum erga rem publicam sperare posse fieri ut contra voluntatem quoque eius quae vindica-
2 tur oculos defendat. Nam et hic dolor gravissima passae convenisset, et illud naturale est, ut bona oculorum intellegant etiam qui eruerunt. Id omne diversum est: haec quae excaecata est, cui erepta lux est, cui omnis vita in tenebris[1]

---

[1] *coni. Wi.*: tormentis Aβ

---

[1] How this happened we are left guessing.

son in his time of adversity. He could not even breathe his last in his country, in his house. But the most insulting thing of all is that he was killed by the hands of a parasite and with impunity: that he should even have been insulted with impunity would have been outrageous.

297

Prostitute blinded by hero lover

Let one who has blinded another either render eye-for-eye or be the guide of the person blinded. The lover of a prostitute became a hero. Meeting the prostitute, he blinded her.[1] She asks that she use him as a guide. He refuses and offers eye-for-eye.

DECLAMATION

Seeing that the law against persons committing a blinding is so framed that they may either render eye-for-eye or make some amends for the injury, suppose, gentlemen, one were to hear of a case in which one party demanded equality of condition while the other appropriated the more lenient part of the law, he would surely think that this woman would be demanding that the man who gouged her eyes out be blinded while the hero, relying on his services to the commonwealth, would hope that he might be able to defend his eyes even against the will of the woman to be avenged. For such indignation would have been fitting to one who had suffered so grievous an injury, while it is natural that the value of eyes should be appreciated even by those who have gouged them out. All that is the reverse of our situation. The blinded woman, whose daylight has been torn away, who must live all her life in darkness, pities

agenda est, miseretur quondam amatoris sui, ille qui ex-
3 caecavit vult istam nimium vindicari. Idque si faceret
paenitentia, utcumque consolandus nobis esset. Nam et
poteramus suspicari hanc istius postulationis esse rationem cum excaecaverit meretricem quam amavit, ⟨quod⟩[2]
4 nunc oculos offerat, causa ambitus fieri. Negat fas esse ut
vir fortis manum meretrici praestet, ut iter demonstret.
⟨At⟩[3] apparet illam esse caecatam. Atque id tamen prae-
tenditur modo, iudices. Ceterum causa postulationis istius
manifesta est: videt miseram feminam durare in hoc non
posse, ut excaecet, neque id agit, ut graviorem patiatur
poenam, sed ut neutram: oculos habeat,[4] quos haec eruere
noluit, ⟨nec⟩[5] ducis opera fungatur, quoniam recusat.
5   Nos tamen necesse habemus his respondere quae pro-
ponuntur, et adversus fallacem[6] sic agere tamquam excaecari voluerit.[7] Illa etiam quae ab ipso iactata sunt nos
quoque referemus, fuisse istum virum fortem, pugnasse
pro re publica, plurimum nobis profuisse manus eius atque
6 oculos. His enim omnibus profecto hoc efficitur, ut illum
excaecari non necesse sit. Neque ei ⟨non⟩[8] nocuit illa

[2] *hic add SB*[1], *post* nunc *Aer., ante* cum (*supra*) *Ri.*
[3] *SB*[4]   [4] *Gron.*: -eret A: -ere β
[5] *Gron.*   [6] *Wi.* (-ciam *iam Hå.*[1]): aliquem Aβ
[7] *Gron.*: no- Aβ   [8] *Wi.*

[2] Before the woman had made her petition it might have been
thought that an offer of *talio* against himself by the gouger could
be taken as an act of remorse, while his present offer, after the petition, might pass for a gesture to court sympathy. But the reason
he gives for it shows otherwise.

her one-time lover, while her blinder wants her overmuch avenged. If he did that out of remorse, he would somehow or other deserve our consolation; for we might have suspected that this was the reason for that demand when he blinded a prostitute whom he loved; but that the present offering of his eyes is done for ostentation.[2] <But> he says that it would not do for a hero to give his hand to a prostitute for to show her the way. <But> it is evident that she has been blinded.[3] However, this is only humbug, gentlemen. Anyhow, the reason for that demand is clear: he sees that the poor woman cannot long be resolved to blind him[4] and it is not his object to suffer the worst punishment, but to suffer neither—to keep his eyes, which she didn't want to gouge out, <and not> serve as guide, since he refuses.[5]

However, we have to answer these proposals and in dealing with this cheat to act as though he wanted to be blinded. We too shall recall even those points which he himself has made much of: that he was a hero, that he fought for the commonwealth, that his hands and eyes were of signal benefit to us. For all this, I suppose, amounts to saying that it is not necessary for him to be blinded. And that highly creditable military service did

---

[3] Wi. would like to delete the words, but something is needed to counter *negat . . . demonstrat*. Adding *at* I understand: "that would ordinarily be so, but she is obviously blind, so that helping her would not demean the 'hero.'"

[4] Her only remaining option if he is not to go free. It seems to be assumed that the "hero" cannot be *forced* to act as guide.

[5] But in s.9 he says that the law requires that one of the two options be put into effect.

honestissima militia: propugnator fuit civitatis; quondam[9]
partem aliquam voluptatis in hanc impenderat. Sed fecit
7 illum arrogantiorem ipsa virtus. Neque tamen nobis adhuc
persuaderi potest ut vir fortis, qui amaverit aperte, qui non
erat laesus ulla meretricis iniuria, oculos volens eruerit.
Fortunam illud putamus fuisse; et,[10] si lex permitteret
neutram ultionem, forsitan totum ius remitteremus. Nunc
oculos eius servamus qua possumus.

8 Lex ita scripta est ut is qui excaecaverit aut talionem patiatur aut ducis opera fungatur. Inter has duas res quaestio
est. Antequam comparo, illud interrogare volo: cuius causa
scriptam esse legem putatis[11]? Dubitari non potest quin
scripta sit ei quae vindicanda est. Ne illud quidem in dubium veniet, optionem[12] quidem harum duarum (ut ita ap-
9 pellem) poenarum esse in potestate exigentis. Quid enim
aliud cogitasse legum latorem putamus? Illum utique qui
excaecasset credidit esse puniendum, adeo ut ne illi quidem ipsi qui vindicabatur permiserit totam legem remittere. Illa igitur fuit cogitatio: 'meruit quidem qui eruit oculos ut et ipse perdat; si tamen habuerit misericordem, si
inciderit in eum qui aliquatenus reddere irae suae rationem posset, gratiam referat huic postea.' Eligi ergo ab ea
10 poena debet quae gravissimam iniuriam passa est. Puta istud esse asperius quod recusas: fortasse propter hoc ipsum

[9] *Ro.*: quoniam Aβ   [10] *Ro.*: ut Aβ
[11] *Ro.*: putas Aβ   [12] *Lat.*: ultio- Aβ

---

[6] *Hanc = civitatem*. But as Wi. says, the sentence is problem-
atic.

[7] Leaving open the possibility that a motive might turn up
later on.

[8] The feminine refers anomalously to the particular case.

him harm. He was a champion of the community. At one time he had expended part of his pleasure on it.[6] But his very valor made him more arrogant. All the same, we cannot be persuaded as yet[7] that a hero, whose love was no secret, who had not been in any way injured by the prostitute, intentionally gouged out her eyes. We think that was Fortune; and if the law permitted abstention from either vengeance, perhaps we should waive our right entirely. As it is, we save his eyes the way we can.

The text of the law says that one who has blinded another should either suffer eye-for-eye or discharge the function of guide. The question lies between these two. Before comparing them, I want to ask for whose sake do you think the law was written? Unquestionably it was written for the woman[8] who is to be avenged. Neither will there be any question but that the option between these two penalties (so to term them) is in the power of the person exacting. For what else do we suppose the lawgiver had in mind? He believed that the person who did the blinding should in any case be punished, so much so that he did not allow even the person who was avenged to waive the whole law. This then was in his mind: he that gouged out eyes has deserved to lose his own. If, however, he has a compassionate victim, if he happens on one who might to some extent come to terms with his anger,[9] let him repay the same later on. So the woman who has suffered a most grievous injury ought to choose the punishment. Suppose the one you refuse is the harsher: perhaps you should suffer it for

---

[9] Lit. "render an account to," i.e. tell it how far it could go. Håkanson compares *Decl. Mai.* 6.17 init. *Fortunae suae rationem reddit.*

pati debeas. Oculos eruisti mulierculae sine dubio, et adice, si vis, meretrici: tamen quos eruere non licebat. Non es dignus qui patiaris quod vis.

11   Haec dicerem si tecum asperius contenderem; nunc ante omnia rei publicae causa tecum ago. Aequum est salvos esse hos oculos et incolumes: multa adferunt casus, 12 frequens bellum est. Detegemus tibi etiam huius mulierculae adfectus, quo magis te rem tam gravem fecisse paeniteat. Haec excaecare te non potuit. Meminit temporum superiorum, meminit illarum quas aliquando communes habuit voluptatum, meminit amoris tui. Digna est cui manum commodes. Nam id quoque lex iustissime constituit: praestet oculos qui eruerit, et in vicem erutorum luminum 13 ipse succedat. 'At enim forti viro turpe est hoc officium subire.' Scilicet illa honestiora, debilitatem pati et ferre infestos numinibus oculos. Non erit talis ista debilitas qualis esset si illam in acie passus esses. Tu qui recusas dux esse meretricis, non cogitas futurum ut tibi oculi propter meretricem eruantur? Verum meretur hic ipse pudor tuus propter quem parcamus oculis tuis.

298

Rusticus parasitus

Rusticus parasitum filium abdicat. CD.

1   DECLAMATIO

Non ignoro, iudices, quamquam non a forensi contentione solum sed ab universa civitatis conversatione longe remo-

---

10 Or "eyes of ill omen," reading *infaustos*.

that very reason. You gouged a little woman's eyes out, no doubt about that, and add, if you will, a prostitute's: all the same, you were not entitled to gouge them. You do not deserve to suffer the punishment of your choice.

This is what I should say if I were contending with you harshly. As it is, first and foremost I am arguing with you for the sake of the commonwealth. It is fair that these eyes be safe and unharmed. Chance brings many things, war is frequent. I shall now also reveal to you this little woman's feelings, to make you the more sorry for having done such a dreadful thing. She could not blind you. She remembers times gone by, remembers the pleasures she once had in common with you, remembers your love. She deserves that you lend her a hand. For this too the law laid down most justly: let him that gouged eyes provide them, and himself take the place of the organs he gouged. "But it's shameful for a hero to take on such an office." Is it more respectable to suffer a mutilation and cast angry[10] eyes upon the gods? This deformity will not be as it would have been if you had suffered it in battle. You refuse to be a prostitute's guide, but doesn't it occur to you that your eyes will be gouged out because of a prostitute? But this very shame of yours deserves that we spare your eyes.

298

The rustic parasite

A rustic disowns his parasite son. He opposes.

DECLAMATION

I am aware, gentlemen of the jury, far removed though I am not only from contention in court but from the general

tus, hoc praecipue fieri miserabiles eos qui paternae animadversionis notam deprecantur, quod periclitari de prae-
terita dignitate videantur: de qua certe sollicitum esse
filium meum incredibile est. Quantulum est enim quod
2 abdicatus erit qui iam parasitus est! Quem ego, iudices,
tam obstinate non praeceptis solum meis sed etiam precibus resistentem utinam possem dicere contumacem: nunc
hanc licentiam concepit animo servitutis. Multum enim
illi, ut res est, fiduciae facit gratia adulescentis locupletis et
prodigi, qui non aliter quam si de proprio mancipio ageretur in hoc vires suas ostendit. Infelix et ille: tam turpem
3 enim filium habeo ut etiam ipsi obiciatur. Nec me praeterit
unde haec frequentia: concurrerunt ad spectandos duos
rusticos, et id forsitan hoc ipso indicante. Merito: sic iste
ridetur. Cuius nomen equidem nec intellego nec interpre-
tari possum [quod vocatur],[1] verum[2] nescio quid esse turpius quam luxuriam puto.

4   Quo magis autem hac eius vita erubescam fecit memoria nostrae.[3] Mihi rus paternum erga labores gratissimum,
non frugalitati tantum suffecturum sed et delectationi, si
coleretur a dominis duobus. Hoc cum diu exercuissem,[4] ne
haec quidem ducendae uxoris et educandorum liberorum
onera recusavi, ut relictum a parentibus meis relinquerem
5 filio meo. De quo ipso[5] non questus sum; nam videbatur
laboriosus. Misi in civitatem; delicatior venit, et redire

[1] *SB*[3]   [2] *Lat.*: unum Aβ
[3] *Gron.*: -ri Aβ
[4] d. e. *SB*[1]: dio evenissem Aβ
[5] *Hå.*[2]: ipse Aβ

[1] παράσιτος. The rustic knows no Greek. The derivation

intercourse of the community, that persons deprecating the stigma of paternal punishment become objects of pity most of all because their past status seems imperiled. That my son should be concerned on that account is certainly incredible. How little will it matter that he will be disowned when he is already a parasite! Would that I could call him contumacious, gentlemen, resisting as he does so obstinately not only my admonishments but my entreaties. As it is, he took this license into his head because of a slave mentality. The fact is that the favor of a rich young prodigal, who displays his power over my son as if a chattel of his own were concerned, greatly emboldens him. This person too is unfortunate; for I have so shocking a son that he himself is reproached with the connection. Nor does the reason for this large gathering escape me; they have flocked here to look at two bumpkins, and perhaps he himself passed the word. Well he might: this is how he gets his laughs. His name[1] I don't understand and can't translate, but I think it means something more disgraceful than loose living.

I blush the more for this life of his from my memory of my own. I have a family property that gives an excellent return for work. It would yield enough not only for frugality but even for enjoyment if it were cultivated by two owners. After I had worked it for a long time,[2] I did not refuse the burden of taking a wife and raising children in order to leave to my son what my parents left to me. Of himself I made no complaint; he seemed a hard worker. I sent him into town. He returned less countrified and was in a hurry

(from παρά, "beside," and σῖτος, "food") is actually quite innocuous.   [2] See crit. note.

properavit. Et primo quidem deformavit tantum diligen-
tior cultus; dehinc procedente tempore saepe fragrantem
mero vidi, redolentem unguenta, et iam plura perditae
6 vitae signa. Cum interrogarem, respondebat esse locupletem amicum. Dispiciebam[6] eam[7] amicitiam, dicebamque:
'quamdiu iste locuples erit?' donec ⟨eo⟩ res redît[8] ut etiam
de salute eius timerem. Ad domum divitis veni, [non
enim][9] nomen inter non agnoscentes requisivi: parasitus
inventus est. Id[10] placeret rustico patri? Erubui.

7   Nondum te, iuvenis,[11] ad comparationem voco utriusque vitae; in praesentia hoc uno contentus sum: suscipe la-
boris tui partem. Satis sine[12] te laboravimus. Iam deficit
aetas, iam quietem poscit senectus: et ego delicatus sum.
Abdicent te[13] licet boni mores, tamen clamo: 'ego te mihi
genui.' Non ergo cogitabis quid mihi debeas? Illae terrae
gratiam referunt, nec quicquam inveniri potest in rerum
8 natura in quo labor pereat. De abdicatione tu quereris?
Prior patrem reliquisti. Quando enim videre te mihi licet?
Quantum absum ab orbitate? Impono, iudices, adfectibus
meis, qui nihil adhuc inter querelas habeo nisi desiderium:
iam irasci necesse est. Nondum tamen ad ultimam tui con-
9 tumeliam venio. Obicio tibi luxuriam; ⟨satis erat⟩[14] si
hoc tantum diceremus: 'vivis inter meretrices et lenones.'

---

6 *SB*[3]: des- Aβ   7 *Gron.*: etiam Aβ
8 e. r. r. *Ro., auct. Aer., Sch.*: resedit Aβ   9 *Ro.*
10 *Wi.*: et Aβ   11 *Sch.*: invenissem Aβ
12 *Obr.*: in Aβ   13 *SB*[3]: me Aβ
14 *SB*[3], sufficeret *iam Wi.*

---

3 Cf. 283.2 init.
4 The son. They knew him as "the parasite."

to go back. At first the only ugly sign was a greater attention to how he dressed. Then as time went on I often saw him smelling of wine, reeking with perfume, and other evidences of wastrel life. When I questioned him, he would answer that he had a rich friend. I looked into[3] that friendship and I used to say: "how long is he going to be rich?"—until it got ‹to the point› that I actually feared for my son's welfare. I went to the rich man's house and asked for him[4] by name, which they did not recognize. The parasite was found. Was it likely to please a rustic father? I blushed.

I am not yet challenging you, young man, to a comparison of our respective lifestyles. For the present I am content with just this: take your part of the work. I have worked without you long enough. I am growing old and weak, my age needs rest. I too need pampering. Morality may disown you, but I proclaim it: "I gave you birth for me." So will you not think of what you owe me? That land repays us; nothing can be found in nature on which work is wasted. Do you complain about being disowned? You left your father first. When am I allowed to see you? Am I not practically childless? Gentlemen, I trick my feelings:[5] so far all that I complain of is that I miss you, but now I must really wax angry. But I have not yet come to the ultimate insult.[6] I tax you with loose living: ‹it would have been enough› if I only said: "you live among prostitutes and

---

[5] "By pretending to be angry when I am only feeling loss" (Wi.). Rather "by pretending to feel only loss when I am really angry, or getting to be."

[6] Acceptance of insults is a parasite's stock in trade, but to be called "parasite" is the worst insult of all.

Dignus es abdicatione etiamsi parasitum habes. Inter aliena servitia numeraris, et tibi luxuria obicitur etiam non tua.
Omitto interim ex quo genere vitae in istud transieris, sub
quo institutus patre; dissimulata et remota persona mea
10 parasitum abdico. Num me irasci putas? Misereor. [ubi][15]
Haeserunt tibi vitia civitatis, ⟨ubi⟩[16] videtur habere hoc
primum odium, rusticitas. Si bona paterna consumpsisses,
iure abdicareris: libertatem et ingenuum pudorem con-
sumpsisti. Quis ⟨est⟩[17] melior ille cui servis? Pudet dicere
quo pretio hereditatem emancipaveris: gulae servis, et sicut muta animalia obiectis cibis in istam cecidisti servi-
11 tutem. Iuvat autem cibus post opus. Multa quidem video
diversa genera vitae, nec probabilia omnia; ceterum tamen
hoc novum est et inauditum, contumelias in quaestu habere et iniuria pasci. Iuvat illa te residua potio et ex locupletis
cena nescio quid intactum. Caedentis manus oscularis et
ferrum portas, fame periturus si ille nihil mali fecerit.[18]
Alios enim fortasse parasitos ars[19] aliqua commendet: tu
12 quid potes, miser, nisi vapulare? Habent hoc quoque deliciae divitum malum, quaerere omnia contra naturam.
Gratus est ille debilitate; illa ipsa infelicitate distorti corporis placet. Alter emitur quia coloris alieni est. Haec, ut res
est, accessit nova elegantia, inter perversas delicias habere
rusticum. Ridiculum hoc, quod durus, quod inhabilis,
quod filius meus.

15 *Ri.*   16 *SB*[1]   17 q. e. *SB*[3]: qui Aβ
18 m. f. *SB*[3]: malef- Aβ   19 *Pith*: pars Aβ

7 A slave must have a master. The parasite's master is his belly.
8 Your chains.   9 *À rebours*, like the decadents of nine-
teenth-century *fin de siècle*.

pimps." You deserve to be disowned even if you *keep* a parasite. You are counted among another man's slaves, you are taxed with loose living which is not even your own. Meanwhile I say nothing about the kind of life from which you passed into your present one, under what sort of father you were trained. I conceal my own persona, put it out of the way, as I disown a parasite. Do you think I am angry? I pity you. The vices of the town clung to you, in which this seems to be the first among things odious—rusticity. If you had consumed your father's goods, you would be justly disowned: you have consumed liberty and freeborn modesty. Who is that superior being whom you serve?[7] I am ashamed to name the price for which you have alienated your heritage: you serve your stomach, and like dumb animals when food is offered them you fell into your present servitude. But food is relished after work. I see many different ways of life, and not all of them to be approved; but this one is novel and unheard-of, to turn insults to profit and live off outrage. You love that residual drink, that something untouched from a wealthy man's dinner. You kiss the hand that beats you and carry the iron.[8] You'll starve to death if he doesn't hurt you. Perhaps other parasites have some skill to recommend them: but you, wretched creature, what can you do except take a thrashing? Rich exquisites have this godsent malady among others, a hankering for everything unnatural.[9] Deformity is one passport to favor—the very infelicity of a twisted body pleases. Another is bought because of his foreign color. The fact is that this has become another new chic, to keep a rustic among one's fancy perversities. It's risible— he's tough and clumsy and my son.

13   Qualia, di deaeque, damnas[20]! Intellego cum quo mihi filio res est: non commendabo illi laborem honestum et bonam cotidie conscientiam et operam etiam civitatibus servientem. Agam causam per vices anni, [non][21] numerabo

14   fructus: luxuriosum filium ad delicias voco paratas. Ingentis pecuniae concupiscis feras? Demens, ipse venare. Avibus onerari fercula gaudes? Fructus nostros, nisi succurris, infestant. Quidquid illic lautum est, nos misimus, et fructus curvatis ramis ad manum paratos habemus. Compara, si videtur, vestris nivibus meos[22] fontes, compara inclusis intra parietes aquis perennes fluminum lapsus. Quae tanta vobis nemora? Quid est istic admirabile nisi ruris imitatio?

15   Ad has te delicias pater voco. Ipse durum desidia solum sulcis aperiam et aratro senex incumbam: tu tantum impera. Non misereris paterni avitique fundi, obsiti sentibus? Circa beati fructus: nos desidia male audimus. Quot iam

16   perdidimus annos! Tu vivis aliena liberalitate. At si te nulla[23] horum miseratio tenet, ignoscas mihi: ducimus quendam adversus ipsas terras consuetudine adfectum. Non vendes tu agellum meum, non paternos avitosque cineres et ossa alicui pretio cenae unius addices. Quatenus infeliciter filium sustuli, quaeram aliquem qui colat.

[20] *SB*[1]: -na Aβ
[21] *Ri., auct. Obr.*
[22] *Gron.*: vestros . . . meis Aβ
[23] *Gron.*: ulla Aβ

Gods and goddesses, what things you despise! I realize what sort of son I have to deal with. I shan't recommend honest toil to him and a good conscience every day and work that serves even the towns. I shall plead my case with the changes of the seasons, I shall number our products; I summon my loose-living son to the delights that await him. Have you a fancy for wild animals that cost a mint? You crazy fellow, do your own hunting. You like your dishes loaded with birds? Well, they infest our crops unless you come to the rescue. Whatever is sumptuous over there, we sent it. Fruits? We have them bending the branches, ready to pick. Compare, if you will, my springs with your snows,[10] compare perennially flowing rivers with waters shut in between walls. These big walls of yours, what of them? What's wonderful with you except imitation of the countryside? To these delights I summon you, your father. I myself, the old man, shall open up the soil—it's hard from lying fallow—with furrows and bend over the plough: you only give the orders. Aren't you sorry for the farm, your father's and your grandfather's, overgrown with brambles? All around is wealth of produce: we are criticized as lazybones. How many years have we wasted! You live on another man's charity. But if you have no commiseration for these things, you must forgive me: familiarity gives us a certain affection for the land itself. You shall not sell my little farm, you shall not make over your father's and your grandfather's ashes and bones to somebody for the price of a single dinner. Since I was unfortunate in the son I acknowledged, I shall look for someone to till the soil.

[10] For cooling wine etc.

299

Ossa eruta parricidae

Parricidae insepulti abiciantur. Sepulcri violati sit actio.
Decedens pater mandavit filiae ultionem, dicens se duorum filiorum veneno perire. Puella reos postulavit. Inter
moras unus se occidit et sepultus est in monumentis maiorum. Alterum cum damnasset et insepultum proiecisset,
eius quoque qui sepultus fuerat ossa eruit et abiecit. Accusatur violati sepulcri.

1   SERMO

An utcumque sepultum eruere non liceat; an ei non licuerit quae potuit prohibere; an etiam ⟨ut⟩[1] non iure fuerit sepultus. Hinc speciales quaestiones, utrum lex damnatum
tantum parricidii an revera parricidam prohibeat sepeliri;
an ille parricida fuerit. In hoc probativae duae, altera pa-
thetice, altera pragmatice, id est, adfectus et iuris quaestiones: an damnatus sit sua sententia qui sibi manus attulit;
2   an et de illo iudicatum sit cum frater eius convictus sit. An
non possit quisquam mortuus damnari; etiam ut alius
nemo possit, an is utique potuerit qui in reatu periit. Ultima [pelagi][2] qualitas, in qua totius controversiae vires
sunt: quale huius factum, utrum venia dignum an damnatione sit; in qua tractatione patheticos pro re publica in-
dignandum.

    [1] *Ri.*
    [2] *Wi.*

---

    [1] An "emotional" question.
    [2] A legal question.

299

A parricide's bones dug up

Let parricides be cast away unburied. Let there be an action for tomb-violation. A father on his deathbed charged his daughter to avenge him, saying he was dying of poison administered by his two sons. The girl brought an accusation against them. During the delays one of them committed suicide and was buried in the family mausoleum. She convicted the other and threw him out unburied, after which she also dug up and threw away the bones of the one who had been buried. She is accused of tomb-violation.

DISCUSSION

Is it in any circumstances lawful to dig a person up after burial? Was this not lawful for somebody who had the power to forbid the burial? Or even if the burial was not lawful? Then come special questions: does the law forbid burial only of one convicted of parricide or of one who in fact committed it? Was the person a parricide? In this case there are two types of probative questions, one emotional, the other juristic, that is the questions of feeling and questions of law. Was the suicide condemned by his own verdict?[1] Was judgment passed on him as well when his brother was convicted?[2] Is it impossible for a dead man to be convicted? Even if no one else, could not a person at least who died while under prosecution? Last comes quality, in which lies the force of the entire controversy: of what quality was her fact, forgivable or condemnable? In handling that, emotional indignation on behalf of the commonwealth is in order.

3

DECLAMATIO

Sepulti ergo essent et aeterna quiete conditi iacuissent
parricidae manes iuxta patris latus, ut, quod diis homini-
busque videatur indignum, tumulo tectus videretur cui leges terram negant, in cuius cruciatus cum omnia commen-
ta sit antiquitas citerior est tamen poena quam scelus,
cuius statim ora oculosque a iudicio lex iussit obduci, ne

4 hunc iucundum caeli aspectum polluerent taetri oculi, cui
lucem vivo, fluitanti mare, naufrago portum, morienti terram, defuncto sepulcrum negat? Quem in poena sua iubet
vivere, huic tumulum et exequias persolvi fas fuit? Adeone
omnia ‹iura›[3] perierunt ut ex duobus meliore loco haben-
dus sit manifestior parricida?

5 Tu vero, puella tam honesti adfectus, quidquid tacita
pietate suggeritur[4] vel his audientibus refer, mihi crede.
Modo approbasti nihil te de fratribus tuis solere mentiri.
'Dies' inquit 'noctesque miseranda patris umbra circum-
volabat,[5] qualis erat cum mandatum daret. Modo minax
atque effera, repente summissa, his me vocibus, ut sciatis,

6 appellabat[5]: "Tu quidem, filia, parricidam postulasti; eodem crimine, isdem argumentis, communibus utrique legibus iudiciisque qui supererat damnatus est. Nunc unus
superest dolor, quod parricida sepultus est, quod aeterna
quiete compositus sepulcro meo parricida patrem premit.
Aude nunc aliquid, puella, fortius, et ab hoc utique me vin-

---

[3] Ro.
[4] SB[1]: -ris Aβ: -it Fr.
[5] SB[4]: -lat Aβ

DECLAMATION

So the parricide's spirit would have been buried and hidden in eternal rest side by side with his father. An outrage in the eyes of gods and men, one would have been seen covered by a tomb to whom the laws deny earth, one for whom antiquity had devised all manner of tortures but whose punishment falls short of his crime, whose face and eyes the law ordered covered immediately after trial lest his direful eyes pollute the pleasant vision of the sky; light to the living it denies, sea to the floating, harbor to the cast adrift, earth to the dying, sepulchre to the dead.[3] It orders him to live in his punishment; could he be permitted the due of tomb and funeral? Have all ⟨laws⟩ so perished that the more manifest parricide of the two should be the better treated?

But you, girl, whose emotions do you so much credit, whatever a daughter's silent feelings suggest, speak, yes, in the hearing of these gentlemen, trust me. You have just proved that you tell no lies about your brothers. "Day and night," she says, "the shade of my poor father used to flit around me, as he was when he gave me his charge. Sometimes threatening and fierce, then suddenly meek, he addressed me (so you may know) thus: 'My daughter, you prosecuted a parricide; the survivor was found guilty on the same charge by the laws and courts common to both. Now one grief remains: a parricide has been buried; laid in eternal rest in my tomb, the parricide presses upon his father. Now, girl, dare a bolder thing and avenge me at any

---

[3] Parricides were sewn up in sacks and thrown into a river; cf. Cic. *Rosc. Am.* 71, the source of this purple patch.

dica quem ego occidi. Expulsus sedibus meis contactum illius fugio.'"

Quid agis, infelix puella? Ecquid agnoscis alterum pa-
7 tris mandatum? Itaque ut primum accessit ad tumulum, sponte resoluta lapidum compage, impios cineres in editum terrae[6] suggessit, onerosa etiam inferis monstra in lu-
8 cem redundare visa sunt. Dii boni, post haec quisquam queretur cur ex duobus parricidis neuter iaceat[7] tamquam pater, uterque tamquam frater?

300

Adultera apud filium iudicem rea

Apud communem filium iudicem ream adulterii fecit maritus uxorem. Matrem absolvit adulescens. Pater eandem detulit in iudicium publicum et damnavit. Abdicat filium.

1 SERMO

De ante actis temporibus non tantum est quod adulescenti nihil obicitur, sed etiam quod proxime iudex placuit patri. Quorum ratio cum constet, poterit[1] non improbi vel non manifesti erroris peti venia. Sed prius iure defendendus est.

2 DECLAMATIO

Obicis sententiam; non dico qualem: iudex pronuntiavi.[2] Dispiciendum tibi fortasse fuerit ad quem venires, diligen-

6 SB[4]: -a Aβ   7 Ro.: -et Aβ
1 SB[3]: -rat Aβ   2 Sch.: -avit *vel sim.* Aβ

---

4 I.e. drove to suicide. *Utique* has been found baffling, but the

cost of this one whom I killed.[4] Driven from my dwelling, I flee his contact.'"

What are you about, unhappy girl? Do you recognize your father's second charge? So as soon as she got to the tomb, the stone structure collapsed of its own accord. She heaped the impious ashes on a mound of earth. It seemed as if the monstrosity, oppressive even to the underworld, had flowed back into the daylight. Kind gods, shall anybody after this find fault in that neither of the two parricides lies like his father, each like his brother?

300

An adulteress prosecuted before her son as judge

A husband prosecuted his wife for adultery before their common son as judge. The young man acquitted his mother. The father brought her before a public court and convicted her. He disowns his son.

DISCUSSION

As for times past, it is not only that nothing is alleged against the son but also that quite recently the father approved him as judge. All that being established, pardon may be sought for an error that was not immoral or not manifest. But first he is to be defended on legal grounds.

DECLAMATION

You tax me with my verdict, never mind what kind of verdict: I pronounced it as judge. Perhaps you should have taken a closer look at the man you resorted to, examined

father means that this son must be dealt with even more than the other because he is an actual annoyance.

tius excutiendi mores: nulla iudici libertas est nisi pronuntiare licet utrum voluerit.

Fortasse erraverim in dispiciendis causis, minus pru-
dentiae habuerim iuvenis: ego nihil aliud debeo quam
3 fidem. An tu ea condicione litigabas, ut pronuntiare pro te
necesse esset? Hoc dicerem si in quocumque iudicio sententiam tulissem; aliquanto fortius ⟨agendum⟩[3] est cum
iudex a te sim electus: hanc quam nunc eripis libertatem[4]
in iudicio dedisti.

4 Quid tamen pronuntiavi, et in qua causa? Ream absolvi. Non dico quam ream, nec cuius criminis. Hoc dico:
male audire plerumque iudicum nimia severitas solet, nec
umquam in convicium nisi asperae sententiae veniunt.
Ideo absolutos publica illa acclamatio prosequitur; a damnato tristes recedunt, et victricis quoque partis silentium
est. Absolvi. Si hoc invidiosum, si hoc criminosum est,
quomodo me putem potuisse defendi si damnassem?
5 Absolvi matrem meam. Hoc non eo pertinet fortasse, ut
debuerim crimen remittere. Multa ignorantes facimus[5]:
mihi mater innocens visa est. Obiciebas tu adulterium. Nihil necesse est tractare de causa, praesertim cum ius[6] sit
ablatum defensionis: mihi tamen omnia quaecumque in
6 matrem meam dicebantur incredibilia sunt visa. Respue-
bat illa *[7] magis apud me agebat causam mater mea, dicens: 'Scis quomodo te amaverim, quomodo educaverim.

[3] *Ro.*   [4] *SB*[1]: clarita- Aβ
[5] *SB*[2]: patimur Aβ   [6] *SB*[3]: nihil Aβ
[7] *lac. ind. Ro.*: mens (*an* mea mens?) *add. Schenkl*

[1] As Wi. says, there was only one (I do not think *causis* can be
taken as "motives").

his character with more care. A judge has no freedom unless he is allowed to pronounce which way he likes.

Perhaps I made a mistake when I looked into the cases,[1] lacked wisdom, young as I was. I have no other obligation than good faith. Were you litigating on condition that the verdict had to go in your favor? That is what I should be saying if I had given a verdict in just any case. <I must plead> somewhat more forcefully since it was you who chose me as judge. The liberty which you take from me now you gave me at the trial.

But what did I pronounce and in what case? I acquitted a woman on trial. I don't say who she was or what she was accused of. I do say this: generally judges are criticized for excessive severity; verdicts never get to be quarreled with except harsh ones. So public applause follows those acquitted; people go away sad from a man convicted, and even the winning side keeps silence. I acquitted. If this makes me unpopular, a target for criticism, what defense am I to think I could have had if I had convicted? I acquitted my mother. This does not mean perhaps that I ought to have remitted the charge. We often act in ignorance. I thought my mother innocent. You taxed her with adultery. There is no need to go into the case, especially since her right to a defense has been taken away.[2] But to me all the things that were being said against my mother seemed unbelievable. My <mind>[3] rejected them. Rather,[4] my mother was pleading her case before me: "You know how I loved you,

[2] By her conviction.
[3] See crit. note.
[4] Rather than listen to them, I listened to her.

Nihil mihi obiectum est in aetate prima, nulla fabula
[ante][8] partum secuta est: ream facit anum et iuvenis ma-
7 trem.' Tu me iudicem faciebas, illa testem. Accedebat his
illud etiam, quod non existimabam tam asperam illam dis-
sensionem, nec veram esse litem quae ad filium ducebatur.
Videbamini mihi quaerere intercessorem. Aliud fortasse
fuerit quod te postea concitavit[9]; illo tempore nihil facere
melioris mariti, nihil indulgentioris potuisti: ad eum iudicem perduxeras uxorem qui damnare non posset.

8   'At enim postea hoc crimen probavi.' ⟦Non iam respon-
deo ista quae dixi: †aliis muneribus accipere iudices extra-
neorum naturam qua†[10] 'fortasse iratior existi.'⟧[11] Non
semper erroris odium penes cognoscentes est: aliquando
causa perfertur neglegentius, interim defenditur. Si matrem meam nunc audias, dicit se ad illos iudices venisse se-
9 curam, et obstitisse sibi fiduciam prioris sententiae. Utitur
[in defensione][12] claris ac nobilibus exemplis, damnatos
mihi Camillos et Rutilios narrat. Verum quicumque iste
exitus fuit, habuerit suum finem. Si crimina in me exples[13]
(neque vereor), plura confitebor quam obicis: et cum dam-
nata esset mater mea, flevi et graviter tuli.

301

Rapta a divite pro ancilla

Pauper divitem invitavit ad cenam. Erat in ministerio
puella[1] pauperis. Interrogatus pauper a divite quaenam

---

[8] *SB*[3]   [9] *SB*[3]: -ant A[1]: -arit A[2]β: -aret D
[10] *inter cruces pos. Wi., Ri.*   [11] *ita secl. SB*[3]
[12] *SB*[1]   [13] *Aer.*: -let Aβ
[1] filia *SB*[1]

how I brought you up. Nothing was said against me in my youth, no scandal followed the birth. He is prosecuting an old woman, the mother of a young man." You made me a judge, she a witness. There was another thing: I did not think that that quarrel was so bitter or that a dispute brought to your son was real. It seemed to me that the two of you were looking for an intermediary. Something else may have happened later to rouse your ire; at that time you could not have shown yourself a better, more loving husband. You had brought your wife before a judge who could not find her guilty.

"But later I established the charge." [[In answer I won't say what I said. . .]] The blame for a mistake does not always lie with the tribunal. Sometimes the prosecution is negligent, sometimes the defense. If you were now to listen to my mother, she says she was confident when she came before that jury and that her reliance on the previous verdict worked against her. She uses illustrious and famous examples, tells me about the convictions of a Camillus and a Rutilius.[5] But whatever the outcome, let it be over and done with. If you are filling out your charge against me (I am not afraid), I'll confess more than you allege: when my mother was found guilty, I shed tears, I bore it hard.

301

Girl raped as a slave by rich man

A poor man invited a rich man to dinner. The poor man's daughter was waiting at table. Asked who she was by the

---

5 M. Furius Camillus and P. Rutilius Rufus, standard examples of good men wrongfully convicted.

esset, dixit ancillam. Discedens a cena dives eam rapuit. Educta ad magistratus puella ex lege raptarum nuptias optavit. Dives accusat pauperem circumscriptionis.

1   SERMO

Etiamsi reus est hic pauper, non tamen mihi videtur aspere et concitate contra divitem acturus; non tantum accusator dives illi sed gener est, et nos non sumus iracundi: rapta nuptias optavit.

2   DECLAMATIO

Si alio accusante dicerem causam, sciebam et expertus proxime eram esse nobis aequam etiam adversus divites libertatem. Sed me, quamquam indignissime petar, non tam
3   lex quam ratio prohibet a conviciis. Ego hunc amicum semper optavi, etiam antequam essem socer, et colui et aliquid etiam supra vires facultatium mearum in excipiendo eo ausus sum. Atque id me fecisse ante omnia confiteor ut patronum[2] haberet filia mea. Nunc vero eum mihi Fortuna ipsa generum dedit quem maxime diligebam. Tota itaque haec quae pro innocentia mea adhibebitur non tam defensio erit quam satisfactio.
4   Fortasse detrectet, sed tamen audebo: ne nos fastidiat. Non sum quidem locuples; sed quotus quisque? Inops censu, sed[3] integer, sine crimine, sine fabula, non indignus aliquando huic diviti visus qui amicus vocarer, ad cuius mensae quoque societatem abundans et locuples accede-

---

² *Sch., Gron.*: potiorem Aβ   ³ *Pith.*: et Aβ

---

[1] At the option.   [2] Ironically, the present case turns on the girl's pretended slave status.

[3] Directed to his son-in-law as well as the court.

rich man, the poor man said she was a slave girl. As he was leaving after dinner, the rich man raped her. Brought before the magistrates, the girl opted for marriage under the law governing raped women. The rich man accuses the poor man of fraud.

DISCUSSION

Although the poor man is on trial, I don't think he will go against the rich man bitterly and vehemently. The rich man is not only his accuser but his son-in-law, and we are not angry: the raped girl chose marriage.

DECLAMATION

If I were pleading my case with another prosecutor, I knew (and had recently so found)[1] that we have fair freedom of speech even against the rich. But though I am being most unwarrantably attacked, abuse is forbidden to me, not so much by the law as by reason. I always longed for this man as my friend; even before I was his father-in-law, I paid him attentions and in having him as my guest I ventured somewhat beyond what my means permitted. And I confess that I did so primarily in order that my daughter might have a patron.[2] But now Fortune herself has given me as a son-in-law the man I liked more than anyone. So all that I am about to bring forward to prove my innocence will not be a defense so much as an explanation.[3]

Perhaps he belittles me, but I shall venture. He had better not look down on us. True, I am not wealthy, but how few are! My means are meager, but there is nothing against me, no charge, no scandal; the rich man once thought me not unworthy to be called his friend, someone whom in his affluence and wealth he would even join at

5   ret. Et existimaram[4] fore hoc quoque inter causas amicitiae, si cenulam diviti pauper fecisset, non illam beatam,
nec qualem hic potest, non instructam ministeriis—unde
enim nobis? Omnia proferenda sunt in medium, cum
praesertim iste nos propius cognoverit. Quidquid illud
fuit, ne dedignaretur dives, ⟨ipse⟩[5] maxima parte curavi,
ipse composui, et post securitatem modo conviva serus ac-
6   cessi. Sed opus erat ministerio. Hoc paraveram mihi non
pecunia, non emptione, sed uxorem ducendo, educando
hanc puellam. Admiratum credidi quod hic sexus ministraret; eoque magis mihi pudori fuit confiteri esse filiam
meam. Nam neque erat is cultus et notitia nobis adhuc
nova. ⟦Et tamen, si de me quoque interrogasset, respon-
7   dissem: 'servuli tui sumus.'⟧[6] Non persuadeo tamen mihi
ut crediderit. Neque enim[7] irritare tam delicatas eius cupiditates potuisset ancilla, nec fecit quod adversus hanc
condicionem fieri fortasse potuisset: rapuit tamquam ingenuam. Ideoque cum educeretur ad magistratus, nihil recu-
8   savit, nihil iuri nostro opposuit: nisi forte hoc quoque in
causa erat, quod ducebatur securus; unde enim nobis adversus istum tantos animos ut vindicaremur? Quomodo
hanc invidiam potuisset ferre paupertas, si occidere filia
mea voluisset iuvenem inter principes civitatis? Non tamen usque eo[8] hoc, iudices, valet, ut non dederim beneficium.

---

4 *Ro.*: -ret Aβ   5 *SB3, monente* Wi. (*post* curavi *Ro.*)
6 *ita secl. SB4*   7 *Aer.*: tamen Aβ   8 *Ro.*: in Aβ

---

4 And so must have known who the waitress was. But this is
hardly consistent with s.6 fin. and 14 *novus usus*.

table. I had thought that it would be another factor making for friendship if the poor man did a little dinner for the rich man: not your slap-up affair, not such as *he* can lay on, with a lot of servants—how's that possible for the likes of us? Everything to be out in the middle, especially as he knew us quite intimately.[4] Whatever there was to do, I <myself> for the most part took care that the rich man should not scorn us, I put it together and joined my guest late, only after I felt comfortable. But I needed someone to wait on us. That I had ready for me, not got by money, not by purchase, but by taking a wife and bringing up this girl. I thought he was surprised that a female should be waiting on us, and I was therefore the more embarrassed to admit that it was my daughter. For she wasn't dressed accordingly, and our acquaintance was still recent. ⟦And all the same, if he had asked me as well, I should have replied: "We are your humble servants."⟧[5] All the same, I don't persuade myself that he believed. A slave girl would not have provoked his so fastidious desires, and he did not do what perhaps could have been done with a person of that condition:[6] he raped her as if she was freeborn. So when he was brought before the magistrates, he made no objection, made no opposition to our law, unless perhaps he had another reason—he thought he had nothing to worry about. For how should we get up the courage to avenge ourselves against *him*? How could poverty have born such odium, had my daughter wanted to kill a young man who ranked among the leaders of the community? Not, gentlemen, that this can change the fact that I did him kindness.

5 Double-bracketed as inconsistent with the previous sentence and the theme.   6 Bribe her.

9   Ubi ergo circumscriptio est? Quam quidem legem arbitror propter eos maxime latam qui circa forenses insidias aliquem scripto callidiore cepissent. Ceterum, ut longius interpretatio veniat, non tamen erit dubium circumscriptionem esse inevitabilem fraudem, id est, in qua factum

10   eius demum aestimetur qui accusatur. Singula ergo aestimemus. Invitavi ad cenam—quae hic circumscriptio est?—pauper divitem. Venisti. Ago gratias: habuisti honorem, et illud humile limen intrasti, et adisti mensam, ad quam cum venire coepimus deos invocamus. Alicuius[9] †in me† humanitatis est nostra frugalitas, quae vobis utique velut refectionem quandam et quietem praebet. Inter vestras quoque epulas non semper illa ponuntur peregrinis petita litoribus et silvis: aliquando haec vilia quae rure mit-

11   tuntur adhibetis, quae emere nos pauperes possumus. Cenasti tamen hilaris; ut vis videri, etiam liberalius bibisti. Quare tamen invitavi? Quoniam promerenda nobis est vestra potentia. Si qui me detulisset reum, defenderes; si quam iniuriam timerem, rogassem te per ius[10] mensae communis. Non est igitur in hoc circumscriptio, quod ad cenam invitavi.

12   Cetera utique ad crimen legemque non pertinent. Sequitur ergo ut sit proximum crimen quod in ministerio fuerit filia mea. Iterum accusabitur paupertas. Quid ergo nos facere iubes? Emere non possumus; etiam si quid ex cotidianis supererat laboribus, educatio exhausit. Mutuemur ergo et alienis ministeriis lautitias vestras imitemur, quan-

---

[9] *SB[1], Watt[1]*: alioqui ius Aβ   [10] *Pith.*: prius Aβ

---

[7] Of fraud.

So where is the fraud? I think that law[7] was passed chiefly because of the people who in the way of legal chicanery had entrapped somebody with a cunning document. But even if interpretation were to go further, yet there will be no doubt that fraud is a cheat that could not be avoided, that is, in which only the action of the party accused is to be judged. So let us consider point by point. I asked you to dinner (what fraud in that?), I poor, you rich. You came: I thank you. You did me honor and you entered that humble threshold and you came to the table, which approaching we invoke the gods.[8] There is a certain thoughtfulness in our frugality: it gives you folk a sort of recreation and rest. In you rich men's banquets too, you don't always serve those items fetched from foreign seas and forests; sometimes you call upon these inexpensive products from the countryside, which we poor men can buy. However, you made a cheerful meal; as you want us to think, you also drank rather freely. But why my invitation? Because we poor men need to stake a claim on you rich men's power. If somebody brought a charge against me, you would have defended me. If I were afraid of some injury, I should have asked your help, invoking the table we shared. So there's no fraud in my inviting you to dinner.

Other items have nothing at all to do with your accusation and the law. So it follows that the next charge is that my daughter was part of the service. Once more poverty will be under fire. So what would you have us do? We can't buy. Even if anything was left over from our daily labors, upbringing exhausted it. Should not we borrow then, and imitate your elegances with other people's servants, as far

---

[8] A custom, like saying grace. Wi. cites Plato, *Laws* 666b3.

tum potest? ⟨A⟩[11] quis? Apud vos illi greges ministrorum,

13   apud vos aurum et argentum. Ministerium ergo fuit ex meo. Non est istud deforme pauperibus; nam et si in aliud diei tempus incidisses, tum quoque tibi videretur ancilla: vidisses pensa facientem. Filia igitur ministravit, sicut mihi solet. Nisi veritus essem ne tibi invidiam fieri putares, nisi me frequenti humanitate in honore posuisses, ego minis-

14   trassem. Hinc quoque remove quod tu fecisti: non est circumscriptio quod interrogatus verecunde respondi, et, cum mihi tecum coepisset novus usus, erubui videri sine ancilla. Hoc mali habet ambitus. Peccasse me fateor; dicendum fuit verum. Sed hac poena potes esse contentus:

15   non impune feci. Et quae a me facta sunt haec sunt; hic me circumscriptionis accusa, nihil ipse feceris. Num enim, si tu nihil concupisses, non rapuisses, poterat mihi obici circumscriptio? Hoc ergo exigis, ut ego nocens sim non ex meo facto sed ex tuo.

16   Age, res quidem ipsa crimine caret sed animus suspectus est. Quid est igitur? Me credibile est circumscribendi mente fecisse? Invitavi ut raperes? Neque enim poterat dubitari quin quaereres quae ministraret; et, cum interrogasses, certum erat fore ut protinus cupiditas aliqua in animum tuum descenderet; et, cum concupisses, ut raperes. Quae si nulla ratione, nulla divinatione provideri potuerunt, apparet non propter id factum quod sperari non po-

11 SB4

---

9 Rich men would not be apt to lend.

10 The rape; cf. s.9.   11 Cf. s.6.

12 My daughter was raped.   13 Once admitted what you did, your charge will be void.   14 Irony.

as possible? Borrow ⟨from⟩ whom?[9] *You* people have the flocks of servants, the gold and silver. So the service came from my own resources. For poor folk that is not unbecoming; if you had happened in at some other time of day, you would likewise have thought she was a slave: you would have seen her spinning. Well then, my daughter waited on us, as she usually does for me. If I had not been afraid of your thinking that I was embarrassing you, if you had not done me honor with frequent courtesies, *I* would have been waiter. Here too, take away what you did.[10] It is not fraud that I made a bashful answer when questioned[11] and that when our familiarity had only just begun I was ashamed to be seen without a maid-servant. This is the trouble with vanity. I confess I did wrong; I ought to have told the truth. But you can be content with this punishment; I did not do it with impunity.[12] So much for what *I* did. Accuse me of fraud at this point, assume you yourself did nothing.[13] For if you had not had an impulse of lust, not committed rape, could I have been taxed with fraud? So what you are demanding is that I be guilty not because of what I did but because of what you did.

Come then, there is no guilt in the thing itself, but the intention is suspect. Well, consider. Is it credible that I acted with fraudulent intent? Did I invite you in order that you should commit rape? For of course there could be no doubt that you would ask who was waiting on us, and, when you had asked, it was certain that a desire would immediately enter your mind and that once you had formed the desire you would rape![14] If all this could not be foreseen by any calculation or divining, it is evident that what was done was not done because of what could not be expected. For

tuit. Quid enim in causa fuit cur raperes? Cultus videlicet
te illexit? Hic enim adici solet ad speciem. Talis ministra-
bat ut necesse esset ancillam esse mentiri.

17   Tu porro (permittis enim[12] aliquid mihi libertatis) ra-
piebas velut[13] ancillam? Tu raperes ancillam eius apud
quem paulo ante cenaveras? Sed non credidisti ancillam
esse. Possis tu fortasse huc usque descendere, ut non fasti-
dias pauperes: numquam cupiditas tua usque ad mancipia
descendet. Ac si forte cepisset oculos tuos [petisses],[14]
quid opus erat vi? Non munusculo sollicitasses? Non, si
contumacior esset, pro tua illa comitate a domino petis-
18   ses[15]? Potuisti ergo scire, etiam antequam rapere incipe-
res. In ipso vero raptu non apparuit tibi ancillam non esse?
Non tamquam libera repugnavit? Non proclamavit patrem? Nullam vocem †meam†[16] audisti? Fieri non potest
ut non eruperit ingenuitas quae aditura erat magistratus.

19   Aut ego fallor aut de hac tota causa iudicatum est: nam
si quid feceram fraudis, apud magistratum agere debuisti:
'circumscriptus sum, ancillam putavi.' Necessitatem raptoris agnovisti.

20   Non puto te obicere quod nuptias optavit. Sed nec ego
imputo, sicut ne gratulor quidem hoc matrimonio. Mihi
magis convenisset gener cum quo mihi par convictus, apud
quem, si forte cenarem, uxor ministraret. Tu tamen quid
circumscriptione ista perdidisti? Uxorem non habes locu-

---

12 *SB*[1]: etiam Aβ
13 *Gron.*: ut Aβ
14 *Gron.*
15 *Gron.*: sollicitasti . . . –isti Aβ
16 ingenuam *SB*[1]

what cause had you to rape? It was her get-up that lured you, I suppose! That is often an extra, on top of beauty. Well, she waited on us so dressed that I had to lie and say she was a slave.

But (you allow me some degree of freedom) were you raping her as a slave? Would you have raped a slave belonging to your dinner-host of a little while back? But no, you didn't believe she was a slave. You might perhaps condescend so far as to not look down on poor folk, but your lust will never stoop to chattels. And if by chance she had taken your fancy, what need was there for force? Should you not have tempted her with some little present? If she was contumacious, wouldn't you, courteous gentleman that you are, have asked her master to let you have her? So you could have known even before you started to rape her. But in the actual assault was it not evident to you that she was no slave? Didn't she fight back like a free woman? Did she not cry out "father"? Didn't you hear a word that sounded like a freeborn (?) girl? It simply had to break out—the free birth that was to go before the magistrates.

I am much mistaken if this whole case has not been judged. For if I had committed any fraud, you should have spoken before the magistrate: "I was cheated, I thought she was a slave." But you acknowledged a rapist's constraint.

I don't suppose you bring it against me that she opted for a wedding. But I don't expect you to be grateful, just as I don't even take satisfaction in this marriage. A son-in-law with whom I could live on equal terms and whose wife would wait at table if I happened to be dining with him would have suited me better. But you, what did you lose by this "fraud"? You don't have a rich wife: don't you stand in

pletem. Nihilne[17] magis quam pecuniam desideras? O te
dignum qui duceres parem! Tunc scires quae discordiae,
quae contentiones, quam frequens mentio dotis, quam
21 erecta ex aequo cervix. Utique in his tuis deliciis, in his cupiditatibus tibi liceret amare aliquam ancillam, deperire
aliquam ministrarum. At nunc habes uxorem non ambitio-
sam, non exacturam comitatus, sed quae tota ex tuo vultu
22 pendeat. Laborare consuevit: habebis ancillam. Tu tantum, etiam si quid ego offendi, mihi irascere: nihil illa fecit,
nihil peccavit. Iussa fuit, in ministerio patri paruit: ad illam
hoc tantum pertinet quod optavit.

302

Auctoratus ob sepeliendum patrem

Gladiator in quattuordecim gradibus ne sedeat. Quidam ut
patrem sepeliret auctoravit se. Die muneris productus sub
titulo causae rudem postulante populo accepit. Postea patrimonium statutum[1] per leges equitibus acquisivit. Prohi-
betur gradibus.

1   DECLAMATIO

Postea dicam qua causa paene gladiator factus sit, postea
hoc quod obicitur in laudem vertam; interim incipere libet
ab ipsa lege. Ius certe sedendi implet ingenuitas et census.

---

17 *Wi.*: nihil enim Aβ
1 *Aer.*: statum Aβ

---

1 Reserved for Knights in the theater.
2 Symbol of discharge.

need of anything more than money? Well did you deserve
to marry an equal! Then you would have known the quar-
rels, the fights, the constant mention of dowry, the stuck-
up neck on a level with yours. Well, amid your luxuries and
lusts you would at all events have been free to choose some
slave, to fall madly in love with one of the maid-servants.
But as it is, you have an unostentatious wife who won't demand companions but have eyes for your face only. She is
accustomed to work: you will have a maid-servant. Even if
I have offended you, be angry only with me; she has done
nothing, done naught amiss. She was under orders, did her
waiting in obedience to her father. The only thing in which
she is concerned is what she opted for.

302

Turned gladiator to bury his father

Let a gladiator sit in the fourteen rows.[1] A man hired himself as a gladiator in order to bury his father. Exhibited on
the day of a show with a notice to show the reason, he accepted the wooden sword[2] at the people's instance. Later
he acquired the means laid down for Knights under the
law. He is barred from the rows.[3]

DECLAMATION

Later I shall say why he almost became a gladiator, later I
shall turn this imputation to his credit. For the time being I
want to begin from the law itself. Free birth and means
certainly satisfy the seating law. So we have to ask whether

[3] And according to s.5 (*isti accusatores*) prosecuted for sitting
in them.

Quaerendum est ergo an hic gladiator sit aut fuerit. Non sumus magni legis interpretes: non ludum nec arenam nec armorum scientiam complexa est, sed gladium. Cui dubium est id exigendum esse in ea[2] ex quo nomen gladiato-
2 ris ductum est? Gladiator igitur est qui in arena populo spectante pugnavit. Nam neque orator est qui numquam egit causam neque accusator qui reum in iudicium non deduxit neque reus qui causam non dixit. ⟦Videamus et ipsius periculi causam.⟧ Quaero an, si creditor post datam pecuniam operas remisisset, diceres eum gladiatorem fuisse?
3 'In ludo fuit.' Fuerunt doctores et medici et ministri, neque tamen [in][3] illo nomine tenentur. 'Productus est.' Et alii multi, spectaculi gratia. 'Sed adfuit pugnae.[4]' Sed animum tenetis, cum praesertim hic ordo ex laude militiae hoc nomen acceperit. Non ergo pugna per se turpis est, sed inhonesta pugna. Dedit enim et familiis nomina: hinc
4 Corvini, hinc Torquati, hinc Opimii. Illum ergo maiores prohibuerunt theatro qui vilitate, qui gula se auctorasset. Videamus et ipsius periculi causam[5]: mutuatus est pecuniam ut patrem sepeliret, mutuatus unde potuit; et quo

---

2 *SB*[2]: eo Aβ   3 *Lat.*   4 *Aer.*: -na Aβ
5 videamus . . . causam *huc transp. SB*[4]: *post* dixit (s. 2) Aβ

---

4 *Gladius.*   5 Owner of the "school," *ludus*, with whom the accused had taken service (s.4).

6 So that he would never have come into the arena.

7 As actors or acrobats.   8 He did not actually fight. Wi. obelizes *sed animum tenetis*, unnecessarily as I now think.

9 Of Knights (*equites*).

10 An irrelevance. The only fighting with which the jury was here concerned *was* discreditable.

he is a gladiator, or was. We are not great interpreters of the law: it doesn't cover training school or arena or martial skill, but the sword.[4] Who questions that the thing to be required in it is the thing from which the name of gladiator is derived? So a gladiator is someone who has fought in the arena with people watching. For a man who never conducted a case is no barrister and a man who never brought a defendant into court is no prosecutor, nor is a man who has not pleaded his case a defendant. [[Let us see why he himself took the risk.]] I ask you: if the creditor[5] after giving him money had remitted services,[6] would you say he was a gladiator? "He was in the school." So were the trainers and doctors and staff, but they are not covered by that name. "He was exhibited." So were many others,[7] for spectacle. "But he was present at the fighting." But you only have intention:[8] especially considering that this order[9] got its name from honorable military service. So fighting is not discreditable in itself, only dishonorable fighting.[10] Fighting gave names to families: hence the Corvini, hence the Torquati, hence the Opimii.[11] So our ancestors barred from the theatre a person who had hired himself as gladiator out of self-contempt[12] or gluttony. Let us see why he himself took the risk. He borrowed money to bury his father, borrowed it where he could; and the more disgraceful

[11] The first two acquired their cognomina in famous combat incidents. As to the Opimii, Wi. rightly suggests that the declaimer connected the name with *spolia opima*, dedicated by a commander who killed his opposite number; although none of the three who did so was an Opimius.

[12] Cf. 260.21 fin.

turpius putas esse sic mutuari, hoc honestius fecit. Vidit
enim quid sibi accidere posset auctorato, sed illud crude-
lius putavit, si pater insepultus iaceret: gladiatores sepe-
5 liuntur. Isti accusatores et Cimoni illi quod[6] patris corpus
vicario corpore redemerit[7] crimini darent. Sed indicavit
populo quare venisset in arenam[8]: non pugnaturus, tantum[9] ut notius fieret exemplum. Num[10] te, popule, iudicii
tui paenitet? Quomodo postea vixit? Quam frugaliter ac-
quisiit, quam parce, quam laboriose! Ausim dicere neminem sic ex hoc ordine, nec ex alio.

303

Proditionis rei fortes

Proditionis rei causam de vinculis dicant. Qui rei facti
erant ruptis vinculis fortiter fecerunt. Praemio petunt ut
soluti causam dicant.

1   SERMO

An reis dandum praemium; an proditionis reis; an his quos
non civitas armavit. An contra legem dandum sit, et hanc
legem, et hoc tempore. An tollatur summa legis, etiam si

---

  [6] *Gron.*: qui AB
  [7] *Gron.*: -mit Aβ
  [8] *SB4*: ludum Aβ
  [9] *Ro.*: tunc Aβ
  [10] *Ro.*: tum Aβ

---

  [13] The theme of Sen. *Contr.* 9.1. Cimon's father Miltiades, victor of Marathon, died in prison (489 B.C.) and a fiction grew up
that Cimon took his place in order to get him burial.

you think it to borrow thus, the more to his credit that he did it. He saw what could happen to him if he hired himself, but he thought it more cruel a thing if his father lay unburied: gladiators are buried. Those prosecutors would have held it against Cimon that he ransomed his father's body with his own.[13] But he gave the people to understand why he had entered the arena[14]: not to fight, only to make the example better known. People, do you regret your judgment[15]? How did he live afterwards? How frugally he made his fortune, how parsimoniously, how laboriously! I would venture to say that no one else in this order or any other did the like.

303

Heroes accused of treason

Let persons accused of treason plead their case in chains. Persons who had been accused broke their chains and became heroes. For reward they ask that they plead their case free of chains.

DISCUSSION

Should a reward be given to persons under prosecution? Or to persons accused of treason? Or to persons whom the community did not arm? Should it be given contrary to law, and to this law, and at this time? Would the law as a whole be annulled, even though its force were to be wa-

---

[14] *Ludum* in the mauscripts. The accused had joined the "school" to get money for his father's burial but he advertised what he had done by appearing in the arena.

[15] In giving the man his discharge.

vis extenuetur. Qua mente petant. Quid utilius.

304

Tria praemia divitis sacerdotis

Sacerdos tria praemia accipiat. Viro forti praemium. Dives
sacerdos inimici pauperis filium sacrilegum uno praemio
liberavit. Eundem in adulterio damnatum secundo praemio absolvit. Bello patriae pauper fortiter fecit, filius ille
deseruit. Vult eundem tertio praemio sacerdos liberare;
petit praemio vir fortis pater ut occidatur.

1   DECLAMATIO

Utra lex antiquior? Tua ad unum pertinet, haec ad omnes.
⟨Utra lex aequior?⟩[1] Mihi lex debet, tu legi. Utrius legis
hoc tempus? Belli utique [prior][1] ⟨mea⟩[1]: sacerdotium
pacis res est.[2] Ego dignior sum praemio quam tu: me viro
forti contigit victoria, te sacerdote admissum sacrilegium.
2 Hactenus de personis: transeamus ad optiones.[3] Ego hodie primum opto, tu bis optasti; et ego ⟨miles⟩[4] melius
opto desertoris mortem quam tu vitam sacrilegi sacerdos.
Castra vindico: disce tu vindicare templa. Quid si contra

---

   [1] SB[2]

   [2] belli . . . est *huc transp.* SB[2] (*post* tempus *lac. ind.* Wi.): *ante*
tua (*supra*) Aβ

   [3] SB[4] (-em *Aer.*): opinionem (opio- A[1]) A[2]β

   [4] Hå.[1], *auct. Obr., Ri.*

---

   [1] Håkanson, followed by Wi., punctuates summa legis etiam,
si . . .

   304: [1] Dig. 34.9.13, *Maevius in adulterio Semproniae damnatus*, is cited.

tered down?[1] With what motive are they asking? What is more expedient?

304

Three rewards of a rich priest

Let a priest receive three rewards. Let there be a reward for a hero. A rich priest with one reward freed the son of a poor man, his enemy, who had committed sacrilege. When the same was found guilty in adultery,[1] he acquitted him with his second reward. In their country's war the poor man became a hero, but that son deserted. The priest wishes to free the son with his third reward. The hero father asks as his reward that he be put to death.

DECLAMATION

Which law has priority? Yours pertains to an individual, this to everybody.[2] ‹Which law is the more just?› The law owes me, you owe the law. Which law is of this time?[3] Certainly ‹my› law is about war; priesthood is an affair of peace. I deserve a reward more than you: when I was a hero, victory came our way, with you as priest a sacrilege was committed. So much for personae: let us pass to the options. I am opting today for the first time, you have opted twice. And I‹, a soldier,› am better opting for the death of a deserter than you, a priest, for the life of a perpetrator of sacrilege. I avenge the army: do you learn to avenge the

---

2 Because, *pace* Wi., the first law pertains to an individual, the priest (priest of a particular deity?), the second to anyone qualifying as "hero."   3 Wartime.

legem petis? Unius vitam iam ter optasti. Comparavi publicas personas; nunc comparemus[5] ⟨privatas⟩.[6] Tu optas
numquam nisi de alieno, ego de meo.

3   Quamquam quid mihi cum lege, dummodo[7] veniat
adulter ille, ille sacrilegus, ille desertor in penates meos?
Sciet quanto meliore patre [natus][8] sit quam inimico. Ar-
miger, da gladium: vindicabo ego illum maritum, vindicabo templum. Legem habeo et viri fortis et patris. Innocentem filium habui ante huius sacerdotium: sub isto primum
expilata templa. Furorem hoc iuvenis mei putabam: fidu-
4 cia erat. Multum est, dives, colere templa: plus tamen sua
tueri,[9] incendere hostium templa. Cur enim, si quicquam
tua vota proficiunt, cliens tuus deseruit? Mihi debetur
praemium quod petiero: possum et tuam mortem, possum
tibi auferre sacerdotium.

305

Exules a divite pugnare inter se coacti

Exulem intra fines deprehensum liceat occidere. Duos
pauperes dives, inimicos suos, imprudentis caedis quinquennii exilio damnatos, intra fines deprehensos dimicare
inter se datis gladiis coegit. Commortui sunt. Accusatur
iniusti supplicii.

[5] *SB*[4]: -em Aβ   [6] *SB*[4]   [7] *SB*[2]: dum ne Aβ
[8] *SB*[2]   [9] s.t. *Ro*.: sustinere Aβ

---

[4] The deserter is his son.

[5] "The feud is regarded as hereditary" Wi. In penalizing his
son the father is behaving as a father should, whereas in interven-
ing for him the rich man is not behaving as an enemy should.

temples. What if your claim is against the law? You have now opted for one man's life three times. I have compared the public personae. Now let us compare ⟨the private⟩. You never opt except at someone else's expense, I opt at mine.[4]

And yet what do I care about the law, if only that perpetrator of adultery and sacrilege comes to my home? He shall know how much better a father he has than an enemy.[5] Squire, give me a sword! I shall avenge that husband, I shall avenge the temple. I have a hero's law and a father's. I had an innocent son before this man became priest. Temples were robbed for the first time under him. I used to think that my young man's behavior was madness: it was confidence.[6] Gentlemen, tending temples is much, but protecting one's own temples and burning the enemy's is more. For if your prayers do any good,[7] why did your protégé desert? The reward that I shall ask is my due. I can even ask for your death, I can deprive you of the priesthood.

305

Exiles forced to fight each other by rich man

Let it be lawful to kill an exile caught inside the borders. A rich man caught two poor men, enemies of his, who had been sentenced to five-year exile for involuntary homicide, inside the borders and compelled them to fight each other, giving them swords. Both died. He is accused of improper punishment.

---

[6] He counted on the priest.　　　[7] I.e. bring us victory.

1

DECLAMATIO

Nisi praecipua, iudices, impotentiae voluptas divitibus
videretur ut sceleribus suis etiam glorientur, fuerat tanti
miserrimorum civium perire vindictam si possit tacere qui
fecit. Haec enim est exacti iniusti supplicii manifesta iniuria, quod excogitavit quomodo ab inimicis mors exigeretur

2 et ipsis imputaretur. Homines innocentes cum damnaren-
tur quoque †confestim† inter se concurrere coegit; quos
etiam in calamitate Fortuna coniunxerat, iussit ut invicem
se occiderent (quod gravissimum illis fuit) scientes. Aestimate, iudices, quid timuerint qui hoc fecerunt. Quamvis
autem, iudices, adicere invidiam sceleribus numerus so-
leat, nos tamen confitebimur inter solacia doloris nostri
esse numerandum quod ambo perierunt: sic miseros commisit ut si unus vicisset post quinquennium redire non pos-

3 set. Sive igitur constare iuri,[1] iudices, debet ultio, nulla
umquam res sic contra leges excogitata est ut intra fines
deprehensum ⟨exulem⟩[2] exul occideret, sive crudelitatis
exigere debet poenam vestra iustitia, non satis habuit quod

4 adversus miseros lex irata conscripserat. Quanto enim gravius tulerint supplicium quam meruerant vel sic aestimate:
hoc inimicus elegit, et inimicus ⟨dives⟩[3] pauperibus iratus;
haec enim odia altissime sedent cum aliquis iis quos con-
tempsit irascitur.

Innocentiae fiducia contra opes istius steterant, non ta-

---

[1] SB[1]: vobis Aβ   [2] Aer.   [3] SB[3]

---

[1] I have ignored the pointless *confestim* ("immediately").
[2] Exile.   [3] Worse than their own deaths.
[4] Of killing, not of being killed.

DECLAMATION

Were it not, gentlemen of the jury, that rich men find the chief pleasure of reckless violence in actually glorying in their crimes, it had been worth while to let vengeance for our most unfortunate fellow citizens go by the board, if only the perpetrator could hold his tongue. For here is the manifest impropriety of the improper punishment that was exacted: he devised how death should be exacted from his enemies and imputed to themselves. He forced men innocent, even though found guilty, to fight each other.[1] Even in their calamity[2] Fortune had joined them: he ordered them to kill each other knowingly, which was for them the worst fate of all.[3] Consider, gentlemen, what those who did this were afraid of.[4] Moreover, gentlemen, while number generally makes crimes appear more hateful, we will admit that the fact that both perished is to be counted as one consolation in our grief: he set them against each other on the terms that if one prevailed he could not go back after five years.[5] So if vengeance should be consistent with the law, gentlemen, never was anything devised so contrary to our laws as that an exile should kill <an exile> caught inside the borders; but if your justice should exact a punishment for cruelty, he was not content with what an angry law had written against unfortunates. For how much heavier punishment they endured than they deserved, judge thus: this an enemy chose, and <a rich> enemy, angry with poor men; for hate sits deepest when a man is angry with those he despises.

They had taken a stand against his wealth in the con-

---

[5] He would incur penalty for intentional homicide.

men futuri pares nisi duo fuissent. Contra gratiam armave-
runt misericordiam sui, donec ambo in periculum capitis
5 adducti: testes enim non defuerunt. Quantum tamen[4] va-
luit innocentia! Constitit inter omnes non potuisse illud
nisi ab imprudentibus fieri.

Incredibile est, iudices, quanto difficilius finibus ca-
reant qui exilium non meruerunt. Amplectebantur miseri
pio furto extremum patriae solum, non mehercule scio an
alicuius insidiis perducti, an aliqua humanitatis facie im-
6 pulsi; nihil probare possum: ambo perierunt. Si tamen intueri naturam ‹rerum›[5] volueritis, apparebit profecto non
casu eos in eum locum potissimum venisse in quo ab inimico deprehenderentur. Deprehendit enim tamquam expec-
tasset. Minus quidem miserrimos cives confuderat istius
aspectus; iugulum contumaciter parabant. ʻIampridem
mortem contempsimus, nec inimicitias adversus te susce-
7 pimus nisi lucis vilitate. Occide: numquid plus potes?ʼ Ri-
sit animos, et ʻadhuc nescitisʼ inquit ʻquantum opes virium
habeant: efficiam vos inimicos.ʼ Tradi utrique gladium iubet et custodiri in primo impetu manus; circa flagella et
ignes et omnis tyrannicae crudelitatis apparatus. Quantos

4 *Gron.*: enim A*β*: autem *Aer.*
5 *SB*3

---

6 On the face of it a vacuous remark. I suspect a conceit, if in-
choate, involving *pares* (“equal”) and *par* (“pair”). Read *par* for
duo?

7 At the trial, presumably suborned by the prosecution.

8 The involuntary homicide for which they had been exiled.
We are told nothing about the particulars.

9 A strange word here. *Penatibus* might have been expected.

sciousness of innocence, but they would not have been his match if there had not been two of them.[6] Against his influence they armed the pity felt for them, until both were brought into peril of their lives; for witnesses were not lacking.[7] But how great was the power of innocence! Everyone agreed that the thing[8] could not have been done except accidentally.

It's unbelievable, gentlemen, how much harder it is for those who have not deserved exile to do without their borders.[9] The poor fellows embraced the edge of their country's soil with a patriotic cheat. Upon my word, I don't know whether they were led on by somebody's trickery or impelled by some show of humanity. [10] I can prove nothing: both are dead. But if you want to look into the Nature ‹of Things›,[11] it will no doubt be evident that it was not by chance that they came to the place of all places where their enemy would catch them. For he caught them as though he had expected them. Our poor fellow citizens were not all that confounded by the look of him; they made their throats ready defiantly: "For a long time past we have despised death, and we only took on enmity with you because we cared nothing for the light of day. Kill us: can you do anything more?" He laughed at their spirit and "you don't know yet," he said, "the power of wealth. I shall make you enemies." He commands that both be given swords and watch kept on their hands in their first impetus.[12] Around are whips and fires and all the appearance of a ty-

10 Some trick of the rich man's. The second alternative narrows down the first.

11 I.e. use common sense.

12 In case they might drop their weapons or attack him (Wi.).

enim fuisse creditis metus qui effecerunt ut concurrere illis expediret? O misera condicio! Magna necessitate victa
8 libertas est. Tunc rogaverunt donec iste crudelis lanista 'concurrite,' inquit; 'in istas [innocentes][6] manus initis prudentes: non continget innocentibus mori.' Quae miserorum inter binos metus cunctationes! Occidere coacti sunt eos quorum miserebantur. Quid ego faciem tristissimi illius temporis narrem, quid vulnera, quid sanguinem, quid gemitus? Tu saltem, Fortuna, melius: uno uterque
9 fato iacet. Te tamen, dives, interrogo quid de illo facturus fueris qui superfuisset? Hoc est puras manus habere, hoc nobis pro innocentia imputas? Nocentem fecisti ipsam infelicitatem et, tamquam parum esset exigere poenas, supplicia infamasti, id denique coegisti quod defendere non potuissent nisi coacti.

10 Iniusti supplicii ago. Non est mihi lex interpretanda: omne iniustum supplicium est quod non est exactum secundum legem. Da igitur ius mihi quo perire debuerint. 'Exulem intra fines liceat occidere.' Quod satis est, non occidisti; quidquid aliud factum est contra legem est. Sit aliquid mitius, sit aliquid clementius: non licet; nec tibi
11 licebit ignoscere. 'Exulem intra fines liceat occidere.' Neminem, iudices, eorum qui iura condiderunt tam asperum et trucem existimo fuisse ut tantum scelus crederet posse fieri. Metu sine dubio fines nostros clusit exulibus;

[6] SB[1], Wi.

---

[13] Whereas the victims had not known what they were doing in the fight for which they had been exiled.

[14] As something, if not innocent, then acceptable.

rant's cruelty. For how dire do you believe were the terrors that made it expedient for them to join combat? What a wretched situation! Freedom was overborne by terrible duress. Then they pleaded until that cruel gladiator-trainer said: "Mix it. You start this fight[13] knowing what you are about. You won't have the good fortune to die innocent." Think of the poor fellows' hesitation between two terrors. They were forced to kill those they pitied. Why should I tell of the aspect of that miserable time, the sounds, the blood, the groans? But at least, Fortune, you managed for the best: each lies in one death. But, rich man, I ask you: what would you have done about a survivor if there had been one? Is this to have clean hands, do you expect us to thank you for it in lieu of innocence?[14] You made misfortune itself guilty, and as though it was not enough to exact penalty, you brought infamy on the very punishments. You forced them to do what they could not have defended if it had not been done under duress.

I prosecute you for improper punishment. I don't have to interpret the law. Every punishment is improper which has not been imposed as the law provides. So tell me the statute under which they should have died. "Let it be lawful to kill an exile inside the borders." It is enough that you did not kill them. Whatever else was done is against the law. Though it be something milder, something more merciful: it is not permitted, nor shall you have license to pardon. "Let it be lawful to kill an exile inside the border." I do not think that any of those who made our laws, gentlemen, was so harsh and ferocious as to believe that so great a crime would be perpetrated. For fear no doubt he[15] closed

15 The lawgiver.

409

magnam tamen illis qui deprehendissent imposuit difficul-
12 tatem. Exulem intra fines deprehendisti: occide, si potes,
sed occide tua manu, sume carnificis animum. Sequetur
quandoque te ista conscientia, et quamquam impunitus
sanguis manabit tamen usque ad animum. Quae sunt istae
deliciae, ut tu velis inimicos tuos incruentis[7] manibus occi-
13 dere? 'Exulem intra fines liceat occidere.' Si deprehensos
detinuisses, iniustum supplicium esset. Nemo inter poenas exulis constituit mortis expectationem. Istud, quod nutum tuum diutius vident, quod arrogantiam ferunt, inius-
14 tum supplicium est. Non licet tibi gladium supra cervices
diu tenere, non licet iugulo necem admovere lente. Tu eos
detineas intra fines quibus venire non licuit? Occide vel
statim vel, si differre potes, miserere. Nondum dico concurrere, praestantis ⟨alterum⟩[8] alterius cervicem ferire
coegisti: iniustum supplicium est.

15   'Mori debent.' Qua lege? In qua scriptum est: 'liceat
occidere.[9]' Putate, iudices, huius furoris ad vos causam re-
ferri: ex duobus exulibus intra fines deprehensis ab altero
occisus est alter. Statim cum hoc agere iniusti supplicii
volo. 'Quis tibi gladium dedit? Quomodo potest fieri ut is
debeat occidere cui ⟨non⟩[10] necesse est mori?' Nemo, ut
opinor, absolvet. Fieri non potest ut, si damnanda fuerit
audacia, non sit vindicanda necessitas. Cum illorum cri-

---

[7] *Ri.*: inprude- A(β)   [8] *Ri., post* cervicem *iam Gron.*
[9] l. o. *Sch., Gron.*: cito occidat Aβ [10] *SB*[1]

---

[16] If you can bring yourself to do it.   [17] It would be
morally outrageous if an exile, whose killing inside the state borders the law permits but does not enjoin, should kill another exile
in the same circumstances as himself. But would it be illegal? The

our borders to exiles; but he put those who caught them in a great difficulty. You caught an exile inside the borders: kill him[16] with your own hand, take the heart of an executioner. One day the guilt will haunt you, and the blood, though unpunished, will flow right into your soul. What squeamishness, that you wish to kill your enemies without getting blood on your hands! "Let it be lawful to kill an exile inside the borders." If you had caught them and held them captive, it would have been improper punishment. No one made waiting for death one of an exile's punishments. That they watch your nod at length, bear your arrogance, is improper punishment. You are not allowed to hold a sword over their necks at length, you are not allowed to move death slowly to their throats. Are you to detain people within the borders who are not permitted to come inside them? Kill them at once, or if you can put it off, pity them. You forced them, I won't yet say to join combat, but to strike ⟨each⟩ the other's neck as he offered it: it's improper punishment.

"They ought to die." By what law? The law in which it is written: "Let it be lawful to kill." Suppose, gentlemen, a case was brought to you this crazy: of two exiles caught inside the borders, one was killed by the other. Right away I want to prosecute him for improper punishment. "Who gave you a sword? How can it be that a person ought to kill who does ⟨not⟩ have to die?" No one, I think, will acquit. It is impossible that if audacity is to be condemned duress is not be avenged.[17] Since it would have been their guilt if

declaimer merely assumes that it would, and goes on to argue that if the act was committed under compulsion by a third person, the guilt and punishment transfer to that person.

men foret si voluissent, tuum sit necesse est quia coegisti.
16 Si concurrissent et viverent, iniusti tamen supplicii agerem. Facile est vitae damnum: abstulisti miseris innocentiae opinionem et ut pessimum gladiatorum genus perire iussisti. Non poteras absolvi si infelicibus missionem
dedisses. Quos composuisti? Homines eiusdem civitatis,
17 eiusdem fortunae, eiusdem inimicos. Plurimum tamen adhuc ad dolorem pertinet quod te spectante pugnarunt; ille
gravissimus dolor, quod ad inimici voluptatem satisfacerent. Misera condicio necessitatis! Gratia[11] infelicibus erat
facere quod velles: quam contumaciam vicisti!

18   Proponite ignes et ‹flagella›,[12] constituite ante oculos
illud crudele spectaculum, sedentem hunc altius, armatos
circa servos. Neque enim profecto sine praesidio magno,
sine certa securitate ferrum commisit inimicis. Qui dolor
miserorum, quod quemquam vulnerarent isto praesente!
Certum habeo, et hortatus est et laudavit illum qui prior
19 percussit. Omnia licet feceris, neuter tamen amicum suum
occidisset nisi scisset expedire ut uterque moreretur.
Si bene miserorum innocentiam novi, non tantum tibi
quantum optaveras contigit: concurrerunt lateribus nudis.
Omnia tu licet crudeliter excogitaveris, fecerunt tamen
bonum exemplum.

11 *SB*[2]: gloria Aβ
12 *Ro.*

they had so wanted it, it must be yours because you forced them. If they had fought and lived, I should prosecute you for improper punishment all the same. The loss of life is easy: you took the reputation of innocence away from the poor wretches and ordered them to die like the worst of gladiators. You could not be acquitted if you had given discharge to the unfortunates. Whom did you pit against each other? Men of the same community, the same fortune, with the same enemy. But in addition the most agonizing feature is that they fought with you looking on; that is what hurt most, that they gave satisfaction[18] at their enemy's pleasure. Sad plight of duress! It was a favor to the unfortunates to do what you wanted. What contumacy did you overcome!

Imagine the fires and ⟨whip,⟩ set before your eyes the cruel spectacle, him sitting aloft, armed slaves around. For surely he did not put steel in his enemies' hands without a large bodyguard, without certain security. What grief to the poor devils to wound anyone with *him* present![19] I'll be bound he urged them on and applauded the one who stabbed first. But do what you might, neither one would have killed his friend if he had not known that it was best for both to die. If I well know the innocence of the unfortunates, you did not get all you had hoped for; they ran together with their flanks bare.[20] For all your cruel devices, they gave a good example.

[18] For their earlier opposition.
[19] *He* was the one they would have liked to get at.
[20] Not trying to defend themselves.

306

Expositus negante[1] matre[2] nuptias petens

Maritus peregre proficiscens praecepit uxori ut partum ex-
poneret. Expositus est puer. Maritus peregre uxore herede
decessit. Post tempus quidam adulescens, cuius aetas cum
expositionis tempore congruebat, coepit dicere se filium et
bona sibi vindicare. Inter moras iudicii bello idem adulescens fortiter fecit. Petit praemio nuptias eius quam matrem dicebat, manente priore iudicio. CD.

1   DECLAMATIO

Non ita me prima frons causae callidissima optionis simulatione decipit ut †mulier ista matrimonio credat†,[3] quod
2 hodie nemo peteret si non recusaretur; illud magis vereor,
ne iuvenis qui eius quam matrem esse dicebat nuptias
optat videatur velle ad verum pervenire, ac vos latentium
natalium credatis experimentum quod mulier, quae post
amissum maritum per tot annos qui facere poterant ab in-
fantia virum fortem sic complexa est viduitatem tamquam
genus pudicitiae, hunc iungere sibi venere sera et polluere
3 complexibus non vult filii sui, si vixisset, aetatem. Intellego
itaque non tam multa mihi contra praemium dicenda
quam contra argumentum; sic componenda actio est tam-
4 quam nos audiant iudices illi. Non tamen iuvenem pari
captione ludemus. Fecisset, fecisset hoc astuta mulier,
anus inverecunda, ut iuveni curioso offerret hanc fatigati

---

¹ A¹: -atae A²β   ² *Dingel*: -ris Aβ   ³ *desideratur*
aliquid velut mulierem istam m. ⟨peti⟩ credam (*SB²*)

---

¹ Because of her age.

306

Exposed child, mother denying, seeking marriage

A husband setting out for foreign parts told his wife to expose her child. The boy was exposed. The husband died abroad leaving his wife as his heir. After some time a certain young man, whose age fitted the time of the exposure, started saying that he was the son and claiming the property. During the trial process the same young man became a hero in war. For reward he asks for marriage with the woman he said was his mother, while the previous trial is still unfinished. Speech in opposition.

DECLAMATION

The first look of the case, with its so cunning pretence of an option, does not deceive me into believing that this woman is being sought in marriage, something that nobody would ask for at this time of day[1] if he was not going to be refused. I am rather afraid that the young man who asks for marriage with the woman he used to say was his mother may appear to want to get to the truth and that you may believe this to be a test of his hidden origin—the fact that a woman who after the loss of her husband embraced widowhood as though it were a kind of chastity throughout as many years as sufficed to make infancy into a hero does not want to join this man to herself in belated sex and pollute a youth of her son's age, had he lived, with her embraces. I realize, therefore, that I do not have to speak against the reward so much as against the argument; my plea must be composed as though that jury were listening. But we shall not mock the young man with a trick like his. Indeed, indeed a crafty woman, a shameless crone, would have gone so far as to

415

corporis partem. Erat dignus qui dum alterius patrimonium petit perderet etiam praemium suum. Sed mulier
simplicissima (si quid mentiri posset, [si][4] non exposuisset)
palam se nolle profitetur. Hoc pudori satis est: si quid ius-
5 seritis, culpa cogentium est. Quid interim proficit adulescens ille? Nam si praeiudicium est quod haec recusat, et
illud sit argumentum, quod hic optat. Cuius quidem pudori propter recentia merita cupio consultum; magna tamen
cupiditatis invidia inquinat laudem, si, cum alienum patrimonium petat, non putat sua referre utrum hereditatem
illud faciat an dotem.

6 Haec quidem minus sollicita fuit priore iudicio: tunc
enim pudor salvus; nunc totos necesse est proferre gemitus. 'Semel' inquit 'infeliciter nupsi. Peregrinabatur maritus; illuc ierat unde non est reversus. Tamen misera con-
cepi, et quantum uterus crescebat tantum accedebant
exequiae. Convenerunt ad parientem consolantes propin-
7 qui. Haec passa sum suasore marito, qui me fecit heredem.
Quis potest illum diem referre sine lacrimis? Vivum funus
gremio tuli: quam paene expiravit in manibus meis! Deinde periit ille qui iusserat: quam paene potui non ex-
ponere! Quid mihi cum hac hereditate? Effecit ut filium
8 magis desiderarem.' Falsas putate voces si postea nupsit:
ille desiderabatur infans. Sic, puto, effectum est ut aliquis

---

4 *Gron.*

---

2 Or "wasted."

3 She would have kept the child alive and made up some story.
We are not told *why* the husband ordered the exposure.

4 As showing that he did not believe he was her son.

5 She had conceived before her husband left.

offer the inquisitive young man this part of her tired body. It would have served him right if in trying to get someone else's patrimony he lost[2] his reward into the bargain. But being quite guileless (if she were capable of lying, she would not have exposed[3]), the woman openly declares she won't do it. That's enough for modesty; if you make it an order, the blame lies with those who force her. Meanwhile, what does that young man gain? If her refusal is prejudicial, *his* option also could be an argument.[4] Because of his recent services I am anxious to spare him embarrassment, but by the great odium attaching to his greed he besmirches his glory if, seeking someone else's patrimony, he thinks it doesn't matter whether it makes it an inheritance or a dowry.

She was less worried by the previous trial, for then her honor had not been touched; now she has no choice but to make all her sorrows public. "Once," she says, "I made an unfortunate marriage. My husband was abroad; he had gone to a place from which he has not returned. All the same, alas, I conceived.[5] As my womb increased, so a funeral drew nearer. My relations gathered to me in my pregnancy, offering consolation. This I suffered at the suasion of my husband, who made me his heir. Who can recall that day without tears? I bore a living corpse in my bosom. How near he came to dying in my hands! Then the one who had given the order perished. How near I came to being able not to expose him! What do I want with this inheritance? It made me miss my son even more." Disbelieve her words if she married later! She was missing that baby.[6] That, I think, is why someone said he was her son; that tale

6 She had no wish for another.

se filium diceret: haec quidem fabula allata est tamquam
temere crediturae. Sed postquam se perspici sensit, iuvenis differre coepit. Nihil iudicium magis trahit quam
diffidentia petitoris. Ante consummavimus bellum. Non
fraudabo te, iuvenis, gloria tua. Tu fugasti hostes. Felices si
qui tibi sunt parentes! Utinam credibilia finxisses! Effece-
9 ras ut te cuperet agnoscere. Hic libet alloqui iuvenem: tu
quidem fortiter fecisti, sed minor corporis virtus, plus est
in animi moderatione: ne quid improbe petas, ne videaris
isto animo litigasse.

10 'Licet' inquit 'mihi optare quod velim.' Nullum manifestius improbae optionis argumentum est quam vim lege[5]
adhibere. Quis enim dicit 'necesse est' qui dicere potest
'oportet'? Non tamen hoc natura recipit, ut tam gravi servitute iuris obstrinxerit rem publicam qui legem dicebat.

11 Sibi sane tulerit iura simplicius aetas vetus, minorque
fuerit verborum custodia cum intellecturi non timebantur.
Has enim primas rudibus illis ac militaribus viris existimo
placuisse leges quibus inter continua bella praemium non
12 avaris virtutibus dabatur. Neque ego crediderim optionem
tunc illam respexisse ad onera rei publicae: liberalis erat
populus ex praeda. Testis carminum antiquitas, ubi illi pri-
mi heroes canebantur. Bellator huic currus, huic ducum
exuviae, nonnulli *.[6] Captivae forma praestantior ultima
sors habebatur [quamlibet nobilis peteret].[7] Legistine cir-

---

5 SB[1]: legi Aβ   6 lac. ind. Wi.   7 SB[3]

---

7 Greed. Formerly I took *isto* as *quo fortiter fecisti*, i.e. audaciously.

8 I.e. constraining other people by the option granted under
the law.

was brought to her in the belief that she would give hasty credence. But after he was seen through, the young man began to slow down. Nothing drags out a trial more than a claimant with cold feet. We finished our war before it was over. Young man, I shall not cheat you of your glory. You routed the enemy. Happy your parents, if you have any! Would that your fiction had been believable! You made her wish to acknowledge you. Here I want to address the young man: "Yes, you became a hero, but physical courage is a lesser thing; there is more to moderation of mind—not to make a shameless claim, not to let it appear that you went to law with that motive."[7]

"I may opt for whatever I want," he says. Nothing is clearer proof of a shameless option than use of violence[8] by means of a law. For who says "must" that can say "ought"? But nature does not admit that the lawgiver constrained the commonwealth in so onerous a legal bondage.

To be sure, in the old days they passed laws for themselves more naïvely, there was less care about the wording when they were not afraid of those who would be understanding them. I judge that those first laws were approved by those unsophisticated military men, laws in which amid continual wars a reward was granted to uncovetous valor. And I should not believe that in those days that option looked to[9] the commonwealth's burdens. The people were generous out of booty. Witness the ancient lays in which those early heroes were sung. To one a war chariot, to another the spoils of commanders, to some *. The outstanding beauty of a captive was considered the bottom lot. Have you not read that the most illustrious kings con-

---

[9] I.e. "was regarded as part of."

[QUINTILIAN]

ca decennis belli exuvias contendisse clarissimos reges?
Haec sacra sunt merita, haec coniurata virtus. Hoc erat il-
13 lud 'quod volo.' Si vero isto verbo immodice abuteris, respondebit tibi res publica: 'Quid mihi prodest vicisse si adhuc aliquid negare non possum? Sic mecum loqueretur
victor hostis. Quid si templorum incendia petas, legum
14 obliviones? Hoc modo et nuptias matris optares.' Quanto
iustius tibi mulier privata respondet: 'Non pro me tantum
militasti: appella rem publicam, appella magistratus. Non
potest a privato dari quod ab omnibus debetur. Haec dicerem si aliquid ex rebus meis concupisses: nunc matrimonium petis, quod tibi contingere non potest sine invidia
15 cupiditatis.[8]' Si tamen urbe capta invocaret manes mariti,
non auferret hostis, et misereretur eius quae amare de-
functum videretur. Tibi cum hac quomodo potest convenire, cuius matrimonium non peteres nisi cum ea litigas-
ses? Vis scire quid sint nuptiae? Aspice illam virginem
quam pater tradidit euntem die celebri, comitante populo.
Non potest quisquam dare quod constat duorum volun-
16 tate. Utcumque tolerabile esset si virginem peteres quae
nullo suspirarat[9] adfectu, quae adhuc rei publicae matrimonium debet. Est praecipuum ius senectutis, quoniam
non omnia[10] subit omnis aetas: non perpetuo senatorem ci-
tat consul; est sua legationibus requies. Cum hos habueris
annos, iam non militabis.

[8] *Aer.*: captivita- Aβ   [9] *SB4*: -irat Aβ: -iravit *Ro.*
[10] *Pith.*: una Aβ

---

[10] Rightly referred by Wi. to the contest between Ajax and
Ulysses about the arms of the dead Achilles.
[11] Cf. s.10 init.

tended with each other about the spoils of a ten-year war?[10] These are sacred merits, this is valor bonded together. That was "whatever I want." But if you abuse that phrase[11] unconscionably, the commonwealth herself will answer you: "What boots my victory if it means I cannot say no to anything? This is how a victorious enemy might talk to me. What if you should ask for a temple to be burned, laws to be put out of mind? In this fashion you might have opted to marry your mother." How much more justly will a private woman answer: "You did not fight only for me: call upon the commonwealth, call upon the magistrates. What is owed by everyone cannot be given by a private individual. This is what I should have said if you had fancied one of my possessions. As it is, you ask for marriage, which cannot be yours without the odium of greed." But if the city had been taken and she invoked her husband's spirit, an enemy would not have carried her off, he would have pitied a woman who seemed to love the dead. How can you and she agree? You would not have sought her hand in marriage if you hadn't sued her. Do you know what marriage is? Look at that maiden there whom her father has handed over as she walks on the festal day with the people keeping her company.[12] Nobody can give what is made out of the will of two. It might be just as tolerable if you were asking for a virgin who has never sighed for love, who still owes the commonwealth matrimony. Old age has its privileges, since every time of life does not carry every burden: the consul does not summon the senator up to any age, there is retirement for ambassadorial missions. When you reach her age, you won't be in the army any more.

---

12 He imagines a bridal procession.

17 Cogis nos agere fortius. Non omnibus praemium debetur: non petet servus, non petet peregrinus. Tu hanc ad-
serendo matrem incertis te parentibus esse confessus es.
Ut optare possis, primum te necesse est filium probes.
Perseveras? Sic agam tamquam velis.[11] Nuptiis tibi opus
non est hoc tempore: militare debes, excubare, vigilare. Ab
18 hac te voluntate non debebat nec mater abducere. Aut[12]
tu, si quietem mavis, duc uxorem parem. Bene †dictam†
compositis aetatibus coacta matrimonia tamen facile fasti-
diuntur,[13] sive non habet omne quod licet voluptatem, seu
continuis vicina satietas, sive durum est quod necesse est.
19 Quid si adfert impares annos? In hac aetate ne olim quidem iuncti se amant. Operies flammeo canos, ut inducta in
cubiculum quomodo blandiatur, quomodo appellet? Nam
20 tu matrem vocabis. ⟦Inter pares quoque annos citius femina senescit, neque amatur anus uxor nisi memoria. Tu fortasse nunc velis: illum annum expecta qui veniet; non eundem gradum ultima aetas facit, nec decedit suprema vita,
sed corruit.⟧ Non ipsam petis, et[14] tua nihil interest uxor sit
an mater.
21 Satis diu fictis respondimus: nunc ars aperienda est.
Non conscientiam nostram temptat sed verecundiam, ut
huic expediat mentiri. Audite igitur tamquam alii iudices.
Iam primum omnium apparet nullam esse generis quod

11 *SB*¹: -it Aβ 12 *Ro.*: ac Aβ
13 *Obr.*: -unt Aβ
14 *Ri.*: sed Aβ

---

13 *Voluntate*, an odd word. *Munere* ("duty") might have been
expected. 14 Sex with your wife.
15 But for her money.

You force me to speak more strongly. Not everybody is entitled to a reward. The slave won't claim, the foreigner won't claim. By claiming her as your mother you admitted that your parentage is unknown. To be capable of opting you have first to prove yourself her son. You persist? I'll pretend that you really want it. Marriage is not for you at this time. You ought to be in the army, standing sentry, keeping watch. Not even your mother ought to have led you away from this choice.[13] Or if you prefer retirement, marry a wife to match. Forced marriage easily breeds contempt even when the ages correspond. Perhaps it is that nothing permitted brings pleasure or that satiety lies close to what goes on and on, or that what is necessary is hard to take. What if she brings disparate years? At that age even old-established couples don't love one another. You will cover grey hairs with the marriage veil, so that when she's taken into the bedroom, how is she to talk sweet, how address you? You will call her mother. ⟦Even when years are equal, the woman ages first, and an old wife is loved only in memory. Now perhaps you might want it,[14] but wait for the year that is to come. Closing age does not keep the same pace; the end of life is not a decline but a collapse.⟧ You are not asking for herself[15] and it does not matter to you whether she is wife or mother.

We have answered fictions long enough. Now I must expose artifice. He is not targeting our conscience but our modesty, to make it better for her to lie.[16] So listen as though you were the other jury. First of all it is evident that proof of the parentage which he is claiming is non-existent;

---

[16] I.e. to appear (by refusing marriage) to endorse the falsehood that he is her son.

adfectat probationem: alioqui praemio opus non esset.

22 Non †anus ulla†,[15] non index. Hinc est illud 'nubat nisi mater est.' Una calumniae origo est, quod hanc exposuisse constat. Rarum igitur est ut expositi vivant: caducum circa initia animal homines sumus. Nam ferarum pecudumque fetibus est statim ingressus et ad ubera impetus; nobis tollendus infans et adversus frigora muniendus[16]: sic quoque inter parentum manus gremiumque nutricis saepius labitur. Unde nobis tantam felicitatem ut ad infantem mors arcessita non veniat? Vos ponite ante oculos puerum statim

23 neglectum, cui mori domi expediret, inde nudum corpus, sub caelo, inter feras et volucres. Video moveri, mulier, lacrimas tuas. Nemo tibi mortalium posset ignoscere nisi

24 iussa fecisses. Alia tamen condicio est eorum quibus obvium patrem quaerit exponentium paupertas; ille relinquitur loco celebri, tunc et libet custodire longe et expectare Fortunam. Aliter abicitur[17] quem iussit exponi qui relin-

25 quere poterat heredem. Sis porro sublatus: ille qui te educat scit parentes, perisse patrem audit. Cur tibi non petit patrimonium? Cur istud tot annos tacet? An expectat donec probare non possit? Age, quid futurum erat si perisset et mater? Age, <quid si>[18] nollet filium mater agnoscere?

26 Nunc[19] huic quidem quanta fuerit materni nominis cupidi-

---

15 anulus ullus *Ro.*, *alii alia*   16 *Aer.*: nutri- Aβ
17 *tempt. Wi.*: abdicatur Aβ   18 *Aer.*
19 *Wi.*: nam Aβ

---

17 See crit. note. The corrupt *anus* will conceal a concrete proof of identity.

18 A baby's life is precarious anyway. How much more so when the baby is exposed!

otherwise there would be no need for a reward. There is no ring[17] (?), no informant. Hence comes that "let her marry me if she is not my mother." The only origin of the falsehood is that she admittedly did an exposing. Well, it's seldom that exposed children live. We humans are fragile creatures at our beginnings. The offspring of wild animals and cattle get going straight away, rush to the dugs, but with us the baby has to be picked up and protected against the cold. Even so there is often a slip between parents' hands and foster-mother's lap. How should we be so lucky that death doesn't come to a baby when invited?[18] Put before your eyes a boy, neglected from the start, who would be better off dying at home; then his naked body under the sky, among wild beasts and birds. Woman, I see you are moved to tears. No mortal could forgive you if you had not been doing as you were ordered. But it is a different story with those for whom the poverty of their exposers seeks for some father to turn up. Such a one is left in a frequented spot, then there's an impulse to watch at a distance and wait for Fortune.[19] One ordered exposed by a man who could leave an heir is quite differently cast away. Suppose moreover you were picked up: whoever rears you knows your parents, hears that your father has died. Why doesn't he claim the estate for you? Why is he silent about it for so many years? Or is he waiting until he can't prove it? Come, what would have happened if the mother had died too? Come, <what if> the mother refused to recognize her son? As it is, I shall prove how much *she* desired the name of

[19] The sentence, pointing to the helpless plight of *this* baby, is deleted by Wi., perhaps without sufficient reason. The repetition *relinquitur . . . relinquere* seems fairly harmless to me.

tas non illis tantum argumentis probabo, quod concepit,
quod sustulit, sed quod maritus numquam mandat expo-
nendum nisi educaturae. Date huic quem vultis adfectum:
si voluit habere, facile agnoscit; si noluit, sic exposuisset ne

27 educaretur. Et tamen fuerit fortis adversus infantem: plura
blandimenta robustior aetas habet. O quantos haec ex alienis liberis cruciatus tulit! Blanditur aliquis puer: 'talis esset
meus.' Laudatur aliquis vultu speciosus: 'talis fuit ille
quem perdidi.' Crescit cotidie dolor: 'iam in foro conspice-

28 retur, iam militaret, iam illi uxorem quaererem.' Nunc
vero propiores admovet stimulos vir fortis. Haec suum
negaret? Te parentes liberis suis monstrant. Scilicet timet
ne ad illum[20] matronae ⟨non⟩[21] conveniant. Si se matrem
fateretur, aliquid fortasse in honorem illius optasses. Ego
miror quod tuo errore non utitur: et uteretur, si errare te
crederet.

29 Cum ergo non nubit, aetatem suam intellegit, quam
impares sitis videt. Est quaedam etiam nubendi impudici-
tia. A viro iam suo secubaret, utique si aetatis huius filius
interveniret. Haec si nubere in istis annis potest quomodo-
cumque, dicam: mulier[22] incesta est, et necesse est umbra

---

[20] *SB*[1], *Watt*[1]: illam A*β*   [21] *coni. SB*[3]
[22] *coni.* Wi.: mater A*β*

---

[20] "Careless verbiage: the father was abroad, and the child was
at once exposed" (Wi.). But the mother could have picked it up before exposing.

[21] Even if she had exposed the claimant, he would have won
her heart as a young man—had he really been her son.

[22] By becoming a hero he gave her additional reason to recognize him as hers—except that she knew otherwise.

mother by arguing not only that she conceived, that she picked up, but that a husband never tells a wife to expose a child unless she is going to rear him.[20] Assign her whatever feelings you like: if she wanted to keep him, she recognizes him, no problem; if she didn't, she would have exposed him in such a way that he would not be reared. And yet, suppose she was strong against a baby: a more advanced age has more blandishments.[21] Oh, what torture she endured from other people's children! Some boy makes up to her: "He's like mine would have been." Some handsome lad is commended: "He's like the one I lost." The pain grows daily: "He would now be seen in the Forum, now be serving in the army, I would now be looking around for a wife for him." But now the hero applies goads at closer quarters.[22] Should she say he wasn't hers? Mothers show you to their children. I suppose she's afraid that married women wouldn⟨n't⟩ flock to him![23] If she confessed to being your mother, perhaps you would have opted for something to honor her. It surprises me that she doesn't take advantage of your mistake; and she would, if she believed it *was* a mistake.[24]

So when she refuses to marry, she realizes her age, sees how ill-matched you two are. Even marrying may involve a sort of wantonness. She would now be sleeping apart from her husband, at all events if a son of this age came between. If she is ever able to marry in any fashion at her time of life, I shall say: "The woman is lewd, and she must be hurt-

[23] Irony. The alleged mother knows that the "hero" would make a coveted parti.   [24] Had she thought that the "hero" really believed he was her son she would have gone along; but she knew he was only after her money.

30 saltem sceleris laboret. Cur in fabulas eat? Cur habeant
materiam maligni? Vix absolvi nuptiae possent si iam contra te iudices illi pronuntiassent. Quid futurum est si haec
31 parata fuerit nubere et illi matrem pronuntiaverint? Quid
autem? Tu, iuvenis, si tibi nuptiae adiudicatae fuerint,
ducturus es? Si non duxeris, non fiet sic generis experimentum; si ducturus es, factum est. ⟦Me miserum! anum
ducis iuvenis! Video quid concupieris: 'mater est: non vult.'
Ergo mater an uxor sit nihil interest?⟧
32   Ceterum²³ iuveni audacia in promptu: nec in hac aetate
mortem quisquam miretur.²⁴ Per fidem, iuvenis, bona potius opta. Consuevit frugalitati; sine marito diu vixit inter
gravissimas vitae calamitates, non sine solacio tamen: paruit marito.²⁵ Et iam in fine vita est; nec de hereditate sollicita est: non habet filium.

307

Conscius veneno proditoris¹

Conscientiae sit actio. Proditor torqueatur donec conscios
indicet. Proditor bis tortus pernegavit. Cum futurum esset
ut tertio torqueretur, amicus ei venenum dedit. Reus est
conscientiae.

²³ *Gron.*: -ra A*β*
²⁴ *coni. SB*³: mirare- A*β*: miratur *Gron.*
²⁵ p. m. *SB*¹: meruit maritum A*β*
¹ *expectares* venenum dans proditori (*SB*²)

---

²⁵ Her sense of guilt (for the exposure) makes her behave ec-
centrically.

ing with the shadow at least of a crime."[25] Why should she get herself talked about? Why should the malicious have their material? Marriage could scarcely be found innocent even if that jury had already pronounced against you. What is going to happen if she is ready to marry and they pronounce her your mother? And again: are you going to wed her, young man, if the marriage is adjudged to you? If you don't marry her, there won't be any test of parentage that way; if you do, the test is made.[26] ⟦Dear, oh dear: a young man like you marrying an old woman! I see your game: "She's my mother, she refuses." So, mother or wife, doesn't it make any difference?⟧

But the young man's audacity is ready to hand; and at her age no one would be surprised if she dies. For faith's sake, young man, opt for the property instead. She's used to frugal ways, she has lived a long while without a husband amidst the heaviest of life's calamities[27]—but not without a consolation all the same: she obeyed her husband. And now her life is at its end, and she doesn't worry about what she has to leave: she has no son.

307

Accomplice by poison of a traitor

Let there be an action for complicity. Let a traitor be tortured until he reveals his accomplices. A traitor twice tortured persisted in denial. When he was about to be tortured a third time, a friend gave him poison. He is tried for complicity.

[26] And your claim proved false.
[27] Loss of husband and son.

[QUINTILIAN]

1

SERMO

Duo nobis efficienda sunt, ut conscium habuerit, ut hunc habuerit.

2

DECLAMATIO

Scio vos, iudices, posse mirari cur ex hoc in iudicio quaeratur. Prospexerat enim lex ut conscius per tormenta potius quaereretur. Sed quatenus nequitia obviam itum[2] est legi, reliquum est ut hic reus sit.

3   Ac primum omnium nego fieri potuisse ut proditor conscios non haberet. Intuemini naturam, intuemini magnitudinem sceleris. Prodere populum, civitatem, exercitum, non est unius. In hoc mihi non[3] est laborandum. Nam lex quae torqueri iubet donec conscios indicet non dubitat

4 conscios esse. Vidit enim quanta esset inter se quodammodo sceleratorum fides, quamdiu tacerent. Itaque non sic scriptum est: 'proditor torqueatur', sed: 'torqueatur donec conscios indicet': adeo ille qui nondum indicavit adhuc non est pro torto. Ergo ut maioribus nostris visum est, [si][4] conscios habuit.

5   Videamus quos habuerit. Nullum factum deprendi, nullum conscientiae signum putemus, mortuum esse antequam torqueretur: quaeramus quos conscios habuerit. Nonne illud genus quaestionis praecipiendum est, quem habuerit amicum? Non temere debet indicasse tantae rei conscientiam. Longa consuetudo, vetus amicitia facit ut

---

     [2] o. i. *Bu.*: -am est A[1]: -atum A[2]β
     [3] *Aer.*: nunc Aβ: non ne B   [4] *del. Ro., Ri.*: iste *Sch.*

---

     [1] *Conscius*, not "put very carelessly for *proditor*" (Wi.).
     [2] I.e. "use common sense." *Natura rerum* is usual.

430

DISCUSSION

We have to establish two things: that he had an accomplice
and that he had this accomplice.

DECLAMATION

I know, gentlemen of the jury, that you may wonder why
this man is being examined in court. For the law had envisaged that an accomplice[1] ought rather to be searched for
through torture. But since the law has been countered by
villainy, it remains that he stand trial.

And to begin with I say that it is impossible that the traitor did not have accomplices. Look at nature,[2] look at the
magnitude of the crime. To betray the people, the community, the army, is not one man's work. I need not labor this
point. The law which orders him[3] to be tortured until he
reveals his accomplices makes no doubt that there *are* accomplices. For it saw how much loyalty (in a way) there
was among criminals, how long they kept silent. So the text
runs, not "let the traitor be tortured," but "be tortured until he reveals his accomplices." So true it is that he who
has not yet "revealed" is still not considered as tortured.[4]
Therefore, as our ancestors thought, he had accomplices.

Let us see whom he had. Let us suppose that no act was
detected, no sign of complicity, that he died before he was
tortured: let us ask whom he had as accomplices. Ought we
not to recommend this line of enquiry: whom did he have
as a friend? He should not have entrusted knowledge of so
great a matter lightly. Long intercourse, old friendship

---

[3] The traitor, understood from *proditor* above.

[4] So the torture must go on. But this interrupts two cohering
sentences and should perhaps be double-bracketed.

6 veniat quis in sceleris societatem. Amicum igitur predito-
ris te fuisse negas? Iam si te interrogavero quare dederis
venenum, respondebis: 'tormenta tertio videre non poteram; meos artus, mea lacerari viscera putabam.' Iungit
enim amicitias similitudo morum: nescio quo modo inter
sese animorum lumina⁵ vident et agnoscunt, nec quisquam amare in altero potest nisi quod tacitus probat. Nec
haec in nobis tantum comparatio: muta animalia si in

7 unum conferantur, genera tamen coibunt. Amicus illius
fuisti, cum illo tibi seria ac ioci: non potes videri non pro-
basse quae⁶ non ignorasti. Amicus proditoris fuisti: plus est

8 hoc quam si dixeris conscium te fuisse. 'At bis tortus pernegavit.' Reddis⁷ nobis rationem quare illi amicus tanto-
pere fueris. Dignum mehercule exemplum quod fieret in
re honestiore: tu ne ille amplius torqueretur periculum
capitis subisti, ille ne te nominaret bis tortus est. Qui non

9 indicat confitetur amicum fuisse. 'Bis tortus negavit.' Nihil
dicam de varietate tormentorum. Nondum erat tortus qui
torqueri poterat. Illa, illa quaestio fuisset quam timuisti.
⟦Difficile est contra dolorem aegris durare corporibus, sed
facile est integro sensu perferre quam semel indueris per-
suasionem. Ideo ars inventa est: illae torquent nocturnae
cogitationes, illa recordatio praeteritorum, illa expectatio
futurorum. Illa est quaestio gravis cum vulnera caeduntur,

⁵ *Obr.*: num- A²β: nom- A¹
⁶ *Ro.*: quem Aβ
⁷ *Ri.*: -des Aβ

---

⁵ *Pace* Wi., *lumina* makes excellent sense, *numina* none.
⁶ The reading and sense remain doubtful.

brings it about that someone comes into fellowship with crime. So do you deny that you were the traitor's friend? If I now ask you why you gave the poison, you will answer: "I could not watch the torments for a third time: I thought it was my limbs, my flesh being torn." For friendships are joined by similarity of character; somehow or other the eyes[5] of men's minds see and recognize, and nobody can love in another except what he silently approves. Nor is this gregariousness found only in mankind: if dumb animals are brought together, the species will still coalesce. You were his friend, you shared work and play with him. You cannot be thought not to have approved of things that were within your knowledge (?).[6] You were a traitor's friend: that's more than if you said you were his accomplice. "But he was tortured twice and still denied." You give me a reason why you were so much his friend. Upon my word, an example worthy of a nobler setting: you risked your life to spare him further torture, he suffered torture twice rather than give your name. He that does not inform confesses that he was a friend. "Twice tortured, he denied." I'll say nothing about the variety of the tortures.[7] A man who could still be tortured had not been tortured. *That* would have been the examination you feared, that would have been the one. ⟦It is hard for sick bodies to endure against pain, but easy when consciousness is unimpaired to persist in a mind-set once assumed. That is why the art was invented; those night thoughts torture, that remembering of the past, that expectancy of things to come. The examination is really serious when wounds are beaten,

[7] Each of the two sessions might be thought to count for several because so many different tortures were employed.

433

cum persuasum est animo nullum esse finem tormentorum. Non igitur peracta quaestio fuit.]

10   Ducit me indignitas rei. Venenum proditori dedisti.
Nisi aliud crimen occupassem, veneficii accusarem: venenum paravit, habuit, dedit. Et primum hoc inquirere[8]
libet: unde tibi venenum, ad quos casus parasti? Sic illud
habuisti tamquam possis ipse torqueri. Age, nondum inva-
do tamquam proditorem; interim ago tecum magistratus
nomine: cur in custodiam irrupisti? Quibus suppliciis hoc
venenum luere poteris? Proditor bene periit.

11   Sed redeamus ad crimen. Venenum dedisti cum scires
futurum ut suspicaremur. Quam valde confessionem timuisti, qui subire maluisti hoc argumentum! 'Amicus' inquit 'erat.[9]' Quid ais? Amicus etiamnum? Patri bono iam
filius non videretur. Antea tibi poterat ignosci, cum ignora-
bas: etiamnum probas proditorem? Amicus ille? Hoc de
12   proditore non est misericordia. Qui misereri proditoris potest, crudelis est. Non ergo istud amicitiae tuae misera-
13   tione fecisti: iam tibi nuntiabatur suprema vox. Vis scire
quam hoc non amicitia feceris? Ne torqueretur non dedisti. Passus es ut ⟨iterum⟩[10] torqueretur. Iam anne tertio
torqueretur minime ad ipsum pertinebat. Bene quod magna scelera iis ipsis quibus occultari videntur aperiuntur.

---

  [8] *SB*[1]: invadere Aβ   [9] *Ro.*: eram Aβ   [10] *Aer.*

---

  [8] I can make nothing apposite of this, and have therefore double-bracketed the passage.
  [9] This question too seems irrelevant, unless *unde tibi* is understood as *quo tibi* ("what did you want with poison?").
  [10] Apparently "in your imagination." They would be a confession implicating the friend.

when the subject is persuaded that there is no end to his torments. So the examination had not been concluded.]][8]

The outrageousness of the thing leads me on. You gave poison to a traitor. If I had not already seized on another charge, I should accuse him of poisoning: he prepared the poison, had it by him, gave it. And first I should like to ask: why did you get the poison,[9] against what contingencies did you prepare it? You had it by you as though you might be tortured yourself. Come now, I am not yet setting on you as a traitor, for the present I ask you in the magistrate's name: why did you break into the prison? With what punishments will you be able to pay for this poison? A traitor had a good death.

But let us come back to the charge. You gave him poison although you knew we were going to suspect you. How you must have feared his confession, that you preferred to face this inference. "He was my friend," he says. What are you saying? Still a friend? A good father would not look on him as a son. Earlier on you might have been forgiven, when you didn't know: do you still approve of the traitor? He a friend? Where a traitor is concerned, this is not compassion. He's a cruel man who can pity a traitor. So you did not do it out of your friendship's compulsion: already you were being told of his last words.[10] Would you like to know how[11] you did not do this out of friendship? You did not give it so that he shouldn't be tortured. You let him be tortured <a second time>. It now mattered very little to *him* whether he be tortured a third time. A good thing that great crimes are laid open by the very means that seem to

[11] I.e. "how evident it is that . . ."

435

Dum hoc agis, ne amicus tuus fateatur, ipse confessus es.

308

Duo testamenta

Testamenta ultima rata sint. Intestatorum sine liberis mortuorum bona proximi teneant. Quidam primo testamento instituit heredem amicum, secundo facto alterum. Decessit. Posterius testamentum damnatum est. Ambigunt de bonis priore testamento heres scriptus et propinqui.

1   DECLAMATIO

Et in more civitatis et in legibus positum est ut, quotiens fieri potuerit, defunctorum testamento stetur, idque non mediocri ratione. Neque enim aliud videtur solacium mortis quam voluntas ultra mortem; alioqui potest grave videri etiam ipsum patrimonium, si non integram legem habet, ut, cum omne ius nobis in id permittatur viventibus, aufe-
2 ratur morientibus. Proximum locum a testamentis habent propinqui, et ita, si intestatus quis ac sine liberis decesserit: non quoniam utique iustum sit ad hos pervenire bona defunctorum, sed quoniam relicta et velut in medio posita nulli proprius[1] videntur contingere. Nihil est ergo quod nos onerare temptent nomine isto propinquitatis, iactatione sanguinis et naturae homines binis iam tabulis ex-
3 heredati. Et sane quotiens quaestio iuris est certi et a maioribus constituti, nihil necesse est laudare leges quibus utimur et ad quas vobis iudicandum est.

---

[1] *SB*[3]: propius Aβ

---

[1] With the knowledge that one's wishes will be honored.

conceal them. In your efforts to stop your friend from confessing you have confessed yourself.

308

Two wills

Let last wills be valid. Let the next of kin have the property of intestates deceased without children. A man made a friend his heir in his first will, then made a second naming someone else. He died. The second will was invalidated. The heir named in the former will and the relatives dispute about the property.

DECLAMATION

Both in the custom of the community and in the laws it is laid down that, whenever possible, the wills of persons deceased be honored, and that for no trivial reason. For no other consolation is seen for death except wish beyond death.[1] Otherwise even patrimony itself may seem a burden if it doesn't have an undiminished law, in which case, while we are allowed complete freedom in its regard during our lifetime, it is taken away when we die. Relatives have second place after wills, and that only if a man dies intestate and childless: not that it is absolutely right that the property of the deceased come to them, but because property left behind, in the middle as it were, doesn't seem to go to anyone else more appropriately. So it's no use their trying to lay a load on us with that word kinship, brandishing blood and nature—people who have already been excluded in two wills. And certainly, whenever the question is about definite law established by our ancestors, there is need to praise the laws under which we live and according to which you gentlemen must give your verdict.

4 Quaestio igitur totius causae nostrae, ut opinor, in eo consistit, an amicus meus intestatus decesserit. In qua parte delector nihil tam obscure, nihil tam clam esse fac-

5 tum ut nobis probandum sit. Interrogo vos igitur, propinqui, an hic quem intestatum decessisse dicitis scripserit aliquando testamentum. Interrogo vos an hae tabulae quae ex parte nostra proferuntur testati sint. Intellegitisne[2] signum? An omni iure conscriptas [vel] tabulas[3] soletis

6 damnare? Non id agunt ut[4] non fecerit testamentum, sed intestatum volunt videri eum quia non semel fecerit. 'Scripsit' inquit 'et alteras tabulas.' Apparet quam noluerit

7 intestatus mori. Neque ego negaverim non uno genere fieri intestatos: aut enim is est intestatus qui non scripsit omnino testamentum, aut qui id scripsit quod valere non possit. Vos eligite quem velitis esse intestatum: si eum qui non scripsit, non est hic cuius de bonis agitur (bis enim scripsit); si eum videri vultis intestatum qui vitiosum scripserit testamentum, hoc confiteamini necesse est, vitiosum

8 testamentum esse pro non scripto. Hoc igitur supremum quaero sitne testamentum. Si confitemini esse testamentum, non potest videri intestatus decessisse; si non est testamentum (sicut non est, quia non iure factum est), nihil obstare priori potest.

9 Venio nunc ad meam legem: 'testamenta ultima rata sint.' Habet sine dubio, si verba tantum ipsa intueri velimus, hoc ius occasionem brevem calumniae. Quid si enim unum aliquis scripserit testamentum? Potest videri non ultimum[5] quod magis iure primum dixerimus. Sed quemadmodum inter plura testamenta ultimum valere opor-

2 Wi.: -tis a me A(β)   3 c. t. Wi., auct. Aer., Fr.: -iptae (-ibitur BD, -ipta C) vel tabulis Aβ   4 Wi.: utrum Aβ

Therefore the question for our whole case, I think, lies in this: did my friend die intestate? In that regard I am glad that nothing has been done so obscurely or secretly that I have to offer proof. So I ask you, kinsfolk, whether the man you say died intestate ever wrote a will. I ask you whether this document produced from our side comes from a testator. Do you understand the seal? Are you in the habit of invalidating documents drafted in total accordance with the law? They are not trying to show that he did not make a will, but they want him to appear intestate because he did not do it only once. "He wrote other wills, too," they say. Very obviously he did not want to die intestate. Nor would I deny that more than one kind of people become intestate: an intestate is either someone who did not make a will at all or who made one which cannot be valid. You choose: whom do you want to be intestate? If someone who did not make a will, it's not the man whose property is at issue, for he made two. If you want an intestate to mean someone who made a faulty will, you have to admit that a faulty will is equivalent to no will. I ask then, is this last a will? If you admit that it is a will, he cannot be considered as having died intestate: if it's not a will (as it isn't, because it was not made legally), it cannot block the former one.

Now I come to *my* law: "Let last wills be valid." No doubt if we choose to look only at the words themselves, this law contains a brief opportunity for a quibble. For what if somebody writes one will? A will may seem not to be the last which we may more properly call first. But just as among several wills the last ought to be valid, so the

---

[5] *Ranc.*: vitium Aβ

tet, ita haec manifesta legis voluntas est, ut id testamentum
10 valeat post quod nullum testamentum est. Neque est incredibile sine dubio, etiam ante hoc testamentum quo ego
heres factus sum, scripsisse illum alia testamenta, hominem frequenter hoc facientem. Ita et ultimum videri potest si post alia scriptum est, et si primum scriptum est,
quia nullum tamen est quod vincat et potentius sit postea
⟨scriptum⟩,[6] pro ultimo habendum est.
11   Sublatum dicunt prius testamentum posteriore testamento; neque ego infitior, si iure factum est testamentum,
hoc est, si testamentum est, potentissimam esse defuncti
proximam quamque voluntatem. Sed nego ullum postea
12 factum testamentum. Quid est enim testamentum? Ut
opinor, voluntas defuncti consignata iure legibusque civitatis. Non dixerim ego testamentum cui numerus signato-
rum deest, non dixerim testamentum cui libripens et emp-
tor familiae et cetera iuri necessaria: tabulae erunt fortasse
et scriptum erit. Et hoc, ut paulo ante dicebam, vestra
quoque manifestum confessione est, non esse illud testamentum: facto enim illo dicitis[7] propinquum vestrum in-
13 testatum fuisse. Hoc propius colligamus. Putemus enim
factum esse unum hoc testamentum quod damnastis: num
dubium erit quin ad vos bona pertinuerint tamquam intes-
tati, id est, quin ita heredes futuri fueritis tamquam ille
omnino testamentum non fecisset? Quod si hoc pro non
14 facto est, nec testamentum quidem videri potest. Fingamus fuisse ultimum testamentum: 'quando?', quaerimus.

---

[6] *SB*[1], factum *Wi*.   [7] *Ro*.: -tur Aβ

---

[2] Terms relating to testamentary procedures (Gaius, *Instit*.
2.104)

clear intention of the law is that a will after which there is no will is valid. Nor doubtless is it incredible that even before the will that made me his heir he wrote other wills, being a man who did this often. So a will can be seen as last both if it has been written after other wills and, if it is the first to be written, since anyway there is none ⟨written⟩ subsequently that trumps it and has more validity, it is to be considered the last.

They say that the former will was cancelled by a later will; and I don't deny that if a will is legally made, that is, if it *is* a will, the latest wish of the deceased is the most valid. But I say that no subsequent will was made. For what is a will? As I suppose, it is the wish of a person deceased sealed according to the law and regulations of the community. I would not call it a will if the number of signatures falls short, I would not call a will something that does not have a balancer and a buyer of the family[2] and what else is legally necessary; it will be a document perhaps, a piece of writing. And this, as I was saying just now,[3] is clear by your own admission, that that was not a will; for after it was made you say that your relative was intestate. Let us draw the conclusion at closer quarters. Let us supposed that the will which you got invalidated was the only one made: will there be any doubt that the property pertains to you, as that of an intestate: that is, that you will be the heirs as though he had never made a will? But if this is reckoned as not having been made, then it cannot be seen as a will. Let us make believe that it *was* the last will:[4] we ask

[3] s.7 fin.
[4] Before it was declared invalid.

Puto cum res in lite est, cum in disputatione. Nec pertinet ad nos quod fuerit ultimum, sed quod sit. Si ius utrique testamento constaret, fuisset illud ultimum quod postea factum est; illo vero sublato incipit ultimum esse quod re- lictum est, ut in contentione[8] cursus qui proximus ab ulti- mo fuerit, si desistat ultimus, in nomen illius locumque
15　succedit. Ergo ut non fuerit ultimum meum aliquando tes- tamentum, nunc ultimum est, et vos id ultimum[9] testa- mentum fecistis damnando id quod postea factum erat.

16　　　　　　　　　　　SERMO

Hoc ad verba legis, illud ad voluntatem.

17　　　　　　　　　　DECLAMATIO

Quid putamus secutam esse legem quae valere voluit ulti- mum testamentum? Plura valere non poterant, et in tam mutabili natura humanorum animorum diversis heredibus media lis relinquebatur. Optimum videbatur esse ut proxi- ma quaeque voluntas duraret; hac vero sublata necesse est
18　eam durare quae sola est. Fecit amicus meus eo tempore quo me instituebat heredem legitimum testamentum. Nam et constabat ei tum iudicium. Quo minus erubesco ista mutatione heredis; in iis tabulis alius legitur quae ius non habuerunt, quae non lege conscriptae sunt, quae for- tasse etiam propter hoc damnatae sunt, quod indignus heres videbatur.

19　　　　　　　　　⟨SERMO⟩[10]

In comparatione summa non recusabo quo minus vel pro- pinquos istos amicitiae conferatis.

---

8 *Sch., Gron.*: intent- A(β)
9 *SB*[3]: id AB: idem C: ultim D　　　10 *Ri.*

"when?" I suppose when the matter was in dispute, being argued.[5] And we are not concerned with what *was* last but with what *is* last. If both wills were legal, that one would have been last which was made after; but when that was cancelled, the remaining one became the last—as in a race, if the last runner falls out, the runner next the last takes his name and place. So if we admit that my will was at one time not the last, it is the last now, and you made it the last will by getting invalidated the one made subsequently.

DISCUSSION

So much as to the words of the law, now as to its intention.

DECLAMATION

What do we suppose guided the law that wanted the last will to be valid? Not more than one could be valid and in the changeable nature of human minds a dispute awaiting decision was being left to different heirs. It seemed best that in each case the most recent wish should hold; but this one being cancelled, the sole remaining one necessarily holds. My friend made a legal will when he made me his heir. For his judgment at that time was sound. That is why I am not much embarrassed by his change of heir. Someone else is read in a document that had no legal standing, that was not drafted conformably to the law, that was perhaps invalidated partly because the heir appeared unworthy.

‹ DISCUSSION ›

In the final comparison I shall not object to your comparing these kinsfolk with friendship.

---

[5] Before the court gave its verdict.

20 ⟨DECLAMATIO⟩[10]

Per se mihi vel sanctius nomen amici videtur. Hoc enim
proficiscitur ab animo, hoc proficiscitur a proposito; istud
dat casus, condicio nascendi et quae non sponte nostra
eliguntur. Me heredem esse amicus meus (quod satis est)
aliquando voluit, vos numquam, ⟨neque⟩[11] eo tempore
quo iudicabat neque eo tempore quo errabat.

21 SERMO

Illa iam communia pro omnibus testamentis.

22 DECLAMATIO

Non tantum ad heredem ista lis pertinet. Aliquem fortasse
amicorum honoravit, aliquem fortasse servulorum manumisit. Vos poenam quandam propinquo vestro constituitis,
ut intestatus decesserit, ut bona tamquam relicta, tamquam deserta invadatis.

309

Raptor convictus

Educta ad magistratum adulescentis a quo esse vitiata dicebatur nuptias optavit. Ille negavit se rapuisse. Iudicio
contendit. Victus est. Non recusat ducere. Illa optare vult.

1 SERMO

Actio debebit huius adulescentis esse summissa. Nam
etiamsi nullo ⟨modo⟩[1] themate ad id alligatur, ut necesse
sit eum raptorem videri, rei tamen iudicatae facere contro-

[11] *Aer.*
[1] *Watt*[2]

In itself the name of friend appears to me actually the more sacred, for it proceeds from the heart, from intention; the other is the gift of chance, of the circumstances of birth, and things that are not of our own choice. My friend wanted me to be his heir at one time (which is enough): he never wanted you, ‹neither› when his judgment was working nor when it was wandering.

DISCUSSION

Now the usual commonplace in favor of all wills.

DECLAMATION

This dispute involves others besides the heir. Perhaps he complimented[6] one of his friends, perhaps he freed one of his slaves. You are in some sort penalizing your relative, making him die intestate, in order to invade his property as though it had been abandoned and forsaken.

309

Rapist convicted

A girl brought up before the magistrates opted for marriage with the young man who was said to have violated her. He denied the rape. He fought it out in court. He lost. He does not refuse to marry. She wants to opt.

DISCUSSION

This young man's style should be restrained. For although the theme in no ‹way› binds him so that he has to appear as a rapist, still he cannot quarrel with the court's decision.

---

[6] With a legacy.

versiam non potest; et videtur mihi hunc modum custodire
debere, ut de raptu nihil neget, nihil tamen sciat.

2   DECLAMATIO

Non aliud, iudices, aut causae meae aptius aut verecundiae necessarium magis est quam ut puellae mitissimae
clementissimaeque gratias agam; lege permittente omnem
in me potestatem, optare nuptias etiam festinavit, nondum
me rogante, nondum (indicare enim simpliciter necesse
est) saltem confitente, ita facile, ita celeriter ut vix mihi
3 verisimile videretur illam iniuriam accepisse. Proxima ab
hac gratiarum actione debet esse confessio: peccasse me
quod dubitaverim fateor. Quid enim mihi contingere opta-
bilius potuerat, etiam si non rapuissem? Sed huius qualis-
cumque culpae meae spes omnis in animo istius est, quae
ignoscere solet. Quantumlibet contradicendo peccaverim,
minus est hoc tamen quam quod rapui.

4   Intellego autem, iudices, hanc primam mihi in hac causa habendam esse rationem, ne me, quod negavi, fecisse
callide ac maligne existimetis. Scitis quam multa faciat error, quam multa permisceat Fortuna, cum praesertim ad
haec ⟨accesserit⟩[2] et obscuritas noctis et paulo liberior
5 usus[3] meri. Quis enim aliter vitiator est? Ignorantem[4] haec
me, antea[5] frugi et innocentem,—non est dubitare iam
fas—fefellerunt: ita vixeram semper, ita custodire probita-
tis meae cupieram famam, ut me peccasse mirarer. Itaque
(confiteor) actum de me erat si in aliam incidissem. Nam
(ut dixi) neque ad genua procubueram neque propinquos
aut amicos advocaveram. Sed movit puellam ipsum (ut

---

[2] *hic add. Wi., alibi Ro. et Lat.*   [3] *Ro.:* liberioris Aβ
[4] *Ro.:* -tia Aβ   [5] me, a. *Ro., Ri.:* mea tea A(β)

It seems to me that he should stick to the line that he doesn't deny anything about the rape but doesn't know anything either.

Nothing, gentlemen of the jury, better suits my case or is more required of my sense of propriety than that I should thank a very gentle and merciful young lady. The law giving her complete power over me, she even made haste to opt for marriage, before I asked, before I even confessed (for I must tell it as it was); so readily, so quickly, that it seemed to me hardly likely that she had been injured. After these thanks should come confession. I admit that I was wrong to doubt. For what could have happened to me more to be desired, even if I hadn't raped her? But whatever this fault of mine, all its hope is in her nature, it being her way to forgive. However wrong I was to oppose, that is a lesser offence than my rape.

I realize, gentlemen, that my first concern in this case should be that you don't think my denial was made in cunning and malice. You know how often mistakes occur, how often Fortune makes confusion, especially when the darkness of night and a rather free indulgence in wine ⟨are added⟩ thereto. For who otherwise is a ravisher? These things deceived me, ignorant as I was, well-conducted and innocent until then (I must not doubt any more). My life had always been such, I had been so anxious to guard my reputation for probity, that I was astonished at my wrongdoing. And so, I confess, it would have been all over with me if I had chanced upon another girl. For as I said, I had not fallen down at her knees nor called my relations and friends to support me. But the girl, as I believe, was moved

credo) ignorantiae meae periculum; persuaserat sibi nihil
6   me fecisse temerariae libidinis causa. Nec me malo hoc
animo negasse ex hoc ipso apparere vobis potest: negavi
postquam ista nuptias optavit. Gratias ago et iudicibus:
emendaverunt contumaciae meae detrimentum: amise-
ram puellae optimae condicionem si vicissem. Ergo, quod
superest, gratulemur.

7   Ius esse raptae optandi adversus raptorem, hoc iam non
negamus; sed illud quoque aeque conveniat necesse est,
bis adversus eundem raptorem optandi non esse ius. Et si
hoc in confesso fuerit, illud quoque teneamus, optasse iam
puellam.

8   SERMO

Haec sunt quae inter utramque partem necessario conve-
niunt.

9   DECLAMATIO

Negat optionis expletum esse ius, quod ante optaverit
quam certum esset rapuisse eum contra quem optabat.
Ego autem in lege nullam animadverto differentiam, et
hoc unum exceptum, ut rapta raptoris mortem ⟨vel nup-
tias⟩[6] optet. Viderimus an in controversiam res adducta sit
postea; interim certum est hunc fuisse raptorem. Ergo
cum et tu rapta esses et hic raptor esset et lex raptae optare
permitteret et tu optaveris, non video quare non finitum
10   ius sit. 'At postea tu negasti te esse raptorem.' Ideo victus
sum. Feci, si vis, improbe (differo enim istius rei defensio-

6 *SB*[3]

---

1 Nor had he denied it, but now he admits that she was such a
victim.

by the very peril of my ignorance; she persuaded herself
that I had not acted out of random lust. And you can see
that I did not deny it with bad intention from the very fact
that I denied after she opted for marriage. I thank the jury
too. They put right the damage done by my contumacy. I
had lost a match with an excellent young lady if I had won.
So nothing is left for me but to rejoice.

That a rape victim has the right of option against the
rapist I don't now[1] deny, but this too must equally be
agreed, that there is no right of option twice against the
same rapist; and if that is admitted, let it also be granted us
that the girl had already opted.

DISCUSSION

These are the points necessarily agreed between both parties.

DECLAMATION

She denies that the right of option has been met in full because she opted before it was certain that the object of
her option had committed rape. But I perceive no difference in the law. The law provides[2] only that the rape victim
opt for the rapist's death <or marriage>. We'll see later
whether the matter was brought into dispute afterwards;
meanwhile it is certain that he was the rapist. Therefore
since you had been raped and the law allows the victim an
option and you opted, I don't see why there is any more to
be said about the law. "But you denied afterwards that you
were the rapist." So I lost. I acted improperly if you like (I
defer my defense on that score), I acted rashly: but what

<hr>

[2] As Wi. points out, *exceptum* is the wrong word; sense calls for
constitutum or equivalent. But the writer may be to blame.

449

nem), feci temere: quid tamen aliud quaeri potuit in illo
iudicio quam hoc, an tu[7] merito optasses? Probasti raptorem fuisse me, hoc est, probasti te recte optasse. Volui
rescindere optionem tuam; non contigit.

11   SERMO

Haec circa ius, illa circa aequitatem.

12   DECLAMATIO

Bis optare vis, quod etiam semel multum est. Potestatem
tibi vitae ac necis lex dedit; ultra regnum omne, ultra tyrannidem omnem est hoc diu licere. Fulmina ipsa veloci-
ter cadunt; habet finem aliquem expectationis securis illa
13 carnificis. Si mortem optasses et nuptias optare velles, videreris [enim][8] facere contra legem, et esset qui diceret:
'ante deliberasses, ante dispexisses; emissa vox est, potestatem tuam ipsa finisti.' Nunc vero cum optaveris nuptias,
mortem optare vis. Quae ista ad crudelitatem paenitentia
14 est? Intellexit et ipsa quam saevum, quam crudele sit. Plus
enim postea mali feci? Ignovisti quod rapueram, ignovisti
quod abstuleram virginitatem; haec nuptiis aestimasti:
15 morte aestimas verecundiam? Neque ego, cum me rapuisse negarem, nuptias tuas recusabam: volebam ducere
non tamquam raptor, cum me hoc modo putarem fore ca-
riorem, si tibi iniuriam non fecissem. Vel fallere animum
tuum volui: ne irascereris.[9]

16   Sed et ipsi iudices hoc pronuntiaverunt, hoc spectave-
runt. Quaestionem enim fuisse putas an ego rapuissem?

---

7 an tu *Wi*.: quam tu A (*ex* quantum?), D: quanto BC
8 D[2]
9 BC: -ceris AD: -caris *coni. SB*[3]

could be asked at that trial except whether your option had been deserved? You established that I had been the rapist, that is, that you had opted correctly. I wanted to rescind your option. I did not succeed.

So much as to law, now as to equity.

You want to opt twice, when even once is much. The law gave you power of life and death; that this license should last long is beyond all monarchy, beyond all tyranny. Even thunderbolts fall quickly. The executioner's axe has a limit to expectancy. If you had opted for death and were wanting to opt for marriage, you would appear to be acting against the law, and somebody would say: "You should have thought about it before, looked into it before; the word has gone out, you have yourself terminated your power." But now, having opted for marriage, you want to opt for death. What is this repentance into cruelty? She realized herself[3] how savage, how cruel it is. Did I offend again afterwards? You forgave me for having raped you, you forgave me for taking away your virginity. You priced these things at a marriage, do you price bashfulness at death? And when I denied the rape, I was not refusing marriage with you; I wanted to wed you not as a rapist, since I thought I should be dearer to you that way, if I had not done you an injury. Or I wanted to deceive your feelings. You should not have been angry.

But the jury itself so pronounced, this was what they had in view. Do you think the enquiry was about whether I

---

[3] When she opted for marriage.

Cum ego dicerem: 'Non rapui, non hi mores sunt mei:
honeste semper vixi, frugaliter vixi. Quae probatio huius
criminis mei, quis testis?', dicebantur illa contra: 'Pericli-
taris, et male tecum agitur? Nuptiae sunt de quibus litigas.'
Fecerunt iudices quod parentes nostri fecissent; id pronuntiaverunt in quo victus gratias ageret.

17   Sed spe suspendit, et vult videri nunc quoque factura
quod fecit. Si beneficium vitae repetere vis, dedisti: non
possum plus debere si repetis. Quam autem causam habes
renovandae optionis si optatura nuptias es? Si vindicari vis
a me metu, timui; si rogari vis, rogo, et rogo per illam cle-
mentiam tuam, rogo iam tamquam maritus; et intellego
tota mihi vita hoc agendum, ut satisfaciam.

310

Fortis bis adulterii damnatus

Bis adulterii notatus ignominiosus sit. Notatus adulterii
fortiter fecit. Petît praemii nomine ut iterum accusaretur.
Impetravit. Accusatus est iterum et damnatus. Dicitur
ignominiosus.

1   DECLAMATIO

Quanta gratia prematur in foro, quam impudenti calumnia
inimicorum suorum vexetur, et hoc ipsum iudicium argumento est; videlicet contemnunt hominem militarem,
nihil minus quam litibus idoneum. Sed †formula†[1] inimi-

---

[1] AB: -le CD: forenses *Morawski*: in forum latae *Hå*.[2]

---

[1] *Notatus*, the term used for the Censor's black mark, here alternative to *damnatus* (see s.2).   [2] See crit. note.

had committed rape? When I said: "I did not rape, it's not my character; I always lived decently and frugally. What proof is there of this offence of mine, who is witness?" this was the answer: "Are you in danger, are you being badly treated? Marriage is what you are disputing about." The jury did what our parents would have done. They brought in a verdict at which the loser could say thank you.

But she is keeping me in hope and wants to look as though now too she is going to do what she did. If you want to repeat your gift of life, you have given it; I cannot owe you more if you repeat it. What reason do you have for re-newing the option if you are going to opt for marriage? If you wish to revenge yourself on me by fear, I have been afraid. If you wish to be begged, I beg you by that clemency of yours, I beg you as already your husband; and I under-stand that throughout my life it must be my endeavor to make amends.

310

Hero twice found guilty of adultery

Let whoso has twice been disgraced[1] for adultery be under stigma. One disgraced for adultery became a hero. He asked by way of reward that he be accused again. It was granted him. He was accused again and found guilty. He was pronounced under stigma.

DECLAMATION

With how much influence he is crushed in the Forum, with what impudent slander his enemies harass him, this very trial is proof. It seems they despise a soldier, the last man to be at home in a lawsuit. But enmities in the courts (?)[2] can

citiae tum valere possunt cum de aliquo facto mentiri licet, cum testes subornare; ceterum in his quae ad intellectum iudicum pertinent, gratia sine vitio cognoscentium nihil est.

2   Nemo igitur nostrum negat ita in lege[2] scriptum esse: 'qui bis adulterii damnatus est, ignominiosus sit.' Ne id quidem negabitur, bis in iudicium hunc descendisse, bis

3 contra hunc latam esse sententiam. Sed si manifestum fuerit legem non ideo esse conscriptam ut hoc genus damnationis ignominiam faciat, si ne in cogitationem quidem cuiusquam cadere omnino potuit aliquem ex eadem causa bis potuisse damnari, profecto manifestum est non in aliud

4 scriptas esse leges, in aliud valere. Quaero igitur ex ipsis adversariis cur bis damnatum adulterii ignominiosum esse voluerint. Ut opinor, iudices, quoniam una damnatio habebat aliam et suam poenam, geminatio criminis adferebat ignominiam. Neque immerito: semel enim errare sane tolerabile sit, in eadem vero incidere, ne damnatione quidem compesci, ultra omnia videbatur. Nihil ergo[3] verba faciunt si[4] voluntas legis diversa atque contraria est; est autem diversa, ut apparet.

5   Atque ego, si descendere ad hoc genus actionum vellem ad quod me pars diversa deducit, possem contendere vim duorum iudiciorum in his non esse. Quare? Quoniam lex viri fortis intervenit, et praemium eam vim habuit ut iudicium prius tolleretur. Itaque etiamsi prius bis[5] damnatus et propter hoc ignominia notatus fortiter fecisset et prae-

[2] in l. *Pith.*: intellege A(β)
[3] β: enim A
[4] *Sch., Gron., auct. Aer.*: set A: sed β
[5] *hic Gron., post* hoc A (his), β

454

be powerful when there is room for lying about some act and suborning witnesses; but in matters pertaining to the understanding of the jury, influence is nothing without fault on the part of those trying the case.

Well, none of us denies that it is written in the law: "Let him who has twice been found guilty of adultery be under stigma." Nor will it be denied that this man has twice gone to trial and that the verdict has twice gone against him. But if it will be clear that the law was not drafted so that this sort of conviction should carry a stigma, if it could not possibly occur to anyone that somebody could have been twice convicted in the same case, it is surely clear that laws are not written for one thing and valid for another. So I ask of my adversaries themselves why they[3] wanted one twice convicted of adultery to be under stigma. As I suppose, gentlemen, a single conviction had a different penalty, one peculiar to itself, whereas the doubling of the offence carried stigma. With reason: for let us say that to err once is tolerable, but to fall twice into the same error and not to be restrained even by a conviction seemed beyond anything. So the words go for nothing if the intention of the law is different and contrary, and it *is* different, as is evident.

If I chose to resort to the type of plea to which the other side is leading me, I could argue that the sense of *two* trials is not present in these. Why? Because the hero's law comes between and the reward carried the sense that the previous trial was cancelled. So even if a man twice previously convicted and on that account marked by stigma had be-

---

[3] The lawgivers. The answer to the question (badly phrased) seems to be the obvious one, that a second offence deserves an additional penalty.

mii nomine restitutionem quaesisset, nihil ne duo quidem
6 vera crimina valuissent. Ergo eo tempore quo optavit ut
accusaretur iterum, hoc optavit, ut esset pro indemnato.[6]
Si ergo prius iudicium hoc illi praestitit, et merito praestitit, *[7] ⟦in summa †quidem secundo iudicio quaesitum sit
an hic adulter esset quare accusatus esset† quoniam tamquam de innocente aut[8] de dubio arbitrabatur ac si prius
iudicium non esset⟧ altero damnari nihil attinuit; erat
7 enim damnatus. Vel[9] elige quod voles, accusator, utique alterum ex duobus: nam, si valuerit[10] illud fuisse sententiam,
alterum ⟨non⟩[11] est pro sententia. Propius[12] utique illud
sic colligite. Non est impunitus is qui semel adulterii damnatus habet suam poenam. Ponamus hanc esse pecuniam.
Num igitur exigis alteram, quae priore iudicio aut debita
aut persoluta erat? Atqui si, tamquam singula, iudicia du-
plicia[13] poenas suas non habent, non possunt pro duobus
numerari.
8 Supererat fortasse ut causam quoque adhuc viri fortis
agere temptarem. Sane ⟨ne⟩[14] dissimulemus ⟨hanc⟩[15]
partem. Quare igitur[16] saepius est[17] damnatus? Erant aliqua quae[18] movere iudices[19] possent: damnatus est adulte-

6 *SB*[3]: damn- A (ne *pro* ut *Aer.*)

7 *lac. ind.* *SB*[3]

8 *SB*[1]: et A*β*

9 *omittendum sive* tu *legendum coni. Wi.*

10 *Ro.*: -uit A*β*   11 *Ro.*

12 *Wi.*: prius A*β*

13 *Obr.*: publica A*β*   14 *SB*[3]

15 *Aer.*   16 q. i. *Gron.*: quaeratur A*β*

17 *Gron.*: esse A*β*

18 a. q. *Ri.*: alioqui que A: alio quoque *β*

19 iud⟨ices⟩ *Wi.*: non A*β*

come a hero and sought restitution by way of reward, even
two real offences would not have had any validity. So when
he opted to be accused a second time, he opted to be as
good as unconvicted. If therefore the previous trial gave
him this, and properly so *[4] [[in fine, since the trial was
considered[5] as concerning an innocent man or one whose
guilt was questionable, as if there had been no previous
trial]]. That he was found guilty in the second trial was irrelevant; for he was already convicted. Choose which you
wish, prosecutor, but at all events choose one of the two:
for if the view prevail that one was a verdict, the other is
<not> to be considered a verdict. Coming closer, at all
events make that conclusion thus: a man who, convicted
once of adultery, has his penalty is not unpunished. Let us
suppose it is a fine. Are you exacting a second—one which
had either been owed or paid in full in the former trial?[6]
And yet if double trials, like single trials, do not have their
own penalties, they cannot be counted as two.

It still remained for me perhaps to try yet further to
plead the case of the hero. To be sure, let me <not> pass
<this> part over. Why then was he found guilty repeatedly?
There were some considerations that might have moved
the jury (?).[7] He was found guilty of adultery; but after-

---

[4] The gap may be substantial. I have not attempted to translate
the words obelized.

[5] On *arbitrabatur* (passive) see Wi.

[6] More clumsy phrasing. Suppose a fine is imposed at the first
trial. Even if was still owing, a second fine could not be imposed at
the second trial for the same offence.

[7] See crit. note. *Vos* and *nos* have been conjectured for *non*,
but this jury was not the same as in the previous trial.

rii. Sed postea fortiter pugnando ostenderat non eos esse
mores suos, non ⟨eam⟩[20] suam vitam ut in illo credibilia
haec crimina forent; sed cum optare illi liceret restitutionem, illud optare maluit, ut accusaretur, ut de vero quaeri
9 posset. Hoc non sine bona conscientia fecit. Cur ergo damnatus est iterum? Quia damnatus erat. Non putaverunt illi
qui cognoscebant priorum iudicum rescindendam esse
sententiam; ita homo qui post praemium accusabatur sic
10 auditus est tamquam nondum fortiter fecisset. Vos ergo
qui duobus iudiciis esse dicitis damnatum explicate quid
aliud obiectum sit altero, quae differentia duorum iudiciorum fuerit. Eadem adultera dicebatur, idem testes pro-
ducebantur, isdem argumentis premebatur. Haec scilicet
improbitas est[21] qua unius causae vultis esse duo iudicia.
11 Potestis et illo modo aestimare, iudices, quam inique ista[22]
poena petatur a viro forti: statuamus duos esse, alterum
qui bis adulterium commiserit, alterum qui bis damnatus
sit. De illo ea dico: 'duo cubicula irruisti, duobus maritis
iniuriam fecisti, duas familias incerta stirpe confudisti.'
Huic tu quid obicis? 'Indignatus es quod damnatus esses,
sententiae iudicum repugnasti, persuadere tibi ipse non
potuisti esse te nocentem.'
12   Egregiam, hercules, gratiam viris fortissimis reddimus.
Hic, si magistratus esse voluisset, honores gessisset, si sacerdos esse, templis praefuisset: hoc egit praemio suo, ut

---

20 *add. Watt*[1] (*pro* suam *Ro.*)   21 *Aer.*: -bitate Aβ
22 *Ri.*: ipsa Aβ

---

8 A man who commits two adulteries deserves the stigma, but
that does not apply to the defendant. He has twice been found
guilty, but the second verdict was merely the consequence of his

wards by fighting bravely he had shown that his character was not such, his life was not ⟨such⟩ as to make these charges credible in his case. But though he might have opted for restitution, he preferred to opt to be prosecuted, so that the truth might be sought. This he did not do without a good conscience. Then why was he found guilty a second time? Because he had been found guilty. The jurors felt that the verdict of the previous jury ought not to be rescinded. So a man accused after his reward was heard as though he had not become a hero. So you that say he was found guilty in two trials, please explain what else was brought against him in the second, what difference there was between the two trials. The same adulteress was alleged, the same witnesses were produced, he was oppressed by the same evidence. It's shameless, your wanting two trials of one case. And you can judge thus, gentlemen, of how unfairly this penalty is sought from the hero: let us assume that there were two persons, one who had twice committed adultery, the other who had twice been found guilty. Of the former I say: "You broke into two bedrooms, you injured two husbands, you confounded two families with uncertain stock." What do you say against the latter? "You were indignant at your conviction, you rebelled against the verdict of the jurors, you could not persuade yourself that you were guilty."[8]

A fine return we make to our bravest, gentlemen. Had this man wanted to be a magistrate, he would have held offices, had he wanted to be a priest, he would have been in charge of temples: what did he achieve with his reward—a

refusal to accept the first. So far as stigma is concerned, he is as clear as if he had never committed adultery at all.

ignominiosus esset? Detrahe illi quod fortiter fecit, detrahe quod optavit: non est ignominia. Nondum atrocitas
erat. *[23]

Qualecumque crimen donari meritis, donari virtuti potest.

311

Addictus manumissus

Addictus donec pecuniam solverit serviat. Qui habebat
domi addictum testamento omnes servos manumisit. Petit
addictus ut liber sit.

1
DECLAMATIO

Intellegimus nihil nobis in hac causa verendum[1] magis
quam communem quendam omnium qui in libertatem ad-
serunt favorem. Contra quem non id modo a nobis intellegimus esse dicendum, ut praecipue ius tueamur, sed illud
etiam, non minus pro eo esse contra quem videmur agere,
2 si tamen explicet fidem, quod nos contendimus. Id enim
hodie quaeritur, an servus sit. De liberalitate eius qui nos
heredes instituit nihil querimur. Servos manumisit. Num
cui controversia movetur? Num inviti eos tristesque in numero civitatis aspicimus? Alia nobis ratio cum debitoribus,
alia cum ingenuis.

---

23 *lac. ind. SB*[3] (erat <in poena. semel adulter erat> *coni. SB*[4],
cf. SB[1])   1 *Aer.*: verecun- Aβ

---

9 And not an adulterer twice over; see crit. note.
1 But the debtor had not been set free and could not be manu-

stigma? Take away his becoming a hero, take away his option: there is no stigma. Nor yet was there ‹savagery in the punishment. He was only once an adulterer›.[9]

Any offence whatever can be forgiven for merit's sake, can be forgiven for valor's.

311

Addicted for debt freed[1]

Let one addicted for debt be in servitude until he pays the money. One who had a person addicted for debt in his house freed all his slaves in his will. The debtor claims his freedom.

DECLAMATION

We[2] realize that we have nothing to be more afraid of in this case than a common predisposition in favor of all who claim their freedom. Against this we realize that we must not only speak as primarily maintaining the law but also in the sense that what we contend is no less to the advantage of the person[3] whom we seem to be opposing, provided that he fulfils his obligation. For the question today is whether he is a slave. We make no complaint of the liberality of the gentleman who made us his heirs. He freed slaves. Is there any quarrel afoot? Are we reluctant and sad to see them as part of the community? Debtors for us are another story, freemen another.

mitted like a slave. The title is therefore incorrect here; but see Calp. Fl. 14.
  [2] The heirs.
  [3] The addicted debtor.

Neque nos fugit velut in contrarium ire litem. Nam si quis ex nobis istum servum vocaret, multa habebat profecto quae pro se diceret, per quae ingenuus videretur. Quid enim lex dicit? 'Addictus donec solverit serviat', ut opinor, non 'servus sit.' Plurimum autem refert. Nam[2] servire merito dicimus et eos qui in piratas inciderint et eos qui ab hoste sint capti: id quidem quod ingenuis natura dedit, nulla Fortunae iniuria eripi potest. Id quamvis nulli non vestrum existimo esse manifestum, quibusdam tamen con-
5 fessis argumentis ostendere volo. Ante omnia [servus][3] hic habet nomen, est in censu, est[4] in tribu: quorum nihil (ut opinor) deprehendi in servo potest. 'At intervenit ea condicio ut servire debeat donec solverit.' Hoc ipsum servi non est, habere in sua potestate quando desinat servire.
6 Fingite enim, iudices, aut oblatam esse ab illo pecuniam aut ex hoc testamento pronuntiatione vestra liberum fieri: num inter libertinos futurus est? Non, ut opinor. Atqui si illud in confesso est, eum qui a servitute in libertatem veniat non esse alio quam libertini loco, hic solutus hac necessitate tam ingenuus futurus sit quam fuit, manifesto ne
7 hodie quidem servus est. Alia quoque complura sunt quae intueri licet, si velitis. Servus aut domi natus est aut relictus hereditate aut emptus. Hunc ex quo genere servorum po-

---

2 *Obr.*: an Aβ 3 *Gron.*   4 *Fr.*: aut Aβ

---

4 Perhaps because, while he was superior to a slave, he was not qualified for freedom as the slaves were (*pace* Wi., whose translation I borrow).

5 A freeman's name—*nomen gentilicium*. When freed, a slave took his master's, along with a praenomen (also regularly his master's), keeping his slave name as a cognomen.

Nor does it escape us that the dispute seems topsy-turvy.[4] For if one of us were calling this man a slave, he surely had many things to say for himself to show he was a freeman. For what says the law? "Let one addicted for debt be in servitude until he pays," I think; not "be a slave." That's very important. For we rightly speak of persons who have fallen into pirates' hands or been captured by the enemy as being in servitude: what nature gave to the freeborn cannot be snatched away by any injury of Fortune. Although I expect that this is clear to every one of you, I want to prove it by certain admitted arguments. First of all, he has a name,[5] is in the census, is in a tribe, none of which, I think, can be found in a slave. "But his condition intervenes, making him be in servitude until he pays." That in itself is not proper in a slave, that he should have it in his own power when he ceases to be in servitude. For imagine, gentlemen, that he has either offered the money or become free under the will by your pronouncement: will he be among the freedmen? I think not. But if it is admitted that a man who passes from slavery to freedom is in no other situation than that of a freedman, while this man once freed from this necessity[6] would be as free as he was before,[7] clearly he is not a slave even today. There are a number of other things you may look at if you will. A slave is either home-born or left by inheritance or purchased. In which category of slaves do you put this man? He says he is

6 Of servitude.

7 *Tam ingenuus futurus sit* irregularly for *tam ingenuum futurum esse.*

nitis? Domi natum esse se non dicit, ne emptum[5] quidem
aut hereditate relictum. Pendet igitur omnis haec condicio
ex faenore. Quid sequitur? Ut non[6] sit ‹servus›.[7]

Haec ad ipsa testamenti verba; libet tamen scrutari
etiam defuncti voluntatem: qua nihil potentius apud nos,
nihil nostro animo sacratius esse debet. Credibile est igitur
hoc eum sensisse, ut liberum esse vellet etiam addictum?

9　Servos cur manumiserit manifestum est: delectatus est
officiis, referre voluit gratiam obsequio. Alius aegrum cu-
raverat, alius peregrinantem secutus erat, alius inter tot
occupationes ‹res›[8] domesticas custodierat, alius hoc ipsum faenus exercuerat: voluit liberos esse quos amaverat, a
quibus amatum esse se crediderat. Huic vero quid debuit
nisi iram?

10　'Durum tamen videtur et inhumanum solum hunc esse
in vinculis et in servitute.' Ante omnia, si quid ‹est›[9] aspe-
ritatis, in lege est, quae addictos servire iussit donec solve-
rent. Num igitur exigitis ut dicamus aliqua pro lege? Non
est nostrae mediocritatis, non officii, ea quae prudentissimi maiores constituerint temptare defendere. Verumtamen si intueri velitis, quid aequius constitui potest, aut
quo alio ‹modo›[10] custodiri patrimonia vestra, fortunae
11　sustineri possunt? An vero pecuniam aliquis acceptam
sic[11] per omnia vitia exhauriet ut non alligetur ad aliquam

---

5 *Ro.*: -tione Aβ　　6 *Ro., Ri.*: nomen Aβ
7 *Ro., Ri.*　　8 *Ro.*　　9 *Sch.*　　10 SB¹, *Hå.²*
11 a. (SB¹) sic SB³: accepturus Aβ

---

8 Not, as Wi., when his master was away, or at least not only
then, but when he was busy with nondomestic matters, public and
private.

not home-born, nor yet purchased or left by will. His condition therefore depends entirely on a loan. What follows? That he is not ‹a slave›.

So much for the actual words of the will. Now I want to scrutinize the intent of the deceased also, than which nothing should carry more weight with us, nothing be more sacred to our minds. Is it then credible that this is what he meant, that he wanted even the man addicted for debt to be free? Why he freed the slaves is clear. He was pleased with their services, he wanted to repay their obedience. One of them had cured him when he was ill, another had followed him travelling abroad, another had kept watch on his domestic ‹affairs› amid so many occupations,[8] another had practiced this very business of loaning money.[9] He wanted those he had loved and whom he believed had loved him to be free. But what did he owe this man except anger?

"But it seems hard and inhumane that he should be in bonds and servitude." First of all, if there ‹is› any harshness, it is in the law which ordered addicted persons to be in servitude until they paid. Do you therefore require me to say something on behalf of the law? It is not for a humble person like myself nor part of my duty to try to defend what our ancestors in their great wisdom determined. All the same, if you care to look into it, what determination can be more equitable or in what other ‹way› can your patrimonies be safeguarded, your fortunes sustained? Or shall a man squander borrowed money in all manner of vices

---

[9] On his master's behalf as *dispensator*; cf. 345.10.

solvendi necessitatem? Dura vincla alicui videntur, dura condicio servitutis? Reddat quod accepit. Istic non servitus constituta est, sed illud quod iustissimum est; reddendae pecuniae causa.

and not be bound by some means to pay it back? Do bonds seem hard to somebody, servitude a hard condition? Let him return what he borrowed. In this law servitude is not laid down, but something eminently just: a reason for returning money.